REMEDIES IN INTERNATIONAL LAW

University of Bristol
Department of Law

EC/International Law Forum
Series Coordinators: Malcolm D. Evans
Stratos V. Konstadinidis

Remedies in International Law:
The Institutional Dilemma

Edited by

MALCOLM D. EVANS

·H A R T·
PUBLISHING
OXFORD
1998

Hart Publishing
Oxford
UK

Distributed in the United States by
Northwestern University Press
625 Colfax, Evanston
Illinois 60208–4210 USA

Distributed in Australia and New Zealand by
Federation Press Pty Ltd
PO Box 45, Annandale
NSW 203, Australia

Distributed in the Netherlands, Belgium and Luxembourg by
Intersentia, Churchillaan 108
B2900 Schoten, Antwerpen
Belgium

Hart Publishing is a specialist legal publisher based in Oxford, England.
To order further copies of this book or to request a list of other
publications please write to:

Hart Publishing, 19 Whitehouse Road, Oxford, OX1 4PA
Telephone: +44 (0)1865 434459 or Fax: +44 (0)1865 794882
e-mail: hartpub@janep.demon.co.uk

British Library Cataloguing in Publication Data
Data Available
ISBN 1–901362–35–3 (cloth)

Typeset in 10pt Sabon
by Hope Services (Abingdon) Ltd.
Printed in Great Britain on acid-free paper
by Bookcraft, Midsomer Norton, Somerset.

Contents

Foreword

The chapters of this book have evolved out of the papers and presentations given at the Fourth EC/International Law Forum hosted by the Department of Law at Bristol University in May 1997. At the outset the organizers wish to acknowledge the generosity of the University of Bristol Alumni Foundation and of the Faculty of Law Trust on whose financial support this event depended. They also wish to express their sincere thanks to Mrs Pat Hammond for the meticulous attention which she devoted to the preparation of the typescript.

The Forum was conceived as the first in a series which would consider various aspects of the quest for a remedy by a state for breach of an international obligation. (It is hoped that remedies sought by individuals against states will be considered at a future Forum). It was decided to commence this investigation by considering a range of issues flowing from the multiplicity of procedures and mechanisms which are currently available to states—hence the theme being 'the institutional dilemma'. At this stage, it was decided not to take a prescriptive view of what might be deemed a 'remedy' for these purposes but to use these terms as a form of shorthand for an acceptable outcome arrived at by a means of an aggrieved state's choosing. There was no pretence to an exhaustive treatment of the topic. Rather, a number of mechanisms and procedures were selected and what might be called their remedial potential considered.

The first chapter, by Judge Rosalyn Higgins, sets the scene by looking at the International Court of Justice 'from the inside' and is followed by a detailed appraisal of the Court from a practitioner's perspective by Malcolm Shaw. In tandem, these chapters point to the range of considerations which potential litigants will need to take into account when determining whether to have recourse to the Court—assuming, of course, that it might be able to exercise jurisdiction in the first place. The third chapter, by John Merrills, takes the theme of remedies further by exploring the manner in which the incidental jurisdiction of the Court can be harnessed to fulfil a remedial purpose, broadly defined.

The following two chapters then turn to the newly established International Tribunal for the Law of the Sea. As with the ICJ, the ITLOS is introduced by one of its Judges, David Anderson. He provides an overview of the genesis of the Tribunal and its approach to the formulation of its rules of procedure, indicating that it is adopting its own persona, and increasing the range of choice available to disputants in matters pertaining to the law of the sea. The question of choice then forms the point of departure for Robin Churchill, who places the ITLOS within the broader context of dispute settlement mechanisms, both within and outside of the framework provided by the 1982 Law of the Sea

Convention. By laying bare the complexity of the relationship between the various mechanisms and procedures, further light is thrown on the true nature of the 'institutional dilemmas' which are likely to arise once the Tribunal's caseload and jurisprudence have evolved.

Of course, resorting to the institutional mechanisms created by the international community is not the only option open to states and, indeed, may not be an option at all. It is a truism that nonjudicial means of dispute settlement remain of paramount importance and so the following three chapters look at the remedial opportunities which they present. David Anderson considers negotiation as a dispute settlement mechanism from both a theoretical and practical perspective and points out that a negotiated settlement can have the potential advantage of avoiding the 'institutional dilemma' altogether, or can play an essential role in fine tuning a settlement the general contours of which have been shaped by recourse to other means. Where negotiation fails to produce an acceptable outcome, there are an ever increasing number of other methods and procedures falling short of judicial settlement and Christine Chinkin looks at a range of these under the umbrella of Alternative Dispute Resolution, with particular emphasis on compliance mechanisms.

ADR is an expression more usually associated with domestic than international dispute settlement and it is consonant with Christine Chinkin's contribution to suppose that there are parallels and lessons to be learnt from other spheres. Although it is not possible to examine the nature and extent of such cross-currents in any depth in a volume of this size and scope, two shorter contributions are included which take on diverse aspects of this theme. First, Michael Furmston illustrates the point that there are trends within the sphere of international commercial arbitration in favour of developing universal principles, the adoption of which is intended to enhance the willingness of would-be litigants to resort to arbitration as an alternative. To the extent that the harmonizing of international commercial arbitration may be seen as the harbinger of similar developments at an inter-state level, this introduction to the reception of the salient issues within the domestic jurisdiction provides interesting food for thought. Secondly, Bernhard Jansen provides an example of the manner in which means of resolution originally set out in counterpoint to more traditional methods have themselves moved towards a more judicial orientation. To this end, he sets out the dispute settlement procedures of the GATT/WTO, tracing its evolution from an essentially negotiating forum into an adjudicative body.

The following chapter draws together a number of the strands of thought so far considered and applies them to a further arena. Phoebe Okowa traces the development of mechanisms for the settlement of environmental disputes. This has often been seen as a self-contained topic but it is pointed out that much depends on the manner in which a given dispute is viewed. Although the environment may form the subject matter of a dispute, it may also be characterized in other ways, such as a question of treaty interpretation, the recent ICJ decision in the case concerning the *Gabčikovo-Nagymaros Project* being a case in point.

In a sense, this chapter brings the book full circle by reuniting us with the first chapter and the function of the ICJ. What has become evident is that a whole range of factors bear upon the 'institutional dilemma', and relate to a multiplicity of factors, structural, procedural and substantive.

The final three chapters can be viewed as something of a coda to the work as a whole. The theme which unites the contributions in the book is the quest for a remedy by a state on the international plane. These final chapters attempt to contextualize 'inter-state' settlement within more general trends within the global community. The chapter by Malcolm Evans looks towards the possible use of domestic courts as alternative fora for 'international' dispute settlement, against a background of the increasing use of national court systems for international offences which attract individual responsibility but for which the state is also concurrently liable. Nanette Neuwahl then considers the extent to which the European Court of Justice can also play a role in settling what have hitherto been considered 'international' as opposed to institutional disputes. This, of course, is at least in part achieved by the passing to the EU of competence over the relevant subject matter but the reordering of the Maastricht system by the Treaty of Amsterdam again leaves open the problems posed by the only partial jurisdiction of the ECJ over the 3rd Pillar issues. The final chapter, by William Robinson, shows that the ECJ itself is steadily advancing into areas which might have been assumed to be 'international' disputes and fall beyond the purview of the Court. Whatever the true nature of these trends, they have the potential within them to revolutionize our concept of what an 'international' dispute actually is, and open up a new series of avenues and issues which states must face when setting out to achieve a 'remedy' for the breach of an international obligation.

Malcolm D Evans

Table of Cases, Treaties and other Materials

Other International Tribunals

ECJ

ECHR

England and Wales

United States of America

International Tribunal for the Former Yugoslavia

International Treaties

Law of the Sea Convention 71, 116, 126
    Article 1 74
    Article 73..89
    Article 74..117, 118
    Article 76..92
    Article 83..117, 118
    Article 101 181
    Article 186..98
    Article 187..75, 91, 98
    Article 188 ....89, 98
    Article 266..89
    Article 279..86
    Article 281 103
    Article 282 ....99–100, 103
    Article 283..106, 118
    Article 285 98–9
    Article 286..105, 118
    Article 287..26–7, 74–8, 169, 170
    Article 288 ....76, 99
    Article 289..81
    Article 290..88
    Article 292 ....26, 75, 78, 88
    Article 293 ....75, 97
    Article 294..78
    Article 295..75
    Article 297 ....78, 89–90, 99–100, 104, 106
    Article 298 ....75, 76, 90–1, 99–100, 104, 106
    Article 299..99
    Article 305..91
    Article 306..91
    Article 319..72

    Annex II..92
    Annex V 86, 90
    Article 2 90
    Article 7..106

    Annex VI (Statute of the International Tribunal for the Law of the Sea)
    Article 2..71, 87
    Article 3 71
    Article 15 ....87, 98
    Article 17..98
    Article 20..91

1

Remedies and the International Court of Justice: An Introduction

ROSALYN HIGGINS, DBE, QC

1. INTRODUCTION

The purpose of this chapter is to identify the advantages and disadvantages of recourse to the International Court of Justice for those seeking a remedy for a violation of international law. Rather than recite the various Charter and Statute provisions, the subject will be tackled from a practitioner perspective.

Certain obvious matters can be cleared out of the way immediately. The International Court can only deal with disputes between States—this is the result of Article 34 of the Statute. So litigation in which individuals or NGOs wish to invoke international law obligations as a cause of action cannot be brought to the Court.

Suggestions have, of course, been made that the Statute be amended to give individuals standing before the Court. But there are very real practical problems. First, the individual would presumably have to show a legal interest—that is to say, that *he* has been damaged by the alleged violation. (It cannot be supposed that, actions *in abstracto* not being permitted for States, they would be permitted for individuals.) And then one immediately enters the theoretical minefield of whether rights under international law (other than human rights) are rights owed to the individual, or rather to his State. Even if there are a limited number of instances where duties owed to the State have been assimilated in practice to duties owed to the individual—such as, for example, questions of expropriation, or physical injury to foreigners—and even if one could set aside the nationality of claims rule, whereby action for harm to an individual can only be brought by his State, the possibilities for litigation seem tiny. Moreover, States would have to agree to this procedure and there is no suggestion that they will allow individuals to bring suits against them in anything other than perhaps the field of human rights.

It is more realistic, in my view, to discuss the position of NGOs before the Court. There is no realistic prospect, for all the reasons already indicated and more, of them being litigants. But it is not impossible that the Court might in the future be able to receive briefs *amicus curiae* from NGOs or from other knowledgeable persons. Very many superior courts do admit these "intervening arguments" in written form, to add to the spectrum of data upon which they are able to base their decision.

The role of NGOs in the recent *Nuclear Weapons* cases[1] was both interesting and important. Although the requests came—as they had to—from the General Assembly of the UN and from the WHO, they were NGO driven. Heavy and well organised lobbying had led to the organisations seeking an opinion from the Court. The United Kingdom government suggested that this reality was a reason for the Court to act circumspectly in deciding whether to give the opinions requested. But the Court rightly rejected this suggestion. All said and done, it is up to the Members of the General Assembly whether or not they act on the lobbying efforts of NGOs.

Under the Statute as it stands, NGOs may not directly participate in advisory opinions, any more than in litigation. Accordingly, the Court took an early decision that it would not make the myriad of briefs and memoranda it was receiving from NGOs on the subject of nuclear weapons part of the docket. At the same time, they were not simply thrown out. They were placed in the library, and every judge knew from week to week what was coming in, and it was up to each judge to decide if he wished to go beyond the already voluminous official pleadings and to read these other materials. At one level this seems progressive and desirable. But it is not without its problems. There is always the possibility that a judge may be influenced by something that those actually making written or oral statements may not know about and have no opportunity to challenge. The matter requires further attention. But, as things stand at the moment, practitioners who advise NGOs should follow the work of the Court closely to see if there is a possibility of making an input, at least on issues which come before the Court in advisory form.

2. THE PROBLEM OF TIMELY DECISIONS

It is undeniable that the greatly increased workload of the Court is presenting it with some difficulties. The Court is required by its Statute—which is annexed to the UN Charter—to work in French and English.[2] And the written pleadings in international litigation are massive, with two rounds usually allowed to each side (occasionally more, especially in submissions by special agreement), and voluminous Annexes to boot. Transcripts are prepared of the oral hearings, in which counsel may plead in the one language or the other. They must be available in both languages. There is thus potential for both delay and considerable expense. The most visible manifestation of the problem has been in the gap—

---

[1] *Legality of the Use by a State of Nuclear Weapons in Armed Conflict*, Advisory Opinion, ICJ Reports 1996, 66; *Legality of the Threat or Use of Nuclear Weapons*, Advisory Opinion, ICJ Reports 1996, 226.
[2] See Art. 39 of the Statute.

sometimes an uncomfortably long gap—between the conclusion of the written phase of proceedings and the beginning of the oral phase. This is because the Court has been dealing with the other, prior cases.

In principle cases are dealt with in their order of submission. But applications for interim measures[3] (international injunctions) always take priority.[4] And there is a tendency to give jurisdictional cases some priority—because, should the Court have no jurisdiction, the defendant State is entitled to know so within a reasonable time. Sometimes, of course, it is learned that settlement discussions are under way; and sometimes the parties themselves will ask the Court for the "clock to be stopped" or even for a case to be withdrawn from the lists.

The traditional method has essentially been this: immediately after the conclusion of the oral hearings, the Court meets to settle a list of issues that must be addressed. The judges then each prepare a "Note", within a stipulated period of time. I went to the Court believing that a Note should be just that—short, an outline of views. I now believe that a Note that does not explain *why* certain views are provisionally held is not useful. And how long it takes to spell out the steps of reasoning—even if the reference to legal authority is light in character—will depend on the issue. It may readily be appreciated that the *Nuclear Weapons* case,[5] with its great complexities of law, its demands of scientific understanding, did not facilitate the writing of very brief Notes. No more did the *Gabčikovo-Nagymaros* case, where sometimes novel and certainly very important points of law required examination, as well as a multitude of scientific and environmental data and reports.

The Notes are then translated and are read by all of the judges, after which the deliberations process begins. The junior judge opens the discussion. Usually it is apparent at the end of the deliberations (which may last over two or three or more days) where the majority view lies. A drafting committee is selected by secret ballot, with the President of the Court always serving *ex officio*. A draft judgment is prepared and circulated. At that moment the other judges may offer, in writing, amendments of form and of substance. In further meetings, the drafting committee will discuss what it is able to accommodate without losing the thrust of its judgment. A second draft judgment is prepared, and the Court then meets in plenary to discuss it in a formal First Reading: that is to say, paragraph by paragraph. Small suggestions may still be made and the drafting committee may make a few further amendments. This is followed shortly after by the Second Reading, and the draft judgment is finally amended, this time page by page. Only technical corrections may now be accepted. Upon arrival at the *dispositif*—which may contain several different provisos—a formal vote is taken, starting again with the junior judge and progressing in order of seniority.

It may readily be seen that there are advantages and disadvantages to this

---

[3] See Art. 73 of the Rules of Court.

[4] Art. 74 of the Rules of Court.

[5] *Legality of the Threat or Use of Nuclear Weapons*, ICJ Reports 1996, 226.

system of work. The traditional system has ensured that every single judge is engaged in the deliberation processes. The preparation of the written Note by everyone is the best guarantee that no point of significance is overlooked and that all possibilities are explored. And the totality of Notes is of the greatest help to the Drafting Committee. The disadvantage is the time the process takes—about four weeks for the preparation of Notes, then translation time, then time for each judge to read another fourteen Notes.

The Court decided to charge its Rules Committee to survey its work methods in the light of the heavy docket. During 1997, using the work of the Rules Committee as a basis, the Court adopted some far reaching changes (albeit some of them on "an experimental basis"), and some of these measures were outlined by President Schwebel in his speech to the General Assembly in October. The Court has now determined that it may proceed without written Notes where it considers it necessary, in suitable cases concerning the jurisdiction of the Court or the admissibility of the application. This has already been the practice in the case of urgent requests for interim measures of protection. This departure will be on an experimental basis. The traditional practice regarding the preparation of written Notes will be continued with regard to cases in which the Court is to decide on the merits.

The Court has made further important decisions directed to accelerating its work. In particular, appropriate cases on jurisdiction may be heard "back to back" (that is to say, in immediate succession), so that work may then proceed on them both concurrently. This innovation will be undertaken on an experimental basis, where there are appropriate cases and a pressing need to proceed rapidly.

The Court has also confirmed its recent practice in trying to give the parties notice of its intended schedule for the next three cases, believing such "forward planning" assists both States and their counsel, and the Court.

In order to respond as best it may to the legitimate aspirations of States to have their cases heard as soon as possible, the Court has decided upon those measures and also upon a series of related and consequential changes in administrative and internal practices.

It is hoped these measures will assist the Court in getting through more cases each year while retaining sufficient time to give the necessary meticulous care to the disposition of issues of great magnitude. And the new work methods (which remain unchanged for the Merits phase) continue to engage every single judge of the Court in each case.

The Court has also taken a cluster of internal decisions, precisely directed to facilitating the "throughput" of cases as expeditiously as possible.

There are also things that States parties will now be expected to do to help avoid the problem of backlog. They will be asked to exercise greater care in the selection of Annexes (because all the documents have to be translated and the increasing size of the Annexes is putting a critical burden upon the Court's translation services and its budget). Other requests, relating to translations and to the possible avoidance of simultaneous submission of pleadings in cases coming by special *compromis*, will also be put to them.

3. FINANCE

The hopes and aspirations for the Court will depend upon its having the necessary means to fulfil its obligations. Regrettably, it is today in severe financial difficulties. As an organ of the United Nations—its judicial organ—it is financed as part of the UN's budget. And the UN is in financial crisis. Unpaid contributions to the UN's regular and peacekeeping budgets stand at about $3.1 billion. The leading defaulter is the United States. As its assessments are an important part of the total, the damage to the United Nations is very significant. Over the last decade, its unpaid assessments have been half and sometimes more of the total unpaid assessments. The United States judge, now the new President of the International Court, has publicly spoken of the manifest illegality of this non-payment.

Non-payment by one is rapidly imitated by others. Only about half the membership pay their regular contributions in full, and an even smaller percentage pay their peacekeeping dues in full. Over two dozen States are currently making no payment at all on the regular budget. Only eight members of 185 last year paid their dues on time.

The ability of the Court to work as efficiently as it would wish is to a degree a matter of proper financing. It may be noted that the intention is that ITLOS[6] will ask for an annual budget of $7.8 million per year from the ratifying parties. The ICJ's UN budget is some $11 million annually, to deal with its entire docket (some ten cases currently), the Bench, the Registry, translations, its publications, its rent for the Peace Palace, etc. The International Criminal Tribunal for the former Yugoslavia is financed mainly from the UN budget, where some $70 million per year is allocated to it. This is topped up by voluntary contributions and the provision of free staff by some governments.

4. THE PROBLEM OF JURISDICTION

One of the contributory elements to a less than speedy service by the International Court is the fact that its jurisdiction is based on the consent of the parties. Acceptance of that jurisdiction can be given either *ad hoc*, by accepting a jurisdictional clause in a treaty,[7] or by the so-called Optional Clause of the Statute.[8] In agreed references to the Court—which, happily, are increasing in number and in proportion to the totality of applications—jurisdictional

---

[6] International Tribunal for the Law of the Sea (ITLOS).
[7] Art. 36(1) of the Statute.
[8] Art. 36(2) of the Statute.

disputes are avoided. The Court can go straight to the merits. Generally, that will be true of a reference made under a treaty—though the recent *Oil Platforms* case[9] shows this is not invariably so. In that case, Iran based its claim that the Court had jurisdiction on the reference clause in the Iran–US Treaty of Amity of 1955. The United States insisted that that Treaty had nothing to do with the events in this case. So the issue of whether the treaty did "cover" the claim had still to be decided by the Court. In the event, the Court has made its jurisdictional finding in favour of Iran.

Invocations of a jurisdiction based on the Optional Clause invariably call forth a challenge to the asserted jurisdiction by the respondent State. And, because these have to be dealt with it can take a long while to move to the merits. Moreover, because hearings on jurisdiction receive a certain priority, in the timetabling, *other* cases on the merits are held up as a consequence. A case like the *Gabčikovo-Nagymaros Project*,[10] for example, which was long ready for its hearing on the merits, was held up not only by provisional measures cases (which always have priority), but also the need to dispose of the jurisdictional phases of the *Genocide* and *Oil Platforms* cases.[11]

It is not easy to see what can be done about jurisdictional objections clogging the Court's calendar—save perhaps for quite radical measures, such as a separate jurisdictional panel. And, ironically, the more people urge States to ratify the Optional Clause, the more likely there is to be an increase in the number of cases that come before the Court with a jurisdictional problem to be resolved.

5. CHOICE OF JUDGES

It is sometimes said, of course, that States like to be able to "choose" their judges—and that this is one of the attractions of arbitration.

The Chambers procedure[12] continues to be available—though it does appear that, since the end of the Cold War, and the increasing confidence of the developing countries in the Court—there seems rather little interest in it. It should be added that although, formally, any Chamber will consist of five judges selected by the President, in reality those judges will be selected with the joint agreement of the litigating parties.

---

[9] *Oil Platforms (Islamic Republic of Iran v. United States of America)*, Preliminary Objections, ICJ Reports 1996, 803.
[10] *Gabčikovo-Nagymaros Project (Hungary/Slovakia)* Judgment of 25 Sept 1997.
[11] *Application of the Convention on the Prevention and Punishment of the Crime of Genocide (Bosnia and Herzegovina v. Yugoslavia)*.
[12] Art. 26 of the Statute.

6. SUBJECT MATTER

It remains the case that the International Court is uniquely well placed so far as possible subject matter is concerned. It may deal with all matters of international law.

Very rarely—with the *Rann of Katch*[13] and *Taba*[14] awards providing examples—the parties go to arbitration to settle boundary matters. But the Court has a very strong record in this subject area. Even now, out of the ten cases currently on its docket, some three concern boundary issues.[15] The jurisprudence is both heavy and well settled: the Court is extremely well placed to apply the law it has done so much to establish.

Maritime issues—including delimitation issues—now have another possible home. This is considered in detail in subsequent chapters.[16] At this point it need only be said that—if the question of standing of non-State parties is not an issue—then the great authority of the Court in this area, and the desirability of it applying its own jurisprudence in any particular controversy, will perhaps have to be weighed against the need for a speedy service which the thoroughly competent judges at Hamburg may be able to provide. Another issue will be how discrete is the law of the sea issue in a particular case. If it is intertwined with other legal controversies, the Court again may be seen as the preferable choice.

There is another range of what can be termed "one-off" issues, these being issues of immense importance and sensitivity that, quite frankly, one cannot imagine any other tribunal dealing with. Examples of such instances are the *Lockerbie* cases,[17] and the case on the *Gabčíkovo-Nagymaros Project*.[18] The Court, with its special position as the principal judicial organ of the UN, and with each of the judges elected by the General Assembly and Security Council, must remain the most appropriate forum for such exceptional litigation.

Mention should also be made of human rights. The International Court is not a human rights court. But it nonetheless has a long involvement in human rights.

After the re-drawing of frontiers at the end of World War II, the Permanent Court of International Justice was to provide the judicial underpinning to the great Minorities Treaties. In so doing it showed a profound insight into what was necessary for the protection of national minorities and its findings contained ideas that were to have a lasting importance in human rights law. A ready

---

[13] 7 ILM 633.

[14] 80 ILR 224.

[15] *Maritime Delimitation and Territorial Questions between Qatar and Bahrain*; *Land and Maritime Boundary between Cameroon and Nigeria (Cameroon v. Nigeria)*; *Kasikili/Sedudu Island (Botswana/Namibia)*.

[16] See below Chs. 4 and 5.

[17] *Questions of Interpretation and Application of the 1971 Montreal Convention arising from the Aerial Incident at Lockerbie (Libyan Arab Jamahiriya v. United Kingdom) (Libyan Arab Jamahiriya v. United States of America)*.

[18] *Gabčíkovo-Nagymaros Project (Hungary/Slovakia)*, Judgment of 25 Sept 1997.

example was the insistence of the Court in the *Polish Upper Silesia* case[19] that what the minority was entitled to was equality in fact as well as in law; and that, while a claim to be a member of a national minority should be based on fact, self identification was the only acceptable method of association.

A further significant contribution made by the Permanent Court to the development of human rights came in the *Minority Schools* case[20] in the idea that special institutions were needed both to protect the special needs of a minority and to ensure equality in fact. The jurisprudence of the UN Human Rights Committee,[21] distinguishing non-identical treatment which is discriminatory from that which is not, has its roots in the jurisprudence of the Permanent Court some 65 years earlier.

Since the end of World War II there has been both a deepening of the substantive law of human rights and a broadening of what is perceived as a human rights entitlement. The Universal Declaration of Human Rights went far beyond minorities protection. The Treaties that were to follow later—universal, regional and single topic—now often have their own dispute-settlement procedures, along with a right of individual application. Nonetheless, only one inter-State case has ever got as far as the European Court of Human Rights[22]; and although the Human Rights Committee can hear inter-State cases under Article 41 of the Covenant on Civil and Political Rights, none has been brought. The International Court of Justice still has a significant role to play in inter-State disputes on human rights. States will want to think carefully about the litigation possibilities open to them.

The Court has clearly played a major and critical role in the development of the concept of self-determination. That legal concept is taken for granted today, but it must be remembered that when the Court addressed this matter in the *South West Africa*, *Namibia* and *Western Sahara* cases, there were still those who insisted that self-determination was nothing more than a political aspiration.

It is, however, still very rare for what might be called a "fully fledged" human rights case to come to the Court—that is to say, a case whose entire essence concerns the violation of customary or treaty law on human rights. The pending litigation in which Bosnia claims that Yugoslavia has committed genocide is one such. Another is the proceedings brought by Paraguay against the USA in April 1998 concerning the murder conviction and subsequent execution—notwithstanding the Court's Order of provisional measures—of Mr Angelo Breard.

Finally, there is an interesting footnote to add which may be of interest to the practitioner. The Court can indicate provisional measures—what we might term international injunctive relief—when certain conditions are met. Once again, these matters are dealt with in detail later in this work.[23] Through the

---

[19] *Certain German Interests in Polish Upper Silesia*, Merits, Judgment No. 7, 1926, PCIJ, Series A, No. 7.

[20] *Minority Schools in Albania*, Advisory Opinion, 1935, PCIJ, Series A/B, No. 64, 4.

[21] See Art. 28 of the International Covenant on Civil and Political Rights.

[22] *Ireland* v. *UK*, Judgment of 18 Jan. 1978, ECHR Series A, No. 25.

[23] See below, Ch. 3.

years of the Permanent Court as well as this Court, it has been clear that this will only be done to protect the subject matter of the dispute. This is sometimes put as ensuring that the Court's judgment can be carried out. But in the *Burkina Faso/Mali Frontier Dispute* case,[24] the Chamber of the Court in granting provisional measures said that the facts "expose the person and property in this disputed area, as well as the interests of both States within that area, to serious risk of irreparable damage". And in the current case brought by Cameroon against Nigeria, the Court developed this thinking further. In ordering interim measures it made clear that the killing of peoples causes irreparable harm to the rights claimed, because disputes about frontiers are not just about lines on the ground but are about the safety and protection of peoples who live there.[25]

7. REMEDIES

So far, the focus of this chapter has been upon those factors which contribute towards achieving a good quality judgment on an appropriate subject within a reasonable period of time. Unless these preconditions are met there can be no meaningful discussion of remedies. Assuming these issues are satisfactorily dealt with, it then becomes necessary to consider the various forms of remedy which have been sought by States from the International Court. These have included mere declarations of a breach, the designation of a boundary line, restitution, the award of damages and performance.

In a variety of cases declaration of a breach has been thought sufficient, or at least central, by a party.[26] The Court is well equipped to perform this task. The Court often combines a declaration of what the law is with an indication of what the parties must do.[27] The Court has determined the legal line of boundaries in innumerable cases—the fixing of that legal line on the ground or at sea sometimes being assisted by specialists or, in the *Chad/Libya case*, by UN personnel.[28]

Sometimes the remedies sought might be more problematic for the Court. In the *Gabčikovo-Nagymaros* case both sides had agreed by treaty in 1977 to build a dam project on the Danube. Hungary refused both to complete its part of a joint construction at Gabčikovo and to build at all the construction for which it was solely responsible at Nagymaros. Slovakia itself completed at Gabčikovo, diverting the Danube to do so, that is, what Hungary was to have completed under the Treaty. Hungary moved before the Court that it lawfully terminated

---

[24] *Frontier Dispute*, Provisional Measures, Order of 10 Jan. 1986, ICJ Reports 1986, 3 at 10.

[25] *Land and Maritime Boundary between Cameroon and Nigeria*, Provisional Measures, Order of 15 Mar. 1996, ICJ Reports 1996, 13, para. 42.

[26] *Legal Status of Eastern Greenland*, Judgment, 1933, PCIJ Series A/B, No. 53, 11; *Diversion of the Waters from the Meuse*, Judgment, 1937, PCIJ A/B, No. 70, 4; *Asylum* case, ICJ Reports 1950, 266.

[27] E.g. *United States Diplomatic and Consular Staff in Tehran*, Order of 12 May 1981, ICJ Reports 1981, 45.

[28] Security Council Resolution 910, 14 Apr. 1994. See also *Temple of Preah Vihear*, ICJ Reports 1962, 6.

the 1977 Treaty and that therefore the construction at Gabčikovo should be dismantled. Slovakia said that the repudiation of the Treaty was unlawful and the Court must therefore order Hungary to build the dam at Nagymaros. The Court was thus faced with requests for remedies which on the one hand sought to destroy a costly existing operational structure; and on the other hand required specific performance of a building contract in the face of deep political and environmental hostility to doing so. The problems are apparent. In the event, the Court required neither the destruction of "Variant C" nor the building of the dam at Nagymaros. It found Hungary's purported termination of the Treaty unlawful. But it also found the construction of Variant C by Slovakia to be unlawful—but the remedy ordered by the Court was for negotiations to be entered into to allow it to operate in a manner that would not deprive Hungary of its essential rights under the Treaty. Thus Variant C would be made to conform to the Treaty. As for the dam at Nagymaros, the Court found that with the effective discarding by both Parties of peak power operation, there was no longer any point in building it.[29]

So far as damages are concerned, it has been clear ever since the *Chorzow* case that the Court will not require any separate basis of jurisdiction to be shown before it will order damages—the existence of jurisdiction to decide the merits carries with it the legal authority to remedy any breach found.[30]

Damages may be asked for injuries to one's nationals or for direct injury to the State itself: the *Corfu Channel*,[31] *Teheran Hostages*[32] and the *Nicaragua* cases[33] are examples of where this element looms large—though because of post-judgment developments in the latter two matters, the question has not been fully developed. The Court has been prepared to use experts for the qualification of damages—though only as a guide, making the final decisions itself. Damages were also very much in issue again in the *Gabčikovo case*—Slovakia's claim was formulated in some detail and Hungary claimed in principle, reserving detailed formulation till after the judgment on the merits, had this been needed.

What may safely be said is that the question of damages does not yet present before the Court the sort of lottery that the practitioner finds in arbitration, where it all seems to depend upon whether the arbitration is an adherent to *damnum emergens* only and/or his views on discounted cash flow.

Where there is more than one possibility for the litigation of a case, States—and the counsel advising them—must carefully weigh all the various advantages and disadvantages. This short chapter has sought to illustrate matters relevant to the use of the International Court of Justice.

---

[29] Judgment of 25 Sept. 1997, especially at paras. 59, 78 and 134.

[30] See the detailed analysis of this point in C. Gray, *Judicial Remedies in International Law* (Clarendon Press, Oxford, 1987) at 58–68.

[31] *Corfu Channel*, Merits, Judgment, ICJ Reports 1949, 4.

[32] *United States Diplomatic and Consular Staff in Tehran*, Order of 12 May 1981, ICJ Reports 1981, 45.

[33] *Military and Paramilitary Activities in and against Nicaragua (Nicaragua v. United States of America)*, Merits, Judgment, ICJ Reports 1986, 14.

2

A Practical Look at the International Court of Justice

MALCOLM N. SHAW*

1. INTRODUCTION

There are many ways in which one may look at the International Court as it moves on beyond its fiftieth anniversary celebrations.[1] This veritable variety of perspectives includes those adopted by the Court itself, academic theorists, practitioners both private and governmental, States more generally, international organisations and individuals. Each of these manifests its own methodology, needs and interests. Academics, for example, are keen to examine the intellectual basis and consistency of decisions and to infer, analyse and criticise the existence and nature of rules and institutions. Practitioners seek to equip themselves with the knowledge and tools necessary in order to enable their clients to win before the Court. States cautiously seek to uphold the role of the Court in general terms without losing any cases or putting themselves in a position where this is a possibility. International organisations and individuals look at the Court with keen and hopeful eyes.

This chapter will try to look at the nature and role of the Court from a practical perspective, that is from the point of view of a potential client and in the light of certain operational factors. The focus will essentially be upon contentious disputes. It is not intended to deal with matters that may require major constitutional changes, such as the question of *locus standi* before the Court of individuals and international organisations,[2] or the suggestion that states and

* This chapter is a revised and extended version of a paper originally delivered at the EU/International Law Forum held at the University of Bristol, May 1997. An earlier version was published as "The International Court of Justice: A Practical Perspective", 46 *ICLQ* 831.

[1] See, e.g., S. Rosenne, *The Law and Practice of the International Court, 1920–1996* (3rd. edn., Nijhoff, Dordrecht, 1997), 4 vols.; V. Lowe and M. Fitzmaurice (eds.), *Fifty Years of the International Court of Justice* (Cambridge University Press, Cambridge, 1996); A.S. Muller, D. Raič and J.M. Thuránszky (eds.), *The International Court of Justice* (Martinus Nijhoff, Dordrecht, 1997); C. Peck and R.S. Lee (eds.), *Increasing the Effectiveness of the International Court of Justice* (Nijhoff/UNITAR, Dordrecht, 1997).

[2] See, e.g., J. Sztucki, "International Organisations as Parties to Contentious Proceedings before the International Court of Justice?" in Muller *et al.*, n. 1 above at 141; P.C. Szasz, "Granting International Organisations *Ius Standi* in the International Court of Justice", *ibid.*, at 169; I. Seidl-Hohenveldern, "Access of International Organisations to the International Court of Justice", *ibid.*,

national courts should be able to ask the Court for advisory opinions.[3] Nor will the proposal to permit the United Nations Secretary-General to ask for advisory opinions from the Court be addressed.[4]

Essentially practitioners and their client States want to win. That is the point of the exercise. No State will go to court, if it can be avoided, if the chances are that it will lose. That is obvious, but too simple. The advantage of third party judicial settlement is that the ultimate responsibility for the decision lies elsewhere than with the States concerned. It thus constitutes an important mechanism to enable a State to come to terms with a losing position in a manner that often entails less political cost than a negotiating strategy producing the same result. Internal political forces are more often inclined to accept losing if the decision has been imposed from elsewhere than if the State concerned has simply conceded from the start. This is especially the case where the result has been arrived at by an unquestionably independent and objective process based on clear norms and processes. At the least, there will be some international benefit to be derived from proceeding to judicial settlement and accepting the consequences. It could be argued that the circumstances of the *Taba* case support this view. The Israeli public accepted with little demur the fact that the Taba stretch of the Sinai coast passed to Egypt after the arbitration decision. It is to be questioned whether the same internal political situation would have obtained if Taba had simply been transferred to Egypt as part of bilateral negotiations.[5] Again, would Libya have so readily withdrawn from the Aouzou Strip without the decision of the International Court on title?[6]

2. STATES, COUNSEL AND INTERNATIONAL COURT

But practitioners, and even States, have an interest in judicial settlement that goes beyond seeking to win (or lose in politically acceptable circumstances).

at 189 and M.W. Janis, *ibid.*, at 205. See also D.W. Bowett, J. Crawford, Sir Ian Sinclair and Sir Arthur Watts, *The International Court of Justice: Process, Practice and Procedure* (The British Institute of International and Comparative Law, London, 1997). Similarly, the question whether the Court should continue to act to hear appeals from certain Appeal Tribunals of international organisations will not be examined: see, e.g., Sir Robert Jennings, "The International Court of Justice After Fifty Years", 89 *AJIL* 493.

[3] See, e.g., S Schwebel, "Preliminary Rulings by the International Court of Justice at the Instance of National Courts", 28 *VaJIL* 495 and S. Rosenne, "Preliminary Rulings by the International Court at the Instance of National Courts: A Reply", 29 *VaJIL* 40.

[4] See, e.g., R. Higgins, "A Comment on the Current Health of Advisory Opinions" in Lowe and Fitzmaurice, n. 1 above at 567 and S. Schwebel, "Authorising the Secretary-General of the United Nations to Request Advisory Opinion", 78 *AJIL* 4. See also the UN Secretary-General, *Agenda for Peace* (1992), para. 38. Although this idea is politically contentious, it may be suggested that there is nothing to prevent the Secretary-General from convening a Judicial Advisory Council, composed of a representative selection of judges from the International Court on a rotating basis, to advise him on pertinent matters.

[5] See 80 *ILR* 244. See also D.W. Bowett, "The Taba Award of 29 September 1988", 23 *Is. LR* 429; G. Lagergren, "The Taba Tribunal 1986–89", 1 *African Journal of International and Comparative Law* 525 and P. Weil, "Some Observations on the Arbitral Award in the Taba Case", 23 *Is. LR* 1.

[6] See n. 33 below.

There is a clear international community interest in supporting and sustaining the International Court of Justice. This operates upon several levels. First, both practitioners and States often look beyond the current case to the next one or to other inter-State dispute situations which may need to be addressed. The success of the resort to the Court may enable other conflicts to be resolved in a similar fashion. The efficacy of the mechanism may prove helpful in relations with other States in other circumstances. Secondly, the elucidation of principles in one case before the Court may prove helpful in bilateral or multilateral negotiations in other situations. States negotiating maritime boundaries, for example, eagerly scour the decisions of earlier cases in an attempt to discover the current internationally acceptable relevant principles. Although the decisions of the International Court bind only the parties in the instant case and for that case,[7] it would be naïve to believe that such decisions are devoid of impact upon other States in similar situations. Thirdly, legal principles expounded on or referred to by the Court in an *obiter dicta* sense may in the appropriate circumstances constitute stepping stones to the development of further norms or the application of existing norms in other areas. Fourthly, new norms may arise as a result of views expressed by the Court, provided the necessary requirements are in place. Finally, many practitioners and States feel a generalised obligation to further the success of the Court as an organ of the international community from a perception or feeling of responsibility to that community. Judges, international practitioners, both private and governmental, and academics are bound together in this sense.

A particular word needs to be said at this point about what Judge Higgins has characterised as "the International Bar".[8] Relatively little has been written about the counsel who plead before the International Court,[9] but they play an important, if rather concealed, part in the role and functioning of the Court. The International Bar is very different from national bars.[10] Membership of the former is not by formal invitation or by examination or by means of complying with any particular formalised requirements. The Statute[11] and Rules[12] of the Court deal only with the existence, role during oral hearings and immunities of

---

[7] Art. 59 of the Statute of the International Court of Justice.

[8] See Bowett *et al.*, n. 2 above, at 102.

[9] But see in particular A. Pellet, "Conseil Devant La Cour Internationale de Justice—Quelques Impressions" in *Mélanges Hubert Thierry* (1998, pending). See also Rosenne, n. 1 above, vol. III, at 1180; R. Monaco, "Représentation des Parties devant les Instances Internationales", *Festschrift für Rudolf Bindschedler* (Stampfli, Bern, 1980), at 373, and Peck and Lee, n. 1 above at 127 ff. (Highet) and 148 ff. (Crawford).

[10] K. Highet has written that the ICJ Bar consists of "those international lawyers who have practised and continue to practice as oral advocates before the Court, who represent a variety of foreign states other than their own governments, who are well known to the Judges and the Registrar of the Court, who know how things work out in practice, and who understand by experience the difficulties, pitfalls and tricks of the trade": see "A Personal Memoir of Eduardo Jiménez de Aréchaga", *ASIL Proceedings*, 1994, 579.

[11] See Arts. 42(2) and (3), 43(5) and 54(1) of the Statute of the International Court.

[12] See Arts. 58(2), 61(2) and (4) and 65 of the Rules of Court.

counsel, with no provision concerning their appointment or qualification or conduct.

The International Bar is composed predominately of university professors of international law and not of persons practising full time. There are therefore both a different atmosphere within the group and different overall approaches than is arguably the case with regard to national professional bars. For reasons mainly concerned with the fact that English and French are the two official languages of the Court, this Bar is primarily anglo-francophone and counsel not proficient in these two languages are at a severe disadvantage. Counsel operate in teams before the Court rather than acting individually, and these teams are invariably multi-national and, at least, bilingual. This must be correct in view of Article 9 of the Statute of the Court, which provides that in the Court "the representation of the main forms of civilisation and of the principal legal systems of the world should be assured". This team activity of itself imposes certain important patterns of conduct and ways of proceeding upon counsel as academic and procedural discussions proceed apace with overtly political considerations. Whether or not one becomes a member of such a team will depend upon a variety of factors ranging from ability to good luck. However, this is not the place to enter into a detailed analysis of the International Bar. Suffice it to point to the importance of the International Bar with regard to the functioning of the Court.

This importance is intangible but in reality significant. It is counsel who advise the governments appearing before the Court not only with regard to the substantive merits of the particular case, but also with regard to tactics, evidential matters and procedure. Whether some arguments and not others are put before the Court and how arguments are framed are traditional duties of the advocate, but members of the International Bar have also to interpret for their clients the meaning and application of the Statute and Rules of the International Court. This necessarily implies a certain view of how, in the broadest sense, the Court operates and what tactics and procedures are and are not advisable. While some of this may be simple conveyance of the terms of relevant provisions contained in the Statute or Rules, other such advice may fall within a broader category of what might be termed a duty of ethical respect by counsel towards the Court. Such a duty is well know to national legal systems, but is barely noted officially at the International Bar and hardly ever discussed as such. Yet it does exist and it is crucial to the Court, for the Court can only decide a case upon the basis of how that case is presented by counsel before it. In this sense, members of the International Bar are guardians of the International Court.

Although the focus is inevitably upon the International Court for present purposes, the existence of other courts should not be ignored.[13] Leaving aside the

---

[13] See as to arbitration, e.g., J.G. Wetter, *The International Arbitral Process: Public and Private* (Oceana, Dobbs Ferry, NY, 1979), 5 vols.; J.L. Simpson and H. Fox, *International Arbitration; Law and Practice* (Stevens, London, 1959); L. Caflisch, "L'Avenir de l'Arbitrage Interétatique", 25 *AFDI* 9; J.G. Merrills, *International Dispute Settlement* (2nd edn., Grotius, Cambridge, 1991), ch. 5;

specialist courts associated with human rights[14] and economic law[15] and certain other particular issues,[16] one must in particular note the establishment of the International Tribunal on the Law of the Sea.[17] Much of its potential work may come from the types of situations that might generate work for the International Court. Whatever view one takes of the question of proliferation of international courts,[18] the reality is that there are now two international courts having potential jurisdiction over law of the sea issues, and litigators are likely to consider a variety of issues before deciding which one to opt for. Leaving aside obvious jurisdictional considerations, practitioners will no doubt consider matters such as experience and established authority, institutional mystique and procedural points. Speed, fluency of procedure and implementation may be high considerations, while availability and enforceability of interim measures may also be relevant in the circumstances.

The rise of the Chambers phenomenon is a factor that is also likely to be in the mind of potential litigators seeking the appropriate forum.[19] The institution of the Chambers system by the International Court[20] was clearly an attempt to

S. Schwebel, *International Arbitration: Three Salient Problems* (Cambridge University Press, Cambridge, 1987); A.M. Stuyt, *Survey of International Arbitrations (1794–1984)* (Nijhoff, Dordrecht, 1990); V. Coussirat-Coustere and P.M. Eisemann, *Repertory of International Arbitral Jurisprudence* (Martinus Nijhoff, Dordrecht, 1989–91), 4 vols.; C. Gray and B. Kingsbury, "Developments in Dispute Settlement: International Arbitration since 1945", 63 *BYIL* 97; L.B. Sohn, "International Arbitration Today", 108 *HR* l; A.H.A. Soons (ed.), *International Arbitration* (Martinus Nijhoff, Dordrecht, 1990), and H. Fox, "States and the Undertaking to Arbitrate", 37 *ICLQ* 1. See also M.N. Shaw, *International Law* (4th edn., Cambridge University Press, Cambridge, 1997), at 737 ff.

[14] See, e.g., the European Court of Human Rights and the Inter-American Court of Human Rights. Note also the proposed international criminal court: see, e.g., J. Crawford, "The ILC's Draft Statute for an International Criminal Court", 88 *AJIL* 140 and Shaw, n. 13 above, at 187 ff.

[15] See, e.g., the EC Court of Justice, the Benelux Court of Justice created in 1965; the Court of Justice of the Cartagena Agreement created in 1976 for members of the Andean Group.

[16] See, e.g., the European Nuclear Energy Tribunal created in 1957 and the European Tribunal on State Immunity, created in 1972.

[17] See, further, n. 266 below.

[18] See, e.g., J.I. Charney, "The Implications of Expanding International Dispute Settlement Systems: The 1982 Convention on the Law of the Sea", 90 *AJIL* 69 and A.E. Boyle, "Dispute Settlement and the Law of the Sea Convention: Problems of Fragmentation and Jurisdiction", 46 *ICLQ* 37. See also S. Oda, "The International Court of Justice from the Bench", 244 *HR* 9 at 139 ff.; G. Guillaume, "The Future of International Judicial Institutions", 44 *ICLQ* 848. Cf. S. Rosenne, "Establishing the International Tribunal for the Law of the Sea", 89 *AJIL* 806. See also Peck and Lee, n. 1 above, at 280 ff. and Rosenne, n. 1 above, at 160.

[19] See, e.g., H. Mosler, "The *Ad Hoc* Chambers of the International Court of Justice" in Y. Dinstein and M. Tabory (eds.), *International Law at a Time of Perplexity* (Nijhoff, Dordrecht, 1989), at 449 and E. McWhinney, *Judicial Settlement of International Disputes* (Nijhoff, Dordrecht, 1991), at 78 ff. See also Jiménez de Aréchaga, "The Amendment to the Rules of Procedure of the International Court of Justice", 67 *AJIL* 1; S. Oda, "Further Thoughts on the Chambers Procedure of the International Court of Justice", 82 *AJIL* 556; S. Schwebel, "Chambers of the International Court of Justice formed for Particular Cases", 82 *AJIL* 739: E. Valencia-Ospina, "The Use of Chambers of the International Court of Justice" in Lowe and Fitzmaurice, n. 1 above, at 503 and T.M. Franck, *Fairness in International Law and Institutions* (Clarendon Press, Oxford, 1995), at 326 ff. As to the precedential value of decisions of Chambers, see M. Shahabuddeen, *Precedent in the World Court* (Cambridge University Press, Cambridge, 1996), at 171 ff.

[20] See Art. 26 of the Statute and Arts. 15–8 and 90–3 of the Rules of Court.

increase the flexibility to the parties that could be offered within the context of the institution. While the composition of the Chamber is a question for the Court, the parties will be consulted and are likely to have a significant influence.[21] On the whole, the additional flexibility may well prove advantageous in attracting clients not wishing their case, for whatever reason, to be heard by the full Court. There are some institutional disadvantages, of course, for the Court, in that certain judges may well be side-lined, whether for personal or national reasons, while there is a potential problem with regard to consistency of judgments. In addition, on a more strategic level, it would be a cause for some concern if a situation were to arise that a significant amount of work was being transacted by the world Court, with all the authority that this implies, by means of Chambers, whose composition was clearly not broadly based. The Court established a Chamber of Summary Procedure for the speedy despatch of business by five judges, but it has not been called upon.[22] A seven-member Chamber for Environmental Matters was created in 1993, but this also remains unused.[23] The particular problem with subject-specific Chambers is that, by agreeing to send a case to such a Chamber, the essential characterisation of that case has been made. In many cases, it is indeed this very characterisation which is at issue.[24] Thus, such Chambers cannot deal with situations where the essential nature of the dispute constitutes the core of the conflict between the parties, and in practice are unlikely to be greatly used.

3. THE PLURALIST CONTEXT

Any State engaged in a dispute with another State will, or should, have a clear view of what the dispute is about and the conditions required for its resolution. In particular, views will be formed on how to achieve the desired result both in terms of general strategic considerations and in the light of tactical methods. Within this general framework, recourse to the International Court might be examined. It is important to realise that, although existing and operating as a discrete and distinct mechanism, the Court finds its place within the larger picture of the peaceful resolution of disputes. Judge Jennings in his address to the General Assembly on 8 November 1991 as President of the Court[25] emphasised that "resort to the Court should be seen . . . as an integral part of the work of

---

[21] See, e.g., *Delimitation of the Maritime Boundary in the Gulf of Maine Area*, Constitution of Chamber, Order of 20 Jan., ICJ Reports 1982, 3 and Judgment, ICJ Reports 1982, 246. See also Merrills, n. 13 above, at 126; N. Singh, *Role and Record*, 110; and R.H. Brauer, "International Conflict Resolution: The ICJ Chambers and the Gulf of Maine Dispute", 23 *VaJIL* 463.

[22] Art. 29 of the Statute. See also *ICJ Yearbook 1994–5* at 17.

[23] *Ibid.*

[24] E.g. the *Gabčikovo-Nagymaros* case between Hungary and Slovakia, where one of the fundamental matters in issue was whether the case was essentially an environmental-law or treaty-law one. See *Gabčikovo-Nagymaros Project (Hungary/Slovakia)*, ICJ Reports 1997, not yet reported.

[25] "The Role and Functioning of the Court", *ICJ Yearbook 1991–2* at 205.

preventive diplomacy in the United Nations".[26] By this was meant the compelling view that the work of the Court had to be appreciated as part of the overall work of the United Nations, of which it is the "principal judicial organ"[27] and not as a totally separate institution operating totally separately from the political organs of the organisation. This realistic approach, that most international disputes have intertwined legal and political elements and that the application of legal and political mechanisms for dispute resolution must be seen as a whole and not as completely discrete elements, is critical to a measured appreciation of the process of peaceful settlement.

As the Court itself noted in the *Iranian Hostages* case,[28] "legal disputes between sovereign states by their very nature are likely to occur in political contexts, and often form only one element in a wider and long-standing political dispute between the states concerned". Thus co-ordinate or parallel consideration of the same factual situation by different legal and political organs is the rule rather than the exception.[29] Judicial settlement and the consequential application of international legal rules is merely one way in which States may settle problems. Other possibilities exist, either alone or in tandem.

Therefore any State in dispute will undoubtedly contemplate the various possibilities laid out by the international community and seek the most advantageous offering or combination. As is well known, the range of possibilities available to States for the peaceful resolution of disputes includes negotiation, enquiry, mediation, conciliation, arbitration, judicial settlement and resort to regional agencies or arrangements or to the United Nations.[30] There is no inherent hierarchy with respect to the methods specified and no specific method required in any given situation. States have a free choice as to the mechanisms adopted for settling their disputes.[31] This approach is also taken in a number of regional instruments.[32] Any issue likely to come before the International Court is therefore likely to form part of a wider context in which the involvement of the Court assumes a vital, but not necessarily exclusive, component. In addition,

[26] *Ibid.*, 211. In his 1993 address to the UN General Assembly, Judge Jennings referred to the Court as "a partner in preventive diplomacy": *ICJ Yearbook 1993–4* at 219–20. See also the address by Judge Schwebel to the General Assembly on 27 Oct. 1997.

[27] Art. 92 of the UN Charter.

[28] *United States Diplomatic and Consular Staff in Tehran*, Judgment, ICJ Reports 1980, 3 at 20.

[29] See, e.g., *Aegean Sea Continental Shelf*, Judgment, ICJ Reports 1978, 3 at 12; *United States Diplomatic and Consular Staff in Tehran*, Judgment, ICJ Reports 1980, 3 at 21–2; *Frontier Dispute*, Provisional Measures, Order of 10 Jan. 1986, 3 at 10 and *Military and Paramilitary Activities in and against Nicaragua (Nicaragua v. USA)*, ICJ Reports 1986, 14 at 392 and 433–5. See also M.N. Shaw, "The Security Council and the ICJ" in Muller *et al.*, n. 1 above, at 236 ff; S. Rosenne, *The World Court* (5th edn., Nijhoff, Dordrecht, 1995), at 37 and n. 2 above, at 149.

[30] See Art. 33(1) UN Charter and the 1970 Declaration on Principles of International Law, GA Res. 2625 (XXV).

[31] See Art. 33(1) of the UN Charter and s. I(3) and (10) of the Manila Declaration on the Peaceful Settlement of International Disputes, GA Res. 37/590.

[32] See, e.g., the American Treaty on Pacific Settlement (the Pact of Bogotá) 1948 of the Organisation of American States, the European Convention for the Peaceful Settlement of Disputes 1957 and the Helsinki Final Act of the Conference on Security and Co-operation in Europe 1975.

the parties to a dispute have the duty to continue to seek a settlement by other peaceful means agreed by them, in the event of the failure of one particular method. Should the means elaborated fail to resolve a dispute, the continuance of which is likely to endanger the maintenance of international peace and security, the parties under Article 37(1) of the Charter, "shall refer it to the Security Council". It is within this larger framework that the role of the Court is to be truly located.[33]

Thus, States, in contemplating the resolution of a dispute, will invariably consider all the relevant circumstances and may resort to the Court as a part of a broader strategy. Of course, not every dispute may be amenable to settlement by judicial means,[34] but judicial mechanisms may play an important part as one approach among others in dispute settlement.[35] Any practical perspective on the Court must take this point on board, and the Court is generally sensitive to this pluralistic context. In the *Fisheries Jurisdiction* case,[36] the Court explicitly declared that it ought not to "refuse to adjudicate merely because the parties, while maintaining their legal positions, have entered into an agreement one of the objects of which was to prevent the continuation of incidents". Moreover, it was emphasised that if the interim agreement between the parties in question was held to prevent it rendering judgment, the effect would be to discourage the making of such interim arrangements and "this would run contrary to the purpose enshrined in the provisions of the United Nations Charter relating to the pacific settlement of disputes".[37] More generally, the Court has clearly held that the fact that negotiations are taking place at the same time as legal proceedings was not a bar to the exercise by the Court of its judicial function.[38] On the contrary, the Court has noted that "pending a decision on the merits, any negotiation between the parties with a view to achieving a direct and friendly settlement

---

[33] A good example of the practical application of a range of methods, including use of the Court, to the task of peacefully settling a dangerous conflict is afforded by the Libya/Chad boundary dispute. Bilateral negotiations were succeeded by an agreed reference to the Court, while the Court's decision was implemented by a bilateral agreement monitored by UN observers. See the Framework Agreement on the Peaceful Settlement of the Territorial Dispute on 31 Aug. 1989; Reports of the UN Secretary-General. S/1994/5129, 27 Apr. 1994, 33 ILM 786 and S/1994/672, 100 ILR 111 ff., and SC Res. 910 (1994), 915 (1994) and 926 (1994). See generally 100 ILR 102 ff.; *Territorial Dispute (Libyan Arab Jamahiriya/Chad)*, Judgment, ICJ Reports 1994, 6, and M. Ricciardi, "Title to the Aouzou Strip: A Legal and Historical Analysis", 17 *Yale Journal of International Law* 301.

[34] See, e.g., Rosenne, n. 29 above, at 7 and Sir Robert Jennings, "The Proper Work and Purposes of the International Court of Justice" in Muller *et al.*, n. 1 above, 33 at 37.

[35] See, e.g., Judge Lachs, in his Separate Opinion in *Aegean Sea Continental Shelf*, Judgment, ICJ Reports 1978, 3 at 52 and in *United States Diplomatic and Consular Staff in Tehran*, Judgment, ICJ Reports, 1980, 3 at 49. See also R.P. Anand, "The Role of International Adjudication" in L. Gross (ed.), *The Future of the International Court of Justice* (Oceana, Dobbs Ferry, NY, 1976), i, at 1.

[36] *Fisheries Jurisdiction (United Kingdom v. Iceland)*, Merits, Judgment, ICJ Reports 1974, 3 at 19.

[37] *Ibid.*, 20.

[38] See *Aegean Sea Continental Shelf*, Judgment, ICJ Reports 1978, 3 at 12 and *Military and Paramilitary Activities in and Against Nicaragua (Nicaragua v. USA)*, ICJ Reports 1986, 14 at 392 and 440.

is to be welcomed".[39] Indeed, cases may well be withdrawn from the Court as a result of a settlement reached during negotiations taking place at the same time as legal proceedings.[40] Judicial settlement may hasten the final resolution of the dispute as a whole,[41] as may simply having the matter before the Court.[42] The latter point does indeed raise the issue whether the Court should itself seek to become more active in achieving a final settlement between the litigating parties. One notes, for example, that Protocol XI to the European Convention on Human Rights allows the newly reconstituted European Court of Human Rights to "place itself at the disposal of the parties concerned with a view to securing a friendly settlement of the matter".[43] However, it is felt that this constitutionally proactive approach would run counter to the established philosophy of the Court and might unnecessarily complicate any negotiations that are taking place either bilaterally or through the United Nations at the same time.[44] The Court itself in reaching a decision may assist in the process of obtaining a settlement, either directly by providing the basis for such resolution or by encouraging negotiations between the parties.[45] Indeed, the Court may also call for the terms of an existing relevant agreement to be observed[46] or for compliance with a particular dispute settlement mechanism.[47]

It is within this pluralistic context that one must view the essential role of the Court. States seeking to resolve a dispute will examine recourse to the Court as part of the totality of methods available in the light of the full situation, with regard to which the legal dispute may only constitute a part. Of course, States

[39] *Passage through the Great Belt (Finland v. Denmark)*, Provisional Measures, Order of 29 July 1991, ICJ Reports 1991, 12 at 20. See also *Free Zones of Upper Savoy and the District of Gex*, Order of 19 Aug. 1929, PCIJ, Series A, No. 22, 13 and *Frontier Dispute*, Judgment, ICJ Reports 1986, 554 at 577.

[40] See, e.g., *Passage through the Great Belt (Finland v. Denmark)*, Order of 10 Sept. 1992, ICJ Reports 1992, 348 and *Aerial Incident of 3 July 1988 (Islamic Republic of Iran v. USA)*, Order of 22 Feb. 1996, ICJ Reports 1996, 9. In the latter case, the parties had asked for the postponement *sine die* of the opening of scheduled oral hearings because of ongoing negotiations to settle the dispute; *ibid.*, 10.

[41] See, e.g., Judge Lachs in *United States Diplomatic and Consular Staff in Tehran*, Judgment, ICJ Reports 1980, 3 at 49.

[42] See, e.g., the second application by Guinea-Bissau against Senegal concerning maritime delimitation introduced on 12 Mar. 1991 and discontinued in 1995 as a result of an agreement between the parties, see *Arbitral Award of 31 July 1989*, Judgment, ICJ Reports 1991, 53 at 75 and *Maritime Delimitation between Guinea Bissau and Senegal*, Order of 8 Nov. 1995, ICJ Reports 1995, 423 and *Report of the International Court of Justice 1995–6*, A/51/4, para. 35 ff.

[43] Art. 38(1)(b) of the Protocol, which entered into force on 1 Nov. 1998. See also D.J. Harris, M. O'Boyle and C. Warbrick, *Law of the European Convention on Human Rights* (Butterworths, London, 1995), ch. 26.

[44] This, of course, is rather a different scenario from the situation where a party might seek subtly to send out hints to the Court on what it might ultimately be prepared to find politically acceptable in the forthcoming judgment.

[45] See, e.g., Judge Broms" Separate Opinion in *Passage through the Great Belt (Finland v. Denmark)*, Provisional Measures, Order of 29 July1991, ICJ Reports 1991, 12 at 39.

[46] See, e.g., *Land and Maritime Boundary between Cameroon and Nigeria*, Provisional Measures, Order of 15 Mar. 1996, ICJ Reports 1996, 13 at 24.

[47] *Ibid.*, 25. The Court here called upon the parties to lend every assistance to the fact-finding mission which the UN Secretary-General had proposed to send to the Bakassi Peninsula.

going to the Court may do so for reasons that are less clearly aimed at the settlement of a dispute upon which they are engaged. This is particularly the case with regard to the situation of third party interventions. A State will intervene in contentious cases either where it considers that it has an interest of a legal nature which may be affected by the decision in the case in question,[48] or where it is a party to a multilateral treaty and the construction of that agreement in is question.[49] However, the situation is more flexible in the case of advisory opinions. Article 66 of the Court's Statute provides that all States entitled to appear before the Court should be notified of the request for the advisory opinion "by means of a special and direct communication" as are international organisations considered by the Court (or the President if the Court is not in session) as "likely to be able to furnish information on the question".[50] Written and/or oral statements may then be made. This opens the possibility for such States and international organisations to act so as to, for example, maintain legal rights, apply or resist political pressure or influence the future development of the law.[51] Accordingly, the Court is able to act in a rather more strategic community way than is often possible in bilateral contentious disputes.

Going to the Court represents one particular strategy for States, but one that possesses special characteristics, which themselves constitute a relevant factor in choosing that option. States in applying to the Court have a variety of expectations in mind. They expect an impartial tribunal composed of independent and appropriately qualified judges applying objective and verifiable rules of law in a reasonably predictable manner. They look for an authoritative decision, which is reasoned and enforceable, binding and final, consistent and coherent.

4. TIMING

An interesting preliminary question is that of the appropriate time to approach the Court. The matter was raised in the *Nauru* case,[52] where the Court took the view that international law did not lay down any specific time limits within which an application should be made, and that it was therefore a matter for the Court to determine in the light of the circumstances of each case "whether the passage of time renders an application inadmissible". Even where in situations of delay the matter is declared admissible, the Court may have to ensure that the

---

[48] Art. 62 of the Statute of the Court. In which case, it is the Court that will decide upon the request.

[49] Art. 63 of the Statute. In this situation, States have the right to intervene.

[50] Note that under Art. 34(3) of the Statute of the Court, where the construction of the constituent instrument of a public international organisation or of an international convention adopted thereunder is in question, the Registrar is to inform the organisation concerned and communicate to it copies of all the written proceedings.

[51] See, e.g., the *Legality of the Threat or Use of Nuclear Weapons*, Advisory Opinion, ICJ Reports 1996, 226.

[52] *Certain Phosphate Lands in Nauru (Nauru v. Australia)*, Preliminary Objections, ICJ Reports 1992, 240 at 253–4.

other party is not thereby prejudiced, particularly in terms of the establishment of facts and the determination of the contents of the applicable law.[53] In certain situations, timing may be all. In the *Northern Cameroons* case,[54] for instance, the Court emphasised that it could only pronounce judgment "in connection with concrete cases where there exists at the time of the adjudication an actual controversy involving a conflict of legal interests between the parties",[55] while in the *Nuclear Tests* case,[56] it was noted, perhaps in more controversial circumstances, that "the dispute brought before it must therefore continue to exist at the time when the Court makes its decision. It must not fail to take cognisance of a situation in which the dispute has disappeared because the object of the claim has been achieved by other means". In addition, one can only point to the impact upon the Order of the Court of 14 April 1992 in the *Lockerbie* case of Security Council resolution 748 (1992), adopted three days after the conclusion of oral hearings.[57] This resolution, adopted under Chapter VII of the UN Charter, imposed binding sanctions upon Libya for failing to comply by the due date with the request to extradite the alleged bombers. However, the initial pleading before the Court was upon the basis of Resolution 731 (1992), which called for the extradition, but which did not constitute a binding decision. The Court in its Order refused to speculate upon the position prior to the adoption of the second resolution,[58] but one wonders what view the Court might have

---

[53] *Ibid.*, at 255.

[54] *Northern Cameroons*, Judgment, ICJ Reports 1963, 15 at 33–4.

[55] It appears sufficient if the dispute becomes manifest at the time of the application, or indeed during proceedings before the Court itself. See *Application of the Convention on the Prevention and Punishment of the Crime of Genocide*, Preliminary Objections, Judgment ICJ Reports 1996, 595, para. 28. *Cf.* the Separate Opinion of Judge Torres Bernárdez in *Land, Island and Maritime Frontier Dispute (El Salvador/Honduras; Nicaragua Intervening)*, Judgment, ICJ Reports 1992, 351 at 659.

[56] *Nuclear Tests (Australia v. France)*, Judgment, ICJ Reports 1974, 253 at 271.

[57] *Questions of Interpretation and Application of the 1971 Montreal Convention arising from the Aerial Incident at Lockerbie (Libyan Arab Jamahiriya v. UK)*, Provisional Measures, ICJ Reports 1992, 3 at 13.

[58] *Ibid.*, 15. The Court emphasised strongly in its preliminary objections decision of 27 Feb. 1998 in this case that the date on which the application was filed was "in fact the only relevant date for determining the admissibility of the Application", so that the adoption of the binding Security Council resolutions 748 (1992) and 883 (1993) could not be taken into consideration (*Questions of Interpretation and Application of the 1971 Montreal Convention arising from the Aerial Incident at Lockerbie (Libyan Arab Jamahiriya v. UK)*, Preliminary Objections, Judgment, ICJ Reports 1998, not yet reported, paras. 43–4). If jurisdiction existed on the date of the application, then this will continue irrespective of events occurring after this date: *ibid.*, para. 38. This reaffirms existing jurisprudence: see, e.g., *Border and Transborder Armed Actions (Nicaragua v. Honduras)*, Jurisdiction and Admissibility, Judgment, ICJ Reports 1988, 69 at 95. However, it should be noted that the paragraph in question from the *Nicaragua* case, the first sentence of which is cited by the Court, is in fact rather less definitive than at first appears. Para. 66 of this *Nicaragua* judgment goes on to state that "[i]t may however be necessary in order to determine with certainty what the situation was at the date of the filing of the Application, to examine the events, and in particular the relations between the Parties, over a period prior to that date, and indeed during the subsequent period. Furthermore, subsequent events may render an application without object, or even take such a course as to preclude the filing of a later application in similar terms".

adopted, had this resolution not appeared before the date of the Order of the Court. Timing was, perhaps, all.[59]

Timing will, however, often be critical in applications for indications of provisional measures in view of the necessity for urgency, and one would expect that States considering such applications would seek to time their applications accordingly. To apply too early might lead to rejection on the basis that the requisite urgency had not been demonstrated,[60] to apply later might indeed adversely impact upon the rights sought to be protected.

Timing may also be crucial with regard to third party interventions.[61] Applications to intervene under Article 62 of the Statute[62] are to be made "as soon as possible and not later than the closure of the written proceedings".[63] However, this may be too late for an intervenor who seeks to intervene as a party.[64] A party may have the right to appoint an *ad hoc* judge and to file pleadings, but the existing parties would have the right to reply to these. Under Articles 85(1) and 86(1) of the Rules of Court,[65] such a State has the right to see the initial memorials and annexed documents only after permission has been given by the Court for the intervention.[66] This is a likely cause of delay and frustration. It is to be envisaged that third party applications to intervene may well increase as a result partly of the successful application by Nicaragua in the *El Salvador/Honduras* case[67] and partly because of the increasing complexity of cases, not least in the maritime field, that may come before the Court.

---

[59] Note that it has been argued that the timing of a judgment of the Court itself may have political repercussions; see McWhinney, n. 19 above, at 137–9.

[60] Compare *Passage through the Great Belt (Finland v. Denmark)*, Provisional Measures, Order of 29 July 1991, ICJ Reports 1991, 12 at 17, where there was held to be no such urgency, and *Land and Maritime Boundary between Cameroon and Nigeria*, Provisional Measures, Order of 15 Mar. 1996, ICJ Reports 1996, 13 at 22, where there was held to be such urgency.

[61] See generally S. Torres Bernárdez, "L'Intervention dans la Procédure de la Cour Internationale de Justice", 256 *HR* 193; S. Rosenne, *Intervention in the International Court of Justice* (Nijhoff, Dordrecht, 1993) and n. 1 above, vol. III, at 1481; J.M. Ruda, "Intervention Before the International Court of Justice" in Lowe and Fitzmaurice, n. 1 above, at 487; C. Chinkin, "Third Party Intervention Before the International Court of Justice", 80 *AJIL* 495, and T.O. Elias, *The International Court of Justice and Some Contemporary Problems* (Nijhoff, The Hague, 1983), ch. 4. See also Rules 81–86 of the Court, 1978, and P.C. Jessup, "Intervention in the International Court", 75 *AJIL* 903.

[62] This provides that where a State considers that it has an interest of a legal nature which may be affected by the decision in the case in question, it may submit a request to the Court to be permitted to intervene. It is for the Court itself to decide upon the request. Note that under Art. 63 where the construction of a convention to which States other than those concerned in the case are parties is in question, the registrar of the Court shall notify all such States forthwith. Every State so notified has the right to intervene in the proceedings: see *SS "Wimbledon"*, Judgments, 1923, PCIJ, Series A, No. 1; *Haya de la Torre*, Judgment, ICJ Reports 1951, 71 at 76–7; and *Military and Paramilitary Activities in and against Nicaragua (Nicaragua v. USA)*, Declaration of Intervention, Order of 4 Oct. 1984, ICJ Reports 1984, 215 at 216.

[63] See also Art. 81 of the Rules of Court.

[64] See Bowett *et al.*, n. 2 above at 65.

[65] Concerning interventions under Arts. 62 and 63 of the Statute respectively.

[66] Although under Art. 53 of the Rules, the Court may furnish copies of the pleadings and documents to a State "entitled to appear before it which has asked to be furnished with such copies".

[67] *Land, Island and Maritime Frontier Dispute (El Salvador/Honduras)*, Application to Intervene, Judgment, ICJ Reports 1990, 92.

Accordingly, some thought may need to be given to whether the Court's current Rules allow sufficiently for multi-party cases, not least with regard to timing issues.

5. THE QUESTION OF REMEDIES

In applying to the Court, States will no doubt consider what may ultimately emerge from the process, in the sense of the remedies that they are able to obtain. In the broadest sense, of course, actually going to Court may constitute a form of remedy by setting the matter down before a high-profile institution in a manner which may assist, stimulate or engage bilateral or multilateral negotiations or regional or global settlement mechanisms. The exercise of the Court's incidental jurisdiction is also itself a form of remedy, whether in the context of an application for indication of provisional measures[68] or third party applications to intervene. Beyond that, it is fair to say that there has been relatively little analysis of the full range of the remedial powers of the Court.[69] In the main, an applicant State will seek a declaratory judgment that the respondent has breached international law. Such declarations may extend to provision for future conduct as well as characterisation of past conduct. Examples might include desisting from particular illegal conduct, withdrawal of forces or the drawing of terrestrial or maritime boundaries. The Court may be asked to lay down the generally applicable principles of international law or simply to resolve the dispute on a technical level. Requests for declaratory judgments may also be coupled with a request for reparation for losses suffered as a consequence of the illegal activities or damages for injury of various kinds, including non-material damage.[70] Such requests for damages may include not only direct injury to the State in question but also with regard to its citizens or their property. The Bosnian application to the Court in the *Genocide Convention (Bosnia v. Yugoslavia)* case, for example,[71] includes a claim that the respondent State is under an obligation "to pay Bosnia and Herzegovina, in its own right and as *parens patriae* for its citizens, reparations for damages to persons and property as well as to the Bosnian economy and environment caused by the foregoing violations of international law in a sum to be determined by the Court".

---

[68] See p. 44 below.

[69] But see, e.g., C. Gray, *Judicial Remedies in International Law* (Clarendon Press, Oxford, 1987) and I. Brownlie, "Remedies in the International Court of Justice" in Lowe and Fitzmaurice, n. 1 above, at 557.

[70] See, e.g., the *I'm Alone* case, 3 RIAA1609 and the *Rainbow Warrior* case, 74 ILR 241 at 274. In the latter case, the subsequent arbitration award provided that "an order for the payment of monetary compensation can be made in respect of the breach of international obligations involving . . . serious moral and legal damage, even though there is no material damage", 82 ILR at 499 and 575.

[71] *Application of the Convention on the Prevention and Punishment of the Crime of Genocide*, Provisional Measures, Order of 8 Apr. 1993, ICJ Reports 1993, 3 at 7.

Reparation may conceivably extend to *restitutio in integrum*, but this has been rather unclear.[72] However, the Court in the *Great Belt* case,[73] faced with a Danish argument that Finland's claims could only be satisfied by damages, since an order for restitution would be excessively onerous, declared that "in principle . . . if it is established that the construction of works involves an infringement of a legal right, the possibility cannot and should not be excluded *a priori* of a judicial finding that such works must not be continued or must be modified or dismantled". The issue of reparation was raised in the *Gabčikovo-Nagymaros (Hungary/Slovakia)* case,[74] where the Court had to consider the consequences of the two parties having breached the relevant treaty concerning the construction of a dam system. One of the consequences in question was the damming up of the Danube river by Slovakia (and the predecessor, the Czech and Slovak Federal Republic) in its unilateral "provisional solution". Hungary, *inter alia*, asked the Court for reparation for damage and loss resulting therefrom. The Court relied upon the definition of reparation provided in the *Chorzow Factory* case,[75] whereby reparation "must, as far as possible, wipe out all the consequences of the illegal act and re-establish the situation which would in all probability have existed if that act had not been committed".[76]

The Court dismissed the possibility of *restitutio in integrum* in the sense of requiring the dismantling of works. The Court emphasised that "it would be an administration of justice altogether out of touch with reality if the Court were to order those obligations to be fully reinstated and the works at Cunovo to be demolished when the objectives of the Treaty [of 1977] can be adequately served by the existing structures".[77] The Court rather underlined the savings clause in the *Chorzow Factory* case, that reparation had "as far as possible" to wipe out the consequences of the illegal act. The Court felt that this could be achieved by the resumption of co-operation in the utilisation of the shared water resources of the Danube in an equitable and reasonable manner.[78]

A party may if it wishes simply leave it open to the Court to apply whatever remedy it feels appropriate beyond a general claim for reparations for damage.[79] In the *Gabčikovo-Nagymaros* case,[80] the Court faced a request by Hungary and Slovakia to determine the consequences of the judgment in so far as it bore upon

---

[72]   See *Factory at Chorzów*, Merits, Judgment No. 13, 1928, PCIJ, Series A, No. 17, and *United States Diplomatic and Consular Staff in Tehran*, Judgment, ICJ Reports, 3 for possible authority for such a power. See also Gray, n. 69 above, at 95–6.

[73]   *Passage through the Great Belt (Finland v. Denmark)*, Provisional Measures, Order of 29 July 1991, ICJ Reports 1991, 12 at 19.

[74]   *Gabčikovo-Nagymaros Project (Hungary/Slovakia)*, ICJ Reports 1997, not yet reported.

[75]   *Factory at Chorzów*, Merits, Judgment No. 13, 1928, PCIJ, Series A, No. 17 at 47.

[76]   *Gabčikovo-Nagymaros Project (Hungary/Slovakia)*, ICJ Reports 1997, not yet reported, para. 149.

[77]   *Ibid.*, para. 136.

[78]   *Ibid.*, para. 150.

[79]   See, e.g., the *Oil Platforms (Islamic Republic of Iran v. US)* case, ICJ Yearbook 1993–4 at 190 ff.

[80]   *Gabčikovo-Nagymaros Project (Hungary/Slovakia)*, ICJ Reports 1997, not yet reported, para. 151 ff.

the payment of damages, which both States had claimed. The Court emphasised that it was a well-established rule of international law that an injured State was entitled to compensation from a State committing an internationally wrongful act for the damage caused to it. However, in the case in question, the Court had concluded that both parties had committed internationally wrongful acts and that therefore both parties were entitled both to receive and to pay compensation. In the light of such "intersecting wrongs", the Court declared that the issue of compensation could be satisfactorily resolved in the framework of an overall settlement by the mutual renunciation or cancellation of all financial claims and counter-claims.[81]

The parties may also confer upon the Court a prescriptive competence in addition to the Court's normal declaratory function of stating what the relevant law is in the given situation. This prescriptive competence consists of requesting the Court's assistance with regard to matters yet to be decided between the parties. Article 5 of the 1993 Special Agreement between Hungary and Slovakia concerning the jurisdiction of the Court in the *Gabčikovo-Nagymaros* case provided that "immediately after the transmission of the Judgement the Parties shall enter into negotiations on the modalities for its execution" and that "if they are unable to reach agreement within six months, either Party may request the Court to render an additional Judgement to determine the modalities for executing its Judgement". The Court, having reached its decision on the past conduct of the Parties, proceeded in its judgment to exercise its prescriptive competence, that is "to determine what the future conduct of the Paries should be".[82]

The Court emphasised that the original 1977 treaty concerning the construction of the dam project remained in force, despite breaches of it by both parties, and continued to govern the relationship of the two States. However, the Court was not prepared to disregard the fact that the treaty had not been fully implemented by the parties "for years", nor could the Court "overlook the factual situation—or the practical possibilities and impossibilities to which it gives rise—when deciding upon the legal requirement for the future conduct of the Parties".[83] Thus, although the Court emphasised that the facts flowing from wrongful conduct were not to determine the law, nevertheless the existing factual situation placed within the context of the treaty relationship was the key. These facts, as the Court noted, flowing from wrongful conduct, did determine in reality the terms of the Court's prescription. As the Court stressed, what might have been a correct application of the law in 1989 or 1992 "could be a miscarriage of justice in 1997" since the fact that the Gabčikovo power plant had been operating for some five years could not be ignored, nor could the fact that the Nagymaros project had not been built and that with the discarding of peak

---

[81] *Ibid.*, para. 153.
[82] *Ibid.*, para. 131.
[83] *Ibid.*, paras. 132–3.

power operation there was no longer any point in building it.[84] The Court concluded that, "It is not for the Court to determine what shall be the final result of these negotiations to be conducted by the Parties. It is for the Parties themselves to find an agreed solution that takes account of the objectives of the Treaty, which must be pursued in a joint and integrated way, as well as the norms of international environmental law and the principles of the law of international watercourses".[85]

The Court did, however, make further suggestions. It asserted that both parties could profit from the assistance and expertise of a third party (such as the Commission of the European Communities), and declared in rather forthright terms that "[t]he readiness of the Parties to accept such assistance would be evidence of the good faith with which they conduct bilateral negotiations in order to give effect to the Judgement of the Court".[86] The Court also made a series of concrete proposals with regard to the operations of the joint regime envisaged under the 1977 Treaty.[87] This provision of guidance, at the express request of the parties of course, is likely to be of considerable assistance to the parties as they proceed with their negotiations. Judge Schwebel, in his address of 27 October 1997 to the General Assembly, expressed the matter thus:

> "So, in a very real sense, the function of the Court in this case has been to provide the Parties with the legal answers within which they may pursue their further negotiations: in other words, to advance the progress of their mutual search for a solution by assuming responsibility for defining the fundamental legal parameters of that process. It is for them to apply the Court's Judgment in taking their negotiations to a new level. In so doing, they will be directed not only by the Court's judgment about the law of the matter, about the legal rights and wrongs of the past. They will also be guided by the Court's view as to the practical contest of future cooperative arrangements.[88]"

It would, of course, be an exaggeration to state that all disputes between States could be so handled. Nevertheless, the way in which the Court has dealt with the request by the parties for a prescriptive as well as a declaratory judgment constitutes an encouraging feature for the future functioning of the Court.

It is clear that applicants to the Court have a wide range of possibilities before them with regard to remedies, since the Court itself has not as yet developed a clear pattern of applicable remedies[89] and doubtless much remains to be done in this field.

---

[84] *Gabčikovo-Nagymaros Project (Hungary/Slovakia)*, ICJ Reports 1997, not yet reported, para. 134.

[85] *Ibid.*, para. 141.

[86] *Ibid.*, para. 143.

[87] *Ibid.*, paras. 145–6.

[88] Transcript, 3.

[89] One should also note here the effect of Art. 292 of the Convention on the Law of the Sea 1982, which provides that the question of the prompt release from detention of a vessel or its crew by another State party to the Convention "may be submitted to any court or tribunal agreed upon by the parties or, failing such agreement within 10 days from the time of detention, to a court or tribunal accepted by the detaining state under Art. 287 . . ." which shall without delay deal with the

6. AN AUTHORITATIVE DECISION BASED ON LAW

States, and their advisers, contemplating an application to the International Court appreciate that what distinguishes the Court from other organs is the fact that they will obtain an authoritative decision based on law. It also raises the issue of the nature of the exercise of the judicial function by the Court. This will include the competence to determine whether a dispute is a legal dispute, in the sense of being capable of resolution by the application of international law.[90] The Court has emphasised that the assessment of the possible conduct of States in relation to international legal obligations is an "essentially judicial task".[91]

Authoritative

The authoritativeness of the decision will essentially be founded upon the constitutional function, perceived role and reputation of the Court. In formal terms, a decision of the Court will be binding upon the parties to the case in question and in respect only of that case,[92] but the reality is that the impact of any decision will range far and wide. It will constitute a precedent in the widest sense, relied upon and cited in subsequent litigation (or indeed in other fora altogether) as an authoritative statement of law.[93] This will be done in the knowledge that the Court itself will with only the greatest hesitation depart from previous decisions.[94] Such judgments may change perceptions and confer authority upon one particular approach to a legal problem, so that that approach becomes accepted as the dominant view. One may take here the *Anglo-Norwegian*

matter. This would include the International Court of Justice by virtue of Art. 287(1)(b). It is unclear how the International Court may deal with such a situation.

[90] *Border and Transborder Armed Actions* (*Nicaragua* v. *Honduras*), Jurisdiction and Admissibility, Judgment, ICJ Reports 1988, 69 at 91. See also *Certain Expenses of the United Nations*, Advisory Opinion, ICJ Reports 1962, 151 at 155 and the *Tadic* (jurisdiction) case before the Appeals Chamber of the Yugoslav War Crimes Tribunal, IT–94–1–AR72, 11. See also R. Higgins, "Policy Considerations and the International Judicial Process", 17 *ICLQ* 58 and 74.

[91] *Legality of the Use by a State of Nuclear Weapons in Armed Conflict*, Advisory Opinion, ICJ Reports 1996, 66 at 73–4.

[92] Art. 59 of the Statute of the Court. Art. 60 states that such decision will be final and without appeal. Note that by virtue of Art. 38(1)(c) judicial decisions are deemed to be "subsidiary means for the determination of rules of law".

[93] Note that Judge Azevedo in his Dissenting Opinion in the *Asylum* case, Judgment. ICJ Reports 1950, 266 at 332, referred to the "quasi-legislative value" of such decisions. See also Judge Tanaka in his Separate Opinion in *Barcelona Traction Light and Power Company, Limited*, Preliminary Objections, Judgment, ICJ Reports 1964, 6 at 67, who referring to the *Aerial Incident of 27 July 1955* (*Israel* v. *Bulgaria*) case, ICJ Reports 1959, 127 at 143, emphasised its "tremendous influence upon the subsequent course of the Court's jurisprudence and the attitude of parties *vis-à-vis* the jurisdiction issues relative to this Court". See also Shahabuddeen, n. 19 above, at 209 ff.

[94] See, e.g., the care taken in *Temple of Preah Vihear*, Preliminary Objections, Judgment, ICJ Reports 1961, 17 at 27–8 and *Barcelona Traction Light and Power Company, Limited*, Preliminary Objections, Judgment, ICJ Reports 1964, 6 at 29–30, to distinguish *Aerial Incident of 27 July 1955* (*Israel* v. *Bulgaria*), Judgment, ICJ Reports 1959, 127.

Fisheries case,[95] or the *Corfu Channel* case[96] or the *Nicaragua* case.[97] When one considers the importance of advisory opinions where no binding element as such exists, the impact of the work of the Court becomes even more evident. Simply to mention by way of example the *Reparation* case[98] or the *Reservations to the Genocide Convention* case[99] will make this point abundantly clear. Thus, the formal role of the Court is the starting point only for a consideration of the authoritativeness of any given judgment.

The International Court rests essentially upon two streams of legitimacy. It is "the principal judicial organ of the United Nations".[100] As such it functions in accord with the terms of its Statute, which "forms an integral part of the present Charter".[101] A series of provisions deal with the position of the Court in relation to other organs and functions of the UN.[102] In addition to its role as the principal judicial organ of the UN, the Court also possesses a more general function. It constitutes, as Judge Lachs in the *Lockerbie* case has noted,[103] "the guardian of legality for the international community as a whole, both within and without the United Nations" and thus possesses both a particular responsibility with regard to the United Nations and a general responsibility towards the international community as a whole. Any State, whether or not a member of the UN, may, if the requisite jurisdictional requirements have been met, ask the Court to settle a dispute between it and another State. In the process of reaching a decision or concluding an advisory opinion, the Court may have resort to the full range of sources of international law and is not restricted to the provisions of the UN Charter itself.

---

[95] *Fisheries*, Judgment, ICJ Reports 1951, 116. See the view expressed by Fitzmaurice that, following this case, "neither the United Kingdom nor any other country could now successfully contest the general *principle* of straight baselines": G. Fitzmaurice, "Some Problems Regarding the Formal Sources of Law" in *Symbolae Verzijl* (Nijhoff, The Hague, 1958), at 170.

[96] *Corfu Channel*, Merits, Judgment, ICJ Reports 1949, 4.

[97] *Military and Paramilitary Activities in and against Nicaragua (Nicaragua v. USA)*, Merits, Judgment, ICJ Reports 1986, 14.

[98] *Reparations for Injuries Suffered in the Service of the United Nations*, Advisory Opinion, ICJ Reports 1949, 174

[99] *Reservations to the Convention on the Prevention and Punishment of the Crime of Genocide*, Advisory Opinion, ICJ Reports 1951, 15.

[100] Art. 92 of the UN Charter and Art. 1 of the Statute.

[101] Art. 92 of the UN Charter.

[102] In particular, under Art. 36(3) it is expressly provided that the Security Council should take into consideration that "legal disputes should as a general rule be referred by the parties to the International Court of Justice" and under Art. 94(2) the Council may, after application by a party to a judgment of the Court, make recommendations or decide upon measures to be taken to give effect to the particular judgment in question. Under Art. 96 the Court may be asked to give an advisory opinion on any legal question by the General Assembly or the Security Council or by other organs of the UN and specialised agencies on legal questions arising within the scope of their activities. The Court submits an annual report to the General Assembly pursuant to Art. 15(2). See e.g. Shaw, n. 29 above, at 219, 236 ff.

[103] *Questions of Interpretation and Application of the 1971 Montreal Convention arising from the Aerial Incident at Lockerbie (Libyan Arab Jamahiriya v. UK)*, Provisional Measures, Order of 14 Apr. 1992, ICJ Reports 1992, 3 at 26.

One of the strengths of the Court, perhaps the prerequisite to its successful functioning as an authoritative world court, lies in the combination of its individual and representative character,[104] the latter being what Jennings has called the "ecumenical quality".[105] The compositional issue is an important part of the recognised authority of the Court.[106] As is well known, Article 2 of the Statute refers to "a body of independent judges" of high moral and legal quality,[107] while Article 9 provides that "in the body as a whole the representation of the main forms of civilisation and of the principal legal systems of the world should be assured". Little more needs to be said of the individual quality of judges, other than that perceived impartiality is indispensable. Judges who have played a part in a case brought before the Court cannot participate in the subsequent decision. While the central core of Article 17(2) of the Statute is clear,[108] there are areas of uncertainty. Judge Zafrullah Khan, for example, was controversially persuaded to recuse himself from the *South West Africa* case[109] on the basis of having participated in UN General Assembly debates on the general questions involved.[110] The Court in the *Namibia* case[111] on the other hand took the view that the participation by members (prior to their election to the Court)

---

[104] See, e.g., M. Shahabuddeen, "The World Court at the Turn of the Century" in Muller *et al.*, n. 1 above, at 9.

[105] "The Internal Judicial Practice of the International Court of Justice", 59 *BYIL* 31 at 35. See also Sir Robert Jennings, "The Collegiate Responsibility and Authority of the International Court of Justice" in Dinstein, n. 19 above, at 343.

[106] See also S. Rosenne, "The Composition of the Court" in Peck and Lee, n. 1 above, at 377 and G. Abi-Saab, "The International Court as a World Court" in Lowe and Fitzmaurice, n. 1 above, at 3.

[107] As to independence, see, e.g., Judge Shahabuddeen's Dissenting Opinion in *Land, Island and Maritime Frontier Dispute (El Salvador/Honduras)*, Application to Intervene, Order of 28 Feb. 1990, ICJ Reports 1990, 3 at 45; Judge Zoricic, *Conditions for Admission of a State to Membership of the United Nations*, Advisory Opinion, 1948, ICJ Reports 1947–8, 57 at 95 and Judge Winiarski, *Judgments of the Administrative Tribunal of the ILO upon Complaints Made against UNESCO*, Advisory Opinion, ICJ Reports 1956, 125 at 104.

[108] "No member may participate in the decision of any case in which he has previously taken part as agent, counsel or advocate for one of the parties, or as a member of a national or international court, or of a commission of enquiry, or in any other capacity". Note that any doubt on this point is to be settled by the decision of the Court: Art. 17(3). Note also that under Art. 24(1) of the Statute, if for some special reason a member of the Court considers that he should not take part in the decision of a particular case, the President should be informed, while under Art. 24(2) "if the President considers that for some special reason one of the members of the Court should not sit in a particular case, he shall give him notice accordingly". Where the President and the member concerned disagree, the matter shall be settled by the decision of the Court (Art. 24(3)).

[109] *South West Africa*, Second Phase, Judgment, ICJ Reports 1966, 6.

[110] See, e.g., McWhinney, n. 19 above, at 92. See also the cases of Judge Sir Benegal Rau, who recused himself in the *Anglo-Iranian Oil* case on the basis that he had represented India on the Security Council when it had dealt with the UK complaint against Iran for failure to comply with the interim measures indicated by the Court; see also Franck, n. 20 above, at 323 and *ICJ Yearbook 1951–2* at 89–90; and Judge Bedjaoui, who recused himself from *Arbitral Award of 31 July 1989*, Judgment, ICJ Reports 1991, 53, on the grounds of having been one of the arbitrators in the award that was the subject of the case before the Court.

[111] *Legal Consequences for States of the Continued Presence of South Africa in Namibia (South West Africa) notwithstanding Security Council Resolution 276 (1970)*, Advisory Opinion, ICJ Reports 1971, 16 at 18–19.

in UN organs in their former capacity as government representatives did not attract the application of Article 17(2), even when in the case of one member this included playing a part in the drafting of a Security Council resolution which referred to a General Assembly resolution that lay at the heart of the case in question.[112] It is to be noted that Article 17(2) refers to recusation within a specific context, that is the "case" with regard to which the Court is to reach a decision. This may pose a particular problem where the general factual background of a case has been the subject of discussion in international organisations, but where the case itself before the Court is focused upon very specific allegations.[113] It may very well be that involvement by members of the Court prior to their election in the former situation should not impel them to recuse themselves from participating in the case itself. It is a matter of fine judgement. There is, of course, a matter of important general interest here. The judges must avoid any hint of partiality or prejudice, and this is a point of fundamental importance for the credibility of the Court, there is also a community interest in sustaining the Court as an institution composed of a wide range of talented and experienced jurists. The loss of such expertise in particular cases needs to be avoided where possible. It is a fact that the Court has been, and is, composed of many judges who have given their views on issues as national legal advisers, representatives at the UN, members of expert bodies, or as academics. Where such issues subsequently give rise to or form the background to specific litigation between particular parties, there is a difficult and sensitive choice often to be made and the greatest care must be shown by the members of the Court. Such members in deciding whether to recuse themselves, or indeed the President in exercising his powers under Article 24(2), need to consider two principles in particular. These are the necessity of avoiding any situation that may give rise to fears of bias, however unjustified in practice, and the need to maintain the basis of the Court as composed of a balanced team of experienced and authoritative members.

Although it is true that the political nature of the election process[114] has sometimes given rise to concern about the independence of judges, examination and empirical research has shown such concerns to be highly exaggerated.[115]

---

[112] But note the criticisms of this by Judges Petrén, Onyeama, Fitzmaurice and Gros, *ibid.*, 16 at 130, 138, 309 and 324.

[113] Note that Judges Higgins and Fleischauer recused themselves from the preliminary objections phase of the *Genocide Convention* case between Bosnia and Yugoslavia. President Bedjaoui at the start of oral hearings put the matter as follows: "Deux membres de la Cour, M. Fleischhauer et Mme Higgins, m'ont fait savoir qu'ayant antérieurement connu, en leur qualité, respectivement, de conseiller juridique des Nations Unies et de membre du Comité des droits de l'homme des Nations Unies, de certaines questions susceptibles d'être pertinentes aux fins de la présente affaire, ils estimaient ne pas pouvoir participer à celle-ci, conformément aux dispositions applicables du Statut de la Cour": CR 96/5, 29 Apr. 1996, 6. It should also be pointed out that at the Counter-Claims stage of this case, Judge Fleischhauer was part of the Bench while Judge Higgins was not. See *Application of the Convention the Prevention and Punishment of the Crime of Genocide*, Counter-Claims, Order of 17 Dec. 1997, not yet reported.

[114] See Arts. 4 to 10 of the Statute of the Court.

[115] See, e.g., E. Brown Weiss, "Judicial Independence and Impartiality: A Preliminary Inquiry" in L.F. Damrosch (ed.), *The International Court of Justice at a Crossroads* (Transnational Publishers,

More than that, one needs to point to the vital significance of the collegiality of the Court. This crucial, if rather indefinable, characteristic permeates the Court and those in professional contact with it. It is a combination of solemn ritual, mutual trust, integrity and professional respect. It conditions the approach of the members of the Court so that they are bound and guided by understood intellectual and moral guidelines in the conduct of their work. The ritual, language and procedures of the law perform an important function in enhancing the separation of the judges from pressures upon them that may tend to affect their consideration of matters before them. Anything which tends to diminish this collegiality is to be avoided. In this context, while one must support the need for additional research assistance to be given to members of the Court,[116] the provision of law clerks, in the very active sense that this is understood and operates in the US, would need very careful thought. The dangers of law clerks negotiating with each other on behalf of "their" judges and thus determining the essential evolution of a decision must be apparent, both for itself and for the distance that it inevitably creates between judges.[117]

As far as professional advisers are concerned, they form part of the outer circle of this collegiality, in that there is undoubtedly a shared sense of community with regard to the work of the Court in its widest sense. In many ways, it is akin to the more formal duty of an advocate to the court found in domestic systems.[118]

Decision

The role of any court is essentially on the basis of the relevant law to decide the case before it. That is what the parties want. The International Court's function, as stated in Article 38 of the Statute, is "to decide in accordance with international law such disputes as are submitted to it"[119] and Judge Weeramantry has referred to the "compelling obligation" to decide.[120]

Dobbs Ferry, NY, 1987), at 123; Franck, n. 19 above, at 319 ff. and McWhinney, n. 19 above, at 91 ff.

[116] See, e.g., the Report of the International Court for 1995–6, A/51/4, para. 193.

[117] See, e.g., the description provided in B. Woodward and S. Armstrong, *The Brethren: Inside the Supreme Court* (Simon and Schuster, New York, 1979). See also W. Richman and W. Reynolds, "Do Not Let the Law Clerks Take Over", *The Lawyer*, 20 May 1997, 149 who criticise in particular the risks in this system of over-delegation to and lack of supervision of law clerks in the US system.

[118] See also above, p. 12 et seq.

[119] See also Art. 94(1) of the United Nations Charter. As to the question whether an indication of provisional measures constitutes a decision of the Court, see, e.g., Judge Weeramantry's Separate Opinion in *Application of the Convention on the Prevention and Punishment of the Crime of Genocide*, Provisional Measures, Order of 13 Sept. 1993, ICJ Reports 1993, 325 at 383 and Rosenne, n. 1 above, at 125.

[120] Dissenting Opinion, *East Timor (Portugal v. Australia)*, Judgment, ICJ Reports 1995, 90 at 159.

Undoubtedly part of the authoritativeness of the decision of the Court in any particular instance relates to the very nature and content of the decision itself. But what is "the decision'? Lawyers, and practitioners in particular, need to know what the court in question has actually decided from the point of view of binding law. Decisions in this sense are important, for that is what will be cited before the court in subsequent litigation as crucial and unavoidable propositions. Other propositions not falling within this precedential equation will be of interest but far less influential. The distinction is therefore important. Of course, the "decision" is something different from the *dispositif*,[121] but how does one identify it from the range of propositions put forward by the Court in any given case? This is an important problem in practice, if only because it could well determine how subsequent cases are argued.

There is some opposition to the notion that the common law concepts of *ratio decidendi* and *obiter dicta* have a place in international law. Lauterpacht was unsympathetic to the view that one could apply to the work of the Court "the supposedly rigid delimitation between *obiter dicta* and *ratio decidendi* applicable to a legal system based on the strict doctrine of precedent",[122] although this was in the context of an approach that called for "a full measure of exhaustiveness of judicial pronouncements of international tribunals".[123] Rosenne has also criticised the "finely drawn distinction" as being not in contemplation with regard to Article 95(1) of the Rules of Court requiring a judgment to set out "the reasons in point of law".[124] Both these seminal authors would, however, distinguish the relevant legal reasons for the decision in question from propositions made which are not necessary for the decision. It is also the case that considerable numbers of judges have in their own separate and dissenting opinions referred to statements made *obiter dicta*.[125] Counsel in putting an argument before the Court are often impelled to determine precisely the identity and legal character of propositions being maintained as support for their views and thus need themselves to distinguish the "decision" in the widest sense of previous judgments, while the Court from time to time is itself required to address an argument that a particular proposition constitutes the *ratio decidendi* of an earlier case.[126] Thus in practice, both counsel and Court may need to address the core issue of what elements in a previous judgment may be deemed to be of precedential value, that is part of the essential reasoning leading up to, and

---

[121] See Art. 95 of the Rules of the Court. *Dispositif* is translated as "the operative provisions of the judgment", *ibid*.

[122] H. Lauterpacht, *The Development of International Law By the International Court* (Stevens, London, 1958), at 61.

[123] *Ibid*., at 37.

[124] Rosenne, n. 1 above, vol. III, at 1613.

[125] See Shahabuddeen, n. 19 above, at 154 ff. See also, generally, Sir Robert Jennings, "The Judiciary, International and National, and the Development of International Law", 45 *ICLQ* 1 at 6 ff.

[126] See *Application for Revision and Interpretation of the Judgement of 24 February 1982 in the Case concerning the Continental Shelf (Tunisia/Libyan Arab Jamahiriya)* (*Tunisia* v. *Libyan Arab Jamahiriya*), Judgment, ICJ Reports 1985, 192 at 208.

including, the *dispositif* itself. Judge Shahabuddeen has indeed in his leading study of precedent in the Court concluded that "it is difficult to deny the existence of a distinction in the jurisprudence of the Court between *ratio decidendi* and *obiter dicta*".[127] Having said that, of course, the question of the precise precedential weight to be accorded to propositions put that do not constitute the *ratio decidendi* of a judgment is another matter entirely, and one to be judged on a case-by-case basis in the light of existing international law.

The issue of the reasoning preceding the formal *dispositif* raises a further question. It is obvious that the process leading up to the decision of the Court needs to be reasoned; that is part of the judicial process itself, but how reasoned? In particular, should the Court adopt a cautious or a charismatic approach? As an example, perhaps, of the former, Jennings has praised "the economy of decision" of the Court in the *Libya/Chad* case,[128] whereby the Court focuses upon those issues considered decisive in the case and ignores the rest. This, it is maintained, is part of a "traditional legal reasoning generally practised by courts of law".[129] Adjudication, it is noted, is "a technical, intellectual, artificial method".[130] This may very well be what Lauterpacht termed "the tendency to compression" in the technique of judicial pronouncement, to be contrasted with the tendency to insist upon "a detailed examination and elaboration of the issues involved".[131] Lauterpacht himself clearly favoured the latter, noting that "there are compelling considerations of international justice and of development of international law which favour a full measure of exhaustiveness of judicial pronouncements of international tribunals".[132] The Court itself emphasised in the *Libya/Malta* case[133] that "it must be open to the Court, and indeed its duty to give the fullest decision it may in the circumstances of each case", while Judge Ranjeva in his Declaration in the *Jan Mayen* case[134] emphasised that "the authority of a decision of the Court cannot but be reinforced whenever, in stating the reasons for its judgment, it reveals the factors which shed light on the operative provisions, i.e. criteria, methods, rules of law, etc.".[135]

One practical reason adduced by Lauterpacht for adopting this broader charismatic approach is that "governments as a rule reconcile themselves to the fact that their case has not been successful—provided the defeat is accompanied

---

[127] *Ibid.*, 157.

[128] *Territorial Dispute (Libyan Arab Jamahiriya/Chad)*, Judgment, ICJ Reports 1994, 6

[129] Jennings, n. 34 above, at 35. See also Abi-Saab, n. 107 above, at 8.

[130] Jennings, n. 34 above, at 36.

[131] Lauterpacht, n. 122 above, at 62. See also G. Fitzmaurice, *The Law and Procedure of the International Court of Justice* (Grotius, Cambridge, 1986), ii, at 647–8.

[132] Lauterpacht, n. 122 above, at 37.

[133] *Continental Shelf (Libyan Arab Jamahiriya/Malta)*, Application for Permission to Intervene, Judgment, ICJ Reports 1984, 3 at 25.

[134] *Maritime Delimitation in the Area between Greenland and Jan Mayen*, Judgment, ICJ Reports 1993, 38 at 87.

[135] Note also the criticism made by Judge Oda in his Separate Opinion in the *Jan Mayen* case, ICJ Reports 1993, 38, 91 at 115, of the lack of reasoning put forward by the Court concerning its views, e.g., on drawing a single line, the relevance of "equitable access" to fishing resources or the adjustment of the median line as a point of departure.

by the conviction that their argument was considered in all its relevant aspects".[136] This is a powerful argument, particularly when allied to the issue of the authoritativeness of the Court and its decisions, for the more a decision is supported by a process of reasoned progression, the more impartial and judicial it appears. Beyond this, there is the question of the overarching function of the International Court within the international community. As Franck has succinctly written, "the International Court of Justice stands at the apex of international legal development".[137] This implies a responsibility perhaps that goes beyond a narrow interpretation of its functions with regard to each particular dispute situation and would suggest that an overly minimalist approach might not rest easily with a broader perception of the role of the Court. One is reminded here of Judge Lachs's Separate Opinion in the interim measures phase of the *Aegean Sea Continental Shelf* case,[138] that "in going further than it has, the Court, with all the weight of its judicial office, could have made its own constructive, albeit indirect, contribution, helping to pave the way to the friendly resolution of a dangerous dispute".

Perhaps in between the minimalist cautious and the maximalist charismatic approaches lies the question of the relationship between the decision and the arguments and submissions of the parties themselves. The Court noted in the *Asylum* case[139] that "one must bear in mind the principle that it is the duty of the Court not only to reply to the questions as stated in the final submissions of the parties, but also to abstain from deciding points not included in those submissions". This has often been interpreted negatively, to preclude the Court from venturing outside the guidelines provided by the parties themselves, particularly in relation to remedies not asked for.[140] It is essentially concerned with the quantum of consent within the jurisdictional framework. However, the positive injunction cannot be overlooked. Judge Lauterpacht stated in the *Norwegian Loans* case[141] that, "in my opinion a party to proceedings before the Court is entitled to expect that its judgment shall give as accurate a picture as possible of the basic aspects of the legal position of that party". While a State cannot expect in all reality for each and every one of its observations to be commented upon by the Court in its judgment, it should be able to expect that its principal lines of argument will be addressed. Reasons of polity as well as those of judicial integrity would appear to suggest this.

The conventional wisdom is that the decision of the Court is constrained by the submissions of the parties to the instant case. It was noted in the *Chorzow*

---

[136] Lauterpacht, n. 122 above, at 39.

[137] Franck, n. 19 above, at 318.

[138] *Aegean Sea Continental Shelf*, Interim Protection, Order of 11 Sept. 1976, 3 at 20.

[139] *Request for Interpretation of the Judgment of 20 November 1950 in the Asylum Case*, Judgment, ICJ Reports 1950, 395 at 402.

[140] See, e.g., Fitzmaurice, n. 131 above, at 524 ff., and Rosenne n. 1 above, vol. II, pp. 594–6. See also *Corfu Channel*, Assessment of Amount of Compensation, Judgment, ICJ Reports 1949, 244 at 249, where the Court declared itself unable to award more compensation than that claimed by the UK government.

[141] *Certain Norwegian Loans*, Judgment, ICJ Reports 1957, 9 at 36.

Factory case that "though it can construe the submissions of the parties, it cannot substitute itself for them and formulate new submissions simply on the basis of arguments and facts advanced".[142] The point was essentially repeated in the *Nuclear Tests* case.[143] This principle, of immense practical importance for the drafting of submissions is a matter over which much care is taken, has two aspects. First, the parties are entitled to expect that their principal submissions will be addressed and dealt with in reasoned conclusions and, secondly, that the parties are entitled to expect that the Court will not reach a decision on the basis of issues not referred to in their submissions and with regard to which they have not had the opportunity to put their views. Each of these propositions has been challenged in recent cases.

One may turn first to the judgment of the Court in the *East Timor* case.[144] Portugal's final submissions[145] were somewhat lengthy, carefully composed and sophisticated. The first submission called upon the Court to declare that the rights of the people of East Timor to self-determination, territorial integrity, national unity and permanent sovereignty over natural resources and that the duties and rights of Portugal as administering power were opposable to Australia, which was bound to respect them. The second submission asked the Court to declare that Australia, by reason of the actions it had taken,[146] had breached these rights of the people of East Timor and the powers of Portugal, and in addition had contravened Security Council resolutions 384 and 389.[147] Australia simply called upon the Court to declare that it lacked jurisdiction or that the application was inadmissible or alternatively that Australia had not breached international law in the circumstances.[148] The case, of course, was complicated by Indonesia's absence.

Portugal sought to argue that there were a series of "givens", arising by virtue of UN resolutions which imposed an obligation upon States not to recognise any authority on the part of Indonesia over East Timor and, as far as that territory was concerned, to deal only with Portugal.[149] The Court, however, interpreted the situation as meaning that any such approach would amount to a determination that Indonesia's entry into and continued presence in East Timor were unlawful and that, as a consequence, Indonesia did not possess any treaty-making power in matters relating to the continental shelf resources of the territory. Thus, Indonesia's rights and obligations would constitute the very subject-matter of a judgment made in the absence of the consent of that State, so that

---

[142] *Factory at Chorzów*, Merits, Judgment No. 13, 1928, PCIJ, Series A, No. 17, 7.

[143] *Nuclear Tests (Australia v. France)*, Judgment, ICJ Reports 1974, 253 at 262–3.

[144] *East Timor (Portugal v. Australia)*, Judgment, ICJ Reports 1995, 90. For comment, see also P. Bekker, 90 *AJIL* 94; C. Chinkin, 45 *ICLQ* 712, and I. Scobbie and C. Drew, "Self-Determination Undermined: The Case of East Timor", 9 *Leiden Journal of International Law* 185.

[145] *East Timor (Portugal v. Australia)*, Judgment, ICJ Reports 1995, 90 at 94–5.

[146] *Ibid.*, 94, i.e. the negotiation, conclusion and implementation of the Agreement of 11 Dec. 1989 with Indonesia and consequential activities.

[147] Submissions 3, 4 and 5 dealt with certain consequential issues.

[148] *Ibid.*, 95.

[149] *Ibid.*, 103.

the *Monetary Gold*[150] principle applied, thus foreclosing jurisdiction.[151] Despite considerable attention having been devoted to this issue by the parties, the essence of the decision by the Court on this crucial, if complex, point rests it would seem upon simple denial of the Portuguese case, unaccompanied by reasoned conclusions. Somewhat confusingly, the rejection of the Portuguese "givens" went hand in hand with the Court's declaration that the right of peoples to self-determination had been recognised both by the UN Charter and in the jurisprudence of the Court and possessed an *erga omnes* character,[152] and the rather coy acceptance by the Court that both the parties had recognised that East Timor remained a non-self-governing territory and that its people had the right to self-determination.[153] One wonders whether Portugal felt that the treatment by the Court of its final submissions was thoroughly satisfactory.

The rather disappointing approach of the Court here might be contrasted with that adopted in the *Qatar* v. *Bahrain* case concerning the relationship between the decision reached by the Court and the submissions made by the parties. The Court in its jurisdiction and admissibility decision of 1 July 1994,[154] inserted in its *dispositif* the provision that it "*decides* to afford the parties the opportunity to submit to the Court the whole of the dispute" (emphasis in original) and then proceeded to fix time limits.[155] This direction did not accord with the submissions of either party. Qatar called for the Court to accept jurisdiction over the dispute referred to in the Application filed by it on 8 July 1991,[156] while Bahrain contested the basis of the jurisdiction invoked by Qatar.[157] The difference between the dispute defined by Qatar and the "whole of the dispute" referred to by the Court was the claim by Bahrain to sovereignty over Zubarah. In other words, the decision of the Court was not to decide on the jurisdiction and admissibility issues but to call upon the parties to submit the whole of the dispute to it.[158] It could be supposed that the Court, which took the decision by 15 votes to one, felt that rather than ignoring or contradicting the submissions of the parties, it was nudging their elbows to add one further disputed issue

---

[150] *Monetary Gold Removed from Rome in 1943*, Judgment, ICJ Reports 1954, 19 at 32.

[151] *East Timor (Portugal v. Australia)*, Judgment, ICJ Reports, 1995, 90 at 104.

[152] *Ibid.*, 102. See, e.g., *Legal Consequences for States of the Continued Presence of South Africa in Namibia (South West Afrcia) notwithstanding Security Council Resolution 276 (1970)*, Advisory Opinion, ICJ Reports 1971, 16 and *Western Sahara*, Advisory Opinion, ICJ Reports 1975, 12.

[153] *East Timor (Portugal v. Australia)*, Judgment, ICJ Reports, 1995, 90 at 103.

[154] In an act termed one of "constructive diplomacy" by E. Lauterpacht, " 'Partial' Judgments and the Inherent Jurisdiction of the International Court of Justice" in Lowe and Fitzmaurice, n. 1 above, 465 at 473.

[155] *Maritime Delimitation and Territorial Questions between Qatar and Bahrain*, Jurisdiction and Admissibility, Judgment, ICJ Reports 1994, 112 at 127.

[156] This concerned disputes between the two parties with regard to sovereignty over the Hawar islands, sovereign rights over the shoals of Dibal and Qit'at Jaradah, and the delimitation of the maritime areas of the two States, *ibid.*, 114.

[157] *Ibid.*

[158] See also *Maritime Delimitation and Territorial Questions between Qatar and Bahrain*, Jurisdiction and Admissibility, Judgment, ICJ Reports 1995, 6.

between the States to the roster. This jurisdictional activism stands in interesting relationship to the de-activist decision in the *East Timor* case.[159]

Based on Law

It is, of course, self-evident that decisions of the Court must be based on law. As Jennings put it, "litigating parties do not resort to judges because they are wise or statesmanlike—very often they are manifestly neither—but because they know the law".[160] The Court has noted that it is no part of the judicial function to make a choice not based on legal consideration, but only on considerations of practicability or of political expediency,[161] while it has emphasised that it is the Court itself which "must be the guardian of the Court's judicial integrity".[162] Although the Court is a court of justice,[163] that justice is one framed and constrained by law. The Court applies international law.[164] This law is temporally constrained, it is the law at the time of the decision in question.[165]

But what if the law is not comprehensive but contains gaps? The issue of *non-liquet* has generated considerable controversy and it was in order to close any such gap that the provision of "the general principles of law recognised by civilised nations" was inserted into Article 38 of the Statute of the Court as a source of law.[166] It is important to appreciate that there may not always be an immediate and obvious rule applicable to every international situation. As Oppenheim has put it, "every international situation is capable of being determined *as a matter of law*".[167] The issue arose, perhaps rather unexpectedly, in the recent *Legality of the Threat or Use of Nuclear Weapons* case,[168] where the

---

[159] *Supra.* n. 144.

[160] Jennings, n. 125 above, at 3.

[161] See *Haya de la Torre*, Judgment, ICJ Reports 1951, 71 at 79. See also the *Free Zones of Upper Savoy and the District of Gex, Judgment, 1932*, PCIJ, Series A/B, No. 46 at 162.

[162] See *Northern Cameroons*, Judgment, ICJ Reports 1963, 15 at 29.

[163] See, e.g., Shahabuddeen, n. 104 above at 4.

[164] See Art. 38(1) of the Statute. Note that the parties may specifically request that the Court take into account particular factors. In *Continental Shelf (Tunisia/Libyan Arab Jamahiriya)*, Judgment, ICJ Reports 1982, 18 at 21, the *compromis* specifically asked the Court to take into account "the recent trends admitted at the Third Conference on the Law of the Sea".

[165] *Fisheries Jurisdiction (United Kingdom v. Iceland)*, Merits, Judgment, ICJ Reports 1974, 3 at 19 and 23–4.

[166] See, e.g., M.O. Hudson, *The Permanent Court of International Justice 1920–1942* (2nd edn. Macmillan, New York, 1943), at 194; J. Stone, *Of Law and Nations* (Hein, Buffalo, NY, 1974), ch. III; H. Lauterpacht, "Some Observations on the Prohibition of *Non-Liquet* and the Completeness of the Legal Order" in *Symbolae Verzijl*, n. 95 above, at 196, and H. Thirlway, "The Law and Procedure of the International Court of Justice", 60 *BYIL* 76. See also *North Sea Continental Shelf*, Judgment, ICJ Reports 1969, 3 at 46, and *Military and Paramilitary Activities in and against Nicaragua (Nicaragua v. USA)*, Merits, Judgment, ICJ Reports 1986, 14 at 135.

[167] Sir Robert Jennings and Sir Arther Watts (eds.), *Oppenheim's International Law* (Longmans, London, 1992), at 13.

[168] *Legality of the Threat or Use of Nuclear Weapons*, Advisory Opinion, ICJ Reports 1996, 226 at 244–5.

Court held that it could not "conclude definitely whether the threat or use of nuclear weapons would be lawful or unlawful in an extreme circumstance of self-defence, in which the very survival of the state would be at stake".[169] This very issue was the subject of a strong rebuttal by Judge Higgins in her Dissenting Opinion.[170]

Without Undue Delay

As the Court has itself emphasised,[171] "it is in the interest of the authority and proper functioning of international justice for cases to be decided without unwarranted delay". Justice must not only be done and be seen to be done,[172] it must be done expeditiously. Justice delayed is justice denied and unwarranted delay impacts upon the credibility of any legal system.

There are many issues connected with the problem in question. The Court will itself set time limits for the production of the various stages of the written pleadings[173] in close consultation with the parties. Generous time limits are clearly inevitable due to the requirement of preparation of relevant material.[174] Such time limits may be extended by the parties themselves for various reasons. On occasions it is genuinely felt that more time is needed in order to prepare the pleadings thoroughly in view of difficulties of obtaining or analysing source materials. On other occasions, delays will be requested in order to permit negotiations to develop.[175] The Court, however, is rightly sensitive to criticisms made of it of undue delay where it is apparent that the fault lies elsewhere.[176]

The expectation that the Court will produce an authoritative reasoned decision based on law in a reasonably predicable manner without undue delay forms the basis of any consideration by potential litigants as to whether or not to make a formal application to the Court.

7. SOME PROCEDURAL ISSUES

Procedure is often one of the keys to success in litigation. Knowledge of it is certainly a crucial practical matter. The formalised system of procedure at the

---

[169] *Ibid.*, 266 (para. 2E of the *dispositif*). See also 263 (para. 97).

[170] *Ibid.*, 583 ff.

[171] In *Barcelona Traction Light and Power Company, Limited*, Second Phase, Judgment, ICJ Reports 1970 3 at 31.

[172] See, e.g., Judge Lachs in his Separate Opinion in *Military and Paramilitary Activities in and against Nicaragua (Nicaragua v. USA)*, Merits, Judgment, ICJ Reports 1986, 14 at 171.

[173] See further p. 39 below.

[174] P. 40 below.

[175] See, e.g., *Aerial Incident of 3 July 1988 (Islamic Republic of Iran v. USA)*, Order of 22 Feb. 1996, ICJ Reports 1996, 9.

[176] See, e.g., *Barcelona Traction Light and Power Company, Limited*, Second Phase, Judgment, ICJ Reports 1970, 3 at 30–1.

International Court is founded upon equality of States and sustains the concept of the equality of arms as between State litigants.[177] The Court has the power to regulate its own procedure,[178] but closely consults the parties to a case on such questions. The parties themselves may jointly propose modifications to many of the Rules of Court in contentious proceedings,[179] while alterations to the normal pattern of proceedings made by the Court may be acceptable upon the basis of the consent of the parties, even where the proposed changes are not specifically authorised by the Rules.[180] It is indeed worth pointing out that the attitude of the Court in general terms to procedural questions of form is less stringent than is the case in domestic legal systems.[181]

There are, however, some procedural issues of particular moment to litigating States. The first is with regard to the structure of pleadings. Written pleadings are governed by Articles 44 to 53 of the Rules of Court. These in effect allow the parties considerable latitude. While it is for the Court itself to determine the number, order and timing of filings of pleadings, this is done in consultation with the parties and the Court is ready to allow parties to extend time-limits or determine whether, for example, there should be further rounds of pleadings. On the precise contents of such written pleadings, the Rules are vague. The memorial is to contain a statement of relevant facts, a statement of law and the submissions. The counter-memorial is to contain an admission or denial of the facts stated in the memorial, any additional facts if necessary, observations upon the statement of law in the memorial and a statement of law in answer thereto and the submissions.[182] The reply and rejoinder, if authorised by the Court, are not intended merely to repeat the contentions of the parties but should be directed at bringing out the issues still dividing them.[183] In practice, this admonition is often neglected.

---

[177] Note Thirlway's view that procedure is "no more than a way of getting somewhere": H. Thirlway, "Procedural Law and the International Court of Justice" in Lowe and Fitzmaurice, n. 1 above, at 389.

[178] See, e.g., Judge Weeramantry's Dissenting Opinion in the *Request for an Examination of the Situation in Accordance with Paragraph 63 of the Court's Judgment of 20 December 1974 in the Nuclear Tests (New Zealand* v. *France)* case, ICJ Reports 1995, 288 at 320, where he noted that this power enabled it to devise a procedure *sui generis*.

[179] See Art. 101 of the Rules of Court.

[180] An example of this was the additional application submitted by the Cameroon in the *Cameroon* v. *Nigeria* case on 6 June 1994 to the original application of 29 Mar. 1994 which had the effect of extending the dispute before the Court. The Agent of Nigeria stated that he had no objection to the additional application being treated as an amendment to the original application, see, e.g., *Land and Maritime Boundary between Cameroon and Nigeria*, Order of 16 June 1994, 105 and Provisional Measures, Order of 15 Mar. 1996, ICJ Reports 1996, 13. Neither the Statute nor the Rules of the Court provide for the amendment of applications, although Rule 47 does permit the joinder of two or more cases. See also Lauterpacht, n. 155 above, at 475–6.

[181] See, e.g., *Mavrommatis Palestine Concessions*, Judgment No. 2, 1924, PCIJ, Series A, No. 2, 34 and *Certain German Interests in Polish Upper Silesia*, Jurisdiction No. 6, 1925, PCIJ, Series A, No. 6, 14.

[182] Arts. 49(1) and (2) of the Rules.

[183] Art. 49(3) of the Rules.

Complaints have been made concerning the length of written pleadings and the time taken to file them, with suggestions for word limits.[184] However, it does need to be appreciated that for litigant states important political as well as legal factors are in play. The Court must be seen to be affording States every reasonable consideration in order to avoid a losing party complaining that no sufficient opportunity was allowed for the full elucidation of its case. The range of primary research required, often amongst documents stored abroad as well as those found within the territory of the litigant State, coupled with the need to organise an international team of counsel and assistants and provide for the necessary logistical and translation support, means that the realistic possibility of curtailing either the time limits for filing or the length of written pleadings is marginal. Even with the best organised and most generously resourced teams in place, much time may be required. It is also believed that the scope for reducing the scale of annexed documents is not large. States, with their national and international advisers, often have a necessarily broad perception of the evidence that must be produced to prove their arguments and disprove those of their adversaries, while modern technological and library developments have meant that more relevant documents are likely to be available than hitherto may have been the case. It also needs to be realised that for many States their written pleadings may have an importance going beyond the immediate case before the Court. They may constitute, and be designed to constitute, a national statement for the record, an exposition of a particular position that will stand as an authoritative commentary for historical purposes. Nevertheless, it may be possible for annexed documents to be better organised for the assistance of the Court. It may be that States could distinguish between those documents that are necessary to prove a particular proposition (or disprove that of the other side) and those that simply add to the weight of existing evidence or merely assist in "setting the scene". Such an arrangement might well prove helpful to the Court as it seeks to digest the extensive materials provided and thus ultimately assist the parties in speeding up the process of consideration.

One controversial issue linking expense and time is that of translation costs. At the moment, the Registry of the Court is responsible for preparing translations of submitted pleadings and documents into the two official languages, as well as for the interpretation of oral hearings. This is time consuming and expensive, although a function which ought to be carried out by the Registry. In view of the serious financial situation faced by the Court,[185] it has been suggested that perhaps the parties to a case might be prepared to submit their written materials in both English and French, rather than in one only of the official languages.[186] There are clearly important cost implications here for litigating States. However, and in the absence of the provision of the necessary resources

---

[184] See, e.g., Highet, n. 9 above, at 131.

[185] Note the concern of the Court expressed in its annual report to the General Assembly covering 1995/6, A/51/4, para. 188 ff.

[186] See, e.g., Highet, n. 9 above, at 131.

by the UN, it might be helpful to seek to establish an expectation or culture whereby parties should, if at all possible and bearing in mind that this might expedite the oral hearing of cases, provide written pleadings in both official languages. Many counsel, for example, have felt frustration where material they have drafted in one official language is translated into the official language used by their client and is then re-translated back into the original language by the Registry of the Court in perhaps a slightly less felicitous form. A modest step might be to permit counsel to submit their original drafts to the Registry at the same time as the written pleadings in the other language are delivered. In addition, it might be possible to use the suggested distinction in the documentary annexes[187] between those deemed essential to a party's case and those that either simply constitute supporting evidence or merely set the scene. It is felt that, in any event, the parties should assume responsibility for the translation of those documents that fall within the second category.

The question of oral pleadings is, however, rather different. Ignoring the determination of counsel to plead before the Court, one must think carefully about the length of oral pleadings.[188] The advantage of an oral proceeding is that it really does provide an opportunity for those representing the State in litigation to put over the essentials of its argument in an appealing and dramatic, if not melodramatic, way. It is indeed true that a more emphatic and nuanced exposition of a State's case orally may bring out elements rather hidden in the dry language of the written pleadings. Oral statements can make a difference. However, there really does appear to be no necessity for a wholesale reiteration of material, both factual and legal, contained in the written pleadings. The view sometimes maintained that one cannot realistically expect a judge to have read the papers, and that therefore one must conduct the case as if essentially there have been no written pleadings, is a little condescending. Oral presentations are important and should take place in order to bring the essentials of the argument to life in a memorable way. They are not needed as talking memorials, counter-memorials, replies and rejoinders.[189] In essence, the provisions of Article 60(1) of the Rules need to be actually applied.

Cases are about law and facts. The Court is expected to know the law, elucidating the facts raises particular problems. The Court has wide powers with regard to evidential matters,[190] and, as Judge Schwebel, the current President of

---

[187] P. 40 above.

[188] See, e.g., Bowett *et al.*, n. 1 above, at 40 ff.

[189] Note that Art. 60(1) of the Rules of the Court provide that "the oral statements made on behalf of each party shall be as succinct as possible within the limits of what is requisite for the adequate presentation of that party's contentions at the hearing. Accordingly, they shall be directed to the issues that still divide the parties, and shall not go over the whole ground covered by the pleadings, or merely repeat the facts and arguments these contain". See also Jiménez de Aréchaga, n. 19 above, at 6.

[190] See e.g. Alford, "Fact-Finding by the World Court", 4 *Vill. LR* 37; S. Schwebel, "Three Cases of Fact-Finding by the International Court of Justice" in Schwebel, *Justice in International Law*, (Cambridge University Press, Cambridge, 1994), at 125; K. Highet, "Evidence, the Court and the Nicaragua Case", 81 *AJIL* 1 and "Evidence and Proof of Facts" in Damrosch, n. 116 above, at 355; R.B. Lillich (ed.), *Fact-Finding Before International Tribunals* (Transnational, Ardsley-on-Hudson,

the Court, has recently remarked "its attitude to evidence is demonstrably flexible".[191] It has under Article 36 of the Statute the competence, *inter alia*, to determine the existence of any fact which if established would constitute a breach of an international obligation. It may make all arrangements with regard to the taking of evidence,[192] call upon the agents to produce any document or to supply any explanations as may be required,[193] or at any time establish an enquiry mechanism or obtain expert opinion.[194] The Court may indeed make on-site visits.[195] This impressive array, however, needs to be qualified. First, it has no power to compel production of evidence generally. Secondly, neither witnesses nor experts can be subpoenaed. Thirdly, there is no equivalent to proceedings for contempt of court.[196] Fourthly, the Court has been reluctant to utilise the powers it possesses. For example, use of experts has been comparatively rare,[197] as has been recourse to witnesses.[198] Agents are rarely asked to produce documents or supply explanations, and there have been only two on-site visits to date.[199] This has produced a situation where the parties feel able to present whatever evidence, primarily documents and maps that they feel would be of assistance in a whole variety of complex circumstances. It has also meant that the Court has sought to evaluate claims primarily upon an assessment of the documentary evidence provided, utilising also legal techniques such as inferences and admissions against interest.[200] In addition, the Court has felt able to take judicial notice of facts which are public knowledge, primarily though media dissemination.[201] Evidence which has been illegally or improperly acquired may also be taken into account, although no doubt where this happens its probative value would be adjusted accordingly.[202] The Court has on the whole been prepared to be flexible with regard to evidential material. In the second provisional measures order in the *Genocide Convention (Bosnia v.*

1991), and D.V. Sandifer, *Evidence Before International Tribunals* (rev. edn. University Press of Virginia, Charlottesville, 1975).

[191]   Address of 27 Oct. 1997 to the UN General Assembly, Transcript, 4.

[192]   Art. 48 of the Statute.

[193]   Art. 49 of the Statute.

[194]   Art. 50 of the Statute. By Art. 43(5), the Court may hear witnesses and experts, as well as agents, counsel and advocates.

[195]   Art. 44(2) of the Statute and Art. 66 of the Rules of Court.

[196]   See Highet, n. 190 above, at 10.

[197]   But see *Corfu Channel*, Merits, Judgment, ICJ Reports 1949, 4.

[198]   But see, e.g., *Corfu Channel*, Merits, Judgment, ICJ Reports 1949, 4; *Continental Shelf (Tunisia/Libyan Arab Jamahiriya)*, Judgment, ICJ Reports 1982, 18; *Continental Shelf (Libyan Arab Jamahiriya/Malta)*, Judgment, ICJ Reports 1985, 13; and *Military and Paramilitary Activities in and against Nicaragua (Nicaragua v. USA)*, Merits, Judgment, ICJ Reports 1986, 14.

[199]   First, in *Diversion of the River Meuse*, Judgment, 1937, PCIJ, Series A/B, No. 70, 4 and secondly in *Gabčikovo-Nagymaros Project (Hungary/Slovakia)*, Order of 5 Feb., ICJ Reports 1997, 3.

[200]   See, e.g., *Military and Paramilitary Activities in and against Nicaragua (Nicaragua v. USA)*, Merits, Judgment, ICJ Reports 1986, 14. The difficulties of proving facts in this case were, of course, exacerbated by the absence of the respondent State during the proceedings on the merits.

[201]   *Ibid.*

[202]   See, e.g., *Corfu Channel*, Merits, Judgment, ICJ Reports 1949, 4 at 32–6. See also H. Thirlway, "Dilemma or Chimerá?—Admissibility of Illegally Obtained Evidence in International Adjudication", 78 *AJIL* 622.

Yugoslavia) case, for example,[203] the Court was prepared to admit a series of documents even though submitted on the eve and during the oral hearings, despite being "difficult to reconcile with an orderly progress of the procedure before the Court, and with respect for the principle of equality of the parties".[204] The admission was actually achieved by virtue of recategorising the material as "observations", which under Article 74(3) of the Rules of Court can be presented before the closure of the oral hearings. This way of proceeding inevitably raises concerns with regard to procedural regularity. Ultimately, the question of production of evidence is one for the parties concerned. They bear the burden of proving their claims to the satisfaction of the Court[205] and in the current circumstances are likely to err on the side of over- rather than under-production of what is regarded as possibly relevant.[206]

Two further issues of practical moment merit brief consideration. Article 79 of the Rules of Court provides for preliminary objections to be made to the jurisdiction of the Court or the admissibility of the application "in writing within the time-limit fixed for the delivery of the counter-memorial". This allows for the respondent State to wait until almost the conclusion of the period allowed for production of the counter-memorial (usually in the order of nine months) before signalling objections to jurisdiction. If such objections are dismissed, the period allowed for production of the counter memorial starts again. This can hardly be equitable. It allows not only for the introduction of unfortunate, albeit legitimate, delaying tactics, but also for the respondent State to have double the usual period for preparation of the counter-memorial. It could perhaps be suggested that if a party wishes to object to jurisdiction or admissibility, then this could be communicated to the Court in short form within two months of the receipt of the memorial. At that point, the Court could then fix time limits for the jurisdictional phase.

It may also be suggested that much tighter time limits would be apposite for the jurisdictional phase than for the merits phase. Clearly the wealth of documentary material usually necessary for the latter stage, which takes so much

---

[203] *Application of the Convention on the Prevention and Punishment of the Crime of Genocide*, Provisional Measures, Order of 13 Sept. 1993, ICJ Reports 1993, 325 at 336–7.

[204] Art. 56 of the Rules provides that after the closure of written proceedings, no further documents may be submitted to the Court by either party, except with the consent of the other party or in the absence of consent where the Court, after hearing the parties, authorises production where it is felt that the documents are necessary.

[205] See, e.g., *Military and Paramilitary Activities in and against Nicaragua (Nicaragua v. USA)*, Merits, Judgment, ICJ Reports 1986, 14 at 392 and 437.

[206] Of particular interest here is the view taken by the Arbitral Tribunal for Dispute over Inter-Entity Boundary in Brcko Area in its Award of 14 Feb. 1997. The Appendix to the Order lays down the Principles Applicable to the Admissibility of Evidence and notes, *inter alia*, that each party bears the burden of proving its own case and in particular facts alleged by it. The party having the burden of proof must not only bring evidence in support of its allegations, but must also convince the Tribunal of their truth. The Tribunal is not bound to adhere to strict judicial rules of evidence, the probative force of evidence being for the Tribunal to determine. Where proof of a fact presents extreme difficulty, the Tribunal may be satisfied with less conclusive, i.e. *prima facie* evidence: see 36 ILM 396 at 402–3.

time to investigate, collate and analyse, is not a factor in jurisdictional problems and the Court should be prepared for speedy hearings on these questions.[207]

The other area which tends to raise important practical issues relates to the application for indication of provisional measures to preserve the rights of the parties under Article 41 of the Statute.[208] Two points only will be briefly noted. First, what is the impact of an application for such measures upon the conduct of the case in practice? Or, in other words, in what circumstances would it be practically advantageous for a party to apply for the indication of provisional measures? It is clear that the Court will not indicate provisional measures unless the provisions invoked by the applicant appear *prima facie* to afford a basis upon which the jurisdiction of the Court might be founded.[209] Often, it is deemed psychologically advantageous to obtain such provisional measures where jurisdiction has been challenged by the other side for the acceptance of a *prima facie* jurisdictional base might be seen as a step forward, not least in domestic political terms where, because of the filing of preliminary objections, it is likely to be many years before the merits may be heard. On the other hand, if the application is refused, then consequential political problems may very well occur. Again, it is possible that the application for provisional measures, although apparently delaying the ultimate merits stage because of the interposition of an additional phase of the case, may in fact have the opposite effect. In the *Great Belt* case,[210] the Court, in rejecting the necessity for interim measures, noted that in the normal course of events the merits stage would be completed before the physical obstruction of the East Channel, which would be not before the end of 1994. Judge Broms in his Separate Opinion[211] pointed out that

---

[207] Note that under Art. 54(2) of the Rules, the Court, in fixing the date for oral hearings, "shall have regard . . . to any other special circumstances, including the urgency of a particular case". This would permit the Court to enable hearings on jurisdiction to have a certain priority.

[208] See also Arts. 73–8 of the Rules of Court. See, e.g., S. Oda, "Provisional Measures", in Lowe and Fitzmaurice, n. 1 above, at 541; B. Oxman, "Jurisdiction and the Power to Indicate Provisional Measures", in Damrosch, n. 115 above, at 323; J.G. Merrills, "Interim Measures of Protection and the Substantive Jurisdiction of the International Court", 36 *CLJ* 86 and "Interim Measures of Protection in the Recent Jurisdiction of the International Court of Justice", 44 *ICLQ* 90; Rosenne, n. 1 above, vol. iii at 1419; L. Gross, "The Case Concerning United States Diplomatic and Consular Staff in Tehran: Phase of Provisional Measures", 74 *AJIL* 395; Gray, n. 69 above, at 69–74; and M. Mendelson, "Interim Measures of Protection in Cases of Contested Jurisdiction", 46 *BYIL* 259.

[209] See the request by Guinea-Bissau for the indication of provisional measures in *Arbitral Award of 31 July 1989*, Provisional Measures, Order of 2 Mar. 1990, ICJ Reports 1990, 64 at 68. See also *Passage through the Great Belt (Finland v. Denmark)*, Provisional Measures, Order of 29 July 1991, ICJ Reports 1991, 12 at 15, where jurisdiction was not at issue and *Land and Maritime Boundary between Cameroon and Nigeria*, Provisional Measures, Order of 15 Mar. 1996, ICJ Reports 1996, 13 at 21, where it was. The Court in *Application of the Convention on the Prevention and Punishment of the Crime of Genocide*, Provisional Measures, Order of 8 Apr. 1993, ICJ Reports 1993, 3 at 12 noted that jurisdiction included both jurisdiction *ratione personae* and *ratione materiae*. Note that Jiménéz de Aréchaga, a former President of the Court, has written that "interim measures will not be granted unless a majority of judges believes at the time that there will be jurisdiction over the merits": "International Law in the Past Third of a Century", 159 *HR* 1 at 161.

[210] *Passage through the Great Belt (Finland v. Denmark)*, Provisional Measures, Order of 29 July 1991, ICJ Reports 1991, 12 at 18.

[211] *Ibid.*, 37 and 38.

"another thing changing the original situation was that later during the deliberations of the case the Court decided to make the final decision of the case expeditiously, probably during the spring of 1992 or at the latest in the fall of 1992". It would therefore appear that the application for provisional measures, although unsuccessful, in fact succeeded in causing an acceleration in the planned timetable. Another advantage in applying for an indication of provisional measures is that it may stimulate the furnishing of assurances from the other party with regard to a critical matter. The *Great Belt* case[212] provides an example of this. During the oral hearing on the application, Denmark gave assurances that no physical hindrance for the passage through the Great Belt would occur before the end of 1994.[213] By "placing on record"[214] such assurances, the Court concluded that the urgency requirement for the indication of provisional measures had not been met. Nevertheless, despite failing to obtain interim relief, Finland in fact achieved an important objective in terms of the assurances.[215] Of course, and upon an analogy with domestic procedures, it may well be open to the party against whom such interim relief is obtained to seek a cross-undertaking in damages whereby it would be compensated for losses suffered as a consequence of complying with provisional measures where it eventually succeeded on the merits.[216]

Less tactically, the applicant State may feel that the deterioration in the situation alleged is such that both it and the Court must be seen to do something or lose credibility. This is particularly so where it is envisaged that several years may elapse before the merits of the case are heard.[217] The Court has set a fairly high threshold for grant of provisional measures. They must protect rights which are the subject of dispute in judicial proceedings,[218] and which are at risk of irreparable damage.[219] The Court has also stated that provisional measures are only justified if there is urgency.[220] Speed is essential and on the whole the Court does respond with adequate rapidity.

---

[212] *Ibid.*

[213] *Ibid.*, 18. See also CR 91/1I, 11, 2 July 1991.

[214] *Ibid.*

[215] See also Merrills, n. 208 above, 44 *ICLQ* 90 at 112.

[216] This was sought by Denmark in *Passage through the Great Belt (Finland v. Denmark)*, Provisional Measures, Order of 29 July 1991, ICJ Reports 1991, 12 at 15, but was not decided upon since Finland's application for the indication of provisional measures failed. See also Merrills, n. 215 above, at 117.

[217] See also the two Orders of the Court in *Application of the Convention on the Prevention and Punishment of the Crime of Genocide*, Provisional Measures, Order of 8 Apr. 1993, ICJ Reports 1993, 3 and Order of 13 Sept. 1993, ICJ Reports 1993, 325.

[218] *Aegean Sea Continental Shelf*, Interim Protection, Order of 11 Sept. 1976, 3 at 9 and *United States Diplomatic and Consular Staff in Tehran*, Provisional Measures, Order of 15 Dec. 1979, ICJ Reports 1979, 7 at 19. See also *Arbitral Award of 31 July 1989*, Provisional Measures, Order of 2 Mar. 1990, ICJ Reports 1990, 64 at 69.

[219] See e.g. Merrills, n. 215 above, at 106 ff.

[220] See *Passage through the Great Belt (Finland v. Denmark)*, Provisional Measures, Order of 29 July 1991, ICJ Reports 1991, 12 at 17. Cf. *Land and Maritime Boundary between Cameroon and Nigeria*, Provisional Measures, Order of 15 Mar. 1996, ICJ Reports 1996, 13 at 22.

The second issue relates to the efficacy of such measures once granted. The record of compliance with provisional measures is not on the whole encouraging,[221] nevertheless, there may be a price for a State ignoring such measures. This will depend upon the Court being willing to refer clearly to the issue at the later stages of the case. For example, the Court was prepared to make some rather critical comments with regard to the attempted US rescue of its hostages in Iran in April 1980,[222] which followed the indication of provisional measures on 15 December 1979 calling for abstention from action which might aggravate tension.[223] Once a party has taken the tactical decision to apply for provisional measures and obtained them, it may consider returning to the Court if such measures have not been respected. However, a second order from the Court may be no more successful in achieving the desired result and may in any event prove logistically counter-productive, in that consideration of the case may be meaningfully delayed by the application.[224] Nevertheless, the Court under Article 78 of its Rules has the authority to request information from the parties on any matter connected with the implementation of any provisional measures it has indicated, and it may be considered whether a formal follow-up mechanism under this provision might not be instituted in order to be seen to be acting in what has already been accepted as an urgent situation.

8. MANAGING CASES

One of the major current concerns with regard to the Court relates to the time taken for deliberation between the close of oral hearings and the announcement of the decision.[225] The process for deliberation is well known.[226] The question,

[221] See, e.g., *Fisheries Jurisdiction (United Kingdom v. Iceland)*, Merits, Judgment, ICJ Reports 1974, 3 at 17.

[222] *United States Diplomatic and Consular Staff in Tehran*, Judgment, ICJ Reports 1980, 3 at 43.

[223] *United States Diplomatic and Consular Staff in Tehran*, Provisional Measures, Order of 15 Dec. 1979, ICJ Reports 1979, 7.

[224] Since under Art. 74(1) of the Rules of the Court a request for the indication of provisional measures has priority over all other cases.

[225] See Bowett *et al*, n. 1 above, at 59, where the six and a half month period between close of oral hearings and delivery of judgment in the *Territorial Dispute (Libyan Arab Jamahiriya/Chad)* case is cited, a judgment which was not complex, relying on one critical ground and taking some 17 pages only of reasoning.

[226] An outline of the procedure is given by R. Higgins in Ch. 1 of this vol. In brief and simple terms, the following constitutes the usual methodology. A meeting of the Court is held before oral arguments begin for an exchange of views on the written pleadings and to identify points on which explanations need to be solicited from the parties. After the close of oral hearings, a meeting is held to discuss the case at which the President will present an Outline of Issues, prepared by the Registry and approved by him. Judges will then prepare written notes on the case if they wish. After a period, a meeting will be held at which the judges will present their opinions orally in reverse order of seniority. A Drafting Committee will be established from among those representing the majority opinion. A preliminary draft will be circulated, which will be revised by the Committee in the light of any amendments and then discussed. Drafts of separate and dissenting opinions will also be circulated. An amended draft of the judgment will be discussed and the final versions of judgment and opinions prepared. See the 1976 Resolution on Practice, International Court of Justice, *Acts and*

however, is what can be done to ensure the rapid completion of the deliberation stage leading to judgment without affecting in any way the authority and weight of that judgment. It is realised by all that such careful deliberation inevitably takes time. However, it may be possible to hasten parts of the process by administrative measures.[227] Judge Schwebel, in his address to the General Assembly on 27 October 1997 as current President of the Court, referred to the recent adoption of a "range of alterations to its working practices".[228] It has been decided to proceed without written Notes where necessary in suitable cases concerning the jurisdiction of the Court of the admissibility of the application. This change is for an experimental period. In addition, appropriate cases on jurisdiction may be heard "back to back", so that work may proceed on them both concurrently. This is also introduced on an experimental basis. The recent practice of giving the parties advance notice of its intended schedule for the next three cases has also been confirmed.

One measure which may be suggested concerns the management of cases from their inception to the implementation of the judgment. One could envisage the establishment of a system whereby a small two- or three-person Case Review Committee would be set up with regard to each case submitted to the Court upon the filing of the application.[229] This Review Committee would keep track of all relevant developments, reporting back to the full Court at regular intervals. The Committee could have a role with regard to oral pleadings. It would be helpful if each litigant State were to provide to the Committee (and to each other) a couple of months prior to the oral hearings,[230] a short, focused

---

Documents Concerning the Organisation of the Court, 1989, 165. See also, e.g., Jennings, n. 105 above; M Bedjaoui, "La 'Fabrication' des Arrêts de la Cour International Internationale de Justice" in *Le Doit international au service de la paix, de la justice et du developpement: mélanges Michel Virally* (Pedone, Paris, 1991), at 87; S. Oda, "The International Court of Justice Viewed from the Bench", 244 *HR* VII, 13 and Bowett *et al.*, n. 1 above, at 51 ff. Compare also the Resolution on Internal Judicial Practice adopted on 31 Oct. 1997 by the International Tribunal for the Law of the Sea, ITLOS/10.

[227] Note the view of Judge Oda that in order for more cases to be dealt with by the Court, "reform of the deliberation procedure will become inevitable", n. 226 above, at 126.

[228] Transcript, 5–6.

[229] This would operate under the overall direction of the President as per Art. 12 of the Rules.

[230] Which should themselves be scheduled soon after the completion of the written proceedings. See, e.g., the call by Bowett *et al.* for an indicative six months maximum between closure of pleadings and commencement of oral argument: n. 1 above, at 40. Note also the view taken by the Court in its Counter-Claims order of 17 Dec. 1997 in the *Genocide Convention* case between Bosnia and Yugoslavia that oral hearings were not necessary at such a stage as the Court was "sufficiently well informed of the positions" the parties held: see para. 25. This controversial finding was criticised by Judge Koroma and by Judge *ad hoc* Lauterpacht in their Separate Opinions. The Court had earlier indicated that both parties contemplated that there would be oral hearings on the question of the admissibility of Yugoslavia's counter-claims after the exchange of written observations: *ibid.*, para 7. Art. 80(3) of the Rules of Court provides that "[i]n the event of doubt as to the connection between the question presented by way of counter-claim and the subject-matter of the claim of the other party the Court shall, after hearing the parties, decide whether or not the question thus presented shall be joined to the original proceedings". While speed is important in reaching a decision, it is felt that where the admissibility of the proposed counter-claim is questioned by the other party and where the Court is aware that the parties expect oral hearings with regard to such important—albeit incidental—proceedings, such hearings should indeed be held. See also Rosenne, n. 1 above, iii, at 1273.

written statement of the essentials of the case in order to highlight the fundamental issues as seen by that State. This would then allow the Committee to signal to the parties which points would be of particular assistance to the judges in oral exposition. Such a short statement to the parties, provided say a month prior to the oral hearings, would no doubt include the fundamental points put by each side, but would allow the parties to be able to identify issues that were felt to be of little importance and which could safely be left in the written arena. This manner of focusing upon the essential issues may very well assist in the reduction of the time spent on oral hearings.

The moment that oral hearings are concluded, a report could be given by the Review Committee to the full Court detailing the key arguments put by each side and indicating the ways in which the matter could be dealt with by the Court. This report might indeed replace the "President's Outline of Issues" document prepared by the Registry and approved by the President.[231] The Committee may also take it upon itself to guide the careful process of preparation of notes, discussions and drafts that invariably and rightly follows. Nothing should be done to impact upon the development of the reasoning of the Court, but the Review Committee system for each case may allow for simultaneous consideration of several cases in on-going review meetings from application onwards, becoming more detailed and substantial as the case progresses. It is also conceivable that the Review Committee would be the appropriate forum to conduct any necessary follow-up activity with regard to provisional measures, reporting as necessary to the full Court. This method of managing cases would at least ensure an up-to-date and full knowledge of each case at each stage and should help reduce the time taken for deliberation.

9. CONCLUSIONS

The Court does not constitute an exclusive, self-contained world, but exists as part of a wide-ranging set of mechanisms and means for the resolution of inter-State disputes. States recognise this and act accordingly. What States seek specifically from the Court is an authoritative decision based on internationally accepted criteria within the bounds of reasonable professional predictability. This means that both the impartiality of the individual judge and the independence and collegiality of the Court as a whole are crucial components in the system. While the substantive law to be applied by the Court is coherent and comprehensive, it is true that there remains a need to elaborate in a more sophisticated fashion a systemic range of remedies that may be provided. It is also felt that community needs and expectations argue for a broader rather than a narrower approach from the Court with regard to its process of reasoning up to and including the *dispositif*. At the very least, the Court must address the major lines of argument from and submissions of the parties.

[231] See n. 226 above.

The relationship between the Court and States within the international system is not at all analogous to the relationship between superior courts and litigants within domestic legal orders. This situation bears certain consequences, including, for example, the need to allow States to develop their arguments as they see fit. Nevertheless, this does not preclude the need for the Court to improve the technical process of considering cases. It may be that the Court should proceed in the future in a rather more proactive fashion in managing cases before it, showing always sensitivity and care. Areas where this may be of advantage would possibly include signalling what the Court feels is important and less important for oral elucidation and indicating to the parties where it is felt that further evidence may be required in order to demonstrate the point being asserted.

The International Court is important. How it works is therefore important. Its operational techniques may be just as significant to a potential litigant State as the content of the substantive rules, so that practical issues simply cannot be neglected or undervalued.

3

Reflections on the Incidental Jurisdiction of the International Court of Justice

JOHN G. MERRILLS

1. INTRODUCTION

The title of this chapter reflects its aim, which is not to attempt to review the International Court's incidental jurisdiction in a comprehensive way, but to focus on certain specific aspects. In keeping with the theme of this book and of the conference for which the chapter was originally prepared, it examines what may be termed the remedial potential of the incidental jurisdiction, that is to say the ways in which, by utilising the relevant provisions of the Court's Statute, a State may be able to obtain a remedy, using that term in its broadest sense to include redress for a wrong, cessation of harm or some other improvement in its position.

At first sight this may seem an unprofitable subject for investigation. Remedies are, of course, normally associated with the Court's power to decide contentious cases under Article 36 where a rich, if somewhat improvised, jurisprudence has developed.[1] The Court's incidental jurisdiction, as the very name indicates, is essentially ancillary to that power, which is plainly the primary remedial source. Moreover, it is clear that some aspects of the incidental jurisdiction, such as the Court's power to resolve disputes concerning its jurisdiction (the *compétence de la compétence*),[2] though vital for its effectiveness, are not in themselves capable of providing a remedy. If we take other aspects, however, it becomes apparent that the position is rather different and a remedial function can be identified. The argument here is not that it is necessarily the main function, let alone the *raison d'être*, of the features concerned to provide States with remedies broadly defined. Rather, the argument is that this is one

---

[1] See I. Brownlie, "Remedies in the International Court of Justice" in V. Lowe and M. Fitzmaurice (eds.), *Fifty Years of the International Court of Justice* (Cambridge University Press, Cambridge, 1996), at 557; and C. Gray, *Judicial Remedies in International Law* (Clarendon Press, Oxford, 1990), at 77–111.

[2] See Art. 36(6) of the Statute of the Court and S. Rosenne, *The Law and Practice of the International Court* (2nd edn., Nijhoff, Dordrecht, 1985), at 438–42.

function which they can, and in practice do, perform. The three aspects of the incidental jurisdiction which will be examined to demonstrate the point are: provisional (or interim) measures of protection under Article 41 of the Statute; intervention under Articles 62 and 63; and interpretation and revision of judgments under Articles 60 and 61.

2. PROVISIONAL MEASURES OF PROTECTION

Article 41 of the Statute provides:

> "The Court shall have power to indicate, if it considers that circumstances so require, any provisional measures which ought to be taken to preserve the rights of either party."[3]

The purpose of this provision is easily stated. It is to safeguard the rights which are in dispute, pending the Court's decision on the merits. The rights, it should be emphasised, are those of both sides. Thus although the tendency is for one side to seek provisional measures and for the other to oppose the request, it is perfectly possible for both parties to make such a request along similar lines, as happened in the *Frontier Dispute* case,[4] or for a request to be met with a denial that those measures are needed, and a counter-claim for measures of a different sort, as happened in the *Genocide Convention* case.[5]

The fact that interim protection is concerned with safeguarding rights, and only with this, has a crucial bearing on what can be granted and means that, like interim injunctions in domestic law, provisional measures have a rather specialised character and are not relevant in every case. Even so, while the ICJ has dealt with many disputes in which provisional measures were never sought, in a significant minority of cases States have relied on Article 41, and on about half of such occasions have been successful.[6] Unfortunately, in several cases in which the Court has made an order for provisional measures it has not been respected.[7] To see how this aspect of the incidental jurisdiction can perform a remedial function we therefore need to consider three distinct possibilities: that an order will be obtained which is respected; that an order will be obtained but proves ineffective; and that an order will be requested but not granted.

If an effective order is secured then it is clear that the requesting State (or States) has obtained a useful, though temporary remedy. A good example is provided by the *Frontier Dispute* case in which Mali and Burkina Faso, having been

---

[3] For discussion of the scope and application of this provision see J.G. Merrills, "Interim Measures of Protection in the Recent Jurisprudence of the International Court of Justice" 44 *ICLQ* 90; J. Sztucki, *Interim Measures in the Hague Court* (Kluwer, Deventer, 1983).

[4] *Frontier Dispute*, Provisional Measures, Order of 10 Jan. 1986, ICJ Reports, 1986, 3.

[5] *Application of the Convention on the Prevention and Punishment of the Crime of Genocide*, Provisional Measures, Orders of 8 Apr. and 13 Sept. 1993, ICJ Reports 1993, 3 and 325.

[6] See Merrills, n. 3 above, at 90–1.

[7] See Sztucki, n. 3 above, at 143–6 and for recent experience Merrills, n. 3 above, at 137–9.

involved in a boundary conflict, agreed to take the dispute to the International Court and then each requested interim protection. Not surprisingly, an order was made the content of which demonstrates the advantages to be derived from using Article 41.[8] For by obtaining it, the two States were able to reinforce their commitment to a cease-fire which had just been negotiated, secure an arrangement for withdrawing their troops from the disputed area and remove suspicion that they might be attempting to pre-empt the Court's judgment. In effect, the order of interim protection was a way of creating a temporary regime for the border area, so allowing a tense situation to cool down.[9] The two States were thus able to use Article 41 to furnish a solution to their immediate problem in much the same way as the subsequent decision on the merits[10] provided them with a solution to the boundary dispute itself.

The recent *Land and Maritime Boundary* case[11] between Cameroon and Nigeria involved a request for provisional measures in a situation that was very similar. Again fighting had broken out in a disputed frontier area, the dispute itself had been referred to the Court, which was asked to settle the boundary and, pending the decision of the merits, provisional measures were requested. A difference between the two cases was that here the Court's jurisdiction was based not on a special agreement, but on the parties' declarations under Article 36(2) of the Statute (the optional clause) and Nigeria, the respondent, not only raised various preliminary objections, but also denied that interim protection was necessary. The Court, however, made an order along the lines requested by Cameroon and, as in the *Frontier Dispute* case, its effect was to calm the situation, confirm a previously agreed cease-fire and encourage the parties to co-operate, pending the next stage of the proceedings.

What about cases in which an order is made and then not respected? This is clearly a different type of situation, but again the order can serve a remedial function as may be seen from the *Genocide Convention* case and the earlier *Nicaragua* case.[12] In the latter the United States never accepted the Court's involvement, strenuously opposed the request for interim measures and challenged both the jurisdiction and admissibility of the claim. The culmination of

---

[8] Both States were ordered to refrain from action which might extend or aggravate the dispute or prejudice compliance with the judgment. Both States were also ordered to refrain from any act likely to impede the gathering of evidence and to withdraw their armed forces behind lines to be agreed. Furthermore, both States were ordered to continue to observe the recently agreed cease-fire, while, in regard to the administration of the disputed areas, the Court indicated that the situation which prevailed before the armed actions that gave rise to the requests for provisional measures should not be modified.

[9] See G.J. Naldi, "Case Concerning the Frontier Dispute between Burkina Faso and Mali: Provisional Measures of Protection", 35 *ICLQ* 970.

[10] *Frontier Dispute*, Judgment, ICJ Reports 1986, 554, and see G.J. Naldi, "The Case Concerning the Frontier Dispute (Burkina Faso/Republic of Mali): *Uti Possidetis* in an African Perspective", 37 *ICLQ* 893.

[11] *Land and Maritime Boundary between Cameroon and Nigeria*, Provisional Measures, Order of 15 Mar. 1996, ICJ Reports 1996, 13, and see J.G. Merrills, Case Note, 46 *ICLQ* 676.

[12] *Military and Paramilitary Activities in and against Nicaragua*, Provisional Measures, Order of 10 May 1984, ICJ Reports 1984, 169.

this opposition was its refusal to participate in the proceedings on the merits, thus ultimately displaying the same attitude to the Court as the respondents in the notorious "non-appearance" cases of the 1970s.[13] In three of those earlier cases provisional measures were ordered but were not effective,[14] and this was also the result here. Nicaragua subsequently sought to reopen the question of interim protection but was unsuccessful,[15] its attempt to do so merely underlining the ineffectiveness of the earlier order.

The *Genocide Convention* case was much the same. In April 1993 the Court made an order for provisional measures which Yugoslavia, against whom the order was mainly directed, strongly opposed, arguing *inter alia* that the Court lacked jurisdiction. In September, following a further request from Bosnia-Herzegovina, the Court renewed the order, stating that it was not satisfied that the parties had done all that they might to comply with its previous order.[16] Again, however, little seems to have changed as a consequence. Throughout this case attention was rightly focused on the key issue of genocide, but it may be noted in passing that the terms in which Bosnia-Herzegovina couched its second request went well beyond that issue, which could in itself be argued to transgress the directive to the applicant to do nothing to aggravate or extend the dispute. This, then, is another poor advertisement for the efficacy of provisional measures.

As it is probable that neither Nicaragua nor Bosnia-Herzegovina had any expectation that a successful application under Article 41 would do much to change the situation on the ground, they presumably made their requests with other objectives in mind. What, then, did they gain? Probably the main benefit was that in both instances the applicant obtained widespread exposure for its claims and, notwithstanding the highly provisional character of the Court's assessments, succeeded in obtaining an order which could be presented as a victory and an embarrassment to the respondent. This was also true of the orders obtained in the earlier *Diplomatic Hostages* case,[17] and the *Nuclear Tests*[18] and *Fisheries Jurisdiction* cases.[19] An order for provisional measures cannot, of course, prejudge issues which belong to the merits and therefore should not be sought as a provisional or interim judgment. Nevertheless, a State which is successful has won the first round of the contest and secured an advantage, even if the order is disregarded.

---

[13] See Sir Gerald Fitzmaurice, "The Problem of the "Non-Appearing" Defendant Government", 51 *BYIL* 89.

[14] For the cases concerned see nn. 17 to 19 below.

[15] See *Military and Paramilitary Activities in and against Nicaragua*, Merits, Judgment, ICJ Reports 1986, 14 at 143–5, and Merrills, n. 3 above, at 138, n. 146.

[16] See the Court's Order of 13 Sept. 1993, ICJ Reports 1993, 325, para. 57.

[17] *United States Diplomatic and Consular Staff in Tehran*, Provisional Measures, Order of 15 Dec. 1979, ICJ Reports 1979, 7.

[18] *Nuclear Tests, Interim Protection*, Orders of 22 June 1973, ICJ Reports 1973, 99 (*Australia v. France*) and 135 (*New Zealand v. France*).

[19] *Fisheries Jurisdiction, Interim Protection*, Orders of 17 Aug. 1972, ICJ Reports 1972, 12 (*UK v. Iceland*) and 30 (*Federal Republic of Germany v. Iceland*).

The remedial value of provisional measures, even in situations where an order is likely to be disregarded, is enhanced by the special characteristics of proceedings under Article 41. In the first place, requests for interim protection have priority over other cases and are always dealt with promptly.[20] Secondly, to enable such requests to be dealt with expeditiously, and provisional measures to perform their function, it is enough for the requesting State to identify an instrument which appears "*prima facie* to afford a basis on which the jurisdiction of the Court might be founded".[21] Thus at this stage any disagreement about whether there is jurisdiction over the merits does not have to be resolved. Thirdly, although the Court cannot give an interim judgment, if the evidence supporting the request for interim protection is similar to that supporting the main claim, this is likely to be reflected in the terms of the Court's order, long before the proceedings on the merits.[22]

The significance of these points can be seen in all the cases just mentioned and also in New Zealand's attempt in the *Nuclear Tests II* case[23] to reopen the 1974 *Nuclear Tests* case[24] In its application New Zealand sought to revive the earlier proceedings on the basis of certain observations in the original judgment, and at the same time made a "further request" for provisional measures,[25] referring to the previous order of June 1973. This bold attempt to repeat its earlier success failed because the Court in its order of 22 September 1995 found that the situation fell outside the terms of the 1974 judgment, with the result that the case could not be reopened. Had its conclusion on that point been different, however, New Zealand's request for provisional measures would have been considered soon afterwards. While the outcome of such proceedings must remain a matter for speculation,[26] the necessary jurisdictional basis had already been established, and here, as in 1973, the measures New Zealand requested were closely related to its main application.[27] The applicant, then, had clearly not forgotten the possibilities offered by Article 41, although the unusual nature of the

[20] See Merrills, n. 3 above, at 142.

[21] See Merrills, n. 3 above, at 91–100. The words quoted are from the orders in the *Nuclear Tests* cases, and have been repeated in many other cases.

[22] This was so, e.g., in both the *Nicaragua* case and the *Genocide* case, as well as in the earlier cases referred to in nn. 17 to 19 above. For discussion of the issues raised by the relationship between provisional measures and the impending judgment see Merrills, n. 3 above, at 104–6 and Sztucki, n. 3 above, at 93–102.

[23] *Request for an Examination of the Situation in Accordance with Paragraph 63 of the Court's Judgment of 20 December 1974 in the Nuclear Tests (New Zealand v. France) Case*, Order of 22 Sept. 1995, ICJ Reports 1995, 288. For comment on the Order see M.C.R. Craven, Case Note, 45 *ICLQ* 725.

[24] *Nuclear Tests*, Judgment, ICJ Reports, 1974, 457.

[25] *Request for an Examination of the Situation in Accordance with Paragraph 63 of the Court's Judgment of 20 December 1974 in the Nuclear Tests (New Zealand v. France) Case*, Order of 22 Sept. 1995, ICJ Reports 1995, 288 at 291.

[26] However, Judge Weeramantry suggested that if, as in 1973, the Court had been called upon to consider provisional measures, its approach "might well have been on similar lines" (*ibid.*, 339).

[27] In both the main application and its request for provisional measures New Zealand sought a cessation of the French tests and a decision requiring France to make an environmental impact assessment.

proceedings meant that in the event the request for provisional measures was never considered.

That there are benefits from using the Court when an order can be obtained is hardly a startling conclusion. Less obvious perhaps is that it may be possible for a State to gain comparable advantages from proceedings under Article 41 even if its request for provisional measures is rejected. The position here, however, is more complicated than in the kinds of cases already considered, and much depends on both the nature of the case and the precise details of the Court's response. Brownlie has suggested that "requests should not be raised without careful consideration" and has pointed out that "an unsuccessful request may produce adverse effects".[28] No doubt this is wise advice, and in this connection it is as well to remember that Article 41 is available to both sides and the Court enjoys a wide discretion in responding to requests. Consequently, an ill-conceived request might be refused but provoke a counter-claim which was accepted, an unwelcome possibility to which we shall return.

There are, nevertheless, circumstances in which even an unsuccessful request for interim protection can perform a remedial function. In the *Lockerbie* cases,[29] for example, Libya, which was under pressure in the Security Council to surrender terrorist suspects, was able to obtain a hearing in a neutral forum by initiating proceedings in the International Court. It is true that the request for interim protection was forestalled when the Security Council adopted a resolution under Chapter VII of the Charter, but it is clear from the individual opinions in the case that Libya's arguments made a strong impression.[30] Moreover here, as in the *Aegean Sea Continental Shelf* case,[31] seising the Court of the dispute went some way to removing the applicant's fear that it was about to be attacked, which was one of the factors prompting its request. Finally, as this was a dispute in which Libya had been made acutely conscious of its vulnerability to measures by the Security Council, bringing the case and provoking a debate on the constitutional limitations of the political organs must also be considered a gain. Proceedings under Article 41 were not, of course, suitable for examining these complex issues exhaustively, but just as in the *Nicaragua* case the request for interim protection enabled the applicant to put the respondent on the defensive at an early stage, offsetting its political and military advantages, so in *Lockerbie* Libya was able to use the law, and specifically Article 41, to redress the weakness of its political position.[32]

---

[28] Brownlie, n.1 above, at 559.

[29] *Questions of Interpretation and Application of the 1971 Montreal Convention arising from the Aerial Incident at Lockerbie*, Provisional Measures, Orders of 14 Apr. 1992, ICJ Reports 1992, 3 (*Libya* v. *UK*) and 114 (*Libya* v. *USA*). Unless otherwise indicated, references to the *Lockerbie* proceedings are to the case involving the UK.

[30] See, e.g., the dissenting opinions of Judges Weeramantry, Ranjeva, Ajibola and El-Kosheri, *ibid.*

[31] *Aegean Sea Continental Shelf*, Interim Protection, Order of 11 Sept. 1976, ICJ Reports, 1976, 3.

[32] On the other hand, it can be argued that by provoking the respondents into obtaining a resolution from the Security Council under Chapter VII of the Charter, Libya's attempt to invoke Art. 41 also escalated the dispute to its disadvantage.

Advantages of a quite different kind accrued to Finland when it made an unsuccessful request for provisional measures in the *Passage through the Great Belt* case.[33] This case concerned a bridge which Denmark proposed to build over one of the straits linking the Baltic to the Kattegat and which, when completed, would impede the movement of oil rigs and similar vessels to and from Finnish shipyards and ports. In its main application Finland disputed Denmark's right to build the bridge, and in its request for provisional measures sought an order directing Denmark to suspend work on it. In response, Denmark indicated that the bridge would not be completed before the end of 1994, while the Court, for its part, formally placed this undertaking on the record and indicated that its decision on the merits would be given well before then.[34] This gave Finland exactly what it wanted, namely a guarantee that it would not be presented with a *fait accompli*. Thus although the request for provisional measures was rejected, because it lacked the necessary element of urgency, the outcome was not very different from if interim protection had been ordered.

A further point of interest is that, when dealing with one of the issues raised by Finland, the Court indicated that a favourable decision on the merits might not merely require Denmark to pay compensation, but could result in its having to abandon the bridge project altogether.[35] Thus the Court was here reassuring Finland that, however far advanced the project might be when the case was decided on the merits, Denmark could not improve its position by continuing the work. This was relevant to the question whether interim protection was a matter of urgency. However, by emphasising that what was at stake was not merely financial compensation, but perhaps the future of the project itself, the Court also appeared to strengthen Finland's bargaining position. As the Court went on to urge the parties to resume negotiation,[36] and they did in fact do so,[37] this too is a matter of some significance. In this respect too, therefore, Finland seems to have gained significant advantages from the proceedings.

While the motives behind a request for provisional measures are no doubt always to improve a State's position and there are numerous ways in which this may be done, in some situations little or nothing will be achieved or, as mentioned earlier, a request may actually be counter-productive. In the *Arbitral Award* case,[38] for example, Guinea-Bissau's motive in seeking interim protection seems to have been to establish that the case was about more than technical issues relating to the validity of an arbitral award and to prepare the ground

---

[33] *Passage through the Great Belt (Finland v. Denmark)*, Provisional Measures, Order of 29 July 1991, ICJ Reports 1991, 12.

[34] *Ibid.*, 18. Moreover, in his separate opinion Judge Broms indicated that during the Court's deliberations it "decided to make the final decision of the case expeditiously, probably during the spring of 1992 or at the latest in the fall of 1992" (*ibid.*, 38).

[35] *Ibid.*, 19. See further on this point Merrills, n. 3 above, at 112–13.

[36] *Ibid.*, 20. See further on this point Merrills, n. 3 above, at 134–6.

[37] The dispute which gave rise to this case was in fact settled by negotiation without the need for a decision from the Court on the merits, see 32 ILM 101.

[38] *Arbitral Award of 31 July 1989*, Provisional Measures, Order of 2 Mar. 1990, ICJ Reports 1990, 64.

for its argument on the merits. It was, however, unsuccessful, and if Guinea-Bissau can be said to have gained anything from the proceedings under Article 41, it was perhaps only an advance indication that at the merits stage the Court was unlikely to be sympathetic to attempts to move the issue away from the validity of the award and towards wider considerations relevant only to a body with appellate functions.[39] Likewise in the *Genocide Convention* case, although Bosnia-Herzegovina gained in the ways already described, it was conspicuously unsuccessful in its attempts to widen the case beyond the issue of genocide by, for example, obtaining an acknowledgment of its right to obtain arms.[40]

The *Genocide Convention* case, in which Yugoslavia, as well as Bosnia-Herzegovina, sought interim protection, is also a reminder of the point made earlier that Article 41 is not just at the disposal of claimants, but in principle is equally available to respondents. A State which is deciding whether to make a request for provisional measures should therefore be aware that by doing so it may provoke a request from the other side by way of counter-attack, in much the same way as initiating litigation can itself provoke a counter-claim. Often, of course, this will be unimportant either because a request from the respondent is very unlikely (as in the *Lockerbie* cases), or because it is not unwelcome (as in the *Frontier Dispute* case). In a situation like that in the *Genocide Convention* case, however, where both sides' actions may be open to criticism, a request for provisional measures from one side may lead to a counter-request from the other and may in turn have the effect of appreciably diminishing the possible advantages.

3. INTERVENTION

Two kinds of intervention are provided for in the Court's Statute. Article 62(1) permits a State to submit a request to be allowed to intervene if it considers that it has "an interest of a legal nature which may be affected by the decision in the case". This kind of intervention has been termed "discretionary" because Article 62(2) provides that it is for the Court to decide upon such a request. On the other hand, Article 63(1) and (2) enables a State to intervene as of right when the construction of a convention to which it is a party is in question.[41] There is less case law in relation to these provisions than in relation to provisional measures because relatively few requests under Article 62 have been made and States'

[39] In its decision on the merits in 1991 the Court did in fact find in favour of Senegal and uphold the validity of the arbitral award: see ICJ Reports 1991, 53. For discussion of the Court's decision on the merits see F. Beveridge, Case Note, 41 *ICLQ* 891.

[40] See on this point Merrills, n. 3 above, at 102–4.

[41] For discussion of the scope and application of these provisions see J.M. Ruda, "Intervention before the International Court of Justice", in Lowe and Fitzmaurice (eds.), n. 1 above, at 487; and S. Rosenne, *Intervention in the International Court of Justice* (Nijhoff, Dordrecht, 1993). On an aspect which has proved particularly important in practice see M.D. Evans, "Intervention, the International Court of Justice and the Law of the Sea", 48 *RHDI* 73.

rights to intervene under Article 63 are usually neglected. From the use which has been made of these facilities it is, however, again possible to see the different ways in which the Court's incidental jurisdiction can in a broad sense serve a remedial function.

The natural place to start is with discretionary intervention under Article 62 and with the situation in which a State makes a request to intervene which is successful. The only case to date in which this has occurred is the *Land, Island and Maritime Frontier* case[42] in 1992 in which Nicaragua was allowed to intervene. However, although the case stands alone, there is much in the proceedings relating to the request and in the final decision of relevance in the present context. Because the case, which involved El Salvador and Honduras, had been referred to a Chamber of the Court, Nicaragua's request was handled in two stages. In an order in February 1990 the full Court decided that the request to intervene must be handled by the Chamber, rather than the Court.[43] In a judgment later in the same year the Chamber accepted the request in part.[44] In the proceedings on the merits in 1992 Nicaragua was therefore able to exercise the limited right of intervention which had been granted.

Since the decision to allow intervention was unprecedented, the Chamber in its 1990 judgment outlined the procedural position of an intervening State in a passage which indicates both the value and the limitations of a successful request.[45] The principal limitation is that the intervening State does not become a party to the case, and consequently does not acquire the rights (or become subject to the obligations) of a party. On the other hand, the intervener does acquire a right to be heard, which, under Article 85 of the Rules, includes the right to submit a written statement and to participate in the hearings. The right to be heard, however, is not unrestricted, but confined to the subject matter of the intervention. This was particularly important in the present case, which involved a number of distinct legal issues, in which Nicaragua claimed to have "an interest of a legal nature". The intervention, however, was admitted only with regard to the legal regime of the waters of the Gulf of Fonseca.

In the light of these general observations it is interesting to see what happened during the proceedings on the merits.[46] Nicaragua, Honduras and El Salvador submitted written statements in accordance with Article 85 of the Rules[47] and

---

[42] *Land, Island and Maritime Frontier Dispute (El Salvador/Honduras: Nicaragua Intervening)*, Judgment, ICJ Reports 1992, 351.

[43] *Land, Island and Maritime Frontier Dispute (El Salvador/Honduras)*, Application to Intervene, Order of 28 Feb. 1990, ICJ Reports 1990, 3.

[44] *Land, Island and Maritime Frontier Dispute (El Salvador/Honduras)*, Application to Intervene, Judgment, ICJ Reports 1990, 92. For discussion of this judgment and the earlier order of the Court see M.D. Evans, Case Note, 41 *ICLQ* 896.

[45] *Land, Island and Maritime Frontier Dispute (El Salvador/Honduras)*, Application to Intervene, Judgment, ICJ Reports 1990, 92 at 135–6.

[46] See further Rosenne, n. 41 above, at 151–2.

[47] Nicaragua had been given access to the parties' pleadings as early as June 1988 and so had been able to use these in formulating its request to intervene, see ICJ Reports 1990, 92 at 98. On the problem which access to the pleadings has presented in other cases see Rosenne, n. 41 above, at 193–5.

when the oral proceedings reached the issue of the Gulf of Fonseca Nicaragua made its oral observations. The Agent of Honduras then protested that these had gone beyond the permitted limits and dealt with matters on which intervention had been denied. Nicaragua also submitted its "formal conclusions" which seemed to be open to similar criticism. In its judgment, however, the Chamber declined to examine this controversy in detail, contenting itself with the observation that as regards both points it had taken account of Nicaragua's statements only where they appeared to be relevant to the legal regime of the Gulf of Fonseca.[48] On the substantive issue it decided that the waters of the Gulf were subject to a condominium in favour of the three coastal States.[49]

In arriving at this conclusion the Court placed considerable reliance on the 1917 judgment of the Central American Court of Justice in the case of *El Salvador* v. *Nicaragua* where the status of the Gulf was the central issue.[50] It is clear that Nicaragua's intervention in the *Land, Island and Maritime Frontier* case served a remedial function by enabling it to present the Chamber with its views on the earlier case, as well as on the status of the Gulf of Fonseca generally. As noted above, despite the limitations imposed on its intervention, Nicaragua was able to take the opportunity to make observations about various other matters. The latter included the status of the waters outside the Gulf, a matter on which it has been suggested that the Chamber's decision indicates that the parameters of its 1990 judgment may have been too circumscribed.[51] In terms of the remedial value of intervention the conclusions to be drawn are perhaps that when, as here, a case involves a number of closely related issues, it may be difficult to ensure that an intervener stays within the prescribed limits and not always desirable to do so.

The decisions which enabled Nicaragua to intervene have been extensively reviewed elsewhere and need not be examined in detail here. However, since the present discussion is concerned with the opportunities offered to a third State by Article 62, a number of points with a bearing on that question should be noted. As regards the Court's order of February 1990 the key point is clearly the ruling that a State requesting permission to intervene must "take the procedural situation in the case as it finds it"[52] which meant that here it was for the Chamber constituted to deal with the case, rather than for the full Court, to respond to the request. It also meant that it was too late for Nicaragua to secure a change in the composition of the Chamber, or alternatively a restriction of its mandate which its application showed were important objectives. While the scope of the Court's ruling should not be exaggerated, it certainly shows that where a case is

---

[48] *Land, Island and Maritime Frontier Dispute (El Salvador/Honduras: Nicaragua Intervening)*, Judgment, ICJ Reports 1992, 351 at 581.

[49] For comment on this and the remainder of the Court's decision see M.N. Shaw, Case Note, 42 *ICLQ* 929.

[50] See ICJ Reports 1992, 351 at 600.

[51] See Rosenne, n. 41 above, at 153 n. 45.

[52] *Land, Island and Maritime Frontier Dispute (El Salvador/Honduras)*, Application to Intervene, Order of 28 Feb. 1990, ICJ Reports 1990, 3 at 5.

being determined by an *ad hoc* Chamber and the application to intervene is submitted at a relatively late stage, the applicant may be able to obtain a hearing, as Nicaragua did, but cannot expect to reconfigure the proceedings.[53]

The Chamber's decision to allow the intervention also holds lessons for the would-be intervener. First, by granting the request in part despite objections from El Salvador, the Chamber demonstrated that intervention under Article 62 is possible, something which many had begun to doubt, following the Court's restrictive approach in earlier cases.[54] Secondly, by accepting the argument of Honduras that intervention was appropriate with regard to the Gulf of Fonseca, but not with regard to other matters, the Chamber indicated the various factors relevant to the application of Article 62 in practice, and thereby gave guidance to States contemplating use of this remedy. Finally, and not least important, by rejecting the argument that an intervening State must be able to point to a jurisdictional link with the parties,[55] the Chamber assimilated intervention under Article 62 with other aspects of the Court's incidental jurisdiction, and laid to rest an issue which had threatened to restrict access to the Court and reduce the opportunities for intervention very significantly.[56]

When a State makes a request to intervene under Article 62 which is unsuccessful, its opportunities to present its views to the Court are obviously more limited, but the remedial function of the provision is still present. This is because even an unsuccessful request enables the would-be intervener to inform the Court of the nature and extent of its putative legal interest, which can then be taken into account when the case is considered on the merits. This can be seen in the two *Continental Shelf* cases involving Libya. In the case between Tunisia and Libya in 1981, Malta sought to intervene under Article 62 but was unsuccessful.[57] In the case between Malta and Libya in 1984 the third State was Italy, but again the application failed.[58] However, in both cases, while rejecting the intervener's request, the Court, having received a great deal of information about its concerns, gave assurances that when it came to consider the merits these would be taken into account.

When the Court gave judgment in these cases in 1982 and 1985 it was as good as its word.[59] For as well as general observations relating to Article 59 of the Statute and the non-prejudicial effect of the decisions on the rights of third

---

[53] See further Rosenne, n. 41 above, at 182–3.

[54] See, e.g., J.G. Merrills, "Intervention in the International Court", 101 *LQR* 11.

[55] See further on this point Rosenne, n. 41 above, at 90–109.

[56] The view that the jurisdictional issue has been "laid to rest" assumes, of course, that the Chamber's decision on this point will in due course be followed by the full Court. On this point see E. Lauterpacht, *Aspects of the Administration of International Justice* (Grotius, Cambridge, 1991), at 26–30.

[57] *Continental Shelf (Tunisia/Libyan Arab Jamahiriya)*, Application for Permission to Intervene, Judgment, ICJ Reports 1981, 3.

[58] *Continental Shelf (Libyan Arab Jamahiriya/Malta)*, Application for Permission to Intervene, Judgment, ICJ Reports 1984, 3. For comment see G.P. McGinley, "Intervention in the International Court: The *Libya/Malta Continental Shelf* Case", 34 *ICLQ* 671.

[59] *Continental Shelf (Tunisia/Libyan Arab Jamahiriya)*, Judgment, ICJ Reports 1982, 18 and *Continental Shelf (Libyan Arab Jamahiriya/Malta)*, Judgment, ICJ Reports 1985, 13.

States, which could have been anticipated, the Court referred in both judgments to the geographical situation of third parties and was careful in each case to avoid trespassing upon the claims of the would-be intervener. As regards the 1982 case it is therefore easy to agree that "[t]he precautionary move by Malta, pending the resolution of its own delimitation problems . . . largely achieved its object as far as this part of Libya's continental shelf delimitation is concerned".[60] A similar conclusion may be drawn from the second case in which indeed the Court's deferential approach to the third State's claims received stinging criticism in the individual opinions. Judge Schwebel, for example, considered the delimitation prescribed by the judgment to be "unduly truncated to defer to the claims of Italy".[61] But this view and others to the same effect were not shared by the majority of the judges.

There is thus ample justification for Rosenne's comment that, despite the rejection of the applications of Malta and Italy in these cases, the requests for permission to intervene in themselves "had a major defensive consequence"[62] for the two States. Moreover, although the Court adopted a rather limited view of the scope of Article 62 in the above cases, by carefully circumscribing its decisions on the merits, it showed the value of making an application and did less to discourage would-be interveners than has sometimes been suggested. Indeed, this was a point which El Salvador sought to exploit in the *Land, Island and Maritime Frontier* case. Opposing Nicaragua's request to intervene, El Salvador argued that the information contained in the application meant that the Court was now so well informed of Nicaragua's position that it was unnecessary to allow the intervention. Not surprisingly, the argument was rejected for, as the Chamber pointed out, were it to be accepted, the purpose of Article 62 would be frustrated.[63]

Before leaving Article 62 it is worth mentioning that this provision was recently invoked in the *Nuclear Tests II* cases where, following New Zealand's initial application, Australia, Samoa, the Solomon Islands, the Marshall Islands and the Federated States of Micronesia all filed requests to intervene claiming to have "an interest of a legal nature" which might be affected by the decision.[64] With the exception of Australia, these States also filed declarations of intervention under Article 63 on the ground that New Zealand was alleging violation of the 1986 Noumea Convention[65] to which they were parties.[66] As already noted,

[60] Rosenne, n. 41 above, at 136.

[61] *Continental Shelf (Libyan Arab Jamahiriya/Malta)*, Judgment, ICJ Reports 1985, 13 at 172, dissenting opinion of Judge Schwebel.

[62] Rosenne, n. 41 above, at 142.

[63] *Land, Island and Maritime Frontier Dispute (El Salvador/Honduras)*, Application to Intervene, Judgment, ICJ Reports 1990, 90 at 130.

[64] See *Request for an Examination of the Situation in Accordance with paragraph 63 of the Court's Judgment of 20 December 1974 in the Nuclear Tests (New Zealand v. France) Case*, ICJ Reports 1995, 288 at 292.

[65] *Convention for the Protection of Natural Resources and the Environment of the South Pacific Region*, 26 ILM 38.

[66] See Craven, n. 23 above, at 727.

the Court dismissed New Zealand's request when it found that the basis of its 1974 judgment had not been affected by French underground nuclear testing. Accordingly, it also dismissed the interveners' requests and declarations. Although no kind of remedy was obtained here, and in that sense the outcome was disappointing for those concerned, the fact that intervention was attempted by a number of States with no previous experience of the International Court, suggests that its remedial possibilities are now widely appreciated.[67]

Intervention under Article 63, which has already been touched on, can be dealt with very briefly. Here, it will be recalled, a State has a right to intervene whenever the construction of a convention to which it is a party is in issue. To facilitate such interventions Article 63(1) of the Statute provides for the Registrar to notify all the other parties to the convention concerned and Article 82(3) of the Rules permits a declaration of intervention to be filed even if a State has not received such notification, which was the position in the *Nuclear Tests II* case. In contrast to intervention under Article 62, a State exercising its right to intervene is, according to Article 63(2), bound by the construction of the convention given in the judgment. Perhaps for this reason there have been few applications relying on this provision and only two cases, the *Wimbledon* case[68] before the Permanent Court and the *Haya de la Torre* case[69] before the present Court, where Article 63 has been used successfully.

As regards the remedial function of intervention under Article 63 only two points need to be made. The first is that while a successful intervention is clearly beneficial, here, as with Article 62, the application itself can sometimes be advantageous. Thus at an early stage in the *Nicaragua* case El Salvador sought to intervene on the basis that the case involved various multilateral treaties to which it was a party. After receiving the parties' observations the Court held the declaration to be inadmissible on the ground that it still had to establish whether it had jurisdiction.[70] However, in spite of this rejection when the Court addressed the merits of the case in 1986 it made extensive reference to El Salvador's declaration in its treatment of both jurisdictional and evidential issues.[71] In view of the fact that here, unlike the *Continental Shelf* cases, the Court did not simply decide that the intervener's request should not be granted,

---

[67] As Craven points out (n. 23 above, at 727, n. 16), for most of the States seeking to intervene the *Nuclear Tests II* case was their first contact with the Court.

[68] *S.S. "Wimbledon"*, Judgments, 1923, PCIJ Series A, No. 1. Poland originally applied to intervene on the basis of Art. 62, but was admitted on the basis of Art. 63, since Poland was a party to the Treaty of Versailles, which was in issue in this case.

[69] *Haya de la Torre*, Judgment, ICJ Reports 1951, 71. Here Cuba was the intervening State.

[70] *Military and Paramilitary Activities in and against Nicaragua (Nicaragua v. USA)*, Declaration of Intervention, Order of 4 Oct. 1984, ICJ Reports 1984, 215. An alternative, and it is suggested preferable, decision would have been for the Court to postpone its consideration of the declaration until the proceedings on the merits, as it did in the *Nuclear Tests* cases; see *Nuclear Tests*, Application for Permission to Intervene, Orders of 12 July 1973, ICJ Reports 1973, 320 (*Australia* v. *France*) and 324 (*New Zealand* v. *France*).

[71] See *Military and Paramilitary Activities in and against Nicaragua (Nicaragua v. USA)*, Merits, Judgment, ICJ Reports 1986, 14 at 34–8 and 44; also Rosenne, n. 41 above, at 146–7.

but went so far as to rule it inadmissible, the *Nicaragua* case provides a particularly striking example of an unsuccessful intervention having effects at a later stage.

If a case is terminated without a decision on the merits then the would-be intervener is likely to leave empty handed. This was the position in the first *Nuclear Tests* cases where Fiji tried to intervene on the basis of Article 62. When the Court held the cases to be moot in 1974 Fiji found its applications to intervene dismissed without its having had an opportunity to be heard.[72] As noted above, this was also the result in the *Nuclear Tests II* case where the interveners under Articles 62 and 63 were dismissed in a similar way. As the Court appears to have a policy of not accepting intervention until the jurisdictional position has been established, this result may well be repeated in future cases. However, it is interesting to note that two members of the Court in the *Nuclear Tests II* case indicated that they would have liked the intervening States to have been given an opportunity to present oral argument before the Court made its order dismissing the case.[73] In the unusual circumstances of this case their approach, if adopted, would have given the interveners the advantage of expressing their support for New Zealand's request at the very beginning of the proceedings.

The second point which needs to be made about Article 63 is that although intervention is a right, the Court is entitled to examine a State's declaration and, as El Salvador found in the *Nicaragua* case, will only admit interventions which it finds are compatible with the Statute. This requirement was important in the *Haya de la Torre* case between Colombia and Peru where Cuba's intervention was only partly admitted. This was because, although Cuba was a party to the 1928 Havana Convention on Asylum, which was in issue in the case, Cuba's declaration sought to reopen questions decided with the authority of *res judicata* in the Court's recent judgment in the *Asylum* case.[74] Thus although intervention under Article 63 can perform a remedial function, this does not extend to interpreting or appealing from the Court's previous judgments.

4. INTERPRETATION AND REVISION OF JUDGMENTS

These aspects of the Court's incidental jurisdiction, which are the last to be considered here, can conveniently be considered together. Article 60 of the Statute lays down that a judgment is final and without appeal, but goes on to state that in the event of a "dispute as to the meaning or scope of a judgment" the Court

---

[72] See *Nuclear Tests*, Application for Permission to Intervene, Orders of 20 Dec. 1974, ICJ Reports 1974, 530 (*Australia v. France*) and 535 (*New Zealand v. France*).

[73] See *Request for an Examination of the Situation in Accordance with Paragraph 63 of the Court's Judgment of 20 December 1974 in the Nuclear Tests (New Zealand v. France) Case*, ICJ Reports 1995 at 288, dissenting opinion of Judge Palmer, 381 at 388–9. Judge Koroma, who also dissented, appeared to support this view, see *ibid.*, 363 at 379–80.

[74] *Asylum*, Judgment, ICJ Reports 1950, 266. For more on this point see Rosenne, n. 41 above, at 127–9.

shall construe it upon the request of either party. The application of this provision is further governed by Articles 98 and 100 of the Rules. Since interpretation is concerned with the scope of the original judgment, including, of course, the specific question of remedies, it is clear that successful requests under Article 60 fulfil a remedial function. Thus in the Tunisia–Libya *Continental Shelf* case[75] in 1985 the Court spelled out the meaning of its 1982 judgment and in the *Chorzów Factory* case[76] showed that interpretation can also establish that a particular point has *not* been settled with binding force.

The request for interpretation in the *Continental Shelf* case was made by Tunisia, but opposed by Libya. As a result the Court had to consider the scope of Article 60 in some detail and its judgment contains much that it is of relevance to States contemplating use of this remedy. It indicated, for example, that to activate this provision a State need not show that a dispute has manifested itself in a formal way so long as "the two Governments have in fact shown themselves as holding opposite views in regard to the meaning or scope of a judgment of the Court"[77] Similarly, it made the significant point that if the parties have made provision for interpretation in a special agreement under which the case was referred to the Court, this does not have the effect of displacing their rights under the Statute.[78] On the other hand, the Court was careful to distinguish between the role of Article 60 and that of Article 61. Thus, although willing to interpret the original judgment, it stressed that this was quite different from revising it, as Tunisia had initially requested.

It is also important to appreciate that interpretation is concerned with establishing the *res judicata* and so Article 60 cannot be used to obtain an answer to a question or questions which have not been decided. This limitation is illustrated by the *Asylum* case[79] in which Colombia sought an "interpretation" of the original judgment, but the Court refused the request on the ground that it concerned new issues which could only be determined in fresh proceedings. These were then initiated and eventually produced the judgment in the *Haya de Torre* case. It has been pointed out, however, that since the rejection of a request always requires a judgment, even a decision like that in the *Asylum* case may constitute an oblique interpretation of the original judgment, if, as here, it shows that something lies outside the original judgment.[80] Thus even a

[75] *Application for Revision and Interpretation of the Judgment of 24 February 1982 in the Case concerning the Continental Shelf (Tunisia/Libyan Arab Jamahiriya) (Tunisia v. Libyan Arab Jamahiriya)* Judgment, ICJ Reports 1985, 192.

[76] *Interpretation of Judgments Nos. 7 and 8 (Factory at Chorzów)*, Judgment No. 11, 1927, PCIJ, Series A, No. 13.

[77] *Application for Revision and Interpretation of the Judgment of 24 February 1982 in the Case concerning the Continental Shelf (Tunisia/Libyan Arab Jamahiriya) (Tunisia v. Libyan Arab Jamahiriya)*, Judgment, ICJ Reports 1985, 192 at 218.

[78] *Ibid.*, 214–16. Art. 3 of the Special Agreement concluded by Tunisia and Libya in 1977 and which was the basis of the Court's jurisdiction in the *Continental Shelf* case provided for the parties to seek "explanations or clarifications" of the judgment in certain circumstances.

[79] *Request for an Interpretation of the Judgment of 20 November 1950 in the Asylum Case*, Judgment, ICJ Reports 1950, 395.

[80] See Rosenne, n. 2 above, at 428.

refusal to interpret a judgment can itself say something about the parties' legal rights.

The interpretive effect of a decision to refuse a request for interpretation can also be seen in two recent cases in which the European Court of Human Rights was asked to interpret decisions in accordance with the relevant provision of its Rules. Both cases, as it happened, concerned the scope of an award of financial compensation made in a previous judgment. In the *Hentrich* case[81] in 1994 the Court held that France had violated two provisions of the European Convention on Human Rights, and in July 1995 awarded the applicant a substantial sum by way of compensation, which the respondent was ordered to pay within three months.[82] Payment was made, but in December, two months after the time limit. The question put by the Commission in its request for interpretation was whether, in view of the delay in making the payment, the French government must pay the applicant interest. The Court, however, rejected the request on the ground that, as the judgment was clear and made no reference to interest, there was no question relating to the "meaning and scope" of the judgment for it to answer.[83] While this may be thought a curious and even self-contradictory piece of reasoning, the effect was plainly to provide the interpretation that was sought, in spite of the Court's denial that this was necessary.

The *Allenet de Ribemont* case,[84] which also involved France, was a little more complicated. Here the applicant had again been awarded financial compensation,[85] but the Commission, when requesting an interpretation of the judgment, presented the Court with three questions. The first question was whether sums awarded as compensation in proceedings at Strasbourg must be paid to the injured party personally and be exempt from attachment. The Court's response was to hold that this was an abstract question which it had no jurisdiction to answer.[86] It added, however, that in its original judgment it had not ruled that any sum awarded to the applicant should be free from attachment. Accordingly, this was an issue for the national authorities. Here, then, the Court, while holding that the issue of interpretation could not be dealt with, again provided the information requested.

The second and third questions were whether in respect of sums subject to claims under French law a distinction should be made between sums awarded

[81] *Hentrich* v. *France*, Judgment of 22 Sept. 1994, ECHR Series A, No. 296A.

[82] *Hentrich* v. *France, Application of Article 50*, Judgment of 3 July 1995, ECHR Series A, No. 320A. For a summary of this judgment and the earlier decision on the merits see J.G. Merrills, "Decisions on the European Convention on Human Rights during 1995", 66 *BYIL* 545 and 558.

[83] *Hentrich* v. *France, Request for Interpretation*, Judgment of 3 July 1997, ECHR Press Release No. 423 (1997). Rule 57 of Rules of Court A provides:

   "1. A Party or the Commission may request the interpretation of a judgment within a period of three years following the delivery of that judgment.

   2. The request shall state precisely the point or points in the operative provisions of the judgment on which interpretation is required . . ."

[84] *Allenet de Ribemont* v. *France, Request for Interpretation* (1996) 22 EHRR 582.

[85] See the Court's judgment of 10 Feb. 1995, ECHR Series A, No. 308, noted in Merrills, n. 82 above, at 531.

[86] Judge De Meyer dissented on this point.

to the applicant for pecuniary and non-pecuniary damage, and, if so, what were the sums which the Court intended to grant the applicant under each head. On this part of the Commission's request the Court took a different line. It explained that in its original judgment it had awarded a sum "for damage", without distinguishing between pecuniary and non-pecuniary loss, as this was unnecessary and often very difficult. Since the earlier judgment was clear on the point, it concluded unanimously that no question of the "meaning and scope" of the judgment arose, with the result that it was unnecessary to answer the second and third questions. The outcome was thus very much like that in the *Hentrich* case. Without formally interpreting its original judgment, the Court indicated that the answer to the Commission's main question was "no", and thereby interpreted its decision.

Revision of judgments is provided for in Article 61 of the Statute, together with Articles 99 and 100 of the Rules, and qualifies the principle of finality contained in Article 60. As such, it provides a potential remedy more extensive than interpretation because it enables a judgment to be changed if new facts are discovered. However, strict conditions must be fulfilled which limit its significance in practice. Not only must there be a new fact "of such a nature as to be a decisive factor", which was unknown to the Court and the party claiming revision, but such ignorance must not be due to negligence. In addition there is a double limitation *ratione temporis* since an application must be made within six months of the discovery of the new fact (Article 61(4)) and within ten years of the original judgment (Article 61(5)). The only case to date in which a request for revision has been made is the Tunisia–Libya *Continental Shelf* case in which Tunisia's request for revision was refused on the ground that the new facts could have been discovered earlier, and in any event were not sufficiently important. As already mentioned, however, the Court did accede to a subsidiary request that it should interpret the judgment.

On the present topic, as with those considered previously, there is also something to be learned from the *Nuclear Tests II* case. In seeking to reopen the 1974 decision New Zealand expressly stated that it was requesting neither an interpretation of the earlier judgment under Article 60 of the Statute, nor a revision of it under Article 61.[87] This denial formed part of New Zealand's argument that the Court's observations in paragraph 63 of the 1974 case provided a right of access to the Court without the need for New Zealand to make a new application under Article 40, or to base itself on some other provision. This submission was rejected by France, but accepted by the Court, which went on to hold that the situation fell outside the terms of the 1974 judgment. Thus, as already noted, the Court rejected the request. What, then, is the relevance of this case in the context of Articles 60 and 61?

---

[87] See *Request for an Examination of the Situation in Accordance with Paragraph 63 of the Court's Judgment of 20 December 1974 in the Nuclear Tests (New Zealand v. France) Case*, ICJ Reports 1995, 288 at 303, para. 50.

As regards Article 61, Judge Koroma recalled that revision requires there to be a new and previously unknown fact of a decisive nature and involves a time limit, conditions which would have barred New Zealand in the present case.[88] Judge Weeramantry similarly pointed out that revision "involves an alteration or modification of the Judgment", whereas what New Zealand sought and the crucial passage in the 1974 case aimed at was "preserving the Judgment in its full integrity in the event that some event had occurred which undermined the basis of the Judgment".[89] In short, ". . . paragraph 63 did not anticipate the discovery of new facts but rather provided for an examination of the subject-matter of the Judgment".[90] The case thus confirms the very specific nature of the remedy furnished by Article 61 and the corollary, that if, as here, a State seeks something else, a basis for the Court's competence must be sought elsewhere.

If the *Nuclear Tests II* case points up the limitations of Article 61, the same can be said of Article 60. New Zealand's intention, as the terms of its request made clear, was not simply to establish what the Court had decided in 1974, but to reopen the case and obtain appropriate remedies. Plainly, this went far beyond anything which might be possible under Article 60. Earlier, however, the point was made that even an unsuccessful request under that provision may provide an oblique interpretation of the original judgment and an analogous point emerged here. For although New Zealand failed to achieve its main objective, it obtained rulings that in paragraph 63 of its 1974 judgment "the Court did not exclude a special procedure, in the event that the circumstances defined in that paragraph were to arise",[91] and that such circumstances had not arisen. Both, it is submitted, were actually interpretations of the earlier judgment, although New Zealand had not relied on Article 60.

Because Tunisia's request for revision was refused in the *Continental Shelf* case and no further requests have been made under Article 61, to see how this provision might be used it is again instructive to turn to the European Court of Human Rights. In the European Court revision, like interpretation, is provided for only in the Rules, which lay down that when a request is made by a Party or by the Commission the first step is to determine its admissibility by considering whether the new facts on which the request must be based "might by [their] nature have a decisive influence".[92] Then, if the claim is admissible, the

---

[88] *Ibid.*, Dissenting opinion of Judge Koroma, 363 at 375–6.

[89] *Ibid.*, Dissenting opinion of Judge Weeramantry, 317 at 320.

[90] *Ibid.*, Dissenting opinion of Judge Koroma, 363 at 376.

[91] *Ibid.*, 303, para. 53.

[92] Rule 58 of Rules of Court A provides:
   "1. A Party or the Commission may, in the event of the discovery of a fact which might by its nature have a decisive influence and which, when a judgment was delivered, was unknown both to the Court and to that Party or the Commission, request the Court, within a period of six months after that Party or the Commission, as the case may be, acquired knowledge of such fact, to revise that judgment. . . .
   4. The request for revision shall be considered by a Chamber . . . which shall decide whether the request is admissible or not under paragraph 1 of this Rule. In the affirmative, the Chamber shall refer the request to the Chamber which gave the original judgment . . ."

Chamber which originally heard the case must decide whether they actually would have had a decisive influence and thus call for revision. The *Pardo* case, which was the first to raise the issue of revision, was originally decided in September 1993. The request for revision was submitted in September 1995 and declared admissible in July 1996, with the final judgment in April 1997.

The complaint in the *Pardo* case concerned commercial litigation in France which the applicant claimed had violated his right to a fair trial as guaranteed by Article 6(1) of the European Convention. According to the applicant the French court had held a hearing at which it decided to postpone consideration of the case, but had then given judgment without holding a further hearing. According to the Government, on the other hand, the court had dealt with the case fully at the hearing and merely reserved its judgment. The Commission accepted the applicant's version of events and unanimously found that Article 6(1) had been violated. However, the Court relied on the record of the hearing and by six votes to three found in favour of the Government.[93] The request for revision was based on the fact that prior to the hearing the Court had requested certain documents which could not then be provided, but two of which had since become available.

In deciding to admit the request the Court decided that the documents in question could be regarded as "facts" for the purpose of the Rules and observed that, while a decision on admissibility in no way prejudged the merits, because revision called into question the finality of judgments the issue required careful scrutiny. However, as the two new developments related to the hearing in the French court, it decided by five votes to four that the request was admissible.[94] Although the case was then remitted to the original Chamber, the latter relinquished jurisdiction in favour of a Grand Chamber of 21 Judges which decided to reject the request. Seeing its task as to decide whether the two new documents cast doubt on the conclusions of the original Chamber, the Court found that the documents in question did not provide any information on the course of the proceedings in the French court. Not surprisingly, therefore it concluded unanimously that they did not constitute grounds for revision.[95]

With so many hurdles to overcome, the revision of judgments by the International Court or other tribunals is likely to be rare. As we have seen, the only attempt to use Article 61 at The Hague was rejected, and though the *Pardo* case narrowly passed the initial requirement of admissibility, this may have had more to do with the novelty of the request than with the strength of the case, a conjecture to which both the reasoning and the unanimity of the Grand Chamber lend support. The European Court's observation that revision is an exceptional procedure to be used with caution would no doubt be echoed in the

[93] *Pardo v. France*, Judgment of 20 Sept. 1993, ECHR Series A, No. 261B. For a note on this case see J.G. Merrills, "Decisions on the European Convention on Human Rights during 1994" 65 *BYIL* 535.

[94] *Pardo v. France, Request for Revision* (1996) 22 EHRR 563.

[95] *Pardo v. France, Request for Revision*, Judgment of 29 Apr. 1997, ECHR Press Release No. 260 (1997).

International Court which adopted just this approach in the *Tunisia–Libya* case. Of all the aspects of the Court's incidental jurisdiction examined here, revision seems therefore to be the least useful as a source of remedies. It does, however, provide both an opportunity for judicial second thoughts and, as the *Pardo* case demonstrates, a chance to confirm that justice has been done. As such, and in the absence of arrangements for appealing from decisions of the International Court, Article 61, like the other provisions of the State we have considered, can be said to have a remedial function.

5. CONCLUSION

Many of the issues which have been dealt with rather cursorily in this chapter could be examined in much more detail. Moreover, nothing at all has been said about counter-claims under Article 80 of the International Court's Rules which are also relevant to the issue of remedies.[96] Perhaps, however, enough has been said to substantiate the thesis that the incidental jurisdiction of the International Court can perform a remedial function in not-so-obvious, as well as in obvious ways. What is true of the ICJ is also true of other international tribunals. The European Court of Human Rights has already been mentioned in the context of interpretation and revision, and relevant too are the Inter-American Court of Human Rights, whose jurisprudence includes cases on provisional measures and interpretation,[97] and arbitral tribunals. Interpretation, for example, raised some difficult issues in the UK–France *Channel Arbitration*[98] and, more recently, together with revision, was the subject of close and detailed attention in the *Heathrow Airport* case.[99] Finally, it is interesting to note that all three aspects of the incidental jurisdiction discussed above are provided for in the constitution of the newest international judicial organ, the International Tribunal for the Law of the Sea,[100] which is due to begin operations shortly. The prospects for that Tribunal and its possible role as a source of international remedies are, however, topics for another occasion.

---

[96] See Rosenne, n. 2 above, at 434–6.

[97] On provisional measures see T. Buergenthal, "Interim Measures in the Inter-American Court of Human Rights", in M. Bernhardt (ed.), *Interim Measures Indicated by International Courts* (Springer-Verlag, Berlin, 1994), at 69; on interpretation see the American Court's decision of 1990 in *Velásquez Rodriguez–Interpretation of the Court's Judgment of July 21, 1989*, Text in 12 HRLJ 14.

[98] *Delimitation of the Continental Shelf (UK/France, 1977/78)*, 54 ILR 6. For analysis and commentary see J.G. Merrills, "The United Kingdom–France Continental Shelf Arbitration", 10 *Calif. Western Int. LJ* 314. The issue of interpretation is discussed at 349–55.

[99] *United States–United Kingdom Arbitration Concerning Heathrow Airport User Charges* (1992/93), 102 ILR 216: see particularly the Tribunal's *Supplementary Decisions and Clarifications* of 1 Nov. 1993: *ibid.*, 564. For comment see S.M. Witten, Case Note, 89 *AJIL* 174.

[100] See Arts. 25, 31, 32 and 33 of the Statute of the Tribunal which forms Annex VI of the 1982 Law of the Sea Convention. For the background to these provisions see S. Rosenne and L.B. Sohn (eds.), *United Nations Convention on the Law of the Sea 1982. A Commentary*, Volume 5 (Nijhoff, Dordrecht, 1988), at 385–8 and 392–8.

4

The International Tribunal for the Law of the Sea

DAVID ANDERSON

The United Nations Convention on the Law of the Sea ("the Convention") constituted several new international institutions of different kinds. Best known, perhaps, is the International Seabed Authority, with its headquarters in Jamaica. Less well known is the Commission on the Limits of the Continental Shelf, elected in March 1997, to consider information from coastal states which have continental shelves extending, as natural prolongations, beyond 200 nautical miles from the baselines of the territorial sea. Particularly relevant to the present study of the institutional dilemma over the settlement of disputes is the International Tribunal for the Law of the Sea, with its seat in Hamburg. The Tribunal forms part of some rather elaborate arrangements for the peaceful settlement of disputes of all kinds which may arise under the Convention.

1. ESTABLISHMENT OF THE TRIBUNAL

The Tribunal was constituted by the Convention as an autonomous international organisation within the wider United Nations system. The Tribunal's statute, contained in Annex VI of the Convention, requires that the judges enjoy "the highest reputation for fairness and integrity and . . . recognised competence in the field of the law of the sea".[1] In other words, it is a special tribunal for the Convention, with specialists as judges. The Tribunal as a whole has to represent the principal legal systems of the world. The composition also has to take account of equitable geographical distribution. On this latter point, according to Article 3 of the Statute, there have to be at least three judges from each of the five geographical groupings used in the United Nations for electoral purposes: Africa, Asia, Eastern Europe, Latin America and the Caribbean, and Western Europe and other States. The members of the Tribunal were elected by the States Parties on 1 August 1996. To secure election, successful candidates had to obtain a two-thirds majority of the votes cast, or at least 67 of the full electorate on the day of exactly 100 States Parties. In the event, the States Parties had

[1] Art. 2 of Annex VI.

decided[2] on the eve of the voting that there should be five judges from Africa, five from Asia, four from Latin America and the Caribbean, four from Western Europe and other States, and three from Eastern Europe. This meant that the United Nations Secretariat could prepare ballot papers divided according to region, and the President of the Meeting could indicate when the "quota" for a particular region had been filled. After as many as eight rounds of voting lasting 12 hours, 21 candidates had achieved a two-thirds majority of the votes cast (a high figure in elections) and all the places had been declared by the President to have been filled. On 2 August 1996, lots were drawn, again according to a scheme for each region, in order to decide who from amongst the successful candidates should have the terms of three, six or nine years in order to prepare for the three year electoral cycle.[3] The 21 successful candidates gathered in Hamburg on 1 October and were sworn in during a public ceremony held in the Rathaus in the presence of the United Nations Secretary General, political figures from Germany and many diplomatic representatives on 18 October 1996.

Because it is new and autonomous, numerous administrative arrangements are required to make the Tribunal an effective body. The Tribunal may well be unique as an autonomous judicial body. The Tribunal has its own budget and organs—ones which differ from those of other international organisations. These organs may be said to include (a) the Judiciary (composed of the members of the full Tribunal, as well as the various chambers) and (b) the Registry, together possibly with (c) the Meeting of the States Parties (convened in accordance with Article 319 of the Convention) which elects the members and funds the Tribunal as a whole.[4] It is endowed with legal personality, including the power to conclude treaties. Negotiations are well advanced with the host country, Germany, for a Headquarters Agreement,[5] the terms of which are likely to follow, broadly speaking, the provisions of the Agreement between the UK and the European Bank for Reconstruction and Development. The Tribunal has been represented in its negotiations with the German Government by the President and Vice President, together with the Registrar, acting in accordance with some broad negotiating guidelines agreed by the Tribunal's members during an administrative meeting.

The Tribunal enjoys close links with the United Nations, links which were strengthened in December 1996 when the General Assembly adopted a Resolution conferring the status of an observer on the Tribunal.[6] The General Assembly holds an annual debate on the Secretary General's report on develop-

---

[2] UN Doc. SPLOS/L. 3/Rev. 1.

[3] For further details of the electoral processes, see UN Doc. SPLOS/14, paras. 13ff.

[4] The States Parties have held seven meetings, starting shortly after the entry into force of the Convention on 16 Nov. 1994, in order to discuss the establishment, status and funding of the Tribunal and the establishment of the Commission on the Limits of the Continental Shelf.

[5] The Meeting of the States Parties recommended a draft of such an agreement to the Tribunal as a basis for the negotiations with the host country: see UN Doc. SPLOS/14.

[6] GA Resolution 51/204 of 17 Dec. 1996.

ments in the law of the sea, a report which includes a section about the work of the Tribunal.[7] The Tribunal may wish to be represented during such debates.

A further negotiation is well under way for an agreement between the United Nations and the Tribunal, defining their future relationship as two separate international organisations. For instance, the two organisations could agree to exchange relevant documentation and the Tribunal will wish to be part of the United Nations' "common system" for conference services, staffing matters, pensions and the like. The Secretary General is the depositary of the convention and the Tribunal has a very obvious interest in having full access to information of all kinds concerning the status of the Convention, declarations by parties, etc. These talks involve members of the United Nations Secretariat and the Registrar.

At their seventh meeting in May 1997 the States Parties to the Convention concluded a multilateral agreement on the Privileges and Immunities of the Tribunal.[8] In addition to conferring privileges and immunities on the Tribunal itself, the Agreement extends certain privileges and immunities also to the Tribunal's elected and *ad hoc* members and its Registry, as well as to persons appearing before the Tribunal as agents, counsel, witnesses and experts. The Agreement contains 25 Articles (plus the usual Final Clauses) recognising the Tribunal's juridical personality, the inviolability of its premises, its immunity from suit, its exemption from taxation and related matters.

To sum up on the question of the Tribunal's status, it is apparent that the various different arrangements, made recently or now in the course of being made, for the operation of the Tribunal bear many similarities with the existing arrangements in regard to courts such as the International Court of Justice, the European Court of Human Rights and the European Court of Justice. However, there is the striking difference in that the Tribunal is a completely separate entity created by the Convention, but not an organ of a larger international organisation, such as the United Nations, the Council of Europe or the European Community. Such autonomy may bring the advantage of genuine independence. At the same time, autonomy increases the number of arrangements which are having to be put in place at present. Autonomy may also mean that the Tribunal has only the periodical meetings of the States Parties from which to seek help should any unexpected problems arise.

2. JURISDICTION OF THE TRIBUNAL

The Tribunal is a standing body with a regular composition (subject to triennial elections for one third of the judges). In contrast to the International Court of

---

[7] See A/51/645 of Dec. 1996.

[8] Discussions were held during the fifth, sixth and seventh meetings of the States Parties in Aug. 1996 and March 1997 (SPLOS/22). The Agreement was adopted by the seventh meeting of the States Parties on 23 May 1997 and opened for signature on I July 1997.

Justice, however, the Tribunal is not a court of general jurisdiction, Instead, the Tribunal will focus on the Convention (in much the same way as the European Court of Human Rights hears cases arising under its Convention), but with the possibility of further jurisdiction being conferred upon the Tribunal by international agreements.

The jurisdiction of the Tribunal is provided for principally in Part XV of the Convention. One of the most significant Articles in that part is Article 287, entitled "Choice of Procedure". According to this provision, States upon signing, ratifying or acceding to the Convention, or at any time thereafter, are free to choose one or more of four different means for the peaceful settlement of disputes concerning the interpretation or application of its terms. The Tribunal is one of these four means, alongside the International Court of Justice, arbitration and a system of structured arbitration known as "special arbitration" for certain categories of disputes. In situations where two disputing States have made different choices or no common choice among the four means, arbitration is the indicated result, unless the parties agree otherwise. At present, the majority of States Parties have not made choices under Article 287, and there remains an "institutionalised dilemma" over the choice of means of dispute settlement in most instances.

The potential jurisdiction of the Tribunal *ratione personae* is extensive. The Tribunal is open to all States Parties to the Convention, of which there are 120 at the time of writing (29 September 1997).[9] In addition, entities other than States Parties have access to the Tribunal in accordance with Part XI dealing with deep seabed mining, including disputes between a State Party and the International Seabed Authority and disputes between mining consortia and the Authority. Moreover, the term "States Parties" is defined in Article 1(2) of the Convention in terms which are wide enough to include the European Community, were it to decide, as seems likely, to confirm formally its signature now that over half of the Member States have become parties. In that event, the European Community could have access to the Tribunal or arbitration in regard to matters within the competence of the Community, as specified in a Declaration to be made under Annex IX of the Convention upon formal confirmation of its signature. The jurisdiction of the Tribunal over non-State entities, such as the International Seabed Authority, mining consortia or the European Community, finds no parallel in the International Court of Justice, the contentious jurisdiction of which is confined by its Statute to States.

The jurisdiction of the Tribunal *ratione materiae* extends to the general law of the sea, practically all of which is regulated in greater or lesser detail in the Convention. Cases could concern issues such as baselines, rights of passage, maritime boundaries and fisheries jurisdiction, all of which have come before the International Court of Justice or *ad hoc* arbitral tribunals in recent years. As a body created by the Convention, the Tribunal will in practice concentrate

---

[9] The last two were the United Kingdom in July 1997 and Chile in Aug. 1997.

upon the true interpretation and application of its terms. However, Article 293 provides that courts and Tribunals with jurisdiction under the Convention are to apply both its terms "and other rules of international law not incompatible with" the Convention. One example of such other rules is provided by Article 295, which imports into the procedures the well-known "local remedies" rule, according to which an available local remedy has to be sought before recourse is had to an international body. Article 293 means, in practice, that the Tribunal will have to consider not only the law of the sea, including customary law on certain matters, but also a wide range of other legal issues. These include: the law of treaties (for instance, the interpretation or application of the Convention as a treaty subject to the Vienna Convention on the Law of Treaties; or the effects of national declarations); the effects of previous judicial decisions (as in the recent case decided by a Chamber of the International Court of Justice about the Gulf of Fonseca[10]); and the law on state responsibility, of which the local remedies rule forms part. Necessarily, the Tribunal will apply the law of its own procedure. The Tribunal will also have to consider certain private law issues to do with deep seabed mining, including activity by consortia under plans of work or contracts. It remains to be seen whether or not the Tribunal will become seised of questions of international law which are connected only indirectly with the law of the sea, e.g. sovereignty over an island disputed between the parties to a general maritime boundary case. Such disputes over islets influencing a short stretch of a lengthy maritime boundary between two States are not uncommon. If the parties request the Tribunal to decide all aspects of a maritime dispute, i.e. both the boundary and the incidental sovereignty question, there appears to be no reason in principle why the Tribunal should decline the invitation. Consent is crucial, a point underlined in this context by the second proviso to Article 298(1)(a)(i).

In addition to its general law of the sea jurisdiction, the Tribunal, including its Seabed Disputes Chamber of 11 judges, has jurisdiction in matters concerning the deep seabed and the realisation under the administration of the International Seabed Authority of the concept of the Common Heritage of Mankind. In regard to disputes about deep sea mining (principally of polymetallic nodules), the Tribunal is the pre-eminent judicial body and it enjoys exclusive jurisdiction. Article 187 of the Convention confers jurisdiction on the Tribunal's Seabed Disputes Chamber over a wide range of disputes arising under Part XI, read with the Agreement on the Implementation of Part XI of 1994. This jurisdiction is exclusive to the Chamber, in the sense that its jurisdiction is not affected by choices made under Article 287 by States Parties. The Tribunal will also have pre-eminent jurisdiction under Article 292 concerning the prompt release of vessels and crews, pursuant to the provisions of the Convention about the release under a system of bonding of fishing vessels and those suspected of having caused marine pollution.

[10] *Land, Island and Maritime Frontier Case* (*El Salvador/Honduras Nicaragua Intervening*), Judgment, ICJ Reports 1992, 351.

In August 1995, the UN Conference on Straddling Fish Stocks adopted an Agreement on that topic which applies the terms of Part XV of the Convention to future disputes about the meaning of that Agreement. The Agreement also provides that disputes about the interpretation or application of regional fisheries agreements or arrangements are subject to the dispute settlement arrangements in Part XV. These provisions, adopted in the light of Article 288 of the Convention, as well as Articles 21 and 22 of Annex VI, reflected a consensus at the Conference over the need to strengthen regional arrangements and organisations. As a result of this new Agreement, the potential jurisdiction of the Tribunal has been greatly expanded in regard to fisheries.[11] The same is true of the International Court of Justice and arbitration since they are both given jurisdiction by Part XV.

3. THE MONTREUX FORMULA AND THE INSTITUTIONAL DILEMMA

As indicated above, much but not all of the above jurisdiction of the Tribunal deriving from the Law of the Sea Convention is shared with the International Court of Justice and also with various arbitral tribunals. Under the so-called "Montreux formula" contained in Article 287 of the Convention, States Parties may choose which dispute-settlement procedures to accept for general law of the sea disputes and, subject to some qualifications, one procedure becomes compulsory for the parties to a dispute. At the informal meeting in Montreux, held during a session of the Conference in Geneva in 1975, many delegates felt this compulsory approach would mark an advance upon the Optional Protocol, such as that adopted at the First UN Conference on the Law of the Sea, on the basis of their assessment that only the existing acceptors of the ICJ's jurisdiction under the optional clause (Article 36(2) of its Statute) would be likely on past experience to accept its jurisdiction under another optional instrument.

The general arrangements for dispute settlement contained in Part XV of the Convention, the terms of Part XI of the Convention on deep seabed mining disputes and subsequently the provisions concerning dispute settlement in the Straddling Fish Stocks Agreement may together lead to an overall increase in the amount of international litigation to do with the law of the sea. The Convention and that Agreement together increase the jurisdictional possibilities (more bilateral connections between pairs of States Parties) for the submission of disputes to compulsory, binding procedures. Simply by ratifying the Convention and the Agreement, additional States are accepting some provisions for compulsory dispute settlement, whether by the ICJ or the Tribunal or some form of arbitration (although Article 298 does permit some opting out from compulsory adjudication). This jurisdictional increase may be seen as an overall advance for the international rule of law. This was the feeling of many of the delegates present

---

[11] For an initial assessment of the Agreement, see the note by the present writer, D. Anderson, "The Straddling Stocks Agreement of 1995—an Initial Assessment", 45 *ICLQ* 463.

at Montreux in the Spring of 1975 when the concept behind Article 287 of the Convention was shaped. Many delegates considered it better to increase the range of commitment to compulsory procedures, even at the cost of creating more "institutional dilemmas". The Soviet and other East European delegations had indicated at the first substantive session of the Conference held in 1974 at Caracas that they had more open minds about arrangements for dispute settlement in the context of a generally accepted new Convention. They signalled that they would not adopt their previous negative stance towards compulsory procedures, thereby going beyond the small advance marked in 1969 by the Vienna Convention on the Law of Treaties, which had provided for such procedures but only in relation to a single issue, that of *jus cogens*.[12] Six years later, there was perceived to be a chance at last, and in a major instrument governing an important part of international law, to secure a greater acceptance of compulsory procedures. However, several objections were voiced to the proposition that the International Court of Justice should be the sole body to which differences must be submitted. The price to be paid for acceptance of some form of binding settlement was the multiplicity of fora seen now in Article 287. The consensus in Montreux was that, in principle, every State Party would be bound to accept some compulsory procedures in the context of the future Convention, and the wishes of the defendant would determine the precise forum. (This latter element was, of course, changed in later negotiations to what appears in Article 287, i.e. in the event of no choices or different choices having been made, arbitration is the default procedure, not that chosen by the defendant. Furthermore, exceptions to compulsory jurisdiction were added later.)

4. THE RULES OF THE TRIBUNAL

At present, the members of the Tribunal are completing work on the Rules of the Tribunal, taking as their basic document the draft Rules prepared by the Preparatory Commission. Those draft Rules were, in turn, drawn largely from the Rules of the International Court of Justice, as revised most recently in 1978.

It is axiomatic that the Rules must be compatible with the Convention and Statute. The Rules will be divided into two parts: organisation or structure, and the conduct of proceedings. As regards, first, the structure of the Tribunal, the Statute provides for 21 members, and that is expected to be the body which will hear the normal case. The Convention and Statute also provide for a Seabed Disputes Chamber of 11 members drawn from the 21; for a chamber of five members to hear cases by Summary Procedure; and for the possibility of setting up other standing or *ad hoc* chambers. At the session held in April 1997, two Resolutions were adopted setting out the terms of reference of two Chambers—

---

[12] Art. 66(a) provides for the reference of disputes involving questions of *jus cogens* to the International Court of Justice upon the application of any one party.

for Fisheries Disputes and for Environmental Disputes, respectively.[13] Each chamber has seven members, a number which gives a cross-section of background and experience. It may be considered that the overall structure is a complex one. In particular, the relationship between the plenary Tribunal and the Seabed Disputes Chamber is unusual. Nonetheless, the Tribunal affords the potential litigants plenty of scope for choice.

Turning to the conduct of proceedings, the Convention and Statute were modelled by the negotiators on the Statute of the International Court of Justice. The basic concepts for the conduct of cases are those of the Hague, rather than Luxembourg or Strasbourg. The Rules naturally reflect this approach. However, the Convention contains some novel provisions concerned with procedures or remedies which are applicable to the various bodies mentioned in Article 287, including therefore the Tribunal. These provisions fall to be considered in framing the Rules. Two examples may be noted.

First, Article 294 introduces in respect of a particular category of disputes the concept of "preliminary proceedings", separate from, logically even prior to or alongside, the familiar concept of preliminary objections to jurisdiction or admissibility. The main intention of the negotiators was to protect coastal states from receiving too many applications challenging the exercise of their sovereign rights or powers and discretions in relation to the Exclusive Economic Zone. (Those are the typical disputes "referred to in Article 297", to which Article 294 itself refers.) The preliminary proceedings are in the nature of a strike-out plea, or possibly of the concept in French administrative law of *abus de droit*. Article 294 links preliminary proceedings to the Application, rather than the Memorial by the applicant, with the possible consequence that unsuccessful preliminary proceedings begun on the basis of the Application could be followed by preliminary objections to jurisdiction or admissibility once the respondent has received the full case of the applicant. This result would have the effect of lengthening the preliminary stages of a case, especially one in which there is an application for the prescription of interim measures of protection.

Secondly, Article 292 makes provision for the consideration of the question of the prompt release of vessels and crews by a court or tribunal, including the Tribunal. The provision contemplates time limits as short as ten days and the consideration of the issue of release on suitable bail without prejudice to the merits of a case before a domestic court in the port State concerned. In other words, the nature of the proceedings is strictly limited and quite different from the normal proceedings, written and oral, for the determination of a dispute concerning the interpretation or application of the Convention.

Those are two examples of provisions in the Convention for new types of proceedings before a court or tribunal with jurisdiction under Part XV. The Rules of the Tribunal need to take account of these provisions. In the absence of detailed rules, reliance could be placed on the general rule according to which

---

[13] See Interim Report prepared by the Tribunal to the Meeting of States Parties, UN Doc. SPLOS/21 of 9 May 1997.

the President ascertains the views of the agents of the parties and makes orders for the procedure to be followed in a particular case.

5. THE "JUDICIAL POLICY" OF THE TRIBUNAL

At its first session, the Tribunal decided that its rules and its procedures should be "user friendly", efficient and cost effective.[14] What do these concepts mean in regard to judicial body? The idea of "user friendliness" covers several matters, including:

—adopting Rules couched in simple, clear language, avoiding repetition of material in the Convention and the Statute;
—complementing the Rules with guidelines for parties to cases;
—flexibility in the procedural decisions for the handling of cases;
—ascertaining the views of the agents on such issues.

"Efficiency" in the case of a judicial body entails following procedures which are effective in determining the disputed issues of law and fact, which are fair to the parties and which avoid unnecessary delays. The procedures must be thorough. Both parties must feel that they have received a full and fair hearing of their arguments. The Tribunal should avoid giving any impression of having pre-judged an issue during the course of the proceedings leading up to its final decision.[15]

The idea of "cost effectiveness" has been taken from the Agreement of July 1994 on the Implementation of Part XI of the Convention.[16] Section I of the Annex to this Agreement requires all institutions constituted by the Convention to be cost effective. This provision applies therefore to the Tribunal. In practice, this provision means that the Tribunal should adopt procedures which avoid unnecessary expense, both for the litigants and the States Parties which fund the Tribunal.

It goes without saying that a tribunal must apply the appropriate rules of law to the cases coming before it. Combining all these elements produces a judicial policy in the following terms: to administer justice diligently, thoroughly and fairly, in accordance with the applicable law, without any unnecessary expense or delay.

---

[14] *Ibid.*, para. 16.
[15] On these points, the comments of Professor Brownlie on the Report of the Study Group of the British Institute of International and Comparative Law are apposite: see D.W. Bowett *et al.* (eds.), *The International Court of Justice: Process, Practice and Procedure* (British Institute of International and Comparative Law, London, 1997), at 105.
[16] Cm 2705.

6. THE EXISTING EXPERIENCE OF INTERNATIONAL COURTS

The 1920s saw an important exercise: the drawing up of the Rules of the Permanent Court of International Justice, no doubt influenced by experience with the Hague Conventions of 1899 and 1907. These Rules served in 1946 as the basis for the Rules of the present Court. The various revisions, most recently in 1978, have not expunged from the content and phrasing (at least, of the English version) of the Rules certain traces of the atmosphere of the early years of this century. Nonetheless, those Rules were used by the Preparatory Commission as a basic text in drawing up the first draft of the Rules for the Tribunal. In considering the draft, the members of the Tribunal decided not to depart unnecessarily from those Rules, which represent the accumulated experience of the judges who have served in the Hague. However, in several places attempts were made to modernise the wording and in others to bring the English more into line with the French (which reads like the original version, possibly going back to the 1920s in some instances).

The members of the Tribunal are also aware of the current debates upon the working methods of the Hague Court. Note was taken of the suggestions made by eminent figures, including former and current members of the Court, by the Study Group of the British Institute of International and Comparative Law[17] composed of experienced Counsel and, last but not least, by Professor Highet.[18] It was decided, in principle, to adopt several of the suggestions, advanced by former members of the Court and Counsel who have appeared before it, to improve the working methods and procedures of the Court. In order to achieve transparency in the conduct of cases about the meaning and effect of the Convention and in order to permit the effective operation of the rules on intervention, the Tribunal decided to make written pleadings available promptly, that is to say, with very little delay after their receipt in the Registry. In an effort to reduce the bulk of annexes to written pleadings, public documents need not be annexed if copies are readily available to the other side and the Tribunal. The Tribunal adopted a six-months rule of thumb, according to which each pleading should be delivered within a maximum of six months and the hearing would follow within the same timescale. The Statute gives the Tribunal the power to "prescribe" interim measures of protection, rather than to "indicate" them: in this perspective, it is proposed to require parties to report on steps taken to comply with prescribed measures. The Tribunal decided to require preliminary objections to be made sooner rather than later, and not at the last possible moment. The Rules will be complemented by Guidelines on written and oral proceedings.

---

[17] See Bowett *et al.* (eds.), n.15 above, containing the Report as well as papers by several judges.
[18] In a paper entitled "Problems in the Preparation and Presentation of a Case from the point of view of counsel and of the Court", 16 Apr. 1996, read at an ICJ/UNITAR Colloquium in the Hague.

Article 289 encourages the use of scientific or technical experts who may sit with the judges but without a vote. Many issues to do with shipping, fishing, the seabed or pollution have a marked scientific or technical content. Boundary disputes are best tackled with the assistance of expert hydrographers or geographers or geodesists. There is a case for making use readily of Article 289, as in the Palena arbitration.[19]

Technological advances permit the simplification of certain aspects of litigation. While the President may summon the agents of the parties to meet at the seat of the Tribunal, there exists also the possibility of video conferencing or conference telephone calling. These techniques could be used, for example, to make second or third contacts following an initial face-to-face meeting, or they may be convenient if the dispute concerns States far removed from Hamburg, such as small island developing states in the Pacific region which may decide to appoint agents resident in the respective capitals. While the Registry will require a minimum number of copies of written pleadings, the submission of a diskette would permit the reproduction of copies, e.g. to satisfy requests from interested governments or members of the public.

7. INTERNAL JUDICIAL PRACTICE

The internal judicial practices of international and European courts vary markedly, especially as regards the conduct of their deliberations, the disclosure of individual opinions and the form of decisions. In the International Court of Justice, the practice is for all 15 or 17 judges sitting to hear a particular case to prepare detailed notes giving their considered opinions on the key issues identified by the Court at the end of the oral hearings. These initial notes together total hundreds of pages and may become the focus of debate in the deliberations. After private deliberation, the President is able to form a drafting committee to put together the draft judgment. In practice, this is often a majority rather than unanimous decision. All judges take part in the discussion of the draft judgment, including those who are about to dissent from its terms or add a separate opinion. The votes of judges are recorded and dissents and separate opinions are accepted. Dissents and separate opinions may, on occasion, be discursive.[20]

The European Court of Justice has a different system. The Court, for each case, is composed of both judges and an Advocate General: the latter puts forward his or her view on the issues following the close of the hearing, before the judges deliberate. The Court appoints a judge rapporteur who has the task of preparing a document for the deliberations of the Court. This document plays a

---

[19] *Argentina–Chile Frontier Case*, 38 ILR 10, where the Court, presided over by Lord McNair, included also a geographer and a land surveyor. On the general issue, see G. White, *The Use of Experts by International Tribunals* (Syracuse University Press, Syracuse, NY, 1965).

[20] For a description of the practice, see Bowett *et al.*, n. 15 above, at 27.

major role in the discussions and each judge rapporteur is no doubt especially influential in the particular case. The Court does not give a record of the voting, nor does it allow separate or dissenting opinions. There is a single judgment which, while it may bear the marks of compromise, does not openly admit to compromise. All judges take part in the discussion of the draft judgment, even those opposed to the decision.[21]

In the case of the European Court of Human Rights, the hearing of cases has been facilitated until now by the Report of the European Commission of Human Rights. When a Report has come before the Court and after the closure of the oral proceedings, the President leads the deliberations and identifies where the weight of opinion lies. The Registrar may assist a drafting committee in producing a decision. The Court produces relatively short judgments which, having stated the relevant facts, discuss the issues under the relevant Articles of the European Convention on Human Rights. The Court gives the voting figures on each part of its decision and permits separate and dissenting opinions. The latter are nearly always short and refer directly to the point or points in the judgment which the dissenting minority does not share.[22]

The International Court of Justice and the European Court of Justice usually allow two rounds of written pleadings. The former gives generous time limits, and pleadings tend to be extensive. The two European Courts limit the time given to each side in oral argument. The Hague Court, perhaps on account of the different nature of its cases, generally does not. All three Courts tend to listen until the end before posing (relatively few) questions. International (as opposed to European) courts tend not to direct the hearings, possibly on account of their collegial nature and their understandable wish to avoid giving the impression of prejudgment of issues.

8. CONCLUDING OBSERVATIONS

Since 1 October 1996, the world has had another standing tribunal applying rules of international law. Leaving aside the recent Yugoslav and Rwanda tribunals, as well as the panels set up by the World Trade Organisation, the Tribunal represents the first world-wide court set up specifically to deal with a major part of international law since the establishment of the International Court of Justice 50 years ago. Some commentators have questioned the wisdom of creating such a new court in the United Nations family alongside the International Court of Justice, which is (and which will remain) the principal judicial organ of the United Nations.[23] Fears have been expressed about the pos-

---

[21] Judge D. Edward, "How the Court of Justice Works", 20 *EL Rev.* 539.

[22] P. Mahoney, "Developments in the Procedure of the European Court of Human Rights: the Revised Rules of Court", 3 *YEL* 127.

[23] E. Lauterpacht, *Aspects of the Administration of International Justice* (Grotius, Cambridge, 1991), at 21.

sible "fragmentation" of the jurisprudence. However, there has long been *ad hoc* arbitration alongside the Permanent Court of International Justice and the present World Court.[24] There is no evidence of inconsistencies: decisions of the Court are sometimes the subject of scholarly criticism, as are those of arbitral tribunals. The fears of inconsistent decisions may prove to be exaggerated. Certainly, the Tribunal should be on its guard against departing unnecessarily from the corpus of existing case law, whether it be a decision by the Hague Court or one given by an arbitral tribunal. At the same time, its primary task will be to apply the Convention of 1982 which introduced many novelties into the law.

The Tribunal will no doubt establish its own pattern and working methods. It is likely to be different from other standing international and European Courts and *ad hoc* arbitral tribunals. This may be no bad thing: it should not live in the shadow of any existing institution. The Tribunal is adopting its own persona or style, based on a modern, business-like approach. The Tribunal should be seen not so much as a rival for the International Court of Justice, but rather as an alternative or complementary body. If States Parties have confidence in its membership and its working methods, they may choose to use it in appropriate circumstances. In that perspective, the Tribunal could strengthen the administration of international justice and thereby the international rule of law. Although its appearance on the international stage may be seen by some commentators to have increased the scope of the institutional dilemma, others may see the Tribunal as having increased the range of choice open to would-be litigants. Freedom of choice amongst a range of options is widely regarded as a good thing.

---

[24] A point made by J. Charney, "The Implications of Expanding International Dispute Settlement Systems: The 1982 Convention on the Law of the Sea", 90 *AJIL* 69 at 72.

5

Dispute Settlement in the Law of the Sea—the Context of the International Tribunal for the Law of the Sea and Alternatives to It

ROBIN R. CHURCHILL

1. INTRODUCTION

The preceding chapter by David Anderson gave an account of how the International Tribunal for the Law of the Sea (ITLOS) is setting about elaborating the way in which it will operate. The aim of this present chapter is to explain the context in which ITLOS has been set up and will function, and to consider the various fora which exist as alternatives to ITLOS for the settlement of disputes in the Law of the Sea and the relationship between ITLOS and those fora.

The chapter is in three main parts. The first part gives an account of the provisions of the 1982 United Nations Convention on the Law of the Sea (hereafter UNCLOS) dealing with dispute settlement, which *inter alia* provide for the creation of ITLOS. This puts ITLOS into its immediate context and explains what alternative fora there are to ITLOS under the UNCLOS dispute-settlement system. The second part examines other means for dispute settlement in the Law of the Sea outside the UNCLOS system. This puts ITLOS and the UNCLOS system into some kind of historical context, as well as exploring a range of alternative means for dispute settlement. The final part of the chapter considers the prospects for the UNCLOS dispute settlement machinery, including ITLOS. This tries to look at the broader politico-legal context within which ITLOS will operate.

At the outset it must be stressed that although UNCLOS entered into force in November 1994, at the time of writing its dispute settlement machinery has not yet been invoked. For this reason some of the discussion in this chapter must of necessity be somewhat speculative.

2. THE DISPUTE SETTLEMENT PROVISIONS OF UNCLOS

For reasons of space the account of the dispute settlement provisions of UNC-LOS which follows must be fairly concise and broad-brush.[1] These provisions are contained in Part XV of UNCLOS and also, as far as disputes relating to the International Sea-Bed Area are concerned, in section 5 of Part XI. Under the general provisions of Part XV, the system of dispute settlement relates to any dispute "[c]oncerning the interpretation or application of this Convention" (Article 279). It seems clear from the jurisprudence of the World Court relating to the meaning of the same and comparable phrases in other treaties that the phrase encompasses disputes relating to alleged breaches of the Convention.[2]

The UNCLOS dispute settlement machinery comprises two phases, the first consensual, the second compulsory. During the first phase the parties to a dispute shall seek to settle it by negotiation or by any agreed third party diplomatic or judicial means of their choice. Such means may also include the conciliation procedure established by section 1 of Annex V of UNCLOS.

Where the consensual first phase procedures do not lead to a settlement of the dispute, the compulsory second phase, dealt with by section 2 of Part XV, comes into play. Under it any party to the dispute may, subject to certain exceptions (discussed in more detail below), refer the dispute to one of four possible fora. These are: ITLOS, the International Court of Justice, an arbitral tribunal constituted in accordance with Annex VII, and a special arbitral tribunal constituted in accordance with Annex VIII. A State at any time following its signature of UNCLOS may make a written declaration specifying one or more of these four fora as its preferred choice for settling disputes: where no such declaration has been made, a State is deemed to have accepted Annex VII arbitration. If the parties to a dispute have chosen the same forum, that will be the forum for hearing the dispute.[3]

Where the parties' choice of forum does not coincide, the dispute will be dealt with by an Annex VII arbitral tribunal. The declarations so far made as to choice of forum are shown in Table 1A. As can be seen, very few parties to the Convention have so far availed themselves of the possibility of making a declaration. This is somewhat surprising, given that this so-called "cafeteria"

---

[1] For detailed accounts of the UNCLOS dispute settlement system, see, from amongst a growing literature, A.O. Adede, *The System for Settlement of Disputes under the UN Convention on the Law of the Sea* (Nijhoff, Dordrecht, 1987); A.E. Boyle, "Settlement of Disputes relating to the Law of the Sea and the Environment" [1996] *Thesaurus Acrosaurium* (forthcoming); E.D. Brown, "Dispute Settlement and the Law of the Sea: The UN Convention Regime," 21 *Marine Policy* 17; and J.G. Merrills, *International Dispute Settlement* (2nd edn., Grotius, Cambridge, 1991) ch. 11.

[2] See, e.g., *Case concerning the Factory at Chorzow,* Judgment No. 8, 1927, PCIJ Series A, No. 9, 4 at 20–5; *Interpretation of Peace Treaties with Bulgaria,Hungary and Romania,* First Phase, Advisory Opinion, ICJ Reports 1950, 65 at 75.

[3] Where the parties to a dispute have each selected two or more fora and listed such fora in order of preference and those lists do not coincide, it is not clear from UNCLOS which is to be the forum for the case. For a suggestion as to what the answer should be, see Boyle, n. 1 (above 31 of original manuscript).

approach to choice of forum was said to be essential in order to obtain agreement on the settlement of dispute provisions during the negotiation of UNCLOS, and the reason for the current lack of declarations is not clear. It may be that States are waiting to see the choices made by other States or that they are waiting to see how ITLOS and the other tribunals function in practice, or that Annex VII arbitration is genuinely their first and only preference. Whatever be the reason, if the present situation is maintained it is very likely that most disputes dealt with under section 2 of Part XV will be referred to Annex VII arbitration.

Of the four possible fora, the International Court of Justice of course needs no further explanation, but it may be useful to say a few words about each of the three new fora. ITLOS, whose seat is in Hamburg, consists of 21 judges elected by the States Parties to UNCLOS from among persons "enjoying the highest reputation for fairness and integrity and of recognised competence in the field of the law of the sea": in ITLOS as a whole the "representation of the principal legal systems of the world and equitable geographical distribution shall be assured".[4] The first set of judges was elected in August 1996.[5] Apart from the Sea-Bed Disputes Chamber, which is established by UNCLOS itself and is discussed in more detail below, ITLOS may sit in such chambers as it may decide or the parties to a case request. So far ITLOS has established a chamber of summary procedure (which is in fact required by UNCLOS[6]) and has formed two seven-person chambers for fisheries and environmental questions. It should also be noted that, unlike the other fora whose jurisdiction is limited to disputes concerning the interpretation or application of UNCLOS or of any other agreement related to the purposes of UNCLOS which are submitted to them in accordance with such agreement, the jurisdiction of ITLOS is wider. Under Article 21 of Annex VI its jurisdiction also includes "all matters specifically provided for in any other agreement which confers jurisdiction" upon it: a number of such agreements are referred to in section 3 below.[7] Similarly under Article 22 ITLOS also has jurisdiction over disputes relating to the interpretation or application of any treaty relating to the Law of the Sea which all the parties to that treaty have agreed shall be submitted to ITLOS. In addition, the Sea-Bed Disputes Chamber, as explained below, also has a wider jurisdiction. Like the International Court of Justice, ITLOS takes its decisions by majority, and such decisions are binding on the parties to the dispute. There is also provision for *ad hoc* judges, intervention by third parties and for ITLOS to decide cases *ex aequo et bono*.

An arbitral tribunal constituted under Annex VII normally consists of five members, one appointed by each of the parties to the dispute and the remaining

---

[4] Annex VI, Art. 2.

[5] For a list of those elected and further details of the elections, see 12 *International Journal of Marine and Coastal Law* (hereafter *IJMCL*) 97.

[6] See Art. 15(3) of Annex VI.

[7] For a discussion of the scope of Art. 21, see A.E. Boyle, "Dispute Settlement and the Law of the Sea Convention: Problems of Fragmentation and Jurisdiction", 46 *ICLQ* 37 at 47–50.

three appointed by agreement between the parties or, failing agreement, by the President of ITLOS. Arbitrators are preferably to be appointed from a list of arbitrators maintained by the UN Secretary-General and to which each State Party to UNCLOS is entitled to nominate four persons "experienced in maritime affairs and enjoying the highest reputation for fairness, competence and integrity".[8] Otherwise the tribunal functions very much like a typical arbitral tribunal, except that its procedure is determined by the tribunal itself and not by the parties, unless the latter agree otherwise.

Arbitral tribunals set up by Annex VIII are limited to hearing four kinds of disputes—those concerning fisheries, protection and preservation of the marine environment, marine scientific research and navigation. Each tribunal normally consists of five members, with each party to the dispute appointing two members and the remaining member, who acts as President of the tribunal, being appointed by agreement between the parties or, failing agreement, by the UN Secretary-General. Arbitrators are preferably to be appointed from a list of experts in each of the four fields referred to above drawn up and maintained by FAO, UNEP, the Inter-Governmental Oceanographic Commission and the IMO, respectively. Each State Party may nominate to each of the four lists two experts in each field "whose competence in the legal, scientific or technical aspects of such field is established and generally recognised and who enjoy the highest reputation for fairness and integrity".[9] Annex VIII tribunals operate in the same way as Annex VII tribunals. In addition to their normal arbitration function, Annex VIII tribunals can also be used at any time, if the parties to a dispute so agree, to "carry out an inquiry and establish the facts giving rise to the dispute", and, if the parties so request, "formulate recommendations".[10]

As well as having jurisdiction to hear a dispute where both parties to the dispute have chosen it as their preferred forum, ITLOS also has jurisdiction in three other situations. First, under Article 290(5) ITLOS has the jurisdiction to prescribe provisional measures in respect of any dispute which is being referred to an arbitral tribunal under Annex VII or VIII where such a tribunal has not yet been constituted and if ITLOS considers that *prima facie* such a tribunal would have jurisdiction and that the urgency of the situation so requires. Obviously ITLOS also has jurisdiction to prescribe provisional measures in relation to disputes where it is the forum chosen by the parties. In both cases provisional measures are binding (Article 290(6)), unlike interim measures of protection indicated by the International Court of Justice. Again, unlike the International Court, ITLOS and other tribunals can prescribe provisional measures not only to preserve the right of the parties to the dispute but also to prevent serious harm to the marine environment. Secondly, under Article 292 where one State has detained the vessel of another State in a manner that is alleged to be contrary to the various provisions of the Convention dealing with the prompt release of ves-

---

[8] Annex VII, Art. 2(1).
[9] Annex VIII, Art. 2(3).
[10] Annex VIII, Art. 5.

sels,[11] the question of release of the vessel from detention may be submitted by the flag State to a court or tribunal accepted by the detaining State or to ITLOS, unless the parties otherwise agree. The court or tribunal concerned can order the prompt release of the detained vessel and determine the bond or other financial security to be posted.[12]

The final, and most important, form of special jurisdiction of ITLOS is that relating to disputes with respect to activities in the International Sea-Bed Area. This jurisdiction, which is governed by section 5 of Part XI of UNCLOS (and also by the 1994 Agreement relating to the Implementation of Part XI of UNCLOS[13]) rather than by Part XV, is to be exercised, not by ITLOS as a whole, but by its Sea-Bed Disputes Chamber. The latter is an 11-member body, selected by and from the judges of ITLOS, who must ensure that there is representation of the principal legal systems and equitable geographical distribution.[14] The Chamber may also establish an *ad hoc* three-member chamber for dealing with certain kinds of dispute.[15] The Sea-Bed Disputes Chamber appears to have exclusive jurisdiction over inter-State disputes relating to activities in the International Sea-Bed Area,[16] and can also have jurisdiction over a variety of other disputes—between States parties and the International Sea-Bed Authority, between parties to a contract (who may be States, the Authority, the Enterprise, State enterprises or natural or juridical persons)[17] or between the Authority and a prospective contractor. The Chamber may also give advisory opinions at the request of the Assembly or the Council of the International Sea-Bed Authority.[18]

As already indicated, the possibility for a party to a dispute to refer the dispute unilaterally to one of the four fora of section 2 of Part XV is subject to a number of significant exceptions. Such exceptions fall into two categories— general exceptions applicable to all parties and optional exceptions of which parties may choose to avail themselves. The former are contained in Article 297.

[11] These provisions comprise Art. 73 (release of vessels arrested for alleged illegal fishing in a coastal State's EEZ) and Art. 226 (release of vessels detained by a coastal or port State in connection with alleged pollution of the marine environment).

[12] For a detailed consideration of these powers, see the special issue of *IJMCL* devoted to this question, vol 11, part 2 (at 137 ff.). For powerful criticism of the powers of ITLOS and other tribunals to order the prompt release of vessels, based on the argument that the exercise of such powers will often involve such bodies in consideration of issues that fall within that area of coastal State powers in the EEZ exempted from the provisions on compulsory dispute settlement (discussed below), see S. Oda, "Dispute Settlement Prospects in the Law of the Sea", 44 *ICLQ* 863 at 865–7.

[13] Cm 2705 (1994).

[14] Annex VI, Art. 35.

[15] Annex VI, Art. 36.

[16] But see the discussion preceding n. 57 above. Note also that the parties may agree to refer a dispute to a special chamber of ITLOS rather than the Sea-Bed Disputes Chamber (Art. 188(1)(a)).

[17] Disputes over contracts may also be submitted to binding commercial arbitration. Any question concerning interpretation of UNCLOS must, however, be referred by the arbitral tribunal to the Sea-Bed Disputes Chamber for a ruling (Art. 188(2)(a)(b)). In addition, disputes concerning the application of GATT/WTO rules to the Authority's production policy are to be settled in accordance with GATT/WTO dispute settlement procedures where the parties to the dispute are parties to GATT/WTO: see 1994 Agreement, n. 13 above, Annex, s. 6, para. 1(f).

[18] For a more detailed analysis of these complex provisions, see Brown, n. 1 above, at 26–8.

This provision is not very well drafted, but essentially what it amounts to (at the risk of some over-simplification) is that disputes concerning the exercise by a coastal State of its rights within its EEZ are exempt from the compulsory dispute settlement provisions of UNCLOS, subject to three qualifications. First, disputes concerning allegations that a coastal State has acted contrary to UNCLOS in regard to other States' rights of navigation, overflight or laying of cables and pipelines or that other States have exercised those rights contrary to UNCLOS or validly adopted coastal State regulations and disputes concerning allegations that a coastal State has acted in contravention of specified international rules for the protection of the marine environment are subject to the full range of compulsory dispute settlement procedures. Secondly, disputes relating to the exercise by a coastal State of its rights to regulate marine scientific research in its EEZ (and on its continental shelf) are exempt from compulsory dispute settlement, except that certain matters may be submitted to compulsory conciliation. Thirdly, the same position obtains in respect of disputes relating to the exercise by a coastal State of its rights to exploit, conserve and manage the living resources of its EEZ. In the last two cases the compulsory conciliation referred to takes place through a conciliation commission established in accordance with Annex V. Such a commission consists of five members, with each party appointing two conciliators and the fifth being appointed by the other four conciliators: in the absence of agreement this appointment is to be made by the UN Secretary-General. Conciliators are preferably to be appointed from a list of conciliators maintained by the Secretary-General to which each State party to UNCLOS may nominate four persons "enjoying the highest reputation for fairness, competence and integrity".[19] The commission, unless the parties agree otherwise, determines its own procedure. Within 12 months the commission is to produce a report recording its conclusions on all questions of fact or law relevant to the dispute and such recommendations as it may deem appropriate for an amicable settlement. The report is not binding on the parties.

Optional exceptions are dealt with by Article 298. Under this provision a State may at any time after signing UNCLOS make a declaration stating that it does not accept the compulsory dispute-settlement provisions of section 2 of Part XV in relation to one or more of the following three categories of disputes: (1) disputes relating to maritime boundaries with neighbouring States or those involving historic bays or titles; (2) disputes concerning military activities and certain kinds of law enforcement activities in the EEZ; (3) disputes in respect of which the Security Council is exercising the functions assigned to it by the UN Charter. In the case of the first category a State making a declaration in respect of such exception must accept conciliation under Annex V if a dispute arises subsequent to the entry into force of UNCLOS, except for a dispute which necessarily involves the concurrent consideration of any unsettled dispute concerning sovereignty or other rights over land territory. Where a conciliation

---

[19] Annex V, Art. 2.

commission has dealt with a dispute and presented its report, the parties are to negotiate an agreement on the basis of that report. If such negotiations do not result in an agreement, the parties are, by mutual consent, to submit the dispute to one of the section 2 fora, unless they agree otherwise. The result of these procedures is that it is still possible for an unwilling State to resist a negotiated or third party settlement of the dispute. The declarations so far made under Article 298 are shown in Table 1B, at the end of this chapter. Even fewer States have made such declarations than those making declarations in respect of choice of forum. Again this is rather surprising, given that the inclusion of such optional exceptions was thought to be necessary in order to obtain agreement on the dispute-settlement provisions of UNCLOS as a whole. On the other hand, since a State can make a declaration under Article 298 at any time and since the consensual first-stage procedures of section 1 must be used before resort may be had to the second-stage compulsory procedures of section 2, there should be no risk of a State which has not yet made a declaration under Article 298 being "ambushed" and having a dispute of one of the kinds listed in Article 298 brought before a third-party forum for settlement against its will.

The system for the settlement of disputes contained in UNCLOS has many traditional features. First, it is based on the traditional bilateral paradigm of dispute settlement. On the other hand, unlike the International Court of Justice, parties to disputes may include entities other than States. Before ITLOS and the Annex VII and VIII arbitral tribunals parties to a dispute can include all parties to UNCLOS: the latter include not only States but also non-independent self-governing territories, such as the Cook Islands,[20] and international organisations, of which the EC is the most likely potential party.[21] Before the Sea-Bed Disputes Chamber parties may also include the International Sea-Bed Authority, its mining arm the Enterprise, State enterprises and natural or juridical persons.[22] Furthermore, it is possible and has been argued that on the basis of Article 20(2) of Annex VI, which refers to ITLOS being open to "entities other than States parties . . . in any case submitted pursuant to any other agreement conferring jurisdiction on the Tribunal which is accepted by all the parties to that case", ITLOS could be open to a variety of non-State parties, "including international organisations, non-governmental organisations, and other entities which are not States or whose international status is doubtful, such as Taiwan".[23] Secondly, the UNCLOS dispute settlement system is traditional because it is based on the adjudicative model. In this it may be contrasted with the non-compliance mechanisms which have recently been or are being developed under various environmental treaties, such as the Montreal Protocol on

---

[20] Arts. 305(1)(c)(d)(e) and 306.

[21] Art. 305(1)(f) and Annex IX. The EC has signed the Convention, but had not as at 26 June 1997 ratified it, although the necessary condition for such ratification, that a majority of its Member States be parties to the Convention (see Art. 3 of Annex IX), had been fulfilled.

[22] Art. 187(b)–(e).

[23] Boyle, n. 7 above, at 53.

Substances that Deplete the Ozone Layer[24] and the various protocols to the Convention on Long-Range Transboundary Air Pollution.[25] Such mechanisms, in contrast to traditional dispute-settlement procedures, are multilateral and largely non-adjudicative. The nearest UNCLOS comes to a non-compliance procedure is the Commission on the Limits of the Continental Shelf, set up by Annex II, which is designed to assist States to determine the outer limit of their continental shelf, where that extends beyond 200 miles, in conformity with the Convention.[26] In general, however, given that UNCLOS imposes few specific and precise obligations on States but is frequently permissive, unlike the environmental agreements referred to, and that a breach of UNCLOS will usually affect one or a limited number of States rather than the international community in general, again unlike the environmental treaties, non-compliance procedures are not so very apposite for UNCLOS. Another contrast may also be drawn with environmental treaties. The latter usually have regular meetings of the parties, either within the framework of an organisation or commission or *ad hoc* like the major multilateral conventions, which can serve as fora for dispute resolution by non-judicial means. UNCLOS, by contrast, makes no provision for regular meetings of its parties, except for its initial phase in order to elect members of various bodies and for meetings of the International Sea-Bed Authority, which of course deals with only one limited area of the Convention's subject matter.

While the system of dispute settlement in UNCLOS may be traditional in much of its basic approach, the extent and complexity of the system are virtually without parallel. No other treaty, except perhaps some regional human rights treaties, has such a comprehensive system for dispute settlement, with a high compulsory element. In the words of Christine Chinkin, "what is important about UNCLOS is that it combines existing processes in a novel way, which combines maximum choice of process with an obligation that some definite process be attempted".[27] It is therefore worth spending a few moments to consider why UNCLOS has such an extensive system for dispute settlement, especially perhaps in view of the fact that, as will be seen in the next section of this chapter, dispute-settlement provisions contained in other Law of the Sea treaties have hardly ever been used—the same is true, too, of most other fields of international law, with the notable exception of human rights.

---

[24] As to which see M. Koskenniemi, "Breach of Treaty or Non-Compliance? Reflections on the Enforcement of the Montreal Protocol", 3 *Yearbook of International Environmental Law* 123, especially at 128–34.

[25] As to which see R.R. Churchill, G. Kütting and L.M. Warren, "The 1994 UNECE Sulphur Protocol", 7 *Journal of Environmental Law* 169 at 190–1.

[26] Further, since limits established on the basis of the Commission's recommendations are "final and binding" (Art. 76(8)), this should also help to prevent disputes. See Brown, n. 1 above, at 40.

[27] C. Chinkin, "Dispute Resolution and the Law of the Sea: Regional Problems and Prospects" in J. Crawford and D.R. Rothwell (eds.), *The Law of the Sea in the Asian-Pacific Region* (Nijhoff, Dordrecht, 1995) at 243.

The reason UNCLOS has a large element of compulsory dispute settlement is because a number of developed States, including the United Kingdom and USA which both made initial and influential proposals for dispute settlement, made it clear that they could not accept some of the proposed innovations of the Convention, which they thought would produce disputes, without compulsory dispute settlement. The latter was also thought necessary in order to preserve the integrity of the Convention text as a universal and comprehensive code for the Law of the Sea, otherwise unilateral and probably conflicting interpretations would result.[28] The reason UNCLOS has a wide "cafeteria" choice of fora for compulsory dispute settlement is because it was thought that States would be more likely to accept such settlement if offered a range of possible mechanisms and fora. As to the different fora, the reason for establishing what is effectively a second international court (ITLOS) as well as utilising the existing International Court of Justice is that at the time UNCLOS was being negotiated there was considerable distrust of the International Court by both developing States (the UNCLOS negotiations began only a few years after the *South-West Africa* case) and Communist States. (This situation has, of course, since changed and, if UNCLOS were being negotiated today, ITLOS might not be thought necessary.) In addition, there was also perceived to be a need for specialist tribunals—hence Annex VIII arbitral tribunals and the Sea-Bed Disputes Chamber of ITLOS, which at one stage was planned as a completely separate tribunal.[29] Annex VII arbitration was chosen as the residual forum because, when delegates were asked to indicate the various possible fora under consideration in the negotiations in order of preference, Annex VII arbitration emerged overwhelmingly as the preferred second choice.[30]

Turning now to the reasons for the inclusion of the various exceptions to compulsory dispute settlement, which of course significantly reduce the scope of such settlement, in general terms the exceptions were included because it was thought that without them many States would not be prepared to accept compulsory dispute settlement. Given the very limited degree to which States parties to UNCLOS have so far availed themselves of the optional exceptions, this premise may possibly be open to some question. More specifically, the reason for excluding most disputes relating to the EEZ is political sensitivity concerning the Convention's provisions, which represent a careful and delicate balance between the interests of coastal States and the interests of other States. Of the optional exceptions, maritime boundaries were included because of fundamental disagreements between States as to the principles on which such boundaries should be delimited, which are also reflected in the vagueness of the Convention's substantive provisions on this question, while the exceptions

---

[28] *Ibid.*, at 245; Boyle, n. 7 above, at 38–9.
[29] L.B. Sohn, "Settlement of Law of the Sea Disputes", 10 *IJMCL* 205 at 211. See also Boyle, n. 1 above, 37–8 of original manuscript.
[30] Sohn, n. 29 above, at 212.

relating to military activities, law enforcement and the Security Council reflect the political and security sensibilities of many States.

Before leaving this account of the provisions of UNCLOS concerning dispute settlement, mention must also be made of the 1995 Agreement for the Implementation of the Provisions of the UN Convention on the Law of the Sea relating to the Conservation and Management of Straddling Fish Stocks and Highly Migratory Fish Stocks,[31] which extends the dispute settlement provisions of UNCLOS to the Agreement. Article 30(1) provides simply that "the provisions relating to the settlement of disputes set out in Part XV of the Convention apply *mutatis mutandis* to any dispute between States Parties to this Agreement concerning the interpretation or application of this Agreement, whether or not they are also Parties to the Convention". Article 30(2) goes on to make the same provision for disputes concerning "the interpretation or application of a sub-regional, regional or global fisheries agreement relating to straddling fish stocks or highly migratory fish stocks". One of the consequences of these provisions is that it may lead to States not parties to UNCLOS utilising its dispute-settlement machinery. A potential example of such a State is the USA, which was one of the first States to ratify the 1995 Agreement but which has not yet acceded to UNCLOS. Finally the 1995 Agreement provides for one other form of dispute settlement. Article 29 provides that "where a dispute concerns a matter of a technical nature, the States concerned may refer the dispute to an *ad hoc* expert panel established by them. The panel shall confer with the States concerned and shall endeavour to resolve the dispute expeditiously without recourse to binding procedures for the settlement of disputes." The 1995 Agreement is not yet in force, so there are obviously no practical examples of the operation of its dispute-settlement procedures.[32]

3. DISPUTE SETTLEMENT OUTSIDE UNCLOS

This section examines the various adjudicative means that existed for third party settlement of disputes in the Law of the Sea prior to the entry into force of UNCLOS and assesses the extent to which such means can still be used, even after the Convention's entry into force. It thus provides some historical context to the UNCLOS dispute-settlement provisions, as well as a survey of alternatives to the UNCLOS section 2 fora. The various adjudicative means for third party settlement outside UNCLOS fall into two broad categories—those of general application and those contained in a variety of particular treaties relating to the Law of the Sea.

[31] Cm 3125 (1995).
[32] For a detailed analysis of the Agreement's provisions on dispute settlement, see A. Tahindro, "Conservation and Management of Transboundary Fish Stocks: Comments in Light of the Adoption of the 1995 Agreement for the Conservation and Management of Straddling Fish Stocks and Highly Migratory Fish Stocks", 28 *ODIL* 1 at 44–9.

Third Party Dispute Settlement Means of General Application

Obviously the traditional adjudicative means for third party dispute settlement—arbitration and international courts—could be used for the settlement of disputes relating to the Law of the Sea prior to the entry into force of UNCLOS, and were in practice relatively frequently used. For example, of the approximately 40 inter-State arbitrations between 1945 and 1994, seven to some degree concern the Law of the Sea.[33] In the case of the International Court of Justice, of the 72 contentious cases referred to the Court before the entry into force of UNCLOS, 22 (or about 31 per cent) were wholly or partly concerned with the Law of the Sea. Of the 39 judgments given on the merits up to the same time, 12 (again about the same percentage) concern, wholly or in part, the Law of the Sea. Many of these judgments have been of major significance for the development of the subject: examples include the *Corfu Channel* case[34] (on passage through straits), the *Anglo-Norwegian Fisheries* case[35] (on the use of straight baselines) and five maritime boundary cases (*North Sea Continental Shelf*,[36] *Tunisia/Libya*,[37] *Gulf of Maine*,[38] *Libya/Malta*[39] and *Greenland/Jan Mayen*[40]).[41] Mention may also be made of the European Court of Justice. The overwhelming majority of cases before the Court are not inter-State cases—indeed the Court has so far given judgment in only one such case, but that was concerned with a marine matter, the mesh size of fishing nets.[42] Nevertheless, a number of the cases brought by the Commission against a Member State under Article 169 of the EC Treaty, by a Member State against the Council or referred

[33] These cases include five maritime boundary delimitations: *Anglo-French Continental Shelf* (1977), 18 ILM 397; *Guinea/Guinea Bissau* (1985), 25 ILM 251; *Guinea Bissau/Senegal* (1989), 83 ILR 1; *Canada/France* (1992), 31 ILM 1145; and *Dubai/Sharjah* (1981), 91 ILR 543), the *Beagle Channel* case (1977), 52 ILR 93, and the *Franco-Canadian Fisheries* case (1986), 82 ILR 590.

[34] *Corfu Channel*, Merits, Judgment, ICJ Reports 1949, 4.

[35] *Fisheries*, Judgment, ICJ Reports 1951, 116.

[36] *North Sea Continental Shelf*, ICJ Reports 1969, 3.

[37] *Continental Shelf (Tunisia/Libyan Arab Jamahiriya)*, Judgment, ICJ Reports 1982, 18.

[38] *Delimitation of the Maritime Boundary in the Gulf of Maine Area*, Judgment, ICJ Reports 1984, 246.

[39] *Continental Shelf (Libyan Arab Jamahiriya/Malta)*, Judgment, ICJ Reports 1985, 13.

[40] *Maritime Delimitation in the Area between Greenland and Jan Mayen*, Judgment, ICJ Reports 1993, 38.

[41] The other five cases are the two *Fisheries Jurisdiction* cases (*UK v. Iceland*; *Federal Republic of Germany v. Iceland*) concerning the extent of fisheries jurisdiction (ICJ Reports 1974, 3 and 175); the *Nicaragua* case concerning access to ports (ICJ Reports 1986, 14); the *Guinea Bissau/Senegal Arbitral Award* case concerning maritime boundaries (ICJ Reports 1991, 53); and the *Land, Island and Maritime Frontier Dispute* case concerning bays (ICJ Reports 1992, 351). The Court has also given one advisory opinion relating to the Law of the Sea concerning the nationality of ships—*the Constitution of the Maritime Safety Committee of the IMCO* (ICJ Reports 1960, 150). For surveys of the Court's jurisprudence relating to the Law of the Sea, see B. Kwiatkowska, "The International Court of Justice and the Law of the Sea—Some Reflections", 11 *IJMCL* 491 and J.-P. Queneudec, "The Role of the International Court of Justice and Other Tribunals in the Development of the Law of the Sea" in A.H.A. Soons (ed.), *Implementation of the Law of the Sea Convention through International Institutions* (Law of the Sea Institute, Honolulu, 1990).

[42] Case 141/78, *France v. United Kingdom* [1979] ECR 2923.

to the European Court by national courts under Article 177 do have an inter-State dimension, in that there is a difference between two or more Member States in the background of the case. Examples from the marine field are the case brought by the Commission against the United Kingdom over changes made to its baselines in 1987,[43] the case brought by Spain against the Council over EC quotas in Norwegian waters,[44] and some of the quota hopping cases.[45] Most cases in the marine area are concerned with the details of the EC's own legislation, but there are occasions on which the European Court has had to concern itself with general Law of the Sea issues, such as baselines,[46] the nationality of ships[47] and the extent of maritime jurisdiction.[48] It must be said that often the European Court does not distinguish itself in the way that it addresses such issues.[49]

Following the entry into force of UNCLOS in 1994, the question arises how far it is possible for States to continue to utilise these general means of third party dispute settlement and how likely it is that they will do so. When one or more of the parties to a dispute is not a party to UNCLOS (and there are still about 70 States which are not parties to UNCLOS), it will not of course be possible for the UNCLOS machinery to be used. If the dispute is to be settled by third party adjudicative means, recourse will have to be had to arbitration or the International Court of Justice, unless one of the particular Law of the Sea treaties containing dispute-settlement machinery (discussed below) is applicable. Examples of disputes currently being settled in this traditional way are the *Fisheries Jurisdiction* case brought by Spain against Canada before the International Court of Justice in March 1995, at which time neither State was a party to UNCLOS, and the maritime boundary arbitration between Eritrea and Yemen, where Eritrea was not a party to UNCLOS at the time the parties agreed to arbitration.[50] In cases such as these the International Court of Justice or an arbitral tribunal will not of course be able to apply UNCLOS *qua* treaty: nevertheless they may well consider UNCLOS in seeking to establish any relevant customary international law, and indeed in the Eritrea–Yemen Arbitration Agreement the tribunal has been specifically directed to do so.

Even where both or all of the parties to a dispute are parties to UNCLOS, they will not be able to use the UNCLOS machinery for Law of the Sea disputes which do not concern the "interpretation or application" of the Convention or

---

[43] Case C–146/89, *Commission v. United Kingdom* [1991] ECR I–2533.

[44] Case C–71/90, *Spain v. Council* [1992] ECR I–5175.

[45] E.g. Case C–246/89, *Commission v. United Kingdom* [1991] ECR I–4585; Case C–221/89, *R v. Secretary of State for Transport, ex parte Factortame* [1991] ECR I–3905.

[46] *Commission v. United Kingdom*, n. 43 above.

[47] See the cases referred to in n. 45 above.

[48] Case C–286/90, *Anklagemyndigheden v. Poulsen* [1992] ECR I–6019.

[49] For example of criticisms of the Court's judgments, see case note on the *Poulsen* case by P.J. Slot, 31 *CMLRev*. 147 at 150–3 and case note by R.R. Churchill on the cases referred to in n. 45 above, 29 *CMLRev*. 405 at 408.

[50] See Agreement on Principles, 21 May 1996 and Arbitration Agreement, 3 Oct. 1996, 100 *RGDIP* 1119 and 1125. The dispute also involves title to territory as well as a maritime boundary.

a related treaty or do not fall within the wider jurisdiction of ITLOS: in practice such disputes are likely to be few and far between. More significantly, since under section 1 of Part XV of UNCLOS States are free to settle disputes by any means of their choice, it would be open to States parties to UNCLOS to choose to settle a dispute by one of the traditional general adjudicative means for third party settlement rather than by one of the new UNCLOS fora. This might particularly be the case where a dispute involved both Law of the Sea and non-Law of the Sea issues, for example a dispute which involved both a maritime boundary and a land boundary or sovereignty over an island in the maritime boundary area. There may also be occasions where the parties might prefer to use an arbitral tribunal of their own choice rather than one of the UNCLOS fora. The difference between such a tribunal and an Annex VII or VIII tribunal, and the possible advantages of the former, are fairly small. With the former the parties have slightly more flexibility and discretion. Thus, in relation to composition, in traditional arbitration the parties have a completely free choice of arbitrators. This can also be so in relation to Annex VII and VIII arbitration. While arbitrators should "preferably" be chosen from the relevant list, the parties are not actually bound to do so: only where they cannot agree on those arbitrators they choose jointly is the third party that makes the choice bound to select arbitrators from the relevant list.[51] In relation to procedure, in traditional arbitration the parties may select any procedure of their choice. This may also be the case with Annex VII and VIII arbitration: whereas the tribunal is normally to determine its own procedure, it is always open to the parties to the dispute to decide otherwise.[52] There may be more difference in relation to the law to be applied. Whereas in traditional arbitration the parties again have a free choice, under Article 293 an Annex VII or VIII arbitral tribunal must apply UNCLOS and "other rules of international law not incompatible" with the Convention in any case where it has "jurisdiction under this section", i.e. section 2 on compulsory dispute settlement. It is not clear whether the same obligation would apply where such a tribunal was acting under section 1 in relation to consensual dispute settlement. Given the extreme latitude afforded to parties to a dispute when acting under section 1, it may well be that such an obligation may not apply and that therefore the parties could determine the law to be applied by an Annex VII or VIII tribunal when acting under Section 1. One advantage commonly ascribed to traditional arbitration is that the parties may, if they so wish, keep the whole procedure private, including the tribunal's decision. There seems no reason why the same position could not also obtain with Annex VII and VIII arbitration since there is no express requirement in UNCLOS for publicity at any stage. One drawback with arbitration, in comparison with, say, the International Court of Justice, is that with the former the parties must pay for the expenses of the arbitrators, the cost of premises for holding the arbitration and the cost of any officials (such as a registrar) to service the arbitration. There

---

[51] Annex VII, Art. 3; Annex VIII, Art. 3.
[52] Annex VII, Art. 5; Annex VIII, Art. 4.

is no difference here between traditional arbitration and Annex VII and VIII arbitration, as in the latter case the parties must also bear the costs of the arbitration.[53] Thus, overall there is little difference between traditional arbitration and Annex VII and VIII arbitration, and therefore no great advantage to the parties to a dispute who have agreed to settle their dispute under section 1 of Part XV through arbitration in choosing traditional arbitration rather than Annex VII or VIII arbitration. On the other hand, the differences between traditional arbitration and ITLOS are more marked. Thus, with ITLOS the parties have no choice over procedure or publicity (ITLOS must give its judgments in open court[54]) and have only a limited choice over composition (the parties can select the composition of a special chamber to hear their dispute, but their choice (apart from judges *ad hoc*) is obviously limited to ITLOS judges[55]). As far as applicable law is concerned, ITLOS is in the same position as Annex VII and VIII arbitral tribunals. Thus, in some cases traditional arbitration may be perceived by the parties to a dispute as having significant advantages over ITLOS as a means of dispute settlement. On the other hand, ITLOS has the advantage that the parties to a dispute do not have to pay for its running costs (other than, of course, their share of the costs that they pay anyway as parties to UNCLOS), neither do they need to spend time and effort in finding a location and officials for the hearing.

One question which arises as a possible qualification on the foregoing is whether parties to a dispute concerning the International Sea-Bed Area can agree to use traditional arbitration as an alternative to the UNCLOS machinery, that is, does the free choice of settlement procedures under section 1 apply to such disputes. At first sight such disputes between parties to UNCLOS would seem to fall exclusively within the jurisdiction of the Sea-Bed Disputes Chamber of ITLOS since Article 187(a) (in Part XI) states that the Chamber "shall have jurisdiction" in the case of such dispute[56]: this impression is reinforced by the fact that under Article 188(2) where disputes involve a contract and are submitted to commercial arbitration any question of interpretation of the Convention "shall be referred" to the Chamber for a ruling. However, it is also necessary to consider Article 285 which provides that "this section [i.e. Section 1 of Part XV] applies to any dispute which pursuant to Part XI, section 5, is to be settled in accordance with procedures provided for in this Part". This provision does not seem so very clear: it would seem to suggest that section 1 applies to any dispute which according to Part XI is to be settled in accordance with the procedures of Part XV. The only reference to Part XV in Part XI is in Article 186, which simply states that the establishment of the Sea-Bed Disputes Chamber and the

---

[53]   Annex VII, Art. 7; Annex VIII, Art. 4.

[54]   Annex VI, Art. 30(4). The parties may, however, request that the hearings be not in public: see Art. 26(2).

[55]   Annex VI, Arts. 15(2) and 17(4).

[56]   As an exception such a dispute may be referred to a special chamber of ITLOS rather than the Sea-Bed Disputes Chamber: see Art. 188(1)(a).

manner in which it exercises its jurisdiction shall be governed by section 5 of
Part XI, Part XV and Annex VI. The only relevant provision of Part XV is in
Article 288(3) which states that the Chamber has jurisdiction in any matter
which is submitted to it in accordance with Part XI. We thus seem to be enter-
ing a world of circularity. The way out seems to lie in considering the drafting
history of the Convention. As a leading commentary on UNCLOS explains, it
became necessary to clarify the applicability of section 1 once it was decided to
make the Chamber part of ITLOS rather than a separate institution. The
intention behind Article 285 is to make all the provisions of section 1 applicable
to all disputes concerning the International Sea-Bed Area.[57] Thus, parties to
UNCLOS to such a dispute (and indeed other entities) could agree to settle such
a dispute by arbitration (or even through the International Court of Justice, provided both parties were States).

A final question is whether traditional dispute-settlement procedures by adjudicative means could be used for disputes which fall within the exceptions to the
UNCLOS dispute-settlement machinery. Since these exceptions relate only to
the compulsory means of section 2 of Part XV and not the consensual means of
section 1, this question arises only where the parties do not agree on a means of
dispute settlement. In practice the only traditional means of dispute settlement
which could be used in this situation would be where both parties had made a
declaration under Article 36(2) of the Statute of the International Court of
Justice. Thus, the question essentially becomes: can Article 36(2) be used to circumvent the exceptions in Articles 297 and 298 of UNCLOS? The answer to this
question is not straightforward. Two provisions of UNCLOS are potentially
relevant in seeking an answer. First, Article 299(2) provides that nothing in section 3, which deals with exceptions and contains Articles 297 and 298, "impairs
the right of the parties to the dispute to agree to some other procedure for the
settlement of such dispute". The question which arises is whether a situation
where a party to a dispute refers a case unilaterally to the International Court
under Article 36(2) can be described as a procedure to which the parties to a dispute have agreed as a means of settlement of that dispute. It seems doubtful that
this can be the case. It might be argued that the fact that both parties to the dispute are parties to the Court's Statute and have made declarations under Article
36(2) indicates an agreement in a broad sense. The problem with this argument
is that, while it may indicate an agreement to refer disputes in general to the
Court, it can hardly be said to indicate an agreement to refer the specific dispute
to the Court. Thus, it seems doubtful that Article 299(2) is relevant. The second
provision which must be considered is Article 282. This provides that if the parties to a dispute "have agreed, through a general, regional or bilateral agreement
or otherwise, that such dispute shall, at the request of any party to the dispute,
be submitted to a procedure that entails a binding decision, that procedure shall
apply in lieu of the procedures provided for in this Part [i.e Part XV]". It seems

---

[57]   M.H. Nordquist, S. Rosenne and L.B. Sohn (eds.), *United Nations Convention on the Law of
the Sea: A Commentary*, (Nijhoff, Dordrecht, 1989), V, at 35–6.

fairly clear that this provision does cover the reference of disputes to the International Court under Article 36(2): as Nordquist *et al.* explain, the phrase "or otherwise" was added specifically to cover declarations made under Article 36(2).[58] Thus, in principle a State Party to UNCLOS which had made a declaration under Article 36(2) could unilaterally refer a dispute concerning a matter falling within one of the exceptions of Articles 297 and 298 to the International Court where the other party to the dispute had also made a declaration, thus effectively circumventing those exceptions. However, it should be noted that some States, such an Honduras and Malta, have made reservations to their declarations excluding a wide range of Law of the Sea matters including all or most of the exceptions, although without referring to them as such, and Norway has specifically excluded any limitations and exceptions contained in any declaration it has made to the Law of the Sea Convention.[59] In addition, a number of States have excluded from their declarations dispute which the parties have agreed to settle by other procedures. This kind of reservation would seem to encompass the totality of the UNCLOS dispute settlement machinery, including the exceptions in Articles 297 and 298 (although in such cases the question might arise as to which has priority, the reservation to Article 36(2) or Article 282).

To sum up briefly: traditional means of dispute settlement, such as arbitration or the International Court of Justice, will continue to be used, even after entry into force of UNCLOS, for the settlement of Law of the Sea disputes where one or more of the parties to a dispute is not a party to UNCLOS or the dispute falls outside the jurisdiction of the UNCLOS dispute-settlement fora. In addition, there may be some consensual use of arbitration and some use of the International Court of Justice, especially for disputes concerning matters covered by the UNCLOS dispute-settlement exceptions, where both parties to the dispute have made declarations under Article 36(2) of the Court's Statute.

Having looked at third party dispute settlement by means of general application, we must now turn to consider the particular means of third party settlement contained in a number of treaties concerned with the Law of the Sea, and consider how far such means can and may be used after the entry into force of UNCLOS.

Third Party Dispute-Settlement Provisions in Law of the Sea Treaties

Before UNCLOS the basic treaty framework governing the Law of the Sea was, of course, that provided by the four 1958 Geneva Conventions on the Law of the

---

[58] M.H. Nordquist, S. Rosenne and L.B. Sohn (eds.), *United Nations Convention on the Law of the Sea: A Commentary*, (Nijhoff, Dordrecht, 1989), V, at 26–7. Art. 282 would also permit Member States of the EC to continue to refer any inter-State disputes concerning the Law of the Sea to the European Court of Justice. Under Art. 219 of the EC Treaty Member States undertake not to submit any dispute concerning the interpretation or application of the Treaty to any method of settlement other than those provided in the Treaty.

[59] *Multilateral Treaties deposited with the Secretary-General: Status as at 31 Dec. 1995* (UN, New York, 1996), at 13–27, updated from the Internet.

Sea. Attached to the Conventions was an Optional Protocol of Signature concerning the Compulsory Settlement of Disputes arising from the Law of the Sea Conventions.[60] This Protocol provided that any dispute relating to the interpretation or application of the four Conventions could be referred by any party to the dispute to the International Court of Justice, unless the parties agreed to arbitration instead. In addition, the parties could also agree to conciliation, and if one of the parties did not accept the recommendation of the conciliation commission, the other party could refer the matter to the International Court. These provisions are almost identical to those contained in the Optional Protocols attached to the Conventions on Diplomatic Relations and Consular Relations, which, like the Geneva Conventions, were based on draft Articles drawn up by the International Law Commission and adopted fairly soon after those Conventions (in 1961 and 1963, respectively). The Optional Protocol has not been widely accepted: of the 70 or so States which are parties to one or more of the Geneva Conventions only 28 have accepted the Protocol. In addition, a further nine States signed the Protocol but did not ratify any of the Conventions. In practice, no party to a dispute has ever made use of the Protocol's provisions.

In addition to the Optional Protocol, one of the four Geneva Conventions—that on Fishing and Conservation of the Living Resources of the High Seas[61]—contains its own dispute settlement provisions. The Convention provides that certain kinds of disputes arising out of its provisions may be submitted by any party to the dispute to a special commission: decisions of the latter are binding. This means of dispute settlement has never been used, mainly because the Convention was never ratified by the major fishing States and has therefore remained largely a dead letter.

As between States parties to it, UNCLOS prevails over the 1958 Geneva Conventions.[62] Thus, the latter apply only to relations between States parties to them and where one or more such States are not parties to UNCLOS. Disputes arising out of such relations could still be settled in accordance with the Optional Protocol to the 1958 Conventions, although given that the latter has never so far been used, it seems unlikely that this will happen, especially as the number of States parties to the Geneva Conventions not party to UNCLOS is likely to continue to decrease.

In addition to the Geneva Conventions, a large number of more specialised treaties concerned with the Law of the Sea, both multilateral and bilateral, contain provisions involving third party dispute settlement by adjudicative means. Such provisions vary considerably, and include the following in multilateral treaties:

—consensual arbitration (most of the UNEP Regional Seas Pollution Agreements[63]);

---

[60] 450 UNTS 169.

[61] 559 UNTS 285.

[62] UNCLOS, Art. 311(1).

[63] As an example of one of these agreements, see Convention for the Protection of the Mediterranean Sea against Pollution, 1976, Art. 22, 15 ILM 290.

—consensual reference to arbitration or the ICJ (London Dumping Convention,[64] Baltic Pollution Conventions 1974 and 1992,[65] CCAMLR 1980,[66] Southern Bluefin Tuna Agreement 1993[67]);

—consensual reference to arbitration, ICJ or ITLOS (FAO Fisheries Compliance Agreement 1993[68]);

—compulsory conciliation, failing that compulsory arbitration (Oil Pollution Intervention Convention 1969[69]);

—compulsory conciliation, failing that compulsory reference to the ICJ (Indian Ocean Tuna Agreement 1993[70]);

—compulsory arbitration (MARPOL Convention 1973,[71] Paris Marine Pollution Conventions 1974 and 1992,[72] USA-Pacific States Tuna Treaty 1987[73]);

—compulsory arbitration or, failing that, compulsory reference to the ICJ (North Atlantic Fisheries Conduct Convention 1967,[74] Maritime Safety Convention 1988[75]);

—compulsory arbitration, unless parties agree to use UNCLOS tribunals (London Dumping Protocol 1996[76]);

—compulsory reference to the ICJ, unless agreement on arbitration (Oil Pollution Convention 1954[77]);

[64] Convention on the Prevention of Marine Pollution by Dumping of Wastes and Other Matter, 1972, Art. 11 (as amended in 1978), UKTS 1976 No. 43 and 1982 No. 20.

[65] Conventions on the Protection of Marine Environment of the Baltic Sea Area, 1974 (Art. 18) and 1992 (Art. 26), 13 ILM 546 and 8 IJMCL 215.

[66] Convention on the Conservation of Antarctic Marine Living Resources, 1980, Art. XXV, 19 ILM 837.

[67] Convention for the Conservation of Southern Bluefin Tuna, 1993, Art. 16, 26 Law of the Sea Bulletin 57.

[68] Agreement to Promote Compliance with International Conservation and Management Measures by Fishing Vessels on the High Seas, 1993, Art. IX, 33 ILM 968.

[69] International Convention relating to Intervention on the High Seas in Cases of Oil Pollution Casualties, 1969, Art. 8, UKTS 1975 No. 77.

[70] Agreement for the Establishment of the Indian Ocean Tuna Commission, 1993, Art. XXIII, Cm 2695 (1994).

[71] International Convention for the Prevention of Pollution from Ships, 1973, Art. 10, UKTS 1983 No. 27.

[72] Convention for the Prevention of Marine Pollution from Landbased Sources, 1974, Art. 21, UKTS 1978 No. 64; Convention for the Protection of the Marine Environment of the North-East Atlantic, 1992, Art. 32, 8 IJMCL 50.

[73] Treaty on Fisheries, 1987, Art. 6, 26 ILM 1048.

[74] Convention on Conduct of Fishing Operations in the North Atlantic, 1967, Art. 13, UKTS 1977 No. 40.

[75] Convention for the Suppression of Unlawful Acts against the Safety of Maritime Navigation, 1988, Art. 16, UKTS 1995 No. 64.

[76] 1996 Protocol to the Convention on the Prevention of Marine Pollution by Dumping of Wastes and Other Matter, 1972, Art. 16, 26 ILM 7.

[77] International Convention for the Prevention of Pollution of the Sea by Oil, 1954, Art. 13, 327 UNTS 3.

—reference to a special committee and, failing resolution there, compulsory reference to the ICJ unless the parties agree otherwise (Indo-Pacific Fisheries Agreement,[78] Mediterranean Fisheries Agreement[79]).

As can be seen, there is considerable variety, both in the procedures themselves and in whether they are consensual or compulsory. It will also be noted that two of the most recent agreements—the 1993 FAO Compliance Agreement and the 1996 London Dumping Protocol—provide for reference to one or more of the UNCLOS dispute-settlement fora. In spite of their richness and diversity, none of these dispute settlement procedures, to the best of the writer's knowledge, has so far ever been utilised in practice.

As to the possible and permissible use of these procedures in future, where a dispute arises in which one or more of the parties is not a party to UNCLOS, the procedures are of course unaffected by UNCLOS. Where, however, both or all of the parties to a dispute are parties to UNCLOS, the position may be different. In the case of the consensual procedures, these may be utilised during the first, consensual stage of dispute settlement under UNCLOS. Where they, or any other agreed procedures, do not lead to a resolution of the dispute, then, to the extent that a dispute arising under one of the treaties concerned involves a question of interpretation or application of UNCLOS,[80] the dispute may be referred by any party to it to the appropriate compulsory dispute-settlement forum of UNCLOS, provided that, as is possible under Article 281(1), the parties have not agreed to exclude the use of the UNCLOS compulsory dispute-settlement procedures. In the case of those treaties referred to above which contain compulsory dispute-settlement procedures, the effect of Article 282 of UNCLOS, quoted earlier, is that such procedures will apply instead of the UNCLOS machinery, unless the parties to the dispute agree otherwise. In some situations this could have the effect of circumventing the exceptions to compulsory dispute settlement in UNCLOS.

4. PROSPECTS FOR THE UNCLOS DISPUTE SETTLEMENT MACHINERY

The final principal section of this chapter speculates on the prospects for the dispute-settlement machinery established by UNCLOS. In doing so it is hoped that this will also help to place this machinery in a broader politico-legal context than the discussion so far.

---

[78] Agreement for the Establishment of the Indo-Pacific Fisheries Council, 1948 (as amended in 1961), Art. III, 418 UNTS 348.

[79] Agreement for the Establishment of the General Fisheries Council for the Mediterranean, 1949 (as amended in 1962), Art. XIII, 490 UNTS 444.

[80] This is quite possible, both because UNCLOS itself is largely of a framework nature and because some of the treaties refer to the Law of the Sea in general (see, e.g., the London Dumping Convention, Art. 13). In addition, application of some of these treaties could also involve questions concerning UNCLOS, e.g. the extent of coastal State jurisdiction.

A first question that may be asked about the prospects for the UNCLOS dispute-settlement machinery is how far it will be used, particularly its compulsory, second phase, procedures. As a treaty text, UNCLOS contains its fair share of ambiguities and imprecision. This is scarcely surprising, since the Convention is to a considerable extent a series of compromises, especially between the interests of coastal States and maritime States. The nature of the Convention text, together with the large number of parties to UNCLOS (now nearly 120) and its scope (the Convention governs, to a greater or lesser extent, virtually all activities at sea) means that there is considerable potential for disputes, especially as differences between States are likely to sharpen with increasing competition for dwindling fish resources and with the marine environment becoming increasingly polluted. Issues which immediately spring to mind as potentially giving rise to disputes include the drawing of baselines (especially straight baselines), the passage of warships through the territorial sea, the extent of coastal State enforcement jurisdiction in straits and archipelagic waters, military activities in the EEZ, research activities in the EEZ, unattributed uses of the EEZ and maritime boundaries: several of these matters, it will be noted, fall within the general or optional exceptions of Articles 297 and 298.

The fact that there is considerable potential for disputes does not mean, of course, that States will necessarily have recourse to the third party dispute-settlement machinery of UNCLOS, especially its compulsory elements. It is, in fact, very difficult to predict what will happen. Traditionally States have generally been reluctant to use third party means for the settlement of disputes. This is borne out by the experience of the Optional Protocol to the 1958 Geneva Conventions and the dispute-settlement provisions of the more specialised Law of the Sea treaties, none of which has ever yet been utilised. On the other hand, some recent trends suggest that States may be more willing to use third party settlement, especially by adjudicative means. Thus, the number of cases referred to the International Court of Justice has increased significantly over the past few years, and the number of declarations made under Article 36(2) of the Court's Statute (the optional clause) now stands at its highest total ever in absolute terms (although not in relative terms as a proportion of the total number of parties to the Statute).

Whatever use is made of the UNCLOS machinery, it is likely that the vast majority of disputes will be settled by direct negotiation between the parties, as they have always been.[81] Indeed, some disputes relating to UNCLOS have already been settled by negotiation, e.g. that between the USA and a variety of Pacific States concerning the extent of coastal State jurisdiction over tuna.[82] In any case the degree of use made of the UNCLOS machinery is a matter of inter-

[81] *Cf.* Boyle, n. 7 above, at 54, who argues that the wide-ranging exceptions to compulsory dispute settlement are such that "procedural fragmentation is inevitable and will lead in practice to greater emphasis on consensual rather than compulsory settlement".

[82] Discussed in W.T. Burke, *The New International Law of Fisheries* (Clarendon Press, Oxford, 1994), at 204–5.

est only and not the test of the system. The most important thing is that States should settle their disputes peacefully: the means by which they do so are of secondary importance. Nevertheless, the existence of the possibility of compulsory third party settlement under UNCLOS will deter some States from breaching the Convention and will induce other States to settle disputes by negotiation.[83]

To the extent that use is made of the compulsory dispute-settlement machinery of UNCLOS, one may ask how likely it is that all the various fora for dispute settlement will be used. As things stand at the moment (*cf.* Table 1A, at the end of this chapter), with only 11 States having selected ITLOS as a possible forum, ten the International Court and five Annex VIII arbitration, by far and away the most likely forum to be used is Annex VII arbitration. The likelihood of ITLOS being used is lessened not only by the small number of States which have selected it as a forum, but also by their diversity: it is difficult to imagine the circumstances in which a dispute might arise between, say, Austria and Cape Verde or between Oman and Uruguay. Furthermore, because mining of the International Sea-Bed Area is not expected to begin until well into the next century, it is likely to be many years before the Sea-Bed Disputes Chamber of ITLOS is used to any degree. In the case of the International Court of Justice and Annex VIII arbitration, their lack of use would not of itself matter very much, since the former has at present plenty of work and the latter are constituted *ad hoc*. The situation of ITLOS, with its 21 semi-permanent judges, is, however, rather different. If it is not used much or at all, the parties to the Convention may begin to query its cost, which is currently about US$ six million a year, and thus its continued existence in its present form. Of course, the situation could easily change if large numbers of parties to UNCLOS were to select ITLOS as their preferred forum.

Assuming, however, that ITLOS and the other UNCLOS fora are used to some degree for compulsory dispute settlement, how likely is it that a possibly unwilling defendant State will contest the jurisdiction of the forum concerned to hear the case? This has frequently been the situation in "compulsory cases" before the International Court of Justice, that is, cases referred to the Court by unilateral application on the basis either of declarations under Article 36(2) or of a compromisory clause in an existing treaty. In the vast majority of such cases the defendant State has contested the jurisdiction of the Court. There is no reason to suppose that the same will not happen, at least to some degree, before the UNCLOS fora. There are several ways in which a forum's jurisdiction could be contested. First, it might be argued that the dispute did not involve the interpretation or application of the Convention. Secondly, it might be argued that the necessary first-stage consensual procedures had not been exhausted. In this respect the Convention is not perhaps particularly helpful in indicating when such procedures have been exhausted. Article 286 provides that a dispute may be referred for compulsory settlement "where no settlement has been reached by

---

[83] *Cf.* Chinkin, n. 27 above, at 248.

recourse to section 1". The defendant State might argue that there was still a chance of settlement being reached by means of section 1 procedures. The forum concerned would then have to decide if this was so. Also relevant is Article 283, which provides that when a dispute arises "the parties shall proceed expeditiously to an exchange of views regarding its settlement by negotiation or other peaceful means": it then goes on to add that "where a procedure for the settlement of such a dispute has been terminated without a settlement" the parties shall again "proceed expeditiously to an exchange of views". Thus, it would seem that no dispute can be referred to an UNCLOS compulsory forum until there has been the double exchange of views referred to in Article 283.[84] Of course there may still be scope for differences between the parties on whether an exchange of views within the meaning of Article 283 has in fact taken place. A third way in which the jurisdiction of an UNCLOS forum could be contested would be to argue that the dispute fell within one of the exceptions of Article 297 and 298 or, more problematically, fell partly within an exception and in so doing could not be properly dealt with by the forum.[85]

The problem raised by defendant States contesting the jurisdiction of an UNCLOS forum is, of course, that it increases the length of time taken to deal with the case. This could be significant in two respects. First, ITLOS is apparently hoping to offer a speedy service, one considerably quicker than that of the International Court of Justice.[86] This may not be possible if defendant States make a habit of contesting its jurisdiction. Secondly, in the case of compulsory conciliation, the conciliation commission is to report within 12 months of the case being brought.[87] Again it may be difficult to meet this timetable if there are challenges to its jurisdiction.

It may also happen that rather than, or as well as, challenging the jurisdiction of the forum concerned, the defendant State absents itself from all or part of the proceedings before the forum, as has happened from time to time with the International Court of Justice. As with the Court, absence of a party or failure of a party to defend its case is not a bar to proceedings before ITLOS or an Annex VII or VIII arbitral tribunal.[88]

---

[84] Note that Nordquist *et al.*, n. 57 above, at 29, appear to suggest that where it becomes clear in the second exchange of views that no settlement has been reached using one kind of section 1 consensual procedure, the parties are under an obligation to utilise further kinds of such procedures before resorting to the compulsory procedures of section 2. It seems difficult to find support for such a view in the text, and this view is not supported by any explicit reference to the *travaux préparatoires*.

[85] The problem of disputes falling partly within and partly outside one or more of the exceptions, what he calls the "salami-slicing" of disputes, and the problem generally of categorising disputes for the purposes of the exceptions have been very well explored by Boyle, n. 7 above, at 41–6.

[86] One ITLOS judge has suggested that the Tribunal should normally be able to decide a case within 12 months, compared with the average five years a case takes before the International Court: see G. Eiriksson, "The Challenges in Fisheries Management", paper given at a symposium on Fisheries Management under Uncertainty, Bergen, Norway, June 1997.

[87] Annex V, Art. 7.

[88] Annex VI, Art. 28; Annex VII, Art. 9; Annex VIII, Art. 4.

A final question which may be asked in assessing the prospects of the UNCLOS dispute-settlement machinery is whether, given the number of different tribunals which may deal with disputes, there is not a risk of a fragmented and diverging jurisprudence developing in the Law of the Sea in general and in interpretation of UNCLOS in particular. This risk has been emphasised especially by two members of the International Court of Justice, Judge Guillaume[89] and Judge Oda,[90] as part of a strongly expressed criticism of the UNCLOS machinery in general and of ITLOS in particular. It must be admitted that a risk of diverging jurisprudence does exist. However, such a risk is not new, nor is it unique to the Law of the Sea. It is not new because for decades Law of the Sea issues have been determined by a variety of arbitral tribunals, regional courts and the World Court. It is not unique because as long as there is a system of decentralised, non-hierarchical courts and tribunals there is a risk of diverging jurisprudence in any field of international law. Indeed, instances of divergence can already be found in areas outside the Law of the Sea, for example the question of the level of compensation to be paid when property belonging to foreigners is expropriated[91] and the effect of reservations to multilateral treaties.[92] As far as the Law of the Sea is concerned, the issue where one might most have expected to find divergence is maritime boundary delimitation because far more cases have been heard by arbitral tribunals and the International Court of Justice on this topic than any other in the Law of the Sea. Yet on the whole there has been relatively little divergence, something which has been helped perhaps by the generality and flexibility of the applicable law. The International Court and arbitral tribunals have each been at pains to take into account the jurisprudence of the other. Thus in the *Guinea/Guinea Bissau* arbitration[93] the tribunal made extensive reference to and followed the approach of the International Court of Justice in the *Gulf of Maine* case,[94] while in the *Greenland/Jan Mayen*

[89] G. Guillaume, "The Future of International Judicial Institutions", 44 *ICLQ* 848 at 854–5.

[90] S. Oda, "The ICJ viewed from the Bench", 244 *Hague Recueil* 9 at 139–55; Oda, n. 11 above. For a spirited rebuttal of Oda's views, see J.I. Charney, "The Implications of Extending International Dispute Settlement Systems: The 1982 Convention on the Law of the Sea", 90 *AJIL* 69. See also Anderson, Ch. 4 above.

[91] Compare the decisions of the arbitral tribunals in *Texaco* v. *Libya* (1977), 53 ILR 389, the *Liamco* case (1981), 20 ILM 1, and the *Amoco International Finance* case (1987), 15 Iran–US CTR 189. See also D.J. Harris, *Cases and Materials on International Law* (4th edn., Sweet and Maxwell, London, 1991), at 543–7.

[92] Compare the approach of the International Court of Justice in *Reservations to the Convention on the Prevention and Punishment of the Crime of Genocide*, Advisory Opinion, ICJ Reports 1951, 15 with the judgment of the European Court of Human Rights in *Belilos* v. *Switzerland*, Judgment of 29 Apr. 1988, Series A, No. 132. *Cf.* also the latter court's judgment in *Loizidou* v. *Turkey*, Judgment of 23 Mar. 1995, Series A, No. 310, where it held that although Art. 46 of the European Convention on Human Rights was modelled on Art. 36 of the International Court's Statute, the International Court's case law on the permissible scope of reservations to Art. 36 was not relevant to the European Court's interpretation of Art. 46. See also R.Y. Jennings, "The Judiciary, International and National, and the Development of International Law", 45 *ICLQ* 1.

[93] See n. 33 above.

[94] See n. 38 above.

case[95] the Court did the same thing in respect of the *Anglo-French Continental Shelf* arbitration.[96] Arguably the most notable inconsistency has come in the jurisprudence of the International Court itself, where the great emphasis laid by the Court on natural prolongation as a relevant factor in lateral continental shelf delimitation in the *North Sea Continental Shelf* cases[97] was completely downplayed in the *Tunisia/Libya* case.[98]

However, in the case of the UNCLOS machinery, the risk of a diverging jurisprudence is greater than it has been in the past. This is so for two reasons. The first is the number of tribunals which will hear cases. These include not only ITLOS itself but also a variety of actual and potential chambers; arbitral tribunals established under Annexes VII and VIII, each of which is likely to be differently constituted on each occasion a case comes before them; the International Court of Justice and possible chambers; and all the possible dispute-settlement fora outside UNCLOS discussed in the previous section which could be faced with having to interpret the Convention. A second, if perhaps less important, reason for an increased risk of diverging jurisprudence is the fact that members of Annex VII and VIII arbitral tribunals (and members of conciliation commissions) do not have to be legally qualified.[99]

In order to counter the risk of diverging jurisprudence one commentator has suggested that ITLOS should establish itself as the central tribunal to which Law of the Sea disputes are referred.[100] However, it is difficult to see how ITLOS could do this itself. The extent to which it hears disputes in preference to other fora is entirely dependent on the actions of the parties to UNCLOS.

5. CONCLUSIONS

As has been seen, UNCLOS establishes an extensive and complex system for settling disputes relating to its interpretation and application. At the same time the system, as far as its compulsory element is concerned, is not comprehensive, as a number of areas where disputes in practice are likely to arise are excluded from its application. Nor is the UNCLOS system wholly exclusive. Its parties could agree to settle a dispute relating to its interpretation or application through traditional arbitration or through one of the means provided by a specialised Law of the Sea treaty to which they were parties. In addition, some of the latter treaties contain provisions for compulsory dispute settlement which take priority over the UNCLOS system, and a State could also use Article 36(2) of the Statute of the International Court of Justice to get round the exceptions of the UNCLOS system.

[95] See n. 40 above.
[96] See n. 33 above.
[97] See n. 36 above.
[98] See n. 37 above.
[99] For their qualifications, see text at nn. 8, 9 and 19 above.
[100] Brown, n. 1 above, at 43.

One of the major themes of this book is the "institutional dilemma" in dispute settlement. As far as the Law of the Sea is concerned, there are perhaps two principal institutional dilemmas, both of which are potential rather than actual. The first is whether, with the parties to UNCLOS having expended considerable effort in conceiving and setting up, and incurring some on-going expense in maintaining, an elaborate institutional structure for dispute settlement, this structure and its institutions will actually be used to any great degree. A particular air of uncertainty hangs over ITLOS because of the few States which have so far accepted it as a possible forum for compulsory dispute settlement. The second potential dilemma is of a rather different kind. If the UNCLOS fora (and fora outside UNCLOS) turn out in fact to be widely used, the question then is whether a diverging jurisprudence will begin to emerge, with different and potentially conflicting interpretations of UNCLOS, when the main reason for establishing an extensive dispute settlement system for UNCLOS was to ensure uniform interpretation of the Convention. At the present time it is impossible to predict whether one or other of these potential institutional dilemmas will materialise (obviously they cannot both do so), we must simply wait and see. Thus, the Law of the Sea will continue to be an area of major interest to students of dispute settlement in international law.

Table 1A—*Choice of Fora under UNCLOS*

ICJ only	Netherlands, Norway, Spain, Sweden
ITLOS only	Greece, Tanzania, Uruguay
ICJ and ITLOS	Cape Verde, Finland, Italy, Oman
ICJ, ITLOS and Annex VIII	Austria, [Belgium], Germany
ITLOS and Annex VIII	Argentina, Chile
Annex VII only	Egypt
Annex VII and Annex VIII	[Belarus], Russia, [Ukraine]

Some of those States choosing more than one forum have stated an order of preference. This is not shown here.

Table 1B—*States availing themselves of Optional Exceptions*

All three	Argentina, [Belarus], Chile, France, Norway (as regards Annex VII arbitration), Russia, Tunisia, [Ukraine]
Maritime boundaries only	Iceland (as regards continental shelf boundaries), Italy
Military activities/law enforcement only	Cape Verde, Uruguay (as regards law enforcement)

The above shows choices made as at 25 September 1997 when there were 120 parties to the Convention. States in square brackets are those which had not ratified the Convention at that date: the choices of these States were made on signature of the Convention.

6

Negotiation and Dispute Settlement

DAVID ANDERSON

1. INTRODUCTION

Article 33 of the Charter of the United Nations lays down a fundamental rule of international law to the effect that States which become parties to disputes, the continuation of which is likely to endanger the maintenance of international peace and security, must first seek a solution by negotiation, by resort to the UN or regional bodies, by arbitration or judicial settlement, or by several other means of their own choice. The Declaration on Principles of International Law concerning Friendly Relations and Co-operation among States in accordance with the Charter[1] repeats the list with the additional glosses that States should seek "early and just settlement" and should agree upon appropriate means of settlement. These two standard listings of the different means of settling disputes include, notably, the possibility of having recourse to a variety of international institutions, both political and legal in character. This possibility raises immediately the "institutional dilemma" which forms a theme of these essays. However, it is a dilemma which presents itself only after some prior attempt has been made to exchange views and to negotiate. Negotiation is perhaps the most effective way of avoiding the dilemma.

Negotiation is established in Article 33 as the first means of settling disputes, but without going so far as to create a general duty to negotiate in order to seek a settlement. Negotiation is also a means which in practice is used to some extent whenever there are efforts to resolve a dispute in some way other than negotiations, e.g. the negotiation of a Compromise. In practice, negotiation may be a means of settlement in itself or it may be simply a prelude to resort to some other means. In other words, negotiation can be resorted to either alone or in combination with one or other of the alternative means of peaceful settlement.[2] It is also the most flexible of all the possible means.

---

[1] General Assembly Resolution 2625(XXV) of 24 Oct. 1970.

[2] A point made by H.G. Darwin in *International Disputes: The Legal Aspects* (published for the David Davies Memorial Institute of International Studies, Europa Publications, London, 1972). See also *Satow's Guide to Diplomatic Practice* (5th edn., by Lord Gore Booth, Longmans, London, 1979), at 349; and J.G. Merrills, "The Principle of Peaceful Settlement of Disputes" in V. Lowe and C. Warbrick (eds.), *The United Nations and the Principles of International Law* (Routledge, London, 1994), ch. 3.

2. SOME ADVANTAGES OF NEGOTIATIONS OVER OTHER MEANS OF SETTLING DISPUTES

Governments normally prefer to seek a negotiated settlement of their differences, rather than have recourse to some third party. The reasons are simple: the parties to a negotiation retain control over the outcome without running the risks inherent in involving an outside body of whatever kind, however wise, just or disinterested it may be. The parties have available to them a full range of possible solutions, both substantive and procedural, subject only to their other international obligations. They can also retain control over the form, content, wording, timing and presentation of a settlement, factors which are ever important in political circles.

Often, it is only when one government adopts an uncompromising position *vis-à-vis* another in their initial contacts that the latter may consider it has little alternative in the circumstances but to move quickly to protect its interests and to seek a judicial remedy or the involvement of some other outside body. Uncompromising positions are sometimes adopted because relations between the two governments are already strained, or because the first government has deliberately set out to change the *status quo,* or to make a point regardless of the consequences. Such instances in international life are comparatively rare. In normal circumstances, governments seek to avoid confrontation and to reach reasonable accommodations of conflicting interests. With the growth of international co-operation and commerce since 1945, a government these days has to balance many different interests *vis-à-vis* another government. A government will usually calculate that creating a sharp dispute may impact negatively upon other national interests: in other words, pursuing a "single issue" foreign policy is rarely a practical option. Interests have to be balanced out.

In some negotiations, political courage is required both to make the concessions needed to resolve the outstanding differences between the parties at the negotiating table and then to secure consent to the settlement as a whole from public opinion or the legislature at home. Politically, it may even be easier in some instances to agree to refer a dispute to arbitration and lose than to make the same concessions across the negotiating table. An arbitral decision is normally accepted by public opinion: the decision may not be liked, but it represents the operation of the rule of law at the international level.

In other cases, there may arise the prior question whether or not to enter into negotiations at all with another government on a particular issue in the circumstances then existing. For example, the Agreement with the Soviet Government about Baltic claims in 1967 was criticised by the Opposition in Parliament during debates in 1968 on the Foreign Compensation Bill on the ground (among others) that the British Government should not have negotiated with Moscow about matters affecting Estonia, Latvia and Lithuania. In other cases, it may be appropriate to decide which aspects of a certain matter are for negotiation with the other government concerned and which others are for purely national action, perhaps coupled with prior notification if only as a matter of courtesy.

Where circumstances are not ripe for negotiations aimed at finding a full settlement of a particular dispute, limited talks may in some instances still be held in order to achieve a *modus vivendi,* or to "manage" the dispute (e.g. to prevent it becoming more serious), or to single out one aspect which can be dealt with in isolation, leaving the rest of the dispute unresolved and for a different time.

Although statistics are hard to find, it seems safe to assert that more disputes are settled by direct negotiation than by any other means of settlement. Moreover, some settlements have involved several hundred individual disputes, for example in the case of the global settlements of property and financial claims following conflicts, or nationalisations or agrarian reforms, as seen in the 1940s or 1950s.

3. NEGOTIATORS

Given the positive qualities of negotiation as a means of seeking to settle disputes, it is perhaps only natural that Article 3(c) of the Convention on Diplomatic Relations lists as a function of a diplomatic mission "negotiating with the government of the receiving state". Bilateral negotiation is a core function of every Embassy and, more generally, a central feature of modem diplomacy.[3] Disputes vary considerably in nature and scope, ranging from minor issues which are readily adjusted and with mutual satisfaction, at one extreme, to serious disputes which attract the attention of the public media because they cause tension or even threats to the peace, at the other extreme. The more straightforward differences are usually resolved by means of talks between an Embassy and the Foreign Ministry. Particularly in the cases of serious disputes or differences over technical issues, however, negotiations are often carried on by means of direct contacts between Ministers or those concerned with the question in the two capitals, including technical experts. In other words, delegations representing the two governments conduct the negotiations, usually with no more than support from the Embassies.

4. DISPUTES

In historical terms and in the wording of Article 33 of the UN Charter, there is a link between the peaceful settlement of disputes and the maintenance of international peace and security. The paragraph about the principle of the non-use of force in the Friendly Relations Declaration to the effect that "every State has the duty to refrain from the threat or use of force . . . as a means of solving

[3] For the history and content of diplomacy, see H. Nicholson, *Diplomacy* (3rd edn., Oxford University Press, London, 1969).

international disputes . . ." is echoed in the articulation of the principle of peaceful settlement of disputes, where it is stated that:

> "Every State shall settle its international disputes . . . by peaceful means, in such a manner that international peace and security, and justice, are not endangered."

Today, there is still such a link in many instances, such as boundary disputes or cases of disputed sovereignty, including disputes over small islands. However, with the growth of arrangements for international co-operation over a wide range of matters, there can now arise disputes of a rather technical nature which, although serious economically or politically, have little or nothing to do with peace or security. Trade disputes, air services disputes and "fish wars" are the best examples of this phenomenon of the modern technical dispute. Disputes of this nature may arise between close allies, neighbours or partners normally enjoying close relations. In such a situation, the question of settling the intrusive dispute has to be approached in terms not so much of maintaining the peace but rather of preventing irritants from arising in otherwise excellent relations.

5. NEGOTIATING PROCEDURES: DIRECT AND INDIRECT CONTACTS

The handling of negotiations over disputes varies greatly from case to case and there is no single pattern or procedure. The most straightforward example is a negotiation between two States which have full diplomatic relations. These days, negotiations to resolve outstanding issues such as boundaries can be conducted, in exceptional circumstances, by telecommunications between Foreign Offices. There is at least one exceptional example of such a boundary which was agreed without a face-to-face meeting.[4] The boundary in the central Pacific between the Pitcairn Islands and French Polynesia was agreed without difficulty through exchanges of fax messages between the two Foreign Ministries in Paris and London. The usual procedures, employed in practically all cases, are negotiations across a table, often extending over several rounds and many months or years. The normal pattern is the holding of a direct, face-to-face meeting (or series of meetings, often in alternating capitals) between two negotiators or delegations, with representatives from one or both Embassies, in which the respective positions are explained and proposals presented.

Slightly more complex than direct talks is the case of a negotiation between two States which have serious disputes or differences but no direct diplomatic relations. Very often, it is precisely the dispute which has prevented the maintenance of formal relations. Here, the two sides may still exchange views or negotiate over the dispute or other items of current business through the medium of their respective protecting powers (which almost invariably have been

---

[4] See Report No. 5–7 by the present writer in J.I. Charney and L.M. Alexander (eds.), *International Maritime Boundaries* (The American Society of International Law/Nijhoff, Dordrecht, 1993), i, at 1003.

appointed) or through a third party (even to the exclusion of the protecting powers). In some instances, agreements have been concluded between two governments represented by their respective protecting powers. In other words, State A, acting as the protecting power for State X, concludes an agreement with State B. acting as the protecting power of State Y: the resulting treaty is between X and Y, even though they do not speak and have not spoken directly to one another. An example is afforded by the Exchange of Notes between Brazil, acting as the protecting power of Argentina, and Switzerland, acting for the United Kingdom, concerning the consolidation of certain Argentine Commercial Debts, concluded at a time when relations had been broken off in 1982. The Notes were exchanged between the Swiss Embassy in Paris, where the so-called "Paris Club" of creditors meets, and the Brazilian Ambassador there.[5] There are also examples of contacts being established through the good offices of a third government, not a protecting power, or through the UN Secretary-General, with a view to the settlement or amelioration of a dispute. To take a similar example again, the resumption of relations between Argentina and the UK in the late 1980s grew from separate contacts between each side and the US Government, followed by the meetings of the two sides in Madrid.[6] And at an even earlier stage, shortly after the severance of diplomatic relations in April 1982, the representatives of the two sides had exchanged views and proposals, in separate meetings with the UN Secretary-General, Señor Perez de Cuellar, in an effort through his good offices to bring an end to the conflict in the Falkland Islands. Clearly, the absence of relations and even the outbreak of a conflict need not, and on occasion should not, represent an obstacle to the discussion of differences with a view to maintaining or restoring international peace and security.

6. TWIN-TRACK NEGOTIATIONS

Negotiation is a means of settlement which is available at all stages of the existence of a dispute or difference. Talks cannot be prevented or excluded by recourse to other means of settlement, including recourse to the United Nations or judicial proceedings, There are many examples now of issues which have been addressed simultaneously in bilateral negotiations and the Security Council or General Assembly. In such a situation, the bilateral talks in private may be more detailed and productive than what amounts to a public debate in the United Nations, where the two sides try to muster support from as many other delegations as possible. Against that, resort to a body such as the Security

---

[5] For the text of this example, see G. Marston (ed.), *United Kingdom Materials in International Law*, 61 *BYBIL* 543.

[6] Joint Statement by the Argentine and British Delegations, dated 19 Oct. 1989, *UKMIL* 60 *BYBIL* 583.

Council may focus international pressure for a peaceful solution or subject a weak case to widespread international criticism leading to a reappraisal.

Different parties may prefer different means of settlement. The "institutional dilemma" may face both sides equally, but its existence does not mean only one means can be used at any one time. Two separate means can be followed: for example, one legal and the other political; or one private and the other public. There are even examples of disputes which have been the subject at the same time of bilateral negotiation, debates in the Security Council and litigation. It is fully permissible to litigate and negotiate over the settlement of a dispute at the same time.[7] Recourse to litigation normally follows talks which have failed to produce a settlement, but talks may also be held after agreement has been reached to litigate the issues or after proceedings have begun. In such circumstances, the negotiations would, in the nature of things, be without prejudice to the positions taken in the proceedings. This would normally be made clear, for the avoidance of doubt or in order to build confidence, in the contacts leading up to the talks, as well as at their outset. Sometimes, negotiators agree and initial some written guidelines or ground rules for the exchanges before substantive talks begin, and especially before any offers of settlement involving the compromise of a position are made. Once made, it may be agreed that such offers of compromise may not be referred to by the other side in any later proceedings which may still ensue. Negotiations both prior to and during legal proceedings are a normal part of international relations. Indeed, it is perhaps a sign of a maturing legal system when a case such as that concerning the proposed bridge over the Danish Straits was completely settled by an agreement reached just before the date fixed for a hearing.[8] Urgency was no doubt given to the contacts by the approach of the due date.

The wish to avoid the delays, uncertainty and expense of litigation has often spurred negotiators to find solutions to previously intractable disputes. Such factors played a role in the conclusion in 1988 of the Agreement between Ireland and the UK concerning the boundary of the continental shelf between the two countries.[9] At one stage, after agreement on the substance had proved elusive during the late 1970s, the talks turned to the terms of reference for arbitration. In the mid-1980s, when these talks had resolved most but not quite all of those issues, a further attempt was made to resolve the substantive differences by resumed negotiations, taking account of the new situation existing following the conclusion of the Third United Nations Conference on the Law of the Sea in 1982. After 23 years of talks between delegations of officials, a mutually satisfactory Agreement was finally signed by the two Foreign Ministers and quickly approved by the two legislatures.

---

[7] Per ICJ in *Aegean Sea Continental Shelf*, Judgment, ICJ Reports 1978, 3, para. 29.

[8] *Passage through the Great Belt (Finland v. Denmark)*, Order of 10 Sept. 1992, ICJ Reports 1992, 348.

[9] Report No. 9–5 by the present writer, in Charney and Alexander (eds.), n. 4 above, ii, at 1767.

7. NEGOTIATION OF A *MODUS VIVENDI*

Short of the complete resolution of a dispute, there have been cases where the successful negotiation of a temporary *modus vivendi* has supervened during the course of proceedings before a court about the underlying issues and before any decisions on the merits. An example was the negotiation of the Interim Agreement between Iceland and the UK in 1973,[10] while the *Fisheries Jurisdiction* Case was pending. The existence of this agreement, which was expressed to be without prejudice to legal positions, was naturally considered by the Court a few months after its conclusion during the hearing on the merits. Questions about it were posed to the UK by several judges. Did not the Agreement place the dispute into suspense? Should not the issues be considered as moot at the time of the hearing? The United Kingdom replied that the judgment could provide a basis for the negotiation of arrangements to follow those in the Interim Agreement. The Court found that the Agreement did not remove the object from the issues dividing the parties. Although on the date of the decision the Interim Agreement had several months still to run, the judgment constituted an authoritative statement of the rights and obligations of the parties under the then existing law. In a valuable passage, the Court indicated that the such agreements were not to be discouraged, being consistent with the terms of the UN Charter concerning the pacific settlement of disputes.[11]

For the past 40 years many States have been trying to negotiate new types of extended maritime boundaries. It is a major task, given the complexity and the sheer overall length of the lines to be drawn. With these considerations in mind, the negotiators at the Third Conference on the Law of the Sea adopted paragraph 3 of Articles 74 and 83 according to which, pending the settlement of maritime boundaries, the States concerned are to make efforts to reach practical, provisional arrangements and to refrain from acting in a manner which would hamper final agreement, all on a "without prejudice" basis.

8. THE SCOPE AND CONTENT OF DUTIES TO NEGOTIATE

The principles in the Charter of the United Nations do not go so far as to lay down a general duty to negotiate at all times and to resolve all outstanding disputes. In its terms, Article 33 is limited in its scope, first, to disputes which are likely to endanger the peace and, secondly, to an obligation to seek a solution by peaceful means, rather than by resort to force. In the words of the Friendly Relations Declaration, "in the event of a failure to reach a solution" by negotiation, "the parties have the duty . . . to continue to seek a settlement of the

---

[10] Exchange of Notes of 13 Nov. 1973.
[11] *Fisheries Jurisdiction (United Kingdom v. Iceland)*, Merits, Judgment, ICJ Reports 1974, 3, para. 41.

dispute by other peaceful means agreed upon by them". In other words, the parties should keep trying, showing patience: in accordance with the law of the UN Charter, they should not resort to forcible means of resolving the problem.[12]

Turning from the general situation to the particular, States may enter into specific treaty obligations with other states which require either an exchange of views, possibly as a first step, or a negotiation between the parties concerned should a dispute arise between them as to the correct interpretation or application of the provisions of the treaty. Such treaties may be bilateral, regional or general multilateral. A leading example of a major multilateral treaty contains somewhat similar terms to those just described is the UN Convention on the Law of the Sea. Article 283 calls upon parties to a dispute to "proceed expeditiously to an exchange of views regarding its settlement by negotiation or other peaceful means". Article 286 provides that where no solution has been reached by negotiation or conciliation, etc., a dispute shall be submitted at the request of any party to the dispute to a court or tribunal.

Other Articles in that Convention also provide, in line with customary law, that boundaries are to be established "by agreement", which presupposes some process of prior negotiation. While there is a specific obligation in this context to negotiate and to seek agreement, the fact remains that the two sides are not obliged to negotiate at any particular time or on any particular terms. Nor are they, as it were, "condemned to agree" at any stage or on a particular basis, although they should seek an equitable solution on the basis of international law.[13] The timing of the start of negotiations can be important for their outcome, as well as for the interests of one or other of the governments concerned (e.g. if one has established a 12-mile territorial sea before the start of talks and the other has not); but the duty to negotiate over maritime boundaries still leaves decisions about timing in the hands of the two sides. The rule of international law that boundaries are to be established by agreement means, primarily, that they cannot be laid down unilaterally by one side, whether in its national law or in its administrative practice, for example by the award of licences. This rule of agreement coupled with an implicit prohibition of unilateral action purporting to lay down a boundary is analogous to the rule of peaceful settlement coupled with the explicit prohibition of the use or threat of force purporting to settle a dispute.

The content of the duty to negotiate can be explained from the dictionary definition: to confer with another so as to reach a compromise or agreement.[14] In some talks, one side may persuade the other of the total correctness of its position in law and agreement may then be reached on that basis. More usually, each side has points which are strong and others not so strong, and each impresses

---

[12] For British practice, see G. Marston (ed.), *United Kingdom Materials in International Law,* in the annual volumes of the *British Yearbook of International Law,* especially that for 1985, 56 *BYIL* 516.

[13] Arts. 74 and 83 of the Convention.

[14] *Concise Oxford Dictionary.*

the other on part of its case but not on the remainder. In such a case, any agreement is likely to amount to a compromise. Negotiation for a maritime boundary under customary law was the subject of judicial explanation in the *North Sea Continental Shelf* Cases. The ICJ concluded that the parties were:

> "under an obligation to enter into negotiations with a view to arriving at an agreement, and not merely to go through a formal process of negotiation as a sort of prior condition for the automatic application of a certain method of delimitation in the absence of agreement."[15]

This was probably the doctrinal issue, laid to rest in the judgment, whether or not the method or principle of equidistance was opposable to Germany. The Court continued:

> "[the parties] are under an obligation so to conduct themselves that the negotiations are meaningful, which will not be the case when either of them insists upon its own position without contemplating any modification of it."[16]

The Court appears to have been contemplating a compromise, which could have been a boundary running somewhere in between the two starting positions or a joint area subject to an agreed regime. The Court's *dicta* about negotiation appear to be applicable both to the first round of negotiations and to negotiations as a second stage, a topic to which is reviewed below.

9. NEGOTIATIONS AS A FINAL STAGE IN A PROCESS OF SETTLEMENT

The outcome of resort to a third party in order to settle a dispute may in some instances be a call to the parties to negotiate. Such a call may be issued by a conciliation commission[17] or be required in the decision of a court. In practice, the call is likely to be for the holding of *a further* round of negotiations, using a new legal basis, since the parties will normally have tried to negotiate a settlement and then have negotiated the terms for the reference of the issue to the court. In such a case, the new negotiations after resort to conciliation or litigation amount to a second or even third stage in the processes of settling the dispute, rather than a complete settlement in themselves. Two decisions by the ICJ illustrate this possibility. The talks between Denmark and Germany about their boundary in the North Sea, as well as those between the Netherlands and Germany, were resumed after the decision of the ICJ in the *North Sea Continental Shelf* cases of 1969.[18] That decision was to the effect that the method of equidistance was not opposable to Germany and that in the circumstances delimitation was to be effected in accordance with equitable principles.

---

[15] *North Sea Continental Shelf*, Judgment, ICJ Reports 1969, 3, para. 85(a).

[16] *Ibid.*, para. 85(b).

[17] As between Iceland and Norway over the maritime boundary near Jan Mayen: Report in 20 ILM 787; comment in Report No. 9–4 in Charney and Alexander (eds.), n. 4 above, ii, at 1755.

[18] *North Sea Continental Shelf Cases*, Judgment, ICJ Reports 1969, 3.

The Court set out some factors which were to be taken into account in negotiations. In practice, both Denmark and the Netherlands abandoned, in the new talks with Germany, their former insistence that the two boundaries should be equidistant lines. However, it is far from clear that the specific findings and directions of the Court for the negotiations were in fact applied in reaching the two final agreements, especially that between Denmark and Germany.[19] A second example is the Court's decision in the *Fisheries Jurisdiction* case between the UK and Iceland to the effect that the parties were under mutual obligations to undertake negotiations in good faith for an equitable solution of their differences, taking some detailed points in mind.[20] While the UK did hold further talks with Iceland after the judgment, and after the expiry of the Interim Agreement in 1975, they did not result in an agreement of the type contemplated by the Court. This difference can be explained partly by the refusal of Iceland to appear before the Court and then accept its decision and partly by the emergence quite soon after the decision of the rule of customary law, based on state practice and the work of the Third Conference on the Law of the Sea on the concept of the EEZ, whereby a fisheries limit of 200 nautical miles could be established. To sum up, the *Icelandic* case may be a rather special one: the *North Sea* cases indicate that the impact of the judgment on the negotiations was not the precise one its terms may have indicated. Negotiators retain their freedom to agree on whatever they can agree on. But the Court's decision that the method of equidistance was not binding upon or opposable to Germany had altered the ground rules for the negotiations, thereby opening the way for the parties to reach agreement at last.

10. CONCLUDING REMARKS

Dispute settlement by the conduct of negotiations is an interesting form of diplomacy. It requires the participants to examine and re-examine both their own starting position and that of the others involved in order to see whether existing divisions could be narrowed to a point where the final gap may be bridgeable or, if not, at least to see whether some aspects of the dispute could be resolved amicably, or whether resort to a third party could help advance matters, or, failing everything else, whether existing conditions could be ameliorated without prejudicing rival positions. Solutions often have to be imaginative: precedents may have to be set or created, rather than found ready-made elsewhere. Patience is usually needed. As Satow concludes:

> " good negotiation is founded on general good sense and good instinct and, of course, a will to succeed. Beyond this, there are great varieties of method and procedure. And

[19] See Report No. 9–18 by the present writer in J.I. Charney and L.M. Alexander (eds.), *International Maritime Boundaries* (The American Society of International Law/Nijhoff, Dordrect, 1998), iii, at 2497.
[20] *Fisheries Jurisdiction* (*United Kingdom* v. *Iceland*), Merits, Judgment, ICJ Reports 1974 3, para. 79(3) and (4).

there are few more rewarding things in diplomacy than a successful negotiation of whatever kind from which both or all parties derive some satisfaction. For mutual satisfaction is the best guarantee of permanence."[21]

This dictum applies to all types of negotiations, whether they are aimed at the establishment of new forms of international cooperation or, particularly, at the settlement of disputes.

---

[21] N. 2 above at 350.

7

Alternative Dispute Resolution under International Law

CHRISTINE CHINKIN

1. DISPUTE RESOLUTION IN NATIONAL AND INTERNATIONAL LAW

Since about the late 1970s alternative dispute resolution (ADR) processes, and in particular forms of mediation, have become fashionable in Western jurisdictions such as the United States, Australia and Canada.[1] They are also becoming more widely known and used within the United Kingdom.[2] This popularity has manifested itself through the introduction of pilot schemes and legislative, administrative and voluntary programmes, within the formal court structures and outside them, for the resolution of disputes in many areas of domestic law.[3] ADR processes comprise forms of third party assisted negotiation (mediation and conciliation), independent expert investigation, appraisal and evaluation, and have been combined or adapted to create a range of innovative methods for the attempted resolution of disputes.

The benefits of ADR processes are regularly extolled by its advocates.[4] Among their most frequently cited advantages are cheapness, flexibility and privacy compared to litigation. The parties' freedom of choice with respect to third party facilitators allows them to draw upon appropriate technical, legal, cultural or other expertise, and even to bring together a balanced team of experts. The consensual nature of the processes is said to be empowering for disputants who can craft for themselves a mutually acceptable outcome, unfettered by the restrictions of legal procedures and remedies. The parties' retention of control over the outcome is thought likely to produce a potentially more durable, forward-looking settlement to the dispute than one imposed by a court, which will

---

[1] See H. Astor and C. Chinkin, *Dispute Resolution in Australia* (Butterworths, Sydney, 1993), especially ch. 1.

[2] See, e.g., *Modern Law Review*, "Special Issue—Dispute Resolution: Civil Justice and its Alternatives", 56 MLR (1993); Lord Woolf, *Access to Justice* (HMSO, London, 1996).

[3] In the UK, ADR processes are especially promoted for family matters and neighbourhood disputes, although there is a growing awareness of their potential in commercial disputes; for a useful summary see Resolving Disputes Without Going to Court (Lord Chancellor's Department, London, 1995).

[4] See Astor and Chinkin, n. 1 at 41.

almost inevitably be framed in a "win/lose" formulation.[5] Further, since the dispute need not be presented in the bilateral model required by litigation, third party and collective interests can be more readily accommodated, at least in theory.

How does this trend translate into the international arena where the paradigmatic disputing parties are sovereign States? ADR processes are not new in international law, as what are more generally termed "diplomatic methods"[6] have been formally part of the framework of international dispute settlement since at least the Hague Treaties of 1899 and 1907,[7] and informally much longer.[8] An optimism that States would co-operate in international relations and seek peaceful methods of dispute resolution motivated the Hague Conferences for the Peaceful Settlement of Disputes, 1899 and 1907 and found expression in provision for third party processes of arbitration, good offices, mediation, inquiry and conciliation. Before World War II these processes were institutionalised, in both multilateral and bilateral treaties, for example through the formation of Permanent Conciliation Commissions,[9] the creation of the Permanent Court of Arbitration,[10] of the fact-finding Commission of Inquiry and of Mixed Arbitral Tribunals.[11] Despite this range of institutional options, their actual use was never extensive. Nevertheless, when the United Nations Charter prohibition on the use of force in international relations necessitated state commitment to the peaceful settlement of disputes,[12] these same processes were reiterated in Article 33 of the Charter.[13]

Despite steady restatement, for example by the revision of the General Act in 1949,[14] further General Assembly resolutions[15] and regional arrange-

---

[5] R. Fisher and W. Ury, *Getting to Yes, Negotiating Agreement Without Giving In* (Houghton Mifflin, Boston, Mass., 1981).

[6] P. Malanczuk, *Akehurst's Modern Introduction to International Law* (7th rev. edn., Routledge, London and New York, 1997), at 273–81.

[7] International Convention for the Pacific Settlement of Disputes, The Hague, 29 July 1899, 32 Stat. 1779; International Convention for the Pacific Settlement of Disputes, The Hague, 18 Oct. 1907; 3 Martens (3rd) 360, 36 Stat. 2199.

[8] J. Merrills, *International Dispute Settlement* (2nd edn., Grotius, Cambridge, 1991).

[9] *Ibid.*

[10] The Permanent Court of Arbitration was set up by the International Convention for the Pacific Settlement of Disputes, 1899, Arts. 20–9, and was only slightly amended by the International Convention for the Pacific Settlement of Disputes, 1907.

[11] Treaty of Versailles, 28 June 1919; 11 Martens (3rd) 323, Arts. 296–7, 304–5.

[12] United Nations Charter, Arts. 2(3) and (4).

[13] Art. 33(1) states: "The parties to any dispute, the continuance of which is likely to endanger the maintenance of international peace and security shall, first of all, seek a solution by negotiation, enquiry, mediation, conciliation, arbitration, judicial settlement, resort to regional agencies or arrangements, or other peaceful means of their own choice." See further *Handbook on the Peaceful Settlement of Disputes Between States* (United Nations, New York, 1992).

[14] General Act for the Pacific Settlement of International Disputes, Geneva, 26 Sept. 1928, 93 LNTS 343 revised on 28 Apr. 1949, GA Res. 268 (A III), GAOR (3rd) Pt II (A/900).

[15] E.g. Declaration on Principles of International Law Concerning Friendly Relations and Cooperation among States in Accordance with the Charter of the United Nations, GA Res. 2625, 24 Oct., 1970; Manila Declaration on the Peaceful Settlement of International Disputes, GA Res. 37/10, 1982; Declaration on the Prevention and Removal of Disputes and Situations which may Threaten International Peace and Security and on the Role of the United Nations in this Field, GA Res. 43/51, 1988.

ments,[16] these processes remained institutionally under-utilised in the cold war years. Recourse tended to be on an *ad hoc* basis where advantage was taken of the inherent flexibility of negotiatory processes to mould dispute-resolution method and outcome to fit the facts, the parties and the political background of the particular dispute. Among the most frequently cited examples of recourse to international arbitration or mediation are inter-State boundary disputes such as those concerning the Rann of Kutch,[17] the Taba,[18] the English Channel,[19] the Beagle Channel[20] and territory between Qatar and Bahrain.[21] While boundary disputes may cause great political tension and be highly emotionally charged,[22] there has also been recourse to such methods in more overtly political disputes, for example the Algerian mediation of the dispute between the US and Iran over the latter's detention of American hostages in Tehran (1980),[23] and that between France and New Zealand over the sinking of the *Rainbow Warrior* in Auckland harbour (1986).[24] There were also many instances where either individual States or the Secretary-General offered their good offices to assist disputing States.[25] The Secretary-General has also exercised his good offices in conjunction with other individuals, representatives from regional organisations[26] and States.

There is currently what has been termed an "obsessive concentration"[27] upon these processes that might be compared with the enthusiasm for ADR manifest in Western domestic law.[28] This concentration can be seen in a number of forms, for example in renewed UN emphasis on the utility of specific

---

[16] E.g. the European Convention for the Peaceful Settlement of Disputes, 1957, 320 UNTS 243; the American Treaty on Pacific Settlement, 1948, 30 UNTS 55; Protocol of the Commission of Mediation and Arbitration of the Organization of African Unity, 1964, 3 ILM 1116.

[17] Indo-Pakistan Western Boundary, Rann of Kutch Award, 50 ILR 2 (1968).

[18] Arbitral Award in the Dispute Concerning Certain Boundary Pillars between the Arab Republic of Egypt and the State of Israel, 80 ILR 224 (1980).

[19] *Delimitation of the Continental Shelf (United Kingdom–France)*, 54 ILR 6 (1977).

[20] *Beagle Channel Award (Argentina v. Chile)* 52 ILR 93 (1977).

[21] The long attempts at mediation by the King of Saudi Arabia are described in the case concerning *Maritime Delimitation and Territorial Questions between Qatar and Bahrain*, Jurisdiction and Admissibility, Judgment, ICJ Reports 1994, 112; Judgment of 15 Feb., ICJ Reports 1995, 6.

[22] E.g. Chile and Argentina were on the brink of war over the Beagle Channel.

[23] See J. Greenburg, "Algerian Intervention in the Iranian Hostage Crisis", 20 *Stanford JIL* 259.

[24] *Ruling pertaining to the Differences between France and New Zealand arising from the Rainbow Warrior Affair*, 74 ILR 241 (1986).

[25] E.g. with respect to Indonesia (1947), Palestine (1956), Tunisia (1958), Cyprus (on-going); n. 13 above, at paras. 112–14; Higgins comments that the "list [of disputes where the Secretary-General has employed his good offices] is almost endless": R. Higgins, *Problems and Process International Law and How We Use It* (Clarendon Press, Oxford, 1994), at 172. See further, Merrills, n. 8 above, at 185–91.

[26] E.g. the joint effort between the Secretary-General of the UN and the Chairperson of the Organisation of African Unity with respect to both the Western Sahara and Mayotte and attempts between the Secretary-General of the UN and the Secretary-General of the Organisation of American States with respect to conflict in Central America: n. 13 above, at para. 115.

[27] M. Koskenniemi, "International Law in a Post-Realist Era", 16 *AYBIL* 1 at 2.

[28] This has been accompanied by greater use of adjudicatory methods of international dispute resolution; see C. Chinkin, "The Peaceful Settlement of Disputes: New Grounds for Optimism?" in R. St John MacDonald (ed.), *Essays in Honour of Wang Tieya* (Nijhoff, Dordrecht, 1994), at 165.

peacemaking processes,[29] and in the proliferation of dispute-resolution clauses in treaties that require some recourse to peaceful settlement. A formula that makes compulsory some form of dispute-resolution process, while allowing parties maximum freedom to specify its form, has been adopted in some sectoral regulatory regimes.[30] Such treaties frequently contain Annexes that facilitate the operation of the chosen process, providing guidelines on such details as the method of selection of third parties, appropriate time limits, applicable procedures, preferred outcomes and third party powers.[31] Similarly, additional institutional mechanisms for dispute resolution have been introduced regionally, especially within Europe at the end of the cold war.[32]

Although there is no doubt cross-fertilisation between the domestic and international arenas, caution should be exercised in drawing comparisons. In domestic legal systems the objective has been to create effective alternatives to what are regarded as the unacceptably high costs and long delays of litigation, while in international law it has been to encourage some form of third party settlement, in the absence of compulsory adjudication.[33] Internationally, diplomatic processes were promoted as alternatives to recourse to armed force, at least in the first instance, rather than as alternatives to international adjudication. The latter was not introduced until the creation of the Permanent Court of International Justice as part of the post-World War I peace settlement.[34] Indeed in the *Great Belt* case the International Court of Justice (ICJ) affirmed that international adjudication is still an alternative to direct and friendly settlement between States,[35] the reverse of the understanding in domestic legal systems. Consequently many domestic debates about the function and efficacy of ADR processes are meaningless in the international context where all third party processes are peaceful alternatives to conflict.[36] Their common consensual basis means that they do not operate in the

[29] E.g. UN Draft Rules on Conciliation of Disputes between States, 30 ILM 231 and, more generally, *An Agenda for Peace, Preventive Diplomacy, Peacemaking and Peace-keeping: Report of the Secretary-General Pursuant to the Statement adopted by the Summit Meeting of the Security Council on 31 January 1992*, 17 June 1992, UN Doc. A/47/277, at paras. 34–45.

[30] The UN Convention on the Law of the Sea, 1982, Part XV, has become a model for this approach; see C. Chinkin, "Dispute Resolution and the Law of the Sea: Regional Problems and Prospects" in J. Crawford and D. Rothwell, *The Law of the Sea in the Asian Pacific Region* (Nijhoff, Dordrecht, 1995), at 237.

[31] Similarly Model Arbitral Rules have been widely adopted for international commercial arbitration, e.g. UN Commission on International Trade Law (UNCITRAL) Model Law on International Commercial Arbitration, 1985, 24 ILM 1302.

[32] E.g. Convention on Conciliation and Arbitration within the Conference on Security and Co-operation in Europe, 1993, 32 ILM 557; *cf.* the Organisation of African Unity, Mechanism for Conflict Prevention, Management and Resolution, 1993, UN Doc. A/47/558. 98 (1993).

[33] Statute of the International Court of Justice, 1945, Art. 36.

[34] Covenant of the League of Nations, Art. 14; Statute of the Permanent Court of International Justice, 16 Dec. 1920.

[35] *Passage through the Great Belt (Finland v. Denmark)*, Provisional Measures, Order of 29 July 1991, ICJ Reports 1991, 12.

[36] One example is the debate whether arbitration is properly perceived as an ADR process, or whether it has more affinity with adjudication. Arbitration by agreement between the parties has been a peaceful alternative to both conflict and diplomatic settlement since at least the UK–US Treaty of Amity, Commerce and Navigation, 1794 (the Jay Treaty).

"shadow of the law" as is the case domestically,[37] although the *Nauru*,[38] *Great Belt*[39] and *Qatar* v. *Bahrain*[40] cases might suggest a change in this respect. On the other hand international adjudication perhaps draws more from negotiatory methods of settlement than does domestic litigation.[41]

This chapter discusses three international institutional contexts where nego-tiatory dispute-resolution processes have been adopted and adapted for differ-ent purposes. The first is the use of similar diplomatic methods for both "compliance control"[42] and dispute resolution in what has been called "dynamic, sectoral legal systems",[43] notably institutional regimes for the regu-lation of the environment and the protection of human rights. The second examines the role of dispute-resolution processes in enhancing institutional good governance and democratic participation within the international finan-cial institutions. The third looks at a more direct alternative to the use of armed force, the practice of good offices by the Secretary-General of the United Nations and the relationship between the concepts of peacemaking and peace-keeping as envisioned by the former Secretary-General.[44] These examples illus-trate the potential tensions between institutional objectives and the assumptions of treaty performance, especially where the latter involve performance of oblig-ations owed *erga omnes* and standing to assert those obligations is narrowly framed. Underlying this tension is the further strain within the international system between the private nature of negotiatory methods, institutional

[37] The expression "bargaining in the shadow of the law" has been used in domestic law to describe how parties negotiate against a backdrop of the likely consequences of litigation and their awareness of that eventuality if they cannot reach a satisfactory conclusion: e.g. R. Mnookin and L. Kornhauser, "Bargaining in the Shadow of the Law: The Case of Divorce", 88 *Yale LJ* 950.

[38] After the ICJ determined that it had jurisdiction to hear Nauru's claims against Australia, a negotiated settlement was reached between the parties and the case withdrawn from the Court: *Certain Phosphate Lands in Nauru* (*Nauru* v. *Australia*), Preliminary Objections, Judgment, ICJ Reports 1992, 240; Australia–Republic of Nauru: Settlement of the Case in the International Court of Justice Concerning Certain Phosphate Lands in Nauru, 10 Aug. 1993, 32 ILM 1471.

[39] Commencement of judicial proceedings may have facilitated the negotiated agreement between Finland and Denmark: P. Magid, "The Post-Adjudicative Phase" in C. Peck and R. Lee (eds.), *Increasing Effectiveness of the International Court of Justice* (Nijhoff/UNITAR, The Hague, 1997), 325 at 343.

[40] The ICJ unusually assumed a case-management role in requiring the parties to negotiate fur-ther about submitting their full dispute to the Court: *Qatar* v. *Bahrain*, n. 21 above; *cf.* E. Lauterpacht, " 'Partial' Judgments and the Inherent Jurisdiction of the International Court of Justice", in V. Lowe and M. Fitzmaurice (eds.), *Fifty Years of the International Court of Justice* (Cambridge University Press, Cambridge, 1996), at 465.

[41] E.g. the ICJ may decide cases *ex aequo et bono*: Statute of the ICJ, Art. 38(2); it has less devel-oped rules of evidence than domestic courts and has recourse to flexible concepts of equity in its judgments. See further T.M. Franck, *Fairness in International Law and Institutions* (Clarendon Press, Oxford, 1995), especially at 47–80 and 316–47.

[42] This expression has been labelled a current "buzz word" of international environmental law: G. Handl, "Compliance Control Mechanisms and International Environmental Obligations", 5 *Tulane Journal of International and Comparative Law* 29 at 30.

[43] T. Gehring, "International Environmental Regimes: Dynamic Sectoral Legal Systems", 1 *YBIEL* 35.

[44] An Agenda for Peace (n. 29 above); Supplement to an Agenda for Peace, 1 January 1995, UNDOC. A/50/60–5/1995/1 .

perspectives and the interests of the wider international community in the visible commitment to the standards required through adherence to treaties.

2. INSTITUTIONAL REGIMES FOR TREATY COMPLIANCE

Innovative procedures for enhancing compliance with, and responding to, non-performance of international obligations have been included within multilateral treaties creating international regulatory regimes, especially within the area of environmental law.[45] The first such model, the Vienna Convention on the Ozone Layer, 1985,[46] and the Montreal Protocol, 1987, will be described as illustration of the major features of such procedures.[47] Article 8 of the Montreal Protocol provided the framework for a non-compliance procedure, the details of which were completed by a working party and adopted by the Fourth Meeting of the Parties to the Protocol in 1992.[48] These procedures allow a party, or the Secretariat, to raise concerns about another party's non-compliance before the Implementation Committee established for this purpose under the Protocol, making each State "a trustee" for other parties' conformity with the Convention.[49] Handl notes that party concern for compliance is not motivated solely by the desire to enhance the efficacy of international legal regulation: as the social and developmental costs of compliance with environmental standards increases, all parties have an incentive in ensuring that others are not gaining an unfair advantage through ignoring those standards.[50] The Implementation Committee considers all submissions, information and observations received with a view to securing "an amicable solution of the matter on the basis of respect for the provisions of the Protocol".

These non-compliance procedures operate through a bureaucratised body integral to the regulatory regime. This has a number of consequences both for the process and for the performance of the relevant obligations. The procedures reject the model of an independent, neutral third party expert by instead bringing together within the institutional framework those who are responsible for the articulation of the substantive norms with those who are working towards agreement as to outcome. Unlike non-institutional mediation or conciliation processes, where the parties alone are responsible for the outcome, any amicable solution must be reached in light of the provisions of the Convention. This

[45] Handl asserts that institutional measures for non-compliance have become an indispensable element of multilateral international environmental treaties: Handl, n. 42 above, at 32.

[46] Vienna Convention for the Protection of the Ozone Layer, 22 Mar. 1985, 26 ILM 1529.

[47] The Montreal Protocol on Substances that Deplete the Ozone Layer, with Annex A., 19 Sept. 1987, 26 ILM 1550.

[48] Report of the Fourth Meeting of the Parties to the Montreal Protocol on Substances that deplete the Ozone Layer, UNEP/OZL.Pro.4/15, 25 Nov. 1992, 3 YBIEL 819.

[49] M. Koskenniemi, "Breach of Treaty or Non-Compliance? Reflections on the Enforcement of the Montreal Protocol", 3 *YBIEL* 123. A party may also bring its own non-compliance to the attention of the Implementation Committee.

[50] Handl, n. 42 above, at 31.

model is similar to the long-established process of a conciliated friendly settlement between the government and petitioner under the European Convention on Human Rights.[51] The replacement of the European Commission on Human Rights by a single-tiered judicial process when Protocol 11 to the European Convention[52] is implemented, does not mean that settlement will no longer be attempted. The first instance Chamber of the newly constituted permanent Court can put itself at the disposal of the parties for the purposes of friendly settlement. This creates the further dilemma of conferring both negotiatory and adjudicatory powers on a single body, a blending of function that has caused disquiet in Western concepts of adjudication but is more common in other systems of law.[53]

Under the Montreal Protocol, the party whose alleged non-compliance has been raised can only submit information and comments to the Implementation Committee. It cannot participate in the elaboration and adoption of the recommendations, an exclusion that detracts both from the voluntariness of the solution and the broader understanding of diplomatic processes. Since the objective is to secure compliance, the solutions adopted tend to be forward-looking and facilitative rather than simply condemnation for failure to perform, although they may include some punitive components such as a caution or even sanctions. This blurring of negotiatory and quasi-adjudicatory function brings issues of institutional accountability and due process back into the picture. Nevertheless, preference for the compliance processes that may avert any more coercive measures is likely to influence the non-complying State's decision with respect to the proposed outcome.

The solution as to recompense or future conduct is worked out within the institutional regulatory framework, but outside the processes of general international law. The non-compliance process of the Montreal Protocol has been commended for its fostering of the dynamic development of a sectoral legal system that takes account of the expectations and understandings developed between participants to the regime, and in light of technical and bureaucratic expertise.[54] In contrast, recourse to dispute-resolution processes outside the institutional framework, such as the ICJ, *ad hoc* arbitration or conciliation would not do this. Use of binding processes (adjudication or arbitration) might be counter-productive to the on-going evolution of the regulatory regime, in that a formal ruling tends to crystallise the law in a fast-changing area, whereas the regime procedures can take into account and contribute to this

---

[51] Friendly settlement has been a primary objective of the European Commission on Human Rights upon receipt of an admissible petition: European Convention for the Protection of Fundamental Rights and Freedoms, 4 Nov. 1950, ETS No. 5, Art. 28(b); *cf.* American Convention on Human Rights, 22 Nov. 1969, OAS TS No. 36, Art. 48(f).

[52] Protocol No. 11 to the European Convention for the Protection of Fundamental Rights and Freedoms, 1994 and Explanatory Report (Council of Europe Press, 1994). Protocol 11 will come into force on 1 Nov. 1998.

[53] Astor and Chinkin, n. 1 above, at 145.

[54] Gehring, n. 43 above.

evolution.[55] Indeed in its judgment in the *Gabčikovo-Nagymaros Project*,[56] the ICJ itself emphasised the importance of parties taking account of developing environmental norms in the performance of their institutional treaty obligations and considered that third party involvement could assist them in doing this, provided they were prepared to be flexible.

There is however another side to this analysis. A treaty is a public prescription of agreed international standards in the performance of which non-parties have an interest, as well as parties. Obligations to decrease emissions damaging to the ozone layer, or to respect human rights, are owed *erga omnes*,[57] not just to the complainant in the particular instance, or even just to other States, parties or non-parties. The concept of amicable solution or friendly settlement, reached through compromise and legitimated by the institutional framework, suggests a bilateralism that might not satisfy others' perceptions of what those obligations should entail.[58] A mediated agreement typically incorporates enough of the interests of both disputants for them to be able to accept it, that is it presents a win/win solution. However a mediated agreement may not take account of the interests of third parties, or of the international community at large.[59] An example is the agreement reached in the inter-State application brought by Denmark, France, the Netherlands, Norway and Sweden against Turkey in 1983.[60] The applicant States claimed violations of a number of Articles of the European Convention on Human Rights, including the prohibition against torture in Article 3. A friendly settlement was reached in which Turkey made general undertakings with respect to future compliance with the Convention and to lifting the state of emergency declared under Article 15. The settlement did not refer to a number of alleged violations that the Commission (which participated in the settlement) had previously found to be admissible. Robertson and Merrills have criticised this settlement on the ground that it "cannot be said to have been reached 'on the basis of respect for Human Rights' as defined in the Convention".[61] They comment further that "in a comparable case brought by an individual it is inconceivable that an arrangement so patently unsatisfactory would have been approved".[62]

---

[55] *Cf.* the development of "transnational commercial law" as described by Prof. Goode: R. Goode, "Usage and its Reception in Transnational Commercial Law", 46 *ICLQ* 1.

[56] *Gabčikovo-Nagymaros Project (Hungary/Slovakia)*, Judgment, ICJ Reports 1997, not yet reported.

[57] *Barcelona Traction, Light and Power Co. Ltd*, 2nd Phase, Judgment, ICJ Reports 1970, 3 at 32.

[58] In the case concerning the *Gabčikovo-Nagymaros Project* Vice President Weeramantry, in his separate Opinion, considered that since claims of environmental damage have *erga omnes* implications, bilateral doctrines such as estoppel might be inappropriate.

[59] The example has been given of quotas agreed by the International Whaling Commission that satisfy the parties (at least to some extent) but do nothing to save the whales: J. Dryzek and S. Hunter, "Environmental Mediation for International Problems", 31 *International Studies Quarterly* 87.

[60] Report of 7 Dec. 1985, 44 Decisions and Reports 31.

[61] A. Robertson and J. Merrills, *Human Rights in Europe* (3rd edn., Manchester University Press, Manchester, 1993), at 284.

[62] *Ibid.*

While appreciating the political dilemma facing the Commission, this is brought about precisely by using private settlement processes within an institutional regulatory regime for performance of treaty obligations, including those owed *erga omnes*, and resurrects the concern about private ordering[63] that has been forcefully expressed in the context of domestic ADR.[64] While the assurance of confidentiality may be an essential factor in reaching an amicable settlement, it prevents open assessment of the parties' compliance with their treaty commitments.[65] Indeed this concern appears even more valid in a decentralised legal system where an amicable solution can generate state practice constitutive of customary international law outside the terms of the treaty. The conclusion that "[i]n inter-state cases, . . . the friendly settlement procedure should be approached with a degree of scepticism" may be equally applicable to all such compliance processes that combine state will with the institutional need for continued credibility.[66] Koskenniemi has warned of the danger that the desire to maintain the treaty and its institutions intact may allow the procedures to become ineffective for achieving their objectives and enable parties to conceal real differences while apparently dealing with them, to the detriment of upholding collective obligations[67] or individual third party interests.[68] Finally, such development can lead to the further fragmentation of the substance of international law and its structures. Views may differ on whether or not such fragmentation is desirable: on the one hand it allows for the development of specialist knowledge and expertise; on the other there is the risk of incoherence between different areas of international law. Whichever way one concludes, at the very least the potential consequences should be recognised.

The Montreal Protocol non-compliance mechanisms co-exist with, or merge into, third party dispute-resolution processes that are contained within the

---

[63] E.g. Turkey agreed to submit reports to the Commission and to participate in dialogue with it on Art. 3 and to prepare a final report on the implementation of the settlement. However all these steps were to remain confidential: *ibid*. at 292, n. 81. Similarly, confidentiality is preserved for the non-compliance procedures under the Montreal Protocol.

[64] Astor and Chinkin, n. 1 above, at 57 and 81–2.

[65] Handl, n. 42 above, at 40, notes that confidentiality may be justified because of the sensitive nature of relevant information.

[66] Similar apprehension may be felt in the context of the purported "constructive dialogue" between human rights treaty bodies and States Parties reporting to them where real concerns about non-compliance with the relevant treaty may not be adequately addressed.

[67] Koskenniemi, n. 49 above.

[68] Despite the flexibility of negotiatory processes that apparently more easily allow participation by third parties, their interests may be more effectively upheld by the more formal procedures before the ICJ. For example in *East Timor (Portugal v. Australia)*, Judgment, ICJ Reports 1995, 90 Indonesia's interests prevented the Court from deciding upon the merits of Portugal's claim and in the *Continental Shelf (Libyan Arab Jamahiriya/Malta)*, Judgment, ICJ Reports 1985, 13 Italy's claims caused the Court to limit its consideration of the maritime areas disputed by the parties, despite its earlier unsuccessful request to intervene. However the protection accorded by the indispensable third party principle is only available to third party States. At the same time, the Court may refuse to consider third party claims such as requests to intervene. See further C. Chinkin, *Third Parties in International Law* (Clarendon Press, Oxford, 1993), especially ch. 12.

Vienna Convention on the Ozone Layer, Article 11.[69] The ICJ has held that a dispute arises when there is "a disagreement on a point of law or fact, a conflict of legal views or interests between parties".[70] The existence of a dispute may assume an allegation of breach, unsatisfactory performance or non-compliance by one party to the Convention with respect to the behaviour of another, and thus overlaps with the concerns that can trigger the non-compliance procedures. Moreover, complaints of non-compliance with the Montreal Protocol may amount to claims of breach within the terms of Article 60 of the Vienna Convention on the Law of Treaties,[71] and raise the substantive options therein specified.[72] The dispute resolution procedures to be followed in the case of claims of breach of the Vienna Convention on the Law of Treaties are those listed in Article 33 of the UN Charter, and especially conciliation.[73] The same techniques, for example consultation, independent expert investigation, seeking further information, negotiations facilitated by a third party, third party expert appraisal of the problem and the formulation of non-binding recommendations on how the issue might be resolved, underlie both compliance and the negotiatory dispute resolution processes. Indeed "amicable solution" is an appropriate description of the preferred outcome of a conciliation process, as well as the objective of the non-compliance procedures. Further, the preference of at least one of the parties in an articulated dispute may be to induce performance rather than to claim termination or redress, and the agreed outcome of conciliation may be devised to maintain the treaty relationship by including inducements for future performance.[74]

---

[69] Art. 11 allows parties to make a declaration accepting compulsory recourse to arbitration or the jurisdiction of the ICJ. If attempts at settlement through negotiation or mediation fail, and no common compulsory process has been accepted, there is compulsory conciliation that leads to a recommendatory award. These provisions follow, to some extent, the model of the UN Convention on the Law of the Sea, Part XV.

[70] *East Timor (Portugal v. Australia)*, Judgment, ICJ Reports 1995, 90 at para. 22.

[71] For full discussion of this point see Koskenniemi, n. 49 above.

[72] Vienna Convention on the Law of Treaties, 23 Mar. 19691 1155 UNTS 331, Art. 60(2) states that "material breach of a multilateral treaty by one of the parties entitles: (a) the other parties by unanimous agreement to suspend the operation of the treaty in whole or in part or to terminate it either (i) in the relations between themselves and the defaulting State or (ii) as between all parties; (b) a party specially affected by the breach to invoke it as a ground for suspending the operation of the treaty in whole or in part in the relations between itself and the defaulting state; (c) any party other than the defaulting State to invoke the breach as a ground for suspending the operation of the treaty in whole or in part with respect to itself if the treaty is of such a character that a material breach of its provisions by one party radically changes the position of every party with respect to the further performance of its obligations under the treaty". For discussion on what actions constitute material breach see the *Gabčikovo-Nagymaros Project (Hungary/Slovakia)*, Judgment, ICJ Reports, not yet reported.

[73] Vienna Convention on the Law of Treaties, Arts. 65–6 and Annex to the Convention (on conciliation procedures).

[74] The outcome may also contain some compensatory element but a win/win formula that takes account of future dealings between the parties is widely associated with non-adjudicatory dispute resolution: see Fisher and Ury, n. 5 above.

Although traditional dispute-resolution processes may not be suitable for inducing compliance,[75] the co-existence of both objectives within a single institutional regime creates a number of legal dilemmas for parties. Koskenniemi raises a number of pertinent questions. For example, can a party "specially affected" by an alleged breach of the Vienna Convention on the Ozone Layer or the Montreal Protocol claim under Article 60 of the Vienna Convention on the Law of Treaties, or must it rely upon Article 11 of the Ozone Treaty? Indeed can there be a "specially affected" State Party in the context of the Ozone Layer treaty, a question that is equally applicable to human rights treaties? Can a party to a dispute continue with the bilateral dispute resolution procedures under Article 11, although another self-designated party has commenced the institutional procedures relating to non-compliance? Standing to commence the latter is broader than that for the dispute resolution procedures. A party to a dispute may thus be pre-empted from exercising its options by the commencement of the institutional non-compliance processes by another party with what a disputing State considers a lesser interest, or even by the non-complying party itself acting deliberately to achieve such an outcome. More broadly, does the coexistence of compliance and dispute resolution procedures, both resting upon similar non-adjudicatory techniques, foster integration into, or development apart from, general international law?

Koskenniemi suggests a practical solution to the procedural dilemmas. He proposes that if a bilateral dispute resolution process progresses to conciliation (where the objective is non-binding recommendations), it should be merged with the procedures of the Implementation Committee, effectively making dispute resolution part of compliance. This does not of course address the concern about private or institutional ordering and deprives the party in dispute of its choice of conciliators and the alleged non-complying party of its active role within the process. However if the chosen dispute resolution process is arbitration or adjudication, the compliance processes should be dropped because their objectives differ and they may frustrate the adjudicatory process. The parties themselves however can always continue to seek friendly settlement. This solution would disadvantage other parties to the treaty that have only limited access to arbitration or adjudication, through the narrowly defined process of intervention,[76] but can participate in Meetings of the Parties with respect to non-compliance.

This discussion reflects the broader debate within the International Law Commission (ILC) on the relationship between state responsibility and dispute resolution.[77] In its Draft Articles on State Responsibility the ILC has extended the concept of an "injured state" in the contexts of breach of a multilateral

---

[75] Handl, n. 42 above, at 34.

[76] Statute of the ICJ, Arts. 62 and 63 (intervention before the ICJ); see Chinkin, n. 68 above, at ch. 11 for intervention in arbitral proceedings.

[77] International Law Commission, Draft Arts. on State Responsibility, provisionally adopted by the Commission on first reading, Draft Report of the ILC on the Work of its Forty-Eighth Session, UN Doc. A/CN.4/L.528/Add. 2, 16 July 1996.

treaty[78] and of an international crime,[79] in order to encompass collective and community interests. An injured State may have recourse to counter measures to induce conforming behaviour.[80] Since the draft definition of international crimes includes a "serious breach of an international obligation of essential importance for the safeguarding and preservation of the human environment"[81] such a claim might come within an environmental treaty with a non-compliance regime. The extensive understanding of "injured" State enhances the possibility of breach being raised at the international level, but may cause friction with a directly injured State that seeks reparation in some other way, or whose interests do not coincide with those of the claimant State. Such a State might not wish to have its claim submerged with those of all other "injured" States. A further debate is whether the legality of counter measures is dependent upon a prior attempt at peaceful settlement, that is a form of compulsory dispute settlement, at least at the level of an obligation to negotiate in good faith.[82] The Draft Articles require "an injured state taking countermeasures . . . to fulfil the obligations in relation to dispute resolution arising under Part Three or any other binding dispute settlement procedure in force between the injured State and the State which has committed the internationally wrongful act".[83] There are differences of opinion in principle whether a directly injured State should be required to attempt peaceful settlement before resorting to countermeasures,[84] but in addition the relationship between the general dispute resolution provisions contained in the ILC Draft Articles and specific treaty regimes for compliance and dispute settlement remains unclear.

3. INSPECTION PANELS OF THE INTERNATIONAL FINANCIAL INSTITUTIONS

Despite the collective nature of non-compliance institutional regimes, access and participation are nevertheless restricted to treaty parties. The second example of where dispute resolution processes have been blended into innovative procedures is the Inspection Panels established by the international financial institutions, the World Bank, the Inter-American Bank and the Asian

---

[78] Draft Arts. on State Responsibility, Art. 40(e). Art. 40(f) states "if the right infringed by the act of a State arises from a multilateral treaty, any other State party to the multilateral treaty, if it is established that the right has been expressly stipulated in that treaty for the protection of the collective interests of the States parties thereto".

[79] Draft Arts. on State Responsibility, Art. 40(3).

[80] Draft Arts. on State Responsibility, Art. 47.

[81] Draft Arts. on State Responsibility, Art. 19(3)(d).

[82] The level of action required to satisfy a requirement to negotiate in good faith remains unclear. A refusal to participate in any form of negotiation could be regarded as an internationally wrongful act, but there remains the possibility of good faith disagreement within the negotiations.

[83] Draft Arts. on State Responsibility, Art. 48.

[84] E.g. B. Simma, "Counter-measures and Dispute Settlement: A Plea for a Different Balance", 5 *EJIL* 102; O. Schachter, "Dispute Settlement and Countermeasures in the International Law Commission", 88 *AJIL* 471; C. Tomuschat, "Are Countermeasures Subject to Prior Recourse to Dispute Settlement Procedures?", 5 *EJIL* 77.

Development Bank.[85] Examination of these Panels shifts the focus of the discussion in two ways: first, the complaint is against the institution itself and, secondly, the process is initiated by non-State actors, that are by definition non-parties to the institutional regime.

In 1993 the World Bank introduced the first of these panels[86] following widespread protests about certain development projects, most famously the Sardar Sarovar Dam on the Narmada river in India.[87] The Panel can be seen as an innovative method of enhancing concepts of effectiveness, good governance, transparency and accountability within international institutions where their activities directly impinge upon peoples, lives and living conditions. Creation of the Inspection Panel constitutes an acknowledgement that disputes arising out of development projects cannot be defined solely by the project State and the relevant lending agency. Thus requests for inspection of a World Bank-financed project can be made by the intended beneficiaries, that is a community, organisation or other group residing in the country in which the project is being implemented, or in an adjacent country, if the group is adversely affected, or likely to be affected, by the project. Requests may also be made by representatives residing in the same State, or in exceptional cases outside the State, if the Board consents.

A request for inspection, even if granted, does not lead to an independent evaluation of the project, nor to an assessment of its conformity with international law, but rather to an examination of the relevant Bank's compliance with its own operational policies and practices, including, for example, the policy of public disclosure adopted by the World Bank's Board in 1993. The focus is upon damage, or likely damage, especially of a social or environmental kind, flowing from non-compliance with Bank policy, not from breach of international law. The World Bank envisaged that recourse to the Panel would be limited to those "exceptional cases where the Bank's own high standards were not met".[88]

Unlike the position of the Implementation Committee described above with respect to the institutional regime for the protection of the ozone layer, the Panel is not an integral part of the World Bank, although the members of the standing panel are selected for their relevant expertise.[89] The Inspection Panel in effect

---

[85] D. Bradlow, "International Organizations and Private Complaints: The Case of the World Bank Inspection Panel", 34 *VJIL* 553; I. Shihata, *The World Bank Inspection Panel* (Clarendon Press, Oxford, 1994). For details of the operation of the Panel see *The Inspection Panel International Bank for Reconstruction and Development Report August 1, 1994 to July 31, 1996* (The World Bank, Washington, DC).

[86] The Inspection Panels each institution has developed vary in detail, so this discussion will focus on the World Bank Inspection Panel.

[87] B. Morse and T. Berger, *Report of the Independent Review, Sardar Sarovar* (Resources Futures International, Ottawa, 1992).

[88] Oxfam, *The World Bank Inspection Panel: Analysis and Recommendations for Review* (Policy Department, UK, Feb. 1996) at 1.

[89] The Inter-American Bank and the Asian Development Bank have adopted a different model, that of a roster of named experts from whom the Board may select a Panel in response to a particular request.

acts as an intermediary between the requesters, the Bank Management and Board. Its processes resemble those for dispute resolution and their flexibility allows them to be adapted to the particular circumstances. Inspection can include impartial investigation, visiting the project site, broad formal and informal consultations, for example with relevant Bank staff, local people, intended project beneficiaries (including indigenous persons), grassroots and international non-governmental organisations and local and central government agencies, appraisal of decision-making, and crafting recommendations for remedial measures. The investigation includes access to the Bank's staff and records. The Panel's findings are sent to the President and Executive Directors of the Bank who determine upon any response. Unlike either non-compliance or dispute resolution processes as such, the objective is not to reach an amicable solution between the requesters and the Bank, but rather a decision by the Board based upon informed, impartial recommendations. This decision might not conform with government aims (for example a decision not to continue financing the project), or might fail to satisfy the requesters and indeed might generate further disputes. In this sense the process is perhaps more akin to an institutional grievance procedure requiring only conformity with Bank policies, and not any re-evaluation of the project.

The bestowal of standing to commence the process upon non-State actors moves away from the traditional state orientation of international dispute resolution by broadening beneficiary participation. It acknowledges that the traditional legal and procedural exclusion of non-State actors from international dispute resolution processes disregards the reality that international decision-making impacts upon peoples' lives,[90] a position the ICJ, for example, has been reluctant to take.[91] It also directly recognises the role of financial institutions as international actors.

However there are limitations to the potential empowerment accorded by the right to request inspection. Single individuals cannot request inspection, but must be part of a community or organisation. Doubts also remain both about the ability of local groups to access the procedures and the receptiveness of the Bank to requests for inspection. Local people may be unaware of the existence and powers of the inspection panels. Even with such knowledge, they may remain unable to access information about the relevant Bank's policies and practices and the potential effects of the project, especially where there are language barriers and the government impedes the flow of information. One response is to facilitate requests from representatives, including non-local representatives, who may have greater resources. The World Bank's reason for limiting non-local representation is a reminder that non-State actors remain outside the project design and management process. The Bank seeks "to prevent

---

[90] *Cf.* "Bank funded projects have an impact upon peoples" lives that is characterised by universal upheaval and yet is uniquely experienced: Oxfam, n. 88 above, at 15.

[91] C. Chinkin, "Increasing the Use and Appeal of the Court", in C. Peck and R. Lee (eds.), n. 39 above, at 43.

well-funded western NGOs from taking up cases and politicising what some borrower governments view as domestic issues".[92] Even if such representation were more readily accorded there is need for some caution. Genuine expression of local people's views cannot be lightly assumed, and care must be taken to ensure that such representation fully encompasses local opinion, including dissenting voices. Procedural rights of the requesters once the process has commenced are poorly defined. Without, for example, the right to be heard or to have access to full documentation, the Inspection Panels may appear to offer more to affected communities than is in fact the case.

Only the World Bank Inspection Panel has to date generated a significant case-load, and by 1997 only one request had resulted in an investigation taking place, although there are others pending. After receiving the Panel's recommendations based on its investigation of the Arun III Hydroelectric project in Nepal,[93] the Board of the World Bank withdrew from the project. In other cases, the Panel has determined requests to be inadmissible or the Board has determined that other internal procedures rendered inspection untimely or otherwise inappropriate. This record has led NGOs to question the World Bank's commitment to the expressed objectives of the process,[94] but a review in 1997 has not recommended substantial change. By 1997 inspection panels had not realised their potential for opening up international institutional policy-making to beneficiary scrutiny, but the model of open access remains the greatest possibility for non-State actors to express their concerns about the impact of international decision-making upon their lives.

4. GOOD OFFICES OF THE SECRETARY-GENERAL

The third example is the institutional relationship between the peaceful settlement of disputes and other actions for the maintenance of international peace and security as exemplified in the mediatory good offices function developed by successive Secretaries-General. Although this role is not explicitly prescribed in the UN Charter,[95] its exercise is pursuant to both the peaceful settlement of disputes under Chapter Six, described in An Agenda for Peace as coming within the concept of peacemaking,[96] and Security Council powers exercised under Chapter Seven, that is peace-keeping.[97] Peace making techniques are also

[92] Oxfam, n. 88 above, at 18.
[93] The Inspection Panel Report , n. 85 above, at 14–18.
[94] Oxfam, n. 88 above.
[95] UN Charter, Art. 98 requires the Secretary-General "to perform such other functions as are entrusted to him" by the organs of the Organization and Art. 99 allows him to "bring to the attention of the Security Council any matter which in his opinion may threaten the maintenance of international peace and security".
[96] Peacemaking constitutes attempts to bring disputing parties to agreement through processes contained in Ch. 6, including Art. 33: *An Agenda for Peace*; *Supplement to An Agenda for Peace*, n. 29 above.
[97] Peace-keeping involves the deployment of UN military, police and civilian personnel in the troubled area, traditionally with the consent of all parties (*ibid.*).

engaged in both preventive diplomacy and peace-building after conflict. Dispute resolution may therefore be attempted alongside and simultaneously with other more coercive operations, directed at other ends.

Tom Franck has argued that when the Secretary-General extends his good offices to disputing parties he deploys the authority of the international community as a whole.[98] This constructed dispute resolution role is therefore integral to the prospects of the UN itself in fulfilling effectively the requirements of peacemaking and peace-keeping in both international and internal disputes that present a threat to international peace and security.[99]

In this context too there are both institutional and process dilemmas. Entwining peacemaking with peace-keeping locates private processes for dispute resolution within the structures for global public ordering. To enhance its potential effectiveness, the exercise of good offices must appear to the parties to be fair: the concept of a mediated agreement rests upon assumptions of neutrality and impartiality between the third party facilitator and the disputants. These qualities require the Secretary-General to distance himself to some extent from the expressed policies of the UN, while working within the purposes and principles of the Charter. This position may become problematic where, for example, the behaviour of one party to the dispute has been condemned by the Security Council, where the Security Council has issued an ultimatum, or has directed that certain actions are required,[100] a situation that is occurring more frequently with the freeing up of the Security Council at the end of the cold war.[101] Franck also points to what he describes as the trend of the Security Council to limit the Secretary-General to delivering its directives to the parties. Such Security Council directives are politically inspired and are generally motivated at addressing the immediate threat to international peace and security. The responses determined upon by the Security Council may leave the Secretary-General with little room to manœuvre as a third party facilitator, while restricting his role to that of messenger undermines his own position. However deployment of the Secretary-General's good offices might secure a mediated outcome which could better achieve long-term resolution of the issues in dispute and thus better conform with international community objectives than the preferred responses of the Security Council.

The Secretary-General may face further thorny questions: with whom should he conduct his good offices? Who are the participants in the dispute whose pres-

[98] T. Franck, "The Secretary-General's Role in Conflict Resolution: Past, Present and Pure Conjecture", 6 *EJIL* 360; for a fuller account of the successful and unsuccessful exercise of good offices see T. Franck, n. 41 above, at 173–217.

[99] Franck, n. 41 above, at 174.

[100] Franck gives the example of the tension between the authorisation given to the Secretary-General to use his good offices in Iraq after the invasion of Kuwait in Aug. 1990 and the demands made upon Iraq in SC Res. 660, 2 Aug. 1990; SC Res. 661, 6 Aug. 1990.

[101] Higgins notes that it is more usual for the Security Council to devise the proposals, and adds that "the tendency for initiatives to flow from the Security Council rather than, even informally, the Secretariat has become more pronounced since the improvement of East-West relations": Higgins, n. 25 above, at 171.

ence is indispensable to an effective process with a realistic prospect of a satisfactory outcome? This question is especially crucial when key players have not received international (UN) recognition. How much institutional support should be provided to the Secretary-General in securing, or performing, an agreement and how does this impinge upon his neutrality? Can the Secretary-General guarantee an outcome, or must he rely upon subsequent Security Council endorsement? If he is unable to offer his own assurances as to the viability of an agreement, the momentum of the process may be lost, but otherwise he may be embarrassed by subsequent lack of political support or by member states' failure to allocate sufficient resources to assure the outcome. Such an eventuality in turn will undermine his credibility, and that of the UN.

5. CONCLUSIONS

Since the commencement of the twentieth century, the international community has evolved a range of tools for dispute settlement that it has continuously adapted, modified and refashioned to meet the demands of new objectives, including those of inducing compliance with treaty regimes and enhancing institutional transparency. These measures have become ever more technically demanding, complex, diversified and streamlined.[102] Inevitably their formulation and use (and projected use) have simultaneously both highlighted problems within institutional structures and contributed to the emergence of an international institutional law. Non-compliance procedures, dispute-resolution processes (both negotiatory and adjudicatory) and peace-keeping measures do not take place sequentially across a continuum but may be attempted separately or simultaneously with respect to a range of different State behaviours. They may merge imperceptibly into one another. Their objectives may coincide or conflict, especially where such objectives are ambiguous, ill-defined and subject to change as the situation unfolds. Since institutional objectives will not necessarily coincide with those of the disputants, they may involve degrees of institutional coercion, even while formally identified as consensual. In addition, the private nature of such processes may disguise lack of conformity with international community interests.

The vitality of international lawyers in designing innovative dispute resolution processes may also obscure real substantive conflict that continues even while the procedures are identified and agreed. It is often easier to reach consensus over the inclusion of a dispute resolution or non-compliance provision in a treaty than it is to resolve the substantive issues involved. This strategy creates the illusion that something is being done to make compliance with their international obligations a high priority for States. Further, since treaty-making remains a State privilege and participation in inter-governmental institutions is

---

[102] The adjectives are Koskenniemi's. See n. 27 above, at 2.

controlled by States, non-State interests are readily excluded or discounted. Where they are exceptionally recognised, as in the power of beneficiaries to request inspection of World Bank-financed projects, the procedures may hold out greater promise for involvement than in fact occurs. As has been the case since at least the Hague Peace Conferences nearly a century ago, the focus must be upon enhancing the political will of States to use the tools they have developed to resolve real differences between disputants, not merely to design elaborate models for their consideration. This problem is not confined to the international legal order but is prevalent within domestic systems where ADR remains more celebrated than engaged. While there are contradictory directions, what is evident is a vibrancy and innovation within the international legal system the structural, procedural and substantive consequences of which cannot yet be fully envisaged.

8

Uniformity in International Commercial Arbitration

MICHAEL FURMSTON

1. INTRODUCTION

The preceding chapters of this volume have raised the question of the manner in which patterns of diplomatic and alternative dispute resolution add to the tapestry of options which are available for dealing with disputes between states and provide viable mechanisms for achieving remedial outcomes. The lists of advantages of such techniques over judicial resolution are well established, and high in the list of attributes of arbitration as a form of settlement in the international sphere is its apparant flexibility. In the sphere of international commercial arbitration, these advantages are also present, but there are matched by tendencies towards uniformity in arbitral practice which, might be thought by some to cut against this. The purpose of this contribution is to consider how these factors have been received and reconciled within the domestic law of England and Wales. In the process, it will highlight a range of specific issues which have emerged and which any further process of harmonization in this field may need to resolve. This in turn may offer some insights which can be of value to those who press the case for the further developement and formalization of arbirtral procedures at the inter-state level. It is not suggested that the parallelisms are exact but there may be profitable analogies.

2. WHAT IS MEANT BY UNIFORMITY IN THE CONTEXT OF INTERNATIONAL COMMERCIAL ARBITRATION?

Is international commercial arbitration becoming more uniform? Is it desirable that it should do so? In the answer to these questions much clearly depends on what we mean by uniform. On one view, uniformity might mean no more than the universal acceptance of the principle of the autonomy of the parties. On this view, a high degree of uniformity exists since this principle is now widely if not universally accepted. Certainly in this country there has been a radical transformation in the things judges say about arbitration. As late as the 1920s, arbitration agreements were discussed in the context of the public policy against agreements to oust the jurisdiction of the courts.[1] Today judges can constantly be found describing arbitration as the private sector for dispute resolution business of which judges are the public sector and saying that if parties choose to have their disputes settled by arbitration, they should in all normal circumstances expect the decision of the arbitrator to be final. So in *Northern Regional Health Authority* v. *Derek Crouch Construction Co Ltd*[2] Sir John Donaldson MR said:

> "Arbitration is usually no more and no less than litigation in the private sector."

Statements such as this are not mere idle rhetoric. Judges have in fact come to behave as if indeed the parties should be, and are, free to choose arbitration as their means of dispute resolution and that a minimalist approach should be taken to judicial intervention. This is most clearly and powerfully demonstrated by the history of appeals against the decisions of arbitrators after the enactment of the Arbitration Act 1979. Before this Act there was, strictly speaking, no appeal against the decisions of arbitrators but there was what, in practice, amounted to an appeal (at least on questions of law) by means of the Case Stated Procedure. Under this Procedure the arbitrator could be required by either party to state a case on a question of law and the court would, if necessary, order the arbitrator to do so. It was widely believed that this Procedure was often abused by parties who wished to delay honouring the arbitrators' award and were prepared to incur the cost of dragging the procedure through the courts in order to do so.

The Arbitration Act 1979 abolished the Case Stated Procedure and substituted an explicit system of appeals on questions of law. Appeals on questions of law however were not granted as of right but were dependant on the granting of leave by a High Court judge. The Act gave very little guidance as to the criteria to be applied in deciding whether to grant leave to appeal. Many people thought that courts would, in practice, readily give leave to appeal, at least in those cases where the appeal stood a plausible chance of success. However, in practice, the House of Lords decided differently. In the two leading cases *The Nema*[3] and *The Antaios*[4] the House of Lords imposed major restrictions on the right to appeal. The position was stated with his usual force and clarity by Lord Diplock in *The Nema* when he said:

> "Where, as in the instant case, a question of law involved is the construction of a 'one-off' clause the application of which to the particular facts of the case is an issue in the arbitration, leave should not normally be given unless it is apparent to the judge upon a mere perusal of the reasoned award itself without the benefit of adversarial argu-

---

[1] *Czarnikow* v. *Roth Schmidt & Co.* [1922] 2 KB 478.

[2] *Northern Regional Health Authority* v. *Derek Crouch Construction Co. Ltd.* [1984] 2 All ER 175 at 189. The decision of the Court of Appeal in this case has recently been overruled by the House of Lords in *Beaufort Developments (NI) Ltd v. Gilbert Ash NI Ltd* [1998] 2 All ER 778 but not in a way which casts doubt on this question.

[3] *The Nema* [1982] AC 724.

[4] *The Antaios* [1985] AC 191.

ment, that the meaning ascribed to the clause by the arbitrator is obviously wrong. But if on such perusal it appears to the judge that it is possible that argument might persuade him, despite first impression to the contrary, that the arbitrator might be right, he should not grant leave; the parties should be left to accept, for better or for worse, the decision of the tribunal that they had chosen to decide the matter in the first instance . . .".[5]

This reasoning shows clearly a judicial policy decision to give great weight, though not necessarily decisive weight, to the decision of the tribunal that the parties had themselves chosen.[6]

If, on the other hand, uniformity meant that all arbitrations were conducted in the same way; that there were always three (or one) arbitrators; that proceedings were always conducted in an adversarial (or inquisitorial) fashion; that there were always oral hearings (or that arbitrations were sometimes (or always) conducted on the documents) then uniformity certainly does not exist and there is no realistic prospect of it being achieved within any relevant time span. Nor, probably, should this degree of uniformity ever be aimed at since one of the advantages of arbitration is (or should be) its flexibility. Some arbitrations call for little more than for the arbitrator to apply his judgement to a particular fact situation with little or no need for evidence or even argument.[7] In other cases, the desire for a quick and cheap solution may make the case for documents only arbitration practically irresistible.

3. TOWARDS UNIFORMITY

The practical question is whether there should be a move towards the widespread (hopefully eventually universal) acceptance of some general notions, other than the notion of the autonomy of the parties. It is in this direction that the UNCITRAL Model Law on International Commercial Arbitration is clearly aimed. Modern developments of English arbitration law derive from the equivocal response of the United Kingdom to the Model Law which was originally that it should be adopted in Scotland but not in England and Wales. The committee which considered the Model Law was initially chaired by Lord Mustill, not only one of our most distinguished judges but also the joint author of an outstanding book on arbitration of which any professor would be inordinately proud. The committee considered that for England, Wales and Northern

---

[5] Later Lord Diplock permits of a rather more relaxed view of appeals in relation to standard form contracts, because of the importance of getting authoritative legal rulings on the meaning of such contracts.

[6] See Sir M.J. Mustill and S.C. Boyd, *The Law and Practice of Commercial Arbitration in England* (2nd edn., Butterworths, London, 1989), at 600–16 for a more detailed exposition. Section 69 of the Arbitration Act 1996 now states these judge-made rules in statutory form.

[7] So in so-called "Look Sniff" arbitrations, all that is called for is for the arbitrator to inspect the goods and pronounce on their quality. Similarly, in many arbitrations under NHBC guarantees the arbitrator's main function is to inspect the building work and assess its quality.

Ireland the law and practice of arbitration was already extremely well developed and that there would be "undoubted disadvantages in introducing a new and untried regime for international commercial arbitration, with all the transitional difficulties that this would entail, and, at the same time, retaining the present regime for domestic arbitration."[8]

In 1990 Lord Steyn succeeded Lord Mustill as Chairman of the Advisory Committee on Arbitration Law. He was in due course succeeded in his turn by Lord Saville. Few committees perhaps have had three such distinguished and appropriately experienced chairmen in succession. Under Lord Steyn's chairmanship, it would perhaps be fair to say that the Committee edged away from its 1989 recommendations. This is clearly brought out by Lord Steyn's 1993 Freshfields' Arbitration Lecture.[9] Debate revealed that although English arbitration law was rich in many respects, it suffered from serious defects of form. The Acts of 1950, 1975 and 1979 were all still in force but between them they covered only a relatively small part of the field. The answer to many questions had to be found in the case law.

Much work was done, first by a private group, led by Arthur Marriott which led first to attempts to consolidate the existing legislation and then to a much more ambitious attempt to produce legislation which sought to cover the whole area, both that governed by existing legislation and by the case law but also to make changes which would make the whole much more coherent and user-friendly. Much of the drafting was done, in the first instance, by Lord Justice Saville and by Mr Toby Landau before the work was taken on board by the Government and the Parliamentary Counsel's Office.

The approach is very clearly stated in section 1 of the Act, which sets out its general approach clearly but in a way which will surprise most readers of English statutes. It stated:

> 1. The provisions of this Part are founded on the following principles, and shall be construed accordingly-
>> (a) the object of arbitration is to obtain the fair resolution of disputes by an impartial tribunal without unnecessary delay or expense;
>> (b) the parties should be free to agree how their disputes are resolved subject only to such safeguards as are necessary in the public interest;
>> (c) in matters governed by this Part the court should not intervene except as provided by this Part.

4. SALIENT QUESTIONS

For the purpose of stimulating debate, I would like to raise the question as to what the agenda for any programme of uniformity should be. Can we isolate half a dozen general issues on which, if all major countries were agreed, one

---

[8]   The Committee's Report (HMSO, London, 1989), para. 89.
[9]   (1994) 60 *Arbitration* 184.

could view arbitration in any such country with equanimity? Let me try and sketch out a list.

Should a Country have a Separate Law for Domestic Arbitration and International Commercial Arbitration?

Although some of the reasons for choosing arbitration over litigation are common to domestic and international arbitrations, others are not. Both in domestic and international arbitrations the parties are often keen to achieve confidentiality which cannot so readily be achieved where the courts are used. It is sometimes also thought that arbitration is cheaper than litigation, though, in general, I am far from certain that this is correct.[10] If both parties want a speedy resolution of the dispute, arbitration will often be quicker since the parties can choose an arbitrator who is available. Unfortunately, in practice, arbitrations in which both sides want a speedy resolution make up only a small fraction of the whole body of disputes.

In general, international arbitral awards are easier to enforce in other states than international judgments; similarly, it is easier to achieve neutrality in an international arbitration than in litigation in a particular country, particularly, as would usually be the case, if the chosen forum is the country in which the defendant resides and does business. In a domestic contract no-one would choose arbitration in preference to litigation because they thought that the arbitrator would be more certainly neutral between the parties than a judge. In general, this is likely to be true in most countries. On the other hand, although no doubt there are many countries where foreigners can sue local defendants in the courts in complete confidence that the courts will be completely neutral, there are undoubtedly other countries where one would need to be very optimistic to believe that this was going to be the case. So in international commercial contracts there are often excellent reasons for choosing arbitration rather than litigation, so as to guarantee neutrality of the dispute resolver.[11]

"Free Floating" Arbitration

Some writers espouse the view that it is possible, and indeed desirable, to have an arbitral regime which has no connection at all with the court system of any

[10] Certainly in construction arbitrations, where my practical experience lies, I can see no clear evidence that arbitration is cheaper than litigation, though this may be because construction arbitration has tended to follow very closely the model of construction litigation. It may be, though this remains to be proved, that the changes made by the 1996 Act will bring about significant financial savings in construction arbitration.

[11] An area in which litigation tends to have significant advantages is multi party disputes which are common for instance in the construction industry, for example, where the employer blames the contractor and the contractor blames the sub-contractor. It is very desirable that all parties appear before the same tribunal and it is easier for courts to produce this result.

state. Clearly the relationship between the arbitral process and the courts is a key question in domestic arbitration and one in which different states have widely differing traditions. Even in its modern form, which is markedly less interventionist than in the past, English law has a noticeably more assertive role in relation to arbitration than many other systems. There are obvious attractions in an arbitrator being able to "float like a butterfly and sting like a bee" and be free from interference by the local courts, particularly if interference involves setting aside a carefully considered award. On the other hand, arbitrators do not have the powers of the state at their disposal and, at the end of the day, it is hard to see how recalcitrant defendants can be forced to honour awards without some assistance from some courts somewhere.

The Doctrine of Kompetenz/Kompetenz

Does the arbitrator have competence to decide his own jurisdiction? A number of answers are possible.

(a) If the arbitrator's jurisdiction is challenged, it is necessary to apply to the court to decide whether the arbitrator has jurisdiction.
(b) If the arbitrator's jurisdiction is challenged, it is open to the arbitrator to decide whether he has jurisdiction but it is open to a party dissatisfied by the arbitrator's decision that he has jurisdiction to challenge this in the courts.
(c) If the arbitrator decides he has jurisdiction, then indeed he has jurisdiction.

The position of English law before 1996 cannot be said to be wholly clear[12] but the matter is now very clearly dealt with by sections 30, 31 and 32 of the Arbitration Act 1996, which adopt solution (b). This is, in my eyes at least, a perfectly satisfactory rule, provided that the dissatisfied party is required to apply to the court very promptly and, provided further, that the court has effective procedures at its disposal for answering the question very quickly. It is submitted that the 1996 Act has passed this test.

Section 30 provides:

"**30**–(1) Unless otherwise agreed by the parties, the arbitral tribunal may rule on its own substantive jurisdiction, that is, as to-
  (a) whether there is a valid arbitration agreement,
  (b) whether the tribunal is properly constituted, and
  (c) what matters have been submitted to arbitration in accordance with the arbitration agreement.
(2) Any such ruling may be challenged by any available arbitral process of appeal or review or in accordance with the provisions of this Part."

Section 31 provides:

---

[12] See Mustill and Boyd, n. 6 at 108–21.

31–(1) An objection that the arbitral tribunal lacks substantive jurisdiction at the outset of the proceedings must be raised by a party not later than the time he takes the first step in the proceedings to contest the merits of any matter in relation to which he challenges the tribunal's jurisdiction.

A party is not precluded from raising such an objection by the fact that he has appointed or participated in the appointment of an arbitrator.

(2) Any objection during the course of the arbitral proceedings that the arbitral tribunal is exceeding its substantive jurisdiction must be made as soon as possible after the matter alleged to be beyond its jurisdiction is raised.

(3) The arbitral tribunal may admit an objection later than the time specified in subsection (1) or (2) if it considers the delay justified.

(4) Where an objection is duly taken to the tribunal's substantive jurisdiction and the tribunal has power to rule on its own jurisdiction, it may:

(a) rule on the matter in an award as to jurisdiction, or

(b) deal with the objection in its award on the merits

(5) The tribunal may in any case, and shall if the parties so agree, stay proceedings whilst an application is made to the court under section 32 (determination of preliminary point of jurisdiction).

Section 32 provides:

"**32**–(1) The court may, on the application of a party to arbitral proceedings (upon notice to the other parties), determine any question as to the substantive jurisdiction of the tribunal.

A party may lose the right to object (see section 73).

(2) An application under this section shall not be considered unless:

(a) it is made with the agreement in writing of all the other parties to the proceedings, or

(b) it is made with the permission of the tribunal and the court is satisfied:

(i) that the determination of the question is likely to produce substantial savings in costs,

(ii) that the application was made without delay, and

(iii) that there is good reason why the matter should be decided by the court.

(3) An application under this section, unless made with the agreement of all the other parties to the proceedings, shall state the grounds on which it is said that the matter should be decided by the court.

(4) Unless otherwise agreed by the parties, the arbitral tribunal may continue the arbitral proceedings and make an award while an application to the court under this section is pending.

(5) Unless the court gives leave, no appeal lies from a decision of the court whether the conditions specified in subsection (2) are met.

(6) The decision of the court on the question of jurisdiction shall be treated as a judgment of the court for the purposes of an appeal.

But no appeal lies without the leave of the court which shall not be given unless the court considers that the question involves a point of law which is one of general importance or is one which for some other special reason should be considered by the Court of Appeal.

The Severability of the Arbitration Agreement

Suppose the arbitration agreement is contained, as is often the case, in a contract and it is alleged that the contract is void or that it is illegal as contrary to public policy. At one time English courts had substantial difficulties with this question but they have now reached, by judicial decision,[13] the position of Article 16(1) of the Model Law that an arbitration clause which forms part of a contract is an agreement independent of the other terms of the contract so that the invalidity of the rest of the contract does not invalidate the agreement to arbitrate. This principle is now clearly stated in statutory form by section 7 of the 1996 Act which provides:

> 7. Unless agreed by the parties an arbitration agreement which forms or was intended to form part of another agreement (whether or not in writing) shall not be regarded as invalid, non-existent or ineffective because that other agreement is invalid, or did not come into existence or has become ineffective, and it shall for that purpose be treated as a distinct agreement.

Procedure

Presumably, the principle of party autonomy means that the parties and the arbitrator, if they all agree at the beginning, can settle for almost any form of procedure. Whether this extends to throwing dice or tossing coins may perhaps be questioned but the limits of such freedom must, on any view, be wide. What is less clear is to what extent the arbitrator is free to impose procedural rules of his own. This would usually be an academic question where the arbitration is under the rules of an established arbitration centre but, of course, not all arbitrations are. It is certainly one of the paradoxes of English domestic arbitration that, although flexibility is one of the great advantages claimed for arbitration, arbitrators in practice are remarkably reluctant to deviate in any way from the pattern of litigation in the courts. The arguments for trying to escape from these constraints seem to me to be overwhelmingly strong, provided that the need to be fair to both parties is always the first consideration. Section 33 and 34 of the 1996 Act are undoubtedly intended to encourage arbitrators to be innovative in procedural terms. Although the arbitrator cannot do what is unfair at all and cannot make procedural innovations if both parties object, it would seem very likely that a determined arbitrator would often find that the parties are unable to agree to reject his proposed course of action sufficiently quickly to stop him pursuing it.

Section 33 provides:

33–(1) The tribunal shall:

[13] *Harbour Assurance* v. *Kansa General International Insurance* [1993] QB 702.

    (a) act fairly and impartially as between the parties, giving each party a reasonable opportunity of putting his case and dealing with that of his opponent, and

    (b) adopt procedures suitable to the circumstances of the particular case, avoiding unnecessary delay or expense, so as to provide a fair means for the resolution of the matters falling to be determined.

(2) The tribunal shall comply with that general duty in conducting the arbitral proceedings, in its decisions on matters of procedure and evidence and in the exercise of all other powers conferred on it.

Section 34 provides:

34–(1) It shall be for the tribunal to decide all procedural and evidential matters, subject to the right of the parties to agree any matter.

(2) Procedural and evidential matters include:

    (a) when and where any part of the proceedings is to be held;

    (b) the language or languages to be used in the proceedings and whether translations of any relevant documents are to be supplied;

    (c) whether any and if so, what form of written statements of claim and defence are to be used, when these should be supplied and the extent to which such statements can be later amended;

    (d) whether any and if so which documents or classes of documents should be disclosed between and procured by the parties and at what stage;

    (e) whether any and if so what questions should be put to and answered by the respective parties and when and in what form this should be done;

    (f) whether to apply strict rules of evidence (or any other rules) as to the admissibility, relevance or weight of any material (oral, written or other) sought to be tendered on any matters of fact or opinion, and the time, manner and form in which such material should be exchanged and presented;

    (g) whether and to what extent the tribunal should itself take the initiative in ascertaining the facts and the law;

    (h) whether and to what extent there should be oral or written evidence or submissions.

(3) The tribunal may fix the time within which any directions given by it are to be complied with, and may if it thinks fit extend the time so fixed (whether or not it has expired).

Governing Law

Traditionally arbitration agreements provided that the dispute was to be governed by a particular national system of law. Such an agreement might be express or implied. In principle, a choice might be made of one law to control the procedure of the arbitration and of another law to control the substance of the dispute. Certainly when it is a matter of implication courts quite often come to different views about what is to be implied as to these two questions.

    (a) In some countries it has long been the practice to empower arbitrators to decide questions in the light of considerations of equity; or to act as *amiable compositeur*. More recently agreements have provided for the arbitrator to apply not a single national system but general principles of international commercial law or as it is sometimes called the *lex mercatoria*. Indeed, a working group set up by ·UNIDROIT published a set of General Principles for International Commercial Contracts in the hope that parties might either expressly choose them by reference or that arbitrators might find them persuasive evidence of what the *lex mercatoria* actually is.

(b) Traditionally it had been assumed that English law rejects all of these possibilities and insists that the only possibility is to choose the law of a defined jurisdiction.[14] More recently there have been cases which indicate some possible retreat from the most entrenched version of this position.

In *Deutsche Schachtbau-Und Tieafbohrgesellschaft* v. *Ras Al Khaimah National Oil Co.*[15] the choice of law in an arbitration in Switzerland was left to the arbitrators who decided to apply "Internationally accepted principles of law governing contractual relations". There was uncontested evidence that this was a valid choice in Switzerland and the English Court of Appeal held that the agreement was not void for uncertainty.

In *Channel Tunnel Group Ltd* v. *Balfour Beatty Construction Ltd.*[16] the agreement for the construction of the Channel Tunnel provided for reference of disputes to those principles of the English and French Law of Contract which were the same and then to General Principles of International Commercial Law. The House of Lords do not appear to have experienced pain in resolving difficult procedural issues arising out of this agreement and neither of the parties argued that it was void for uncertainty.

The question is now dealt with in any case by section 46 of the Act, which provides:

46–(1) The arbitral tribunal shall decide the dispute:
  (a) in accordance with the law chosen by the parties as applicable to the substance of the dispute, or
  (b) if the parties so agree, in accordance with such other considerations as are agreed by them or determined by the tribunal.
(2) For this purpose the choice of the laws of a country shall be understood to refer to the substantive laws of that country and not its conflict of laws rules.
(3) If or to the extent that there is no such choice or agreement, the tribunal shall apply the law determined by the conflict of laws rules which it considers applicable.

---

[14] Mustill and Boyd, n. 6 at 71–86.
[15] *Deutsche Schachtbau-Und Tieafbohrgesellschaft* v. *Ras Al Khaimah National Oil Co.* [1987] 2 All ER 769.
[16] *Channel Tunnel Group Ltd.* v. *Balfour Beatty Construction Ltd.* [1993] AC 334.

9

GATT/WTO Dispute-Settlement Mechanisms: An Introduction

BERNHARD JANSEN*

1. INTRODUCTION

The disputes handled by the GATT or the WTO dispute-settlement mechanism have been associated by others with "chicken wars" that do not really have a bearing on international relations more generally. This may be true for a number of more technical cases that have arisen under the GATT or the WTO, but such a characterisation does not give the full picture or the full range of the types of disputes that may come under the auspices of the GATT/WTO. The purpose of this section is to highlight a number of recent cases that clearly have a bearing beyond trade. A well-known example is the EC import ban for pelts and skins of baby seals from Canada because of the capturing methods in the North of Canada. Another well-known example is the present dispute between the USA and the EC on the EC import ban on US beef where the cattle were raised with growth promoters (hormones). Yet another "high profile" dispute concerns the US Cuban Liberty and Democratic Solidarity (LIBERTAD) Act, better known by the names of its sponsors in Congress ("Helms/Burton"). Similar disputes have in the past been launched by Nicaragua because of a US trade embargo against its socialist regime, and—last but not least—with regard to the Arab boycott of Israel. In all these cases, the borderline between trade disputes and issues of general foreign policy has probably been passed. It may be that such disputes overstretch the capability of the GATT/WTO dispute-settlement mechanism, but such disputes exist and have been brought to the GATT or the WTO, for better or for worse. Since the inception of the WTO at the beginning of 1995, approximately 60 cases have been submitted to it, 12 of which went to panels and four of which have already been handled by the newly-created Appellate Body.

2. THE BACKGROUND

The GATT/WTO dispute-settlement mechanism has developed over the course of the last 50 years, from its instigation in January 1948 until today. It is not the

* The author is a Legal Advisor in the Legal Service of the European Commission. All views expressed in the present article are personal.

intention to describe this historic development in detail. It should be noted how-ever that GATT dispute settlement has always been somewhat different from dispute-settlement mechanisms developed in other international fora. Moreover, GATT/WTO dispute settlement has the reputation of being rela-tively more efficient than other mechanisms. This has to do, at least in part, with the possibilities offered under this mechanism for arriving at internationally approved remedies which may, in the last resort, take the form of "withdrawal of concessions". This expression is a euphemism for very efficient trade sanc-tions in the form of targeted restrictions, such as a penalising increase of cus-toms duties, by the winning party for products imported from the losing party.

The first dispute-settlement procedures in the GATT were handled by so-called "working parties" composed of the delegations of all interested GATT contracting parties. Since such working parties could only take decisions arrived at on the basis of a consensus embracing all of the participants, it quickly became obvious that the parties to the dispute should not have the same status as other participants in the working parties. Their full and equal participation in working groups, coupled with the consensus rule, combined to prevent them from arriving at decisions within a reasonable period of time. Indeed, in trade matters, "time is money" and interminable discussions are generally considered to be a luxury that nobody can afford. Moreover the working parties tended to take on the appearance of a negotiating forum rather than of an adjudicatory body. In the early 1950s it was felt within the GATT that working parties com-prised of a large number of participants, including the parties to the dispute and normally including some allies of the disputants, did not offer the most efficient mechanism for the handling of disputes. It was at that point in time that the idea of establishing GATT "panels" was developed. The parties to the dispute had to agree both on the establishment of such panels and on their composition but these panels were (and still are) composed not of national delegations, but of trade experts from countries other than the parties to the dispute. Panels were usually composed of either three or five individuals, and this remains the case today. Another feature of early practice, and one which is still the case today, is that the experts appointed as members of a GATT panel could not be of the same nationality as a party to the dispute, unless these parties expressly agreed otherwise. In this respect, GATT/WTO dispute-settlement procedures have always been quite different from normal practice in the area of international arbitration where each of the parties to the dispute appoints one of the arbitra-tors and these two arbitrators subsequently are requested to agree on the chair-person.

Like the original working parties, panels saw their main role in the early years of GATT as being catalysts through which the parties might come to an agreed solution. Since they did not see themselves as adjudicatory bodies, early panel reports are rather poor in legal reasoning, their focus being upon trying to indi-cate an acceptable way forward to the parties to the dispute. In that sense, they were still a particular type of a negotiating forum. However, over time, parties to disputes started to present and argue their cases in a more legally oriented fashion and, in order to try and cope with this development, in the early 1960s the GATT Secretariat established a small legal department which assisted panels on legal questions.

A number of developments took place in the context of the Tokyo Round (1972–9), which led to the first consolidated text concerning dispute-settlement procedures under the GATT. In this text, panel procedures are described as being confidential in nature and intended to assist the GATT Contracting Parties in finding adequate solutions for disputes. In practice, however, it remained possible to delay panel procedures in a number of ways, e.g. by not agreeing to the establishment of a panel in the first place, contesting the composition of a panel, objecting to its terms of reference or, last but not least, not agreeing to the adoption of their reports.

In addition, this mechanism was considered by at least one important GATT contracting party, namely the USA, as not being sufficiently efficient to ensure a speedy resolution of disputes. The US administration came under increasing pressure from Congress, particularly following the adoption of the 1974 Trade Act and its amendments, to exercise pressure on other GATT contracting parties who were, rightly or wrongly, accused of not respecting their obligations under the GATT. In spite of criticism made by others opposed to US "unilateralism", the US administration decided on several occasions to impose trade sanctions against its partners under section 301 and other relevant provisions of the 1974 Trade Act for alleged violations of GATT obligations without resorting to the GATT dispute settlement mechanism. A well-known example is the so-called "hormones" case in which the USA in 1987 imposed trade sanctions on the European Community for an alleged breach of GATT disciplines without having sought to bring the dispute before a GATT panel. The justification given for this behaviour by the USA was that the GATT dispute-settlement procedures were known to be inadequate since they did not guarantee a speedy resolution of disputes. In this context, the tight time limits that are built into section 301 of the Trade Act are also relevant, since they are binding on the US administration.

It was against this background that a policy decision was taken within the framework of the Uruguay Round negotiations (1986–94) that there was a compelling need to improve the GATT dispute-settlement mechanism and to follow a quasi-judicial procedure allowing the "Dispute Settlement Body" to adjudicate upon a dispute in the absence of an agreement between the parties, and that this should occur within certain time limits. (It may be noted in passing that these time limits were surprisingly similar to those laid down in section 301 of the 1974 US Trade Act.) The Uruguay Round negotiators considered this to be the only way to reduce the likelihood of the USA resorting to the temptation to use unilateral mechanisms to resolve trade disputes in their favour. As a counterpart, there is now a firm commitment binding on all WTO Members to resort to the WTO dispute-settlement system whenever a violation of obligations under any of the Agreements coming under the auspices of the WTO is alleged: members are obliged to refrain from resorting to trade sanctions other than those approved by the Dispute Settlement Body in application of the WTO Understanding on the Rules and Procedures Governing the Settlement of Disputes (the DSU).

3. PERTINENT FEATURES OF THE WTO SYSTEM

The most striking features of this new quasi-judicial process are summarised below and may conveniently be considered in the context of the three procedural stages to which disputes are subject. At the first stage, whenever a complaint is submitted to the WTO, a compulsory consultation phase of at least 60 days must be respected. Once the consultation phase has expired, and if the parties to the dispute have not been able to settle the dispute in a mutually acceptable manner, the complaining party has an unconditional right to pass to the second stage of the procedure, meaning that a panel has to be established in order to hear the arguments of the parties. There are tight and precise time limits for the procedure leading to the establishment of the panel, for establishing its composition and terms of reference, and regarding the procedure to be followed in presenting the dispute to the panel once it has been established. In total, these steps should not normally last longer than six months, and in no case longer than nine months. The third stage comes when, after nine months at the latest, the panel has to circulate its report to all Members of the WTO, unless the complaining party requests a suspension of the procedure in the meantime. The panel report, once circulated, will be deemed to have been considered and approved by the WTO Dispute Settlement Body, unless during the course of this stage of the procedure an appeal is filed within 60 days following the circulation of the report.

Appeals are considered by the Appellate Body, which is a new institution created as a result of the Uruguay Round trade negotiations. It is a standing body composed of seven individuals who are appointed for a four-year term of office, with the possibility of that term being extended for a second four-year period. The composition of the Appellate Body is therefore quite different from that of the panels which are composed on an *ad hoc* basis. Appeals to the Appellate Body may only be based on points of law. The Appellate Body must deliver its ruling in a Report to be delivered within 60 to 90 days following the filing of the appeal. These reports are circulated to WTO Members and will be deemed to have been approved by the Dispute Settlement Body once it has been considered in a meeting to be held within 30 days of circulation. The Dispute Settlement Understanding provides that such a report, once approved by the DSB, shall be unconditionally accepted by the parties to the dispute. In sum, the DSU provides that the period from the time of the establishment of a panel until the approval of the report by the DSB shall not exceed nine months if the panel report is not subject to appeal, while that period shall not exceed 12 months in cases where an appeal to the standing Appellate Body does occur.

The next step in the procedure relates to the consequences to be drawn from the adoption of an Appellate Body report or a panel report that has become final in the absence of an appeal. In other words, what remedies are available to the party that was successful on the substance of the dispute? This is another aspect which has seen an important improvement as a result of the Uruguay Round trade negotiations. A final panel report or an Appellate Body report that contains a "recommendation" that the losing party take certain measures must be implemented by that party within a "reasonable time period", which should not normally be longer than 15 months after the adoption of the report. If the parties to the dispute cannot agree what constitutes a reasonable time period in the context of an individual case, compulsory arbitration may be resorted to. The arbitration may be carried out either by a panel or by an individual designated by the parties or, in the absence of an agreement between the parties, by the Director-General of the WTO Secretariat.

Once the "reasonable time period" for the implementation of the recommendations of the report has expired, if the necessary action has not been taken by the losing party, the new dispute-settlement mechanism really starts to bite. In such a case, the losing party has to offer (as a temporary solution) adequate compensation, which may, however, be refused by the winning party. Compensation is expressly considered to be a sufficient remedy only for an interim period, pending the operation of domestic procedures that would ultimately lead to full implementation. If the offer of compensation is refused by the winning party, that party may resort to the "withdrawal of concessions", as was mentioned earlier, which means retaliation by adopting trade-restricting measures which have the aim of hitting the exports of the losing party at a level that is commensurate to the violation committed by that party in the case at hand. Should there be a dispute about the commensurate level of the withdrawal of concessions, there is provision for this to be settled by arbitration as well.

4. CONCLUSION

To sum up, the GATT/WTO dispute settlement has undergone a transformation from being primarily a negotiating forum into a body which has features that are more typical of an adjudicatory mechanism. This has become necessary because of the paramount need of trade operators to achieve legal certainty regarding their rights and obligations with regard to market access in an international trading environment that is increasingly global in nature. The mechanism is, however, still something of a hybrid in nature, oscillating between classic diplomacy and a court-like adjudicatory system. This duality is exemplified by rules of confidentiality: whereas a court of law would normally hold its hearings in public, panels and the Appellate Body hold their hearings behind closed doors; while panels are not even fully accessible to so-called third parties (i.e. WTO Members having a trade interest in the dispute), the Appellate Body has allowed third parties full access to its hearings. On the other hand, while panels under the old GATT tended to lay extraordinary weight on the negotiating history when interpreting the GATT, this tendency has now largely been replaced by other means of interpretation. Indeed, since the inception of the WTO and its new dispute-settlement mechanism, the tendency is now to refer to the Vienna Convention on the Law of Treaties when interpreting the WTO rules, thus putting the weight on the treaty texts themselves rather than on the intentions of the drafters of the treaty, which have become of more historic than practical interest.

10

Environmental Dispute Settlement: Some Reflections on Recent Developments

PHOEBE N. OKOWA

1. INTRODUCTION

The proliferation of international environmental agreements has generated much debate on how the effectiveness of these agreements could be ensured. Much of the debate has been conducted against the background of trenchant criticism of existing mechanisms for dispute settlement in the international system. Doubts have been consistently raised as to the ability of the prevailing mechanisms of international dispute settlement to cope with what were perceived as a radically different order of concerns.[1] The purpose of this chapter is to assess the extent to which environmental disputes raise discrete issues or problems for the adjudicatory methods of dispute settlement that exist in the international system. The first part will summarise the legal and policy arguments that are usually advanced against the practical utility of adjudicatory methods in relation to environmental disputes. The second part will assess the strength of these arguments in light of disputes that have been recently considered by the International Court. An attempt will be made to evaluate some of the practical impediments that inevitably arise when disputes that are inherently multilateral are referred to an adjudicatory structure that is designed to operate in a purely bilateral framework. The final section will consider the significance of new adjudicatory forums, including the value of specialised tribunals.

---

[1] C. Gray, *Judicial Remedies in International Law* (Clarendon Press, Oxford, 1987), at 210; K.B. Hoffman, "State Responsibility in International Law and Transboundary Pollution Injuries", 25 ICLQ 508 at 511; S. McCaffrey, "Transboundary Pollution Injuries: Jurisdictional Considerations in Private Litigation Between Canada and the United States", 3 *California Western International Law Journal* 191; R.B. Bilder, "The Settlement of Disputes in the Field of the International Law of the Environment", 144 *HagueRecueil* 141 at 155; A.E. Boyle, "Saving the World? Implementation and Enforcement of International Law Through International Institutions", 4 *JEL* 229.

2. SOME GENERAL OBJECTIONS ADVANCED AGAINST THE SUITABILITY OF THE ADJUDICATORY METHODS OF DISPUTE SETTLEMENT

One of the principal arguments advanced against the suitability of pre-existing mechanisms rests on the idea that disputes in the field of environmental protection raise technical questions that could only be effectively considered by specialised and innovative tribunals. It has been suggested that the International Court lacks this form of expertise. Critics of the Court envisaged the creation of specialised tribunals which would consist not just of lawyers but other technical experts as well. The case was thus consistently made in some of the literature for the creation of a new specialised tribunal to deal with environmental disputes, and emphasis was regularly placed on alternative methods of dispute resolution.[2] It was suggested that any adaptation of the existing systems of dispute settlement would place unimaginable strain on these mechanisms.

Other specific arguments about the inherent limitations of the adjudicatory framework were also advanced. It was suggested, and perhaps rightly, that existing mechanisms of dispute settlement were designed to deal with bilateral disputes, and that as a result they were an ill-suited mechanism for dealing with the multi-party/multilateral character of environmental disputes.[3] In practice there is little doubt that access to the International Court and other arbitral tribunals is predicated on the vindication of private legal rights and is therefore unsuitable for the protection of community values. Yet most environmental disputes, even in the form of a most straightforward case of transboundary pollution, always affect the interests of other States, say in a clean environment, and a bilateral resolution of such a dispute will invariably marginalise the wider community concerns or what Riphagen has elsewhere referred to as *"extra-state interests"*.[4]

Furthermore, it was suggested that issues such as those raised by the prospect of climate change or the depletion of the ozone layer required a more inclusive approach that would take into account the common nature of the interests involved. A bilateral framework was clearly deemed unsuitable, since it presupposed the existence of a clearly identifiable State with *locus standi* which was not possible in the case of harm to common interests. Traditional international law has always restricted standing to those whose proprietary or economic interests were at stake. Quite apart from the question of community values it was in any case doubtful whether a State would be able to have standing in those

---

[2] E. Lauterpacht, *Aspects of the Administration of International Justice* (Grotius Publications, Cambridge, 1992), at 18; A. Postiglione, "An International Court for the Environment?" (1993), 23/2 *EPL* 73–8; Boyle, n. 1 above, at 229.

[3] On the limitations of the bilateral framework see C. Chinkin, *Third Parties in International Law* (Clarendon Press, Oxford, 1993), at 148; Lauterpacht, n. 2 above, at 62; J. Brunnée, "Non-compliance Procedures in Multilateral Environmental Agreements: The Example of the Montreal Protocol on Substances that Deplete The Ozone Layer" [1977], *ASIL/NVIR, Proceedings*, 364.

[4] W. Riphagen, "State Responsibility: New Theories of Obligation in Interstate Relations" in R. St. J. MacDonald and D. M. Johnston (eds), *The Structure and Process of International Law* (Martinus Nijhoff, The Hague, 1983) p. 581 esp. at 602.

instances where, although it has suffered no proprietary harm, there has nevertheless occurred a detrimental alteration in the quality of its environment.

Implicit in some of these arguments was a concern that the role of dispute-settlement forums should not be limited to adjudication of private law rights, but that tribunals should also assume a general supervisory role in ensuring that those on whom obligations are imposed conform to the prescribed standards of conduct. Doubts were also expressed as to viability of adjudicatory mechanisms in the absence of a coherent body of substantive law.[5] It was pointed out that litigation would raise formidable problems of defining and assessing actionable harm, victims, causation, and unacceptable risk.[6] The utility of adjudicatory methods was particularly doubted because environmental damage was invariably due to multiple causes, and usually the result of cumulative processes of degradation over a long period of time.[7] It was suggested that even in the context of domestic law, harm to the environment usually attracted very high damage awards, and that in the international context, cleanup costs and the varied nature of damages would in any case be beyond the compensation capacity of any State.

Most threats to the environment are attributable to the activities of private entities operating on state territory. States have therefore exhibited a marked reluctance to assume responsibility for the activities of these private operators. Thus one finds in a large number of environmental treaties a rejection of traditional methods of state-based dispute-settlement mechanisms and an increased preference for private law solutions.[8] This is the approach taken in the nuclear civil liability conventions[9] and the conventions dealing with oil pollution from ships.[10] In reply to a report of the Working Group of the International Law Commission circulated to governments for comment, the United States opposed any system of direct state accountability, stressing that such responsibility could only work in highly centralised economies where state regulation of private enterprise was the norm.[11]

[5] I. Brownlie, "A Survey of International Customary Rules of Environmental Protection" in L.A. Teclaff and A.E. Utton, *International Environmental Law* (Praeger Publishers, New York, 1974), at 1; N. Singh, *The Role and Record of the International Court of Justice* (Nijhoff, Dordrecht, 1989), at 165; Hoffman, n. 1 above.

[6] P. Sands, *Principles of International Environmental Law* (Manchester University Press, Manchester, 1994), i, at 641; I. Brownlie, "General Course of International Law", 255 *Hague Recueil* 190; A. Hurrell and B. Kingsbury, *The International Politics of the Environment* (Clarendon Press, Oxford, 1992), at 26.

[7] Brownlie, n. 5 above.

[8] P.W. Birnie and A.E. Boyle, *International Law and the Environment* (Clarendon Press, Oxford, 1992), at 137; McCaffrey, n. 1 above, at 191.

[9] See Paris Convention on Third Party Liability in the Field of Nuclear Energy (1961), 55 AJIL 1082; The 1963 Vienna Convention on Civil Liability for Nuclear Damage [1962–3] ILM 727.

[10] See generally, McCaffrey, n. 1 above, at 191; 1969 International Convention on Civil Liability for Oil Pollution Damage, 9 ILM 45, amended by a 1976 Protocol: 16 ILM 617; The 1971 Convention on the Establishment of an International Fund for Compensation for Oil Pollution Damage, 11 ILM 284; The 1969 Tanker Owners Voluntary Agreement on Liability for Oil Pollution (TOVALOP), 8 ILM 497 and the 1974 Offshore Pollution Liability Agreement (OPOL), 13 ILM 1409.

[11] International Liability for Injurious Consequences Arising Out of Acts Not Prohibited by International Law, Comments and Observations received by Governments UNDOC. A/CN 4/481, 14 April 1997, p. 6.

The absence of retrospective remedies either in the form of specific performance or injunction was also seen as a major limitation of the adjudicatory process.[12] It was suggested that a system that hinged heavily on delictual responsibility and which was primarily concerned with compensation after the event was not the most effective way of dealing with things that ought not to happen in the first place. In other words, remedies that were retrospective in character were an ill-suited mechanism for dealing with public-order concerns that could not be compensated by the award of damages.[13] Other suggestions made called for a reconceptualising of international dispute settlement, and moving it away from being a state-centred system towards a more broadly-based regime that would accommodate the interests of individuals, international organisations, and non-governmental organisations.[14] Here the emphasis has been on the establishment of a free-standing international environmental court, which would have special jurisdiction to protect community interests.[15]

Many of these concerns were raised in a wide range of literature as well as in the practice of States at a time when the International Court had not been asked to consider any overtly environmental issues. The picture has changed somewhat and the Court has in the last few years been asked to consider a wide range of environmental arguments in disputes before it. The purpose of this chapter is to evaluate the jurisprudence of the International Court against the background of some of these earlier concerns. What is immediately apparent is that there is no evidence to date of the inherent unsuitability of the International Court, and everything seems to turn on the precise nature of issues before the court. There of course remain a considerable range of practical and conceptual problems in the resolution of environmental disputes within an adjudicatory framework. However, as the cases discussed illustrate, issues pertaining to the protection of the environment have no clear boundaries and usually arise alongside other questions of international law.

3. THE INTERNATIONAL COURT OF JUSTICE AND ENVIRONMENTAL DISPUTES

The International Court may be faced with a dispute relating to environmental protection in a number of ways. In the first place the Court may be asked to adjudicate on a dispute in which the whole essence of the claim is about environmental protection. The Court will in this instance be pronouncing on the illegality or impermissibility of a particular course of conduct by reference primarily to environmental norms. This may be referred to as the *classical environmental dispute*.

---

[12] Gray, n. 1 above, at 64–6, 95; Brownlie, n. 5 above, at 191; Birnie and Boyle, n. 7 above, at 150–1; Hurrell and Kingsbury, n. 6 above, at 26.

[13] Gray, n. 1 above, at 64–6; Brownlie, n. 5 above, at 191; Hurrell and Kingsbury, n. 5 above, at 26; Sir Robert Jennings and Sir Arthur Watts, *Oppenheim's International Law* (Longman, London, 1992), i, pt. 1, at 415.

[14] Postiglione, n. 2 above, at 74; Lauterpacht, n. 2 above, at 62.

[15] *Ibid.*

Alternatively the Court may be asked to rule upon an issue or group of issues which do not in themselves raise questions of environmental protection, but where legality or illegality of a particular cause of action has to be determined by reference to environmental standards. The context may be the legality of the use of a particular weapon, the permissibility of which is then tested by way of *renvoi* to environmental norms. In these instances the environmental standard is usually incidental to a claim under some other head of responsibility.

Few cases raising questions of environmental protection in a direct manner have come before the Court. In fact most of the cases that have come before the court have only raised environmental issues in an incidental manner, where the principal claim is grounded in some other head of responsibility.

Some Recent Cases Raising Issues of Environmental Protection

In the *Advisory Opinion Concerning the Legality of Nuclear Weapons*,[16] the Court was asked by the General Assembly, among other things, whether legal obligations concerning environmental protection had to be taken into account in determining the legality of the use of force. In particular the Court had to consider whether an alleged right to use nuclear weapons was incompatible with the requirements of environmental law given the very serious and devastating effects of such weapons. The Court concluded that developments in the field of environmental law and obligations assumed by States in that context had to be taken into account. It noted that "respect for the environment is one of the elements that go to assessing whether an action is in conformity with the principles of necessity and proportionality"[17] which are basic requirements for a lawful use of force.

In its request to the International Court for an advisory opinion, the World Health Organisation asked the Court to rule on whether "in view of the health and environmental effects, . . . the use of nuclear weapons by a state in war or other armed conflict [would] be a breach of its obligations under international law including the WHO Constitution".[18] The Court was thus again being asked to consider the legal consequences of environmental obligations, and in particular whether they placed any practical restraints on the methods of warfare. The Court declined to give an opinion.[19] In refusing to respond to the request, it noted that questions concerning the legality or illegality of nuclear weapons did not fall within the WHO's sphere of operation as required by Article 96(2) of the UN Charter. It is nevertheless significant that the Court was being asked to consider the compatability of the use of nuclear weapons with environmental obligations.

---

[16] *Legality of the Threat or Use of Nuclear Weapons*, Advisory Opinion, ICJ Reports 1996, 226.
[17] *Ibid.*, 242.
[18] *Legality of the Use by a State of Nuclear Weapons in Armed Conflict*, Advisory Opinion, ICJ Reports 1996, 66 at 73.
[19] In their dissenting opinions Judges Weeramantry and Koroma were unequivocally of the view that obligations in the field of environmental protection placed restraints on the methods and means of waging warfare. See *ibid.*, at 143 and 215 respectively.

In the *Nauru* case,[20] the Court was principally asked to consider the responsibility of Australia as administering authority, for its failure to comply with the principles and standards of the legal regime of trusteeship in relation to the administration of the Trust Territory of Nauru. The items of loss in respect of which Nauru was seeking compensation included costs of rehabilitating damaged lands, which had been rendered completely unusable as a result of phosphate mining. The case was subsequently withdrawn and settled by the parties out of court (no doubt as a result of pressure brought to bear on Australia by the prospect of losing the case). It is nevertheless significant that the Court was considered by the applicant as an appropriate forum for the determination of the relevant legal issues including compensation for harm to the environment. Although the case was an important one from the perspective of environmental protection, it is also clear that environmental questions were intertwined with other questions of general international law arising from the regime of trusteeship.

The *Gabčikovo-Nagymaros* Project (Hungary/Slovakia)

The dispute between Hungary and Slovakia[21] concerning the construction and operation of the *Gabčikovo-Nagymaros* barrage system is widely perceived as the first major environmental dispute to come before the Court. Yet on closer analysis it is immediately apparent that the dispute was concerned with a wide range of international law questions in respect of which the environmental arguments may be described as incidental.

The main issue in respect of which the Court was asked to give an answer was whether Hungary was entitled to terminate its treaty with Slovakia and to refuse to complete the construction of that part of their joint project which the treaty had attributed to it. The project had provided for the construction of a system of locks on the Danube which was to be used for the purpose of hydro-electricity production, flood control and improvement of navigation.

Hungary, it will be recalled justified its termination on various grounds under the law of treaties, including fundamental change of circumstances, and subsequently imposed requirements of international law, these being development of legal norms in the field of environmental protection. It also invoked the principle of "supervening impossibility of performance" as a ground of non-performance. Under this head, it argued that the project was ecologically unsound, and that it was unrealistic to expect it to undertake the completion of a project that entailed serious environmental damage for its territory and its people.[22]

---

[20] *Certain Phosphate Lands in Nauru (Nauru v. Australia)*, Memorial of the Republic of Nauru, Vol. 1, Apr. 1990.

[21] *Gabčikovo-Nagymaros Project (Hungary/Slovakia)*, Judgment, ICJ Reports 1997, not yet reported.

[22] Memorial of the Republic of Hungary, Vol. 1, 2 May 1994, 258–315. Hungary also argued that the treaty had been concluded in furtherance of the principle of socialist integration and under Soviet pressure and that as a result of the radical political and economic circumstances that had

The Court was also asked to determine whether, in the specific circumstances of the bilateral treaty, it could be argued that Slovakia had succeeded to the obligations of Czechoslovakia in accordance with the law of state succession. It was Hungary's principal argument that as the obligations in the treaty were yet to be executed, they could not be regarded as attaching to the territory, and therefore automatically binding on Slovakia as the successor State.[23]

Hungary laid emphasis on the likely environmental damage that the project could give rise, to, and the fact that the nature of these risks had not been evaluated through appropriate environmental-impact assessment procedures. The case is also interesting because it is the first case in which the International Court has been directly asked for orders of specific performance; Slovakia's basic argument was that the termination of the treaty was illegal and Hungary should be ordered to complete the construction of that part of project that the treaty attributed to it.[24] Hungary on the other hand argued that Slovakia's unilateral decision to proceed with a modified form of the project in the face of opposition from Hungary was illegal, and that the Court should order Slovakia to dismantle the project and restore the waters of the Danube to their original state.[25]

So in an indirect way the Court was being called upon to pronounce on the legal implications of developments in the environmental field. Seen in a broader context there is nothing inherently *environmental* about the dispute; it is fact raises a multiplicity of international law questions. At least if there is one thing to be learned from this case it is the fact that, since issues of environmental protection permeate most activities of States and in a wide variety of fields, a large number of environmental issues are going to be raised before the ICJ in this manner. Many questions of state obligations will be decided upon by the Court without any formal characterisation of the obligations as environmental and in relation to disputes which at first sight cannot be characterised as environmental. In this context the ICJ is no less suitable than a specially constituted environmental tribunal.

Nuclear Tests Cases (New Zealand v. France)

The 1995 *Nuclear Tests Cases*[26] brought by New Zealand against France could in principle be characterised as distinctly "environmental". It is true that the formal application was on a narrow point, asking the Court to consider whether circumstances had arisen which necessitated the application and a formal

---

taken place in Eastern Europe, it was no longer under a duty to comply with the terms of a treaty that was not economically viable and was in any case an ecological disaster.

[23] Memorial of the Republic of Hungary, n. 21 above, 321.
[24] Memorial Submitted by the Slovak Republic, Vol. 1, 2 May 1994, 358.
[25] Memorial of the Republic of Hungary, n. 21 above, 338.
[26] *Request for an Examination of the Situation in Accordance with Paragraph 63 of the Court's Judgment of 20 December 1974 in the Nuclear Tests (New Zealand) v. France) Case*, ICJ Reports 1995, 288.

reconsideration of the Court's 1973 judgment.[27] Had the case gone to the merits phase, one of the questions which would have arisen for consideration was whether French underground tests were compatible with its obligations to protect environment under treaty and customary law.

It was New Zealand's argument that any resumption of nuclear testing in the South Pacific was totally unacceptable and contrary to environmental and political developments. New Zealand, in addition to contesting the legality of the French nuclear tests *per se*, also argued that France was under a customary law duty to carry out environmental-impact assessments before proceeding with the conduct of the tests as required by the Noumea Convention,[28] and at customary law.[29] In its judgment of 22 September 1995, the International Court ruled that the basis of its 1974 decision in the *Nuclear Tests (New Zealand v. France)* case had not been affected as required by paragraph 63 of that judgment and that it therefore lacked competence to re-open the dispute which had been declared moot in 1974. That the new application was concerned with underground nuclear tests while the 1974 case was exclusively concerned with atmospheric nuclear tests.[30]

It is nevertheless clear from the pleadings and the pronouncements by the Court that there was nothing inherently technical or radically different about this case to require consideration by the environmental chamber or a more specialised tribunal. In fact in their dissenting opinions, Judges Weeramantry, Koroma and Sir Geoffrey Palmer, eloquently considered the legal consequences of the environmental obligations assumed by France in treaty and customary law.[31]

4. COMMUNITY CONCERNS AND BILATERAL DISPUTES

There are nevertheless certain worrying features of the *Nuclear Tests* cases which go to show that in many ways the multi-faceted nature of environmental disputes is bound to place considerable strain on an institution largely structured to deal with bilateral issues on a private-rights basis. Like in the 1974 case, no fewer than five States sought to intervene, in each case arguing that their own legal interests were affected by the French nuclear tests. Applications for intervention in broadly identical terms were received from the governments of

---

[27] *Nuclear Tests (New Zealand v. France)*, Judgment, ICJ Reports 1974, 457.

[28] Convention for the Protection of Natural Resources and the Environment of the South Pacific (1986), 26 ILM 38.

[29] *Aide Mémoire*, 21 Aug. 1995, 17; see also *Verbatim Record*, 12 Sept. 1995, CR95/20; for comment, see P.N. Okowa, "Procedural Obligations in International Environmental Agreements", 67 *BYIL* 329.

[30] *Request for an Examination of the Situation in Accordance with Paragraph 63 of the Court's Judgment of 20 December 1974 in the Nuclear Tests (New Zealand v. France) Case*, ICJ Reports 1995, 288 at 306.

[31] *Ibid.*, at 317 (Judge Weeramantry), 363 (Judge Koroma) and 381 (Judge *ad hoc* Sir Geoffrey Palmer).

Australia, Samoa, Solomon Islands, Marshall Islands and Federated States of Micronesia.[32]

In its application for permission to intervene, Australia argued that the obligations owed by France to New Zealand had an *erga omnes* character, with the consequence that all States had a right to participate in the proceedings. The application observed in part that, "while the dispute between New Zealand and France is bilateral, it remains the case that in determining the merits of the New Zealand claim, the Court would necessarily be required to pronounce on the rights of all states. The legal interests of every member of the international Community, even of those States not bound by the judgment, are thus 'affected' or 'encause' within the meaning of Article 62 of the Statute."[33] In invoking the jurisdiction of the Court in 1973, New Zealand had also argued that the French nuclear tests violated its right, as well as those of other States, to be free from the risks associated with radioactive contamination especially in the marine environment.[34] As a result all States were entitled to challenge the legality of the French tests.

The Australian application for intervention must be seen as a rather bold attempt to expand its scope. The interventions that have taken place to date have been largely singular in form, usually at the instance of a single state articulating a narrow circumscribed interest.[35] There is nothing in the structure of the Court to indicate that the intervention was designed as a forum for the vindication of wider community values.[36] The International Court has itself in the *Gulf of Fonseca* case[37] indicated the very limited purpose and scope of intervention. According to the Court the intervening State is not formally regarded as a party to the disputes, its rights being limited to what is necessary to protect its interests. It is therefore not be bound by the judgment. Intervention cannot therefore be regarded as an appropriate mechanism for protecting community values. Although the Australian argument was novel, its logic as a matter of principle is immediately apparent. It seems pointless to have a developed concept of *erga omnes* obligations without putting into place any procedural mechanisms for their enforcement.

---

[32] *Ibid.*, 292. The text of the applications are reproduced in *French Nuclear Testing in the Pacific* (New Zealand Ministry of Foreign Affairs and Trade, Wellington, 1996), at 98–125.

[33] Application for Permission to Intervene submitted by the Government of Australia, 23 Aug. 1995, para. 20.

[34] *ICJ Pleadings, Nuclear Tests*, Vol. II, 143, at 209–10 (para. 207).

[35] *Land, Island and Maritime Frontier Dispute (El Salvador/Honduras: Nicaragua Intervening)*, Judgment, ICJ Reports 1992, 351; *Continental Shelf (Tunisia/Libyan Arab Jamahiriya)*, Application for Permission to Intervene, Judgment, ICJ Reports 1981, 3; *Continental Shelf (Libyan Arab Jamahiriya/Malta)*, Application for Permission to Intervene, Judgment, ICJ Reports 1984, 3.

[36] For the argument that intervention in the public interest may be justifiable see the dissenting opinion of Judge Schwebel, *Military and Paramilitary Activities in and against Nicaragua (Nicaragua v. United States)*, Declaration of Intervention, ICJ Reports 1984, 215 at 223; Chinkin, n. 3 above, at 215.

[37] *Land, Island and Maritime Frontier Dispute (El Salvador/Honduras: Nicaragua Intervening)*, Judgment, ICJ Reports 1992, 351.

Since an intervening State is not as such bound by the judgment of the Court given in a case in which it sought to intervene, the benefits of such intervention are limited.[38] For instance in the *Nuclear Tests* cases it would have been incumbent on the intervening States to institute separate proceedings, especially if they had desired to obtain compensation against France for the harm suffered. This raises the prospect of serial litigation, with all the attendant consequences of excessive costs, delay and the risk of conflicting judgments.

In any case it is not clear that Australia or any of the States that sought intervention would have been allowed to institute separate proceedings. The rights they were relying on were owed to all States, and it is very likely that such proceedings could be viewed as an attempt to circumvent the unavailability of an *actio popularis* through a wide formulation of legal interest. The International Court has categorically stated elsewhere that the international system does not as such recognise the right of any member of the international community to vindicate the public interest.[39]

The limited nature of the right of intervention and the general bar to *actio popularis* means that large areas of state activity or those under state control that cause harm to the global environment will be immune from censure, for the sole reason that they affect collective interests, and under circumstances where no State could claim that its proprietary or specific legal interests have been infringed. It is unfortunate that restricted access to the International Court through a narrow formulation of "standing" should remain the norm, despite the fact that such restrictions on standing are generally on the decline in most domestic legal systems and other international fora.[40] The view has been taken in the context of domestic litigation that the law must create a framework for protecting social, non-economic and other community values which cannot be protected through the private-rights model.[41]

Yet even in those cases where States have identifiable proprietary interests, the framework of the International Court is not always the most appropriate for the articulation of those interests. The unsuitability of the Court structure is particularly marked in respect of those injuries that affect a multiplicity of potential claimants. The problem posed by multi-party disputes is most poignantly illustrated by the Chernobyl nuclear accident.[42] In that case it will be recalled that no fewer than 20 States were affected by the accident. No case was formally brought before an international tribunal, the affected States no doubt

[38] But for the view that intervention serves an important remedial function, see J.G. Merrills, Ch. 3 of this vol.

[39] *South West Africa*, Second Phase, Judgment, ICJ Reports 1966, 6 at 47, para. 88.

[40] See D. Robinson and J. Dunkley, *Public Interest Perspectives in Environmental Law* (Wiley Chancery, London, 1995); C. Chinkin, "New Forms of International Dispute Resolution" in *ASIL/NVIR*, n. 3 above, 368 at 370.

[41] See P. Stein, "A Specialist Environmental Court: An Australian Experience" in Robinson and Dunkley, n. 39 above, at 256.

[42] For an illuminating account of the accident and its legal consequences, see P. Sands, *Chernobyl: Law and Communication* (Grotius Publications, Cambridge, 1988).

deterred by the uncertainties concerning the applicable law, as well as inherent difficulties in proving causation. Nevertheless the case also illustrates that where the harm suffered affects a large number of States, the resulting disputes cannot realistically be accommodated within a bilateral framework, access to which is based on the consent of States.[43] In the absence of some flexible rules concerning joinder of parties, it is unlikely that the International Court will be able to deal with these multiple disputes in a comprehensive or satisfactory manner. Furthermore, it remains the case that litigation within an *inter partes* framework is not at all suited to the comprehensive evaluation of extra-state interests; thus where the resulting harm also affects community values these will remain unprotected in any resulting litigation under the present system.

The dispositive part of the judgement in the *Gabčikovo-Nagymaros* dispute also points to the limitations of the Court when faced with issues that call for the evaluation of technical or scientific evidence. An impressive range of scientific and technical arguments on the ecological consequences of the proposed project were presented before the Court. It will be recalled that the thrust of the Hungarian argument was that the project as conceived was environmentally unsound and incompatible with the customary and treaty law obligations. Slovakia, on the other hand, maintained that the treaty regime contained an acceptable framework for evaluating the environmental risks, and such risks as there were had properly been taken into account. The Court, however, refrained from giving an opinion on which of those arguments was scientifically better founded, maintaining that such a choice would not assist it in answering the questions put to it.[44] This was a curious position, since the environmental effect of the project was central to the arguments advanced by both parties, and was in fact the essence of the dispute. It is unfortunate that the Court did not find it necessary to make use of technical assessors, provision for which is made in Articles 30 and 50 of the Statute.[45] Furthermore, although the dispute involved a major international watercourse, nowhere in the judgment does the Court pay any regard to the interests of the other Danube riparian States. While the future direction of the Court in relation to disputes that call for the evaluation of complex scientific evidence in the environmental context must remain a matter of speculation, the precedent set by the *Gabčikovo-Nagymaros* Dam dispute calls at best for cautious optimism.

---

[43] Art. 36(2) of the Statute of the International Court of Justice; Lauterpacht, n. 2 above, at 18.

[44] *Gabčikovo-Nagymaros Project (Hungary/Slovakia)*, Judgment, ICJ Reports 1997, not yet reported, para. 54.

[45] G. White, "The Use of Experts by the International Court" in V. Lowe and M. Fitzmaurice, *Fifty Years of the International Court of Justice* (Cambridge University Press, Cambridge, 1996), at 528.

5. THE ICJ CHAMBER ON ENVIRONMENTAL DISPUTES

In 1993 the International Court, invoking its powers under Article 26(1) of its Statute, decided to set up a technical chamber to deal with environmental disputes. The press release issued by the Court at the time of the establishment of the chamber clearly indicated that the Court wanted to be prepared for a category of disputes that were perceived as technical, and therefore calling for a certain level of expertise.[46] No dispute has been referred to the chamber and a number of criticisms may be levelled at this approach.

First, access to the chamber is subject to the same restrictions that govern access to the Court generally. There is no evidence to suggest that the chamber procedures would be expedient, cheaper or informal. Moreover in its present form, it has not in any way broadened access by allowing non-state actors to be parties to disputes before it, nor is it competent to protect community interests in those instances where the private law rights of States are not at stake.

Furthermore, it could be argued that since the substantive law in this field is still in an inchoate state, and many of the norms have not been defined with any degree of precision, it would have made sense if the first wave of environmental disputes were considered by the full court and that a chamber should be established only after a reasonably coherent jurisprudence was in place. The technical aspects of the dispute could be resolved through consultations with assessors and other technical experts, which it has been noted are expressly provided for under the Court's Statute.[47]

It is also not immediately apparent that those members of the Court who have been selected to date to serve on the Chamber possess particular expertise in environmental matters. The original members of the Chamber elected by the Court in July 1993 were Judges Schwebel, Bedjaoui, Evensen, Shahabuddeen, Weeramantry, Ranjeva, Herczegh. Of these, it is true that Judges Schwebel and Evensen had served as ILC Rapporteurs on the law of Non-navigational Uses of International Watercourses. However there is little evidence that the other members of the Chamber selected to date possessed wide expertise in environmental matters.[48]

It also remains uncertain precisely what method would be used to characterise a dispute as environmental. What happens if the parties choose to refer to the environmental chamber a dispute which in substance cannot be described as environmental? Do parties have a free hand in referring the dispute to the chamber, for instance because they prefer the composition of the chamber? Will the

---

[46] ICJ Communiqué No. 93/20, 19 July 1993.

[47] See Arts. 30 and 50 of the Court's Statute.

[48] For the view that members of the Chamber possess appropriate green credentials, see E. Valencia-Ospina, "The Use of Chambers of the International Court of Justice" in Lowe and FitzMaurice, n. 44 above, at 522, n. 57. The mandate of the Chamber was renewed for a second term, with Judge Fleischhauer replacing Judge Evensen. See ICJ Communiqué No. 94/10, 14 Mar. 1994.

Chamber be prepared to decline a dispute on the basis that it is not the appropriate forum and that the matter should go before the full Court?

There is little doubt that the philosophy underlying the creation of the environmental Chamber was in many ways no different from those extolled by proponents of a free-standing environmental court. However in its present form the Chamber does not appear to be an improvement on the existing adversarial process before the full Court.

6. IS THERE A DISTINCT ROLE FOR TECHNICAL/SPECIALISED FORA?

There is considerable support in some of the literature for the use of specialised tribunals, especially for the settlement of technical disputes.[49] The argument in this context is that, given the wide range of subject matter covered by environmental disputes as well as the very different contexts in which such disputes arise, their resolution can only effectively be realised if they are considered in specialised forums staffed with the requisite expertise.[50] It is also said that quite apart from the question of expertise such forums are likely to be cheap and informal, thus facilitating the settlement of a wide range of disputes. In other contexts, such as in the human rights field where specialised tribunals are widely used, restrictions to access on the basis of specific legal interests are dispensed with. Instead States are generally entitled to bring any action as long as it is designed to ensure general compliance with the relevant treaty obligations.[51]

It has also been suggested that most environmental disputes call for no more than objective evaluation of facts as to the environmental effects of a proposed activity. As the *Gabčikovo-Nagymaros* case illustrates, there may be conflicting scientific evidence as to the effects of a proposed course of conduct. Such disputes it is suggested may be more suited to an inquisitorial than an adversarial process. The argu-

---

[49] The term "tribunal" is used widely and refers to all authoritative legal mechanisms for the settlement of disputes apart from the traditional court system. See, generally, I.A. Shearer, *Starke's International Law* (Butterworths, London, 1994), at 446; Gray, n. 1 above, at 149; C. Gray and B. Kingsbury "Developments in Dispute Settlement: Inter-State Arbitration since 1945", 63 *BYIL* 97; see also the Implementation Committee established under Art. 8 of the 1985 Montreal Protocol on Substances that Deplete the Ozone Layer, 26 ILM 1550; on the Implementation Committee see M. Koskenienni, "Breach of Treaty or Non-Compliance? Reflections on the Enforcement of the Montreal Protocol", 3 *YBIEL* 123. See also the special arbitral procedure for the settlement of disputes relating to the protection of the marine environment provided for under Art. 287 of the 1982 Law of the Sea Convention. See A.E. Boyle, "Dispute Settlement and the Law of the Sea Convention: Problems of Fragmentation and Jurisdiction", 46 *ICLQ* 37.

[50] For the suggestion that environmental disputes are appropriate candidates for consideration by technical forums see Gray and Kingsbury, n. 48 above, at 135; Lauterpacht, n. 2 above, at 18.

[51] See, e.g., Art. 44 of the Inter-American Convention on Human Rights which provides that "any person or group of persons, or any non-governmental entity legally recognized in one or more member states of the Organization, may lodge petitions with the Commission containing denunciations or complaints of violation of this convention by a State Party". *Actio popularis* is also an important feature of the enforcement mechanisms that exist under the EC Treaty: see Arts. 164, 169 and 173 of the EC Treaty; see also D. Wyatt and A. Dashwood, *Substantive Law of the European Communities* (Sweet and Maxwell, London, 1993), at 109.

ment here is that disputes of that nature are better handled by institutions not wedded to *inter partes* combat inherent in the adversarial process.

That there may be some merits in alternative methods of dispute resolution is not in doubt. The limitations inherent in the adjudicatory structure of the International Court have already been noted. However, it seems that there is little agreement on the precise method that should be adopted. There are those who argue that, given the varied nature and different contexts in which environmental disputes arise, it would be unrealistic to expect that they can all be satisfactorily accommodated in one forum. The suggestion here is for the creation of distinct specialised tribunals set up by reference to the subject matter. The second approach sees all environmental disputes as one distinct category, raising broadly similar issues. It is then argued that, in order to prevent the fragmentation of disputes as well as of the applicable substantive law, all such disputes should be referred to the same forum. Proponents of this approach have repeatedly called for the creation of a free-standing environmental court with jurisdiction to resolve disputes referred to it by States as well as non-state actors.[52]

Although no free-standing environmental court has been created to date,[53] provision for dispute-settlement forums of a specialised character is increasingly made in treaty regimes. These usually have a limited mandate, being created as part of the overall framework for the implementation of that particular treaty. The approach has, for instance, been adopted in the 1982 Law of the Sea Convention. Under Article 287 disputes relating to the protection of the marine environment may be referred to the special arbitral procedure provided for in Annex VIII.[54] The United Nations Environment Programme is required to maintain a list from which a choice of arbitrators may be made. Some disputes of an environmental character that arise in the field of nuclear energy are also considered by special tribunals, such as those envisaged under Article 27 of the European Energy treaty.[55] Dispute-settlement frameworks such as those created under the auspices of the WTO are also increasingly used to settle those disputes which raise questions about the compatibility of trade agreements with environmental standards.[56]

It may be asked at this stage whether the creation of a free-standing environmental court will necessarily facilitate the better protection of the environment. It is suggested that the alleged benefits of a specialised court rests on several untested assumptions. First, that existing mechanisms are overburdened and that the creation of a new tribunal is the minimum required if a wide range of

---

[52] Sir Robert Jennings, "Need for Environmental Court?" (1992) 22/5/6 *EPL* at 312–14; Postiglione, n. 2 above, at 73–8; M. Fitzmaurice, "Environmental Protection and the International Court" in Lowe and Fitzmaurice, n. 44 above, at 302.

[53] The nearest equivalent is the Chamber established by the ICJ to consider environmental disputes, for which see ICJ Communiqué No. 93/20, 19 July 1993.

[54] See Boyle, n. 48 above.

[55] 33 ILM 360 (1995) at p. 401.

[56] See Sands, n. 5 above, at 687.

disputes are to be submitted to adjudication. In truth States have exhibited a marked reluctance to resort to binding forms of dispute settlement, and disputes in the field of environmental protection are no exception. The virtually unused ICJ chamber on environmental disputes bears testimony to this reluctance, and it is not immediately obvious why the picture should change through the creation of a new court.

Secondly, such a specialised environmental court would only make a difference if States parties to it were prepared to broaden access and extend standing to a wide category of litigants. It is widely accepted that the main actors in the environmental field are NGOs, individuals and corporations. It is the activities of these categories of actors that impact most directly on the environment. Moreover, it has already been noted that in relation to environmental damages such as those due to climate change or depletion of the ozone layer, no particular litigant would be able to establish a legal interest for the purpose of invoking the jurisdiction of the International Court. Extension of standing to permit litigation in the public interest must therefore be an indispensable part of any new arrangements. This may take the form of empowering an international organisation such as UNEP with the mandate to institute litigation in the public interest. UNEP would in this instance be performing a role not dissimilar to that performed by the European Commission in relation to the general enforcement and supervision of compliance with European Community law. However, if experience in the human rights field is anything to go by, it is clear that there is no general political will to allow non-state actors direct access to dispute-settlement forums.

The case for a specialised tribunal also rests on the rather dubious assumption that a broad range of legal and technical expertise can be effectively achieved in the composition of a single tribunal. Given the varied nature of the subject matter of most environmental disputes, as well as the different contexts in which they arise, it is unlikely that the requisite expertise can be determined beforehand. In this regard the procedure for the use of technical assessors that already exists in the ICJ Statute is to be preferred. The procedure, it will be recalled, enables the ICJ to make use of use of technical assessors as and when the circumstances of the dispute require. In any case, the argument has already been made that although environmental disputes have an identifiable core, in practice the disputes are usually intertwined with other questions of international law and cannot be determined in isolation.[57] The *Gabčíkovo-Nagymaros* dispute bears testimony to this fact.

7. SOME CONCLUSIONS

It is suggested that there is little evidence that existing dispute-settlement mechanisms are unable to cope with environmental disputes as a distinct category.

[57] Jennings, n. 51 above; Fitzmaurice, n. 51 above, at 302.

The limitations inherent in the ICJ structure and other arbitral procedures have already been noted. However, there is no evidence to suggest that these limitations will be overcome by the creation of a new tribunal. It is suggested that the case for a free-standing environmental court can only be rationalised if the conclusion is reached that the present limitations on the ICJ cannot be overcome through large-scale reform. New institutions are not cost free, and it would be pointless to set up a new elaborate structure when the advantages of such a process are not obvious.

How then might the ICJ be reformed? Several ideas spring to mind. The first is to develop/expand on the specialised chambers approach. Environmental disputes would be referred to the specialised chamber which, like the full Court, would have a wide mandate to make use of technical assessors as and when the circumstances of the case require. However, the contribution of such a chamber is likely to be meaningful only if it is also accompanied by a revision of the present rules on access. It is perhaps time that the international system recognised the concept of *actio popularis*, even if it is of a restricted kind vested in an identifiable institution which would have the mandate to litigate in the public interest. If there is enough political will to justify creation of a new court with expanded jurisdiction, then one would assume that such a will ought to exist for the revision of the restrictive rules that govern access to the court.

It has been noted that the present rules on intervention before the Court are restricted to those with an identifiable legal interest, and are therefore a logical extension of the present adversarial model. As part of general reform of rules on standing the right to intervene should also be liberalised, to permit intervention in the limited circumstances in which it is apparent that the State in question is intervening in the public interest. In order to prevent the risk of abuse, the right to intervene in these circumstances should not be available as of right, but should be left to the discretion of the court. In addition to broadening access, it may also be necessary to have some flexible rules governing joinder of parties especially in relation to those disputes arising from the same cause of action and where the plaintiffs and defendants are also identical. The suggested reforms are not intended to be exclusive avenues for the settlement of disputes. It is in fact envisaged that they will go hand in hand with the many institutional mechanisms set up to supervise compliance with environmental treaties.[58]

[58] There is a vast literature on these mechanisms. See for instance, Boyle, n. 1 above; C. Chinkin, Ch. 7 of this vol.; G. Handl, "Compliance Control Mechanisms and International Environmental Obligations", 5 *Tulane Journal of International and Comparative Law* 29.

11

International Wrongs and National Jurisdiction

MALCOLM D. EVANS

1. INTRODUCTION

There is nothing particularly novel in pointing out that domestic courts can pro-vide a forum in which a remedy can be sought for a breach of certain forms of international obligations and an area in which this technique has been widely used, and seems to have acquired a certain potency, concerns the individual lia-bility (criminal or otherwise) of the individual.[1] The purpose of this chapter is to raise the question whether there is a danger of individual responsibility under international law being used—*de facto*, if not *de iure*—as a cloak behind which the responsibility of the State can shelter. While it is clearly correct that the international community should have effective means at its disposal for exercis-ing jurisdiction over individuals in instances where individual responsibility exists, it must also be correct that the exercise of such jurisdiction ought not to be at the expense of holding the State itself to account in circumstances when its own responsibility is engaged by the act in question.[2] If individuals have respon-sibilities under international law, States do too. Where individual and state responsibility co-exist under international law, the efficacy of international law as a body of law is not enhanced—and, indeed, may be undermined, if the indi-vidual becomes the focus of attention to the exclusion of the State. There are further questions—which are beyond the scope of this chapter—concerning the degree to which this tendency to transfer responsibility from the State to the individual calls into question our understanding of what international law is all about.

---

[1] See C. Gray, *Judicial Remedies in International Law* (Clarendon Press, Oxford, 1987), at 219.

[2] See the view expressed in the ILC that "a State could cause such damage to the international community as a whole that a society should not be allowed to shift the responsibility for crimes com-mitted in its name on to mere individuals" [1994] ILCYB Vol. II, Pt. 2, 139. But *cf.* Judges Shi and Vereshchetin, who questioned the wisdom of pursing States rather than individuals, agreeing with Hartley Shawcross (*International Herald Tribune*, 23 May 1996, 3) that "[t]here can be no recon-ciliation unless individual guilt for appalling crimes . . . replaces the pernicious theory of collective guilt": *Application of the Convention on the Prevention and Punishment of Genocide (Bosnia and Herzegovina v. Yugoslavia)*, Preliminary Objections, Judgment, ICJ Reports 1996, 595 at 632. *Cf.* also the Declaration of Judge Oda in that case, where he questions whether the ICJ was the appro-priate forum for such questions (ibid, at 629).

What we think international law is and what we think international law does depends very largely on who we are and what we do. When forced to theorise, ultra-traditionalists will see it as a normative system the primary function of which is to lay down the parameters, and oil the wheels, of inter-State relations.[3] Other entities may gain a footing: they may be "states in the making", such as "National Liberation Movement",[4] or entities which, although in many/most/ (all?) respects may be qualified to participate as states within the international community, are unable to do so, usually for political reasons.[5] In a benign, paternalistic fashion, the international community permits the rigours of its own fictions to be ameliorated in the interests of the practical reality.[6] The subordinate creatures of this system, the international organisations which are the creation of States, are allowed their entry in a similar manner. And then at the bottom of the pile come individuals.[7] The international system may set limits on the freedoms and fetters that States can legitimately set. But individuals remain passive beneficiaries unless States themselves provide otherwise.

This model has, of course, been widely criticised and rejected for not reflecting the dynamic that exists within the international system in which the individual is neither a subject nor an object, but a participant.[8] It is certainly true that, even if the individual has not gained an equal standing alongside that enjoyed by States within the international system, international law is no longer neutral (if it ever was) in the sense of being indifferent to the interests of individuals. Pleas of domestic jurisdiction no longer invalidate the legality of the interest shown by one State in the treatment of the citizens of another in the

---

[3] A classic statement of this position was given by the PCIJ in the "*Lotus*", Judgment No. 9, 1927, PCIJ, Ser. A, No. 10 at 18:

"International law governs relations between independent States. The rules of law binding upon States therefore emanate from their own free will as expressed in convention or by usages generally accepted as expressing principles of law and established in order to regulate the relations between these coexisting independent communities or with a view to the achievement of common aims."

[4] E.g. the PLO and SWAPO. For National Liberation Movements as subjects of international law see A. Cassese, *International Law in a Divided World* (Oxford, Clarendon Press, 1986), at 90–9.

[5] Among many examples which might be cited, mention might be made of Taiwan, the Turkish Federal Republic of Northern Cyprus and the Republic of Ciskei.

[6] Thus the practical consequences of the non-recognition of Taiwan, either as an independent State or as the authentic voice of China, have not prevented its being embraced by the 1995 Agreement for the Implementation of the provisions of the United Nations Convention on the Law of the Sea on 10 Dec. 1982 Relating to the Conservation and Management of Straddling Fish Stocks and Highly Migratory Species, Art. 1(3) of which extends the ambit of the Agreement beyond "States Parties", and "to other fishing entities whose vessels fish on the high seas": see D. Anderson, "The Straddling Stocks Agreement of 1995—An Initial Assessment", 45 *ICLQ* 463 at 468. The legal consequences flowing from the non-recognition of the *de facto* situation in Northern Cyprus were ameliorated by the Court of Appeal in *Hesperides Hotels Ltd.* v. *Aegean Turkish Holidays* [1978] 1 All ER 277 and by Parliament in the Foreign Corporations Act (1991, c.44). In *Gur Corporation* v. *Trust Bank of Africa* [1987] 1 QB 599, the "Republic of Ciskei" was given standing to sue and be sued, notwithstanding its non-recognition.

[7] Characterised as "puny young Davids confronted by overpowering Goliaths holding all the instruments of power" by Cassese, n. 4 above, at 9.

[8] See R. Higgins, *Problems and Process: International Law and How We Use It* (Clarendon Press, Oxford, 1994), 48–55.

political fora of the international system.[9] The exponential growth in "human rights" protection under international law and the evolution of concepts such as *ius cogens* and *erga omnes* obligations evidence the manner in which this concern has, in turn, affected the very fabric of the international legal order itself. Be that as it may, in one way or another the individual as a discrete conceptual entity has become enmeshed within the international legal system.

But on what basis? There is a need to scrutinise the new orthodoxy that the rise of the individual within the international system is an unqualified good. This is not because the rights and responsibilities of individuals cannot or should not be a matter of international concern. Paradoxically, it is because they should. There is, however, a danger that the international community is becoming so interested in working through the consequences of individual responsibility that it is failing to pay sufficient attention to the need to hold States to account for their failures to respect international law. On a broader level, this tendency threatens to distort the picture of the international legal system and results in insufficient attention being given to the cogency and efficacy of its fundamental components. Certainly, as the assertion of jurisdiction over individuals is becoming more common, the lack of similar assertions of jurisdiction over States becomes all the more apparent. Moreover, the assertions of jurisdiction over delinquent States that do take place are primarily mediated through the political organs of the international community[10] rather than through its judicial organs.[11]

Thus, when it is the State which is acting in violation of its international obligations, judicial redress is only available if the State in breach has accepted that this be so—unless there is an overwhelming display of political will that this be otherwise.[12]

[9] See, e.g. A.H. Robertson and J.G. Merrills, *Human Rights in the World* (4th edn., Manchester University Press, Manchester, 1996), at 32. I. Brownlie, *Principles of Public International Law* (4th edn., Clarendon Press, Oxford, 1990), at 554 warns that "[i]f care is not taken, too much can be proved, and the substance of Article 2, paragraph 7 [of the UN Charter], will disappear".

[10] E.g. the mandatory UN Security Council resolutions in relation to Iraq and the former Yugoslavia and other examples of sanctions.

[11] The reason, of course, is that States must have expressed their consent before a judicial body can exercise jurisdiction over them. This radically reduces the number of disputes which are dealt with though an international judicial (or arbitral) process. Although the authority of the Security Council over a State is itself ultimately derived from the voluntary participation of the State in the UN organisation, the nexus between that generalised consent and the assertion of jurisdiction in a concrete situation is of an entirely different order.

[12] Thus in Security Council Resolution 827 of 23 May 1993, the Security Council created the International Criminal Tribunal for the Former Yugoslavia, acting under Ch. VII of the UN Charter. It should be noted that although the Tribunal does not exercise a juridical jurisdiction over States (Art. 6 of the Statute limits its jurisdiction to natural persons), Art. 9(2) grants it primacy over national courts, and the right to request national courts to defer to its jurisdiction.

2. THE EXERCISE OF JURISDICTION

States and individuals can both be liable in the international arena and judicial fora exist in which they can be held to account for their allegedly wrongful international acts. There are, of course, many gaps in the system: the jurisdiction of the ICJ is limited to those States which have expressed some form of consent to its exercise; the ICTFY and ICTFRwanda have jurisdiction only over natural persons and in respect of a limited number of offences committed in defined areas and within prescribed periods. Doubtless this is unfortunate, and the answer might lie in the creation of an International Court with a compulsory jurisdiction over States and individuals for all breaches of international law. However, the individual is a comparatively "soft" target whereas the State is not, and what is currently on offer is rather different. A draft Statute for an International Criminal Court was adopted by the ILC in 1994[13] and is currently under considerable by governments, with a view to its being adopted and opened for signature in the course of 1998.[14] This will be a profoundly significant event, but since the draft Statute is, once again, directed towards natural persons rather than States,[15] this further reinforces the tendency to develop mechanisms through which the responsibility of the individual can be enforced, while leaving the State whose responsibility might also be engaged by the very acts in question beyond the reach of the judicial machinery.

Nor will the Statute, once adopted, set the parameters of criminal liability under international law. The proposed Statute, like the war crimes tribunals before them, focuses upon a comparatively narrow range of serious violations of international law. Putting the procedural questions whether the relevant consents have been made by the custodial State and the State in which the offence took place,[16] there still remain a significant number of offences which might

---

[13]   See [1994] YBILC, Vol. II, Pt. 2, 20.

[14]   In 1994 the General Assembly established an *ad hoc* committee in order to "review the major substantive and administrative issues arising out of the draft statute" (see General Assembly Resolution 49/53, 9 Dec. 1994). This was followed in 1995 by a decision to establish a preparatory commission (see General Assembly Resolutions 50/46, 11 Dec. 1995 and 21/207, 17 Dec. 1996) which is currently refining the draft for presentation at the inter-governmental conference. For an examination of the first two sessions of the preparatory commission see C.K. Hall, "The First Two Sessions on the UN Preparatory Committee on the Establishment of an International Criminal Court", 91 *AJIL* 177.

[15]   The ICC draft Statute does not have an equivalent of Art. 8 of the Statute of the ICTFY, which makes this point explicitly, but it is inherent in the entire structure of the ICC draft Statute that this is the case.

[16]   In the model proposed by the ILC the State which has custody of the suspect and the State in which the act in question occurred would both have to have given their consent to the Court's exercising its jurisdiction unless the offence in question is genocide, over which the Court has inherent jurisdiction (ICC draft Statute, Art. 21(1)(a) and (b)). The ICC would become seised of a case once a complaint had been made by a State Party itself accepting the jurisdiction of the Court (Art. 25) or by decision of the Security Council acting under Ch. VII of the UN Charter (Art. 23). These "Trigger Mechanisms" are a matter of particular dispute in the preparatory committee: see Hall, n. 14 above, at 181.

well be categorised as "criminal" but which will fall beyond its scope. This is not surprising. In addition of the draft Statute, the ILC has also recently adopted the text of its Draft Code of Crimes Against the Peace and Security of Mankind.[17] Article 8 of the Draft Code would require a State to assert universal jurisdiction over crimes set out in Articles 17–20 of that Code, these being genocide, crimes against humanity, crimes against United Nations and associated personnel and war crimes. In these cases, the Code envisages an ICC exercising a concurrent jurisdiction with national courts, the so-called principle of "complementarity". The Code's jurisdictional structure aims at the "[b]roadest jurisdiction of national Courts together with the possible jurisdiction of an International Criminal Court".[18] This makes it clear that there is to be no "withering away" of the role of the national court as regards the enforcement of international crimes. Indeed, there could not be. The Commentary to Article 20 of the ICC draft Statute, which sets out the crimes which will fall within the jurisdiction of the Court, stresses that:

> "Article 20(a)–(e) are not intended as an exhaustive list of crimes under general international law. It is limited to those crimes under general international law which the Commission believes should be within the reach jurisdiction of the court at this stage, whether by reason of their magnitude, the continuing reality of their occurrence or their inevitable international consequences."

The ICC goes beyond the jurisdictional framework of the Code by including in Article 20(e) "treaty" crimes, these being offences established by Conventions and for which there exists "either universal jurisdiction based on the principle *aut dedere, aut judicare* [extradite or punish] or the possibility for an international court to try the crime, or both, thus recognizing clearly the principle of international concern".[19] In all these instances, however, the ICC would exercise jurisdiction only to the extent that "having regard to the conduct alleged, [they] constitute exceptionally serious crimes of international concern".[20] The commentary explains, in a rather opaque passage, that:

> "many of those treaties could cover conduct which, though serious in itself, was within the competence of national courts to deal with and which (in the context of an individual case) did not require elevation to the level of an international jurisdiction".[21]

It is clearly going to be interesting to observe how this develops, and there is likely to be to considerable controversy surrounding the question of what

---

[17] See Report of the ILC to the General Assembly on the Work of its 48th Session (1996), GAOR Doc. A/51/50, ch. 2.

[18] *Ibid.*, Art. 8, Commentary (5).

[19] ICC Draft Statute, n. 13 above, Art. 20, Commentary, para. (18)(b). The Annex to the Draft exhaustively lists the crimes concerned.

[20] *Ibid.*, Art. 20(e).

[21] *Ibid.*, Art. 20, Commentary, para. (20).

justifies "ratcheting up" a particular case to the international sphere.[22] However, the point to be noted here is that the international community continues to be entirely at ease with placing responsibility upon individuals as a matter of international law and leaving the execution of that responsibility in the hands of domestic legal fora in all but the most serious of instances.

Of course, it would be wrong to suggest that the international community has overlooked the responsibility of the State for serious breaches of its international obligations. During the same period as it has been working on the draft ICC Statute and Code of Crimes, the ILC has also been continuing its work on its draft Articles on State Responsibility. It was in 1976 that the text of draft Article 19(2) was adopted. It provides that[23]:

> "An internationally wrongful act which results from the breach by a State of an international obligation so essential for the protection of fundamental interests of the international community that its breach is recognized as a crimes by that community as a whole constitutes an international crime."

The very idea that a State can be subject to criminal liability has been the subject of strong criticism,[24] and although the ILC decided to retain the existing formulation when it revisited the issue while considering what consequences were to flow from criminal responsibility attaching to a State,[25] there remains considerable unease at the prospect of characterising a State's actions as "criminal".[26] It has been argued that it is inappropriate to draw upon the "municipal law" distinction of civil and criminal responsibility and that it should be accepted that there exists in the international arena a single notion of internationally wrongful acts.[27] For some, this is reflected in the "continuum" theory, in which there is a single regime of responsibility extending from minor breaches . . . to exceptionally serious breaches . . . marked by an essentially qualitative difference".[28] This leads to the question of the consequences attaching to a breach and at least a part of the problem associated with "criminal" responsibility is that it is taken to entail a "criminal"—punitive—sanction against the entire community which, since it would penalise all within the State irrespective of their degree of participation in the act in question, is generally considered problematic. However, another facet of the nature of international responsibility

---

[22] The Commentary suggests that "the systematic factor" will be of relevance, particularly in connection with terrorist activities. Along with drug-trafficking, these are given as examples where "the requirements of subparagraph (e) in terms of the exceptionally serious character of the crime will readily be satisfied": *ibid.*, paras. (21)–(22).

[23] For the text of Art. 19 and commentary see [1976] YBILC, Vol. II, Pt. 2, 95–122.

[24] E.g. I. Brownlie, *System of Law of Nations: State Responsibility Part I* (Clarendon Press, Oxford, 1983), at 32–3 and works cited therein.

[25] See [1994] YBILC, Vol. II, Pt. 2, paras. 230–46.

[26] This is further reflected in the text adopted by the ILC in 1996 which, when defining the term "injured state" for the purposes of Part II of the daft, noted that "alternative phases such as 'an international wrongful act of a serious nature' or 'an exceptionally serious wrongful act' could be substituted for the term 'crime', thus, *inter alia*, avoiding the penal implication: A/CN.4/L.528/Add 2, 18).

[27] [1994] YBILC, Vol. II, Pt. 2, para. 245.

[28] *Ibid.*, para. 236.

was said to be "that some internationally wrongful acts, instead of entailing the responsibility of the State alone, also entailed the individual responsibility of their perpetrators, who could not hide behind the immunities conferred on them by their functions".[29] In other words, it is thought possible to distinguish between those internationally wrongful acts which are "crimes" and those which are not, on the basis of whether the international community imposes individual responsibility for their breach. It is not the intention to debate the case for and against the concept of the criminal responsibility of States in this chapter. However, it is evident that there is a strong body of opinion in favour of abandoning this approach altogether, while at the same time preserving the criminal responsibility of the individual as a matter of international law—in short, the view that while the individual can be "criminal", the State cannot (or ought not). Others see a solution in allowing what might be called the burden of criminal responsibility to fall chiefly upon the individual. Certainly, if Article 19 is finally adopted in its current form there is force in the criticism that it draws the distinction between criminal and delictual responsibility without attributing any particularly significant consequences to that distinction—apart, perhaps, from moral opprobrium—for the State in beach.[30] The position for the individual is, however, currently very different, both on the international[31] and domestic plane.[32]

3. NO HIDING PLACE FOR THE INDIVIDUAL—UNIVERSAL JURISDICTION

There seems to be a tendency to consider international crimes—of an individual or of a State—as comprising any action in relation to which the international community is prepared to allow municipal legal fora to exercise the broadest forms of jurisdiction over those individuals who might commit them, i.e. actions which attract universal jurisdiction.[33] This correlation is certainly not exact and

---

[29] *Ibid.*, para. 245.

[30] The further consequences of an international crime are provided for in Draft Arts. 51–3. These amount to an obligation on all States to refrain from recognising the situation created by the criminal act and to co-operate in efforts aimed at its elimination. In the context of crimes such as "aggression" and genocide it is difficult to see how this goes beyond existing obligations and raises difficult questions of auto-interpretation of the criminality of actions. Other "extra" consequences include the non-applicability of certain restrictions upon the availability of restitution in kind and satisfaction under Arts. 43 and 45. There is, however, no lifting of Art. 42(3) which prevents an award of reparations from "depriving the population of a State of its own means of subsistence".

[31] *Cf.* the fate of Drazen Erdemovic who was sentenced by the ICTFY to 10 years' imprisonment for crimes against humanity and violations of the laws and customs of war (case No. IT–96–22–T, Judgment of Trial Chamber, 29 Nov. 1996, subsequently reduced on appeal to 5 years in Mar. 1998), and Dusko Tadic (case No. IT–94–T, Judgment of Trial Chamber, 7 May 1996, 36 ILM 908).

[32] See news reports of a 5-year sentence of imprisonment passed upon an individual found guilty of genocide in Bosnia by a German court (*The Times*, 24 May 1997) and the death penalty passed upon Froduald Karamira, a ringleader of the 1994 genocide in Rwanda by a Rwandan Court (*The Times*, 15 Feb. 1997, 14) and in April 1998 the first of a series of executions commended, with 22 people being put to death by firing squad.

[33] See, e.g., *Restatement of US Foreign Relations Law* (*Third*), para. 404, Reporter's note 1.

the ILC itself drew a distinction between international crimes, which it considered to be "international wrongs which are more serious that others and which as such, should entail more severe legal consequences", and expressions "such as 'crime under international law', 'war crime', 'crime against peace' and 'crime against humanity' etc., which are used in a certain number of international instruments to designate certain heinous individual crimes, for which those instruments require States to punish the guilty persons adequately, in accordance with their internal law".[34] At the same time, there is a further temptation to identify international crimes with norms of *ius cogens*. Again, the ILC has cautioned against this,[35] but there is, at the very least, a gravitational pull in the direction of uniting *ius cogens*, universal jurisdiction and international crimes. While this has the attraction of simplicity, it also has the effect of transporting the burden of responsibility away from the State and towards the individual. The ILC saw international crimes as serious breaches committed by States, whereas crimes under international law were offences committed by individuals. As generally understood, universal jurisdiction attaches to the latter rather than the former, in that it amounts to an acceptance by the international community that domestic courts are entitled to assert their authority over those individuals who have committed such acts.[36] However, the international community is not renouncing its right to assert jurisdiction in such cases, as the emergence of the ICTFY, ICTFRwanda and the moves towards the establishment of an ICC demonstrate. Rather, in recognising the right of States to assert universal jurisdiction, it is delegating its capacity (or, indeed, responsibility) to respond to such breaches of international law to the domestic legal tribunals of whichever State appears willing and able to do so. At the same time, the international community reserves its right to reclaim that jurisdiction for itself should it wish to do so.[37] To that extent, universal jurisdiction is permissive. It

---

[34] [1976] YBILC, Vol. II, Pt. 2, 119.

[35] *Ibid.*, 120.

[36] But *cf.* Brownlie, n. 9 above, at 304–5 who argues that since the domestic court is in such cases punishing the commission of a crime under international law, universal jurisdiction is not at issue, since universal jurisdiction describes the punishment under national law of acts which the international community does not itself consider criminal. Even if technically this is correct, it must also be recognised that offences which attract universal jurisdiction are, at the very least, "crimes under international law in the making", as is evidenced by their inclusion in Art. 20(e) of the Draft Statute of the ICC—thus rendering this distinction at best of only transitory relevance in any given case. Approaching the question from the other direction, Higgins, n. 8 above, at 62, argues that one of the only purposes served by labelling an action "criminal" in the international sphere is to indicate that an assertion of universal jurisdiction will be tolerated.

[37] For example the draft Code of Crimes Against the Peace and Security of Mankind, Art. 8 would reserve jurisdiction over Crimes of Aggression to an International Criminal Court (with States being allowed to exercise jurisdiction only over their own nationals), while the Statute of the ICTFY, Art. 29(2)(e) and Rules of Procedure 8–11 and the draft Statute of the ICC, Arts. 52 and 53 govern the transfer of cases from the national to the international plane. For comment on the US and UK domestic legislation giving effect to this in the context of the ICTFY and ICTFR, see R. Kushen and K.J. Harris, "Surrender of Fugitives by the United States to the War Crimes Tribunals for Yugoslavia and Rwanda", 90 *AJIL* 510; C. Warbrick, "Co-operation with the International Criminal Tribunal for Yugoslavia", 45 *ICLQ* 947; and H. Fox, "The Objections to the Transfer of Criminal Jurisdiction to the UN Tribunal", 46 *ICLQ* 434.

is also permissive in the sense that it takes little notice of the extent to which the system of justice in the State concerned meets basic standards of fairness or whether the custodial system measures up to international standards.[38] It is the seriousness of the offence which apparently merits the exercise of domestic jurisdiction, behind which lies the concern that the means of punishing the individual upon the international plane are either inadequate or lacking. This means that the "gravitational pull" tends to operate through a broadening of the reach of universal jurisdiction, and with it the responsibility of the individual, rather than towards the concept of an "international crime", behind which (irrespective of whether one accepts the theory of its criminal liability) lies the responsibility of the State.

But just how seriously does the international community regard these offences? It is not necessary to consider the nature of universal jurisdiction at length. It is, however, worth recalling that the example *par excellence* is piracy. The idea that pirates are the common enemy of all mankind is of ancient origins, and it is entirely appropriate that the legal fora of any State should be able to act against those who commit offences beyond the limits of exclusive state competence, in the absence of any other realistic option.[39] Moving away from piracy, there may be disagreements over which offences attract universal jurisdiction (and why), but the series of treaties based upon the *aut dedere aut judicare* principle (which, even if not technically providing for universal jurisdiction,[40] were

---

[38] Schachter has argued that "[i]n the absence of an international criminal court or a generally accepted code of criminal procedures, international law should require that a State exercising universal jurisdiction fully meets the criteria of a fair trail and the limits on punitive action that are part of basic human rights": O. Schachter, *International Law in Theory and Practice* (Nijhoff, Dordrecht, 1991), at 270. The emergence of an ICC might not, however, solve these problems: it has, e.g., been argued that the methods of the ICTFY do not ensure an equivalence with best national practice. See, e.g., Fox, n. 37 above, *passim*. The existing *aut dedere aut judicare* conventions do include a basic requirement of fair treatment (e.g. International Convention Against the Taking of Hostages) 1970), Art. 8(1); Convention Against Torture and other Cruel, Inhuman or Degrading Treatment of Punishment (1984), Art. 7(3)) the meaning of which has been elaborated upon somewhat, notably in the Convention on the Safety of UN and Associated Personnel (1994), Art. 17. Even so, the consequences of non-compliance with these procedural obligations upon the validity of the exercise of jurisdiction is far from clear.

[39] "Piracy . . . is an offence against the law of Nations; and as the scene of the pirate's operations is the high seas, which it is not the right or duty of any nation to police, he is denied the protection of the flag which he may carry, and is treated as an outlaw, as an enemy of mankind—hostis humani generis—whom any nation may in the interest of all capture and punish": Moore J, *The Lotus*, Judgment No. 9, 1927, PCIJ Ser. A, No. 10 at 70. It is, then, rather ironic that the ILC has excluded piracy, as defined in Art. 15 of the 1958 Convention on the High Seas and Art. 101 of the 1982 Law of the Sea Convention, from the list of "treaty crimes" over which the ICC would exercise jurisdiction, on the ground that these Conventions "confer jurisdiction only on the seizing State, and they cover a very wide range of acts": [1994] YBILC Vol. II, Pt. 2, 68. On the other hand, the crimes defined by Art. 3 of the Convention for the Suppression of Unlawful Acts against the Safety of Maritime Navigation, and Art. 2 of the Protocol for the Suppression of Unlawful Acts against the Safety of Fixed Platforms located on the Continental Shelf, both of 10 Mar. 1988, were included: *ibid.*

[40] See, e.g., Higgins, n. 8 above, at 63–4. *Cf.* Schachter, n. 9 above, at 268 who suggests that there might be a necessary implication (or assumption) that universal jurisdiction attaches to those offences over which States choose to oblige themselves to exercise it or that such treaties imply

certainly considered by those that drafted them as achieving this[41]) reflect different preoccupations: the need to indicate the seriousness of the offence; the need to underpin the assertion of an otherwise potentially dubious jurisdiction; and the need to overcome the reluctance or unwillingness of States to take appropriate measures against individuals who perpetrated such acts by obliging them to do so.

4. A HIDING PLACE FOR THE STATE?

In common with so much of international law, however, the nature of the system prevents the logic of these concerns running their course. The *aut dedere aut judicare* conventions—like the Genocide Convention before them—start with the assumption/fiction that States themselves either cannot be or are not behind such "crimes".[42] To take a single, typical, example, the Preamble to the 1971 Montreal Convention for the Suppression of Unlawful Acts against the Safety of Civil Aviation commences by emphasising that the States Parties consider that "for the purpose of deterring such acts, there is an urgent need to provide appropriate measures for punishment of offenders", and, to that end, they go on to agree to apply severe penalties to any person committing an offence as defined in the convention.[43] This portrays the perpetrator as a "rogue individual" against whom the community of States is to close ranks for the common good. The *Lockerbie* incident is eloquent testimony to the fact that this is not what States really think of each other: Libyan requests that it be left to take action within its domestic legal framework against Libyan nationals allegedly involved in the bombing of Pan Am Flight 103 were met by demands for the surrender of the suspects to face charges in either the UK or the USA, and for Libya to accept responsibility for the crime and pay appropriate compensation.[44] The Security Council itself expressed the view that "the suppression of acts of international

advance waivers of claims between parties that such an exercise is impermissible under international law, the third party effect of such waiver (and its truly "universal" character) depending upon the response of non-treaty parties to its exercise over their nationals. Both these arguments indicate a bias towards the universality of jurisdiction in such cases.

[41] See, e.g., J.H. Burgers and H. Danelius, *The UN Convention Against Torture* (Nijhoff, Dordrecht, 1988), which gives an account of the drafting of that instrument which makes it clear that the relevant Arts. were considered to be an embodiment of the principle of universal jurisdiction.

[42] This form of drafting lead to problems in the case concerning the *Application of the Convention of the Prevention and Punishment of the Crime of Genocide (Bosnia and Herzegovina* v. *Yugoslavia)*, Preliminary Objections, Judgment, ICJ Reports 1996, 595. Yugoslavia argued that under the 1948 Convention a State could be liable for the failure to punish an individual, but "the responsibility of a State for an act of genocide perpetrated by the State itself would be excluded from the scope of the Convention" (para. 32). This was rejected by the Court (para. 32) but accepted by Judge *ad hoc* Kreca (Dissenting Opinion, para. 103).

[43] 1971 Montreal Convention, Arts. 1 and 3.

[44] Joint UK/USA Declaration of 27 Nov. 1991. See generally F. Beveridge, "The Lockerbie Affair", 41 *ICLQ* 907.

terrorism, including those in which States are directly or indirectly involved, is essential for the maintenance of international peace and security" and, under Chapter VII of the UN Charter, decided that the Libyan Government "must commit itself definitively to cease all forms of terrorist action and all assistance to terrorist groups and that it must promptly, by concrete action, demonstrate its renunciation of terrorism".[45] To say the least, this ringing denunciation does not sit easily alongside the presumptions underlying the Montreal Convention. A further reflection of the truth that States know that the most serious of violations are the responsibility of States as much as (if not more than) of individuals—if further proof is thought necessary—is provided by the ILC itself, which has said that crimes under international law "are often committed as part of a general plan or policy which involves the participation of a substantial number of individuals in a systematic or massive criminal conduct in relation to a multiplicity of victims".[46] Interesting, and revealingly for the purposes of this chapter, the ILC did not see this as a factor which justified the "ratcheting up" of jurisdiction from the national to the international plane. Rather, it is given as a practical reason why it is necessary to retain the concurrent jurisdiction of national courts.

The extent to which the State is involved in the commission of offences which attract universal jurisdiction becomes quite apparent if one thinks of the definition of torture found in the 1984 UN Convention Against Torture, which provides that:

> "the term 'torture' means any act by which severe pain or suffering, whether physical or mental is intentionally inflicted on a person for such purposes as obtaining from him or a third person information or a confession, punishing him for an act he or a third person has committed or is suspected of having committed, or intimidating or coercing him or a third person, for any reason based on discrimination of any kind, *when such pain or suffering is inflicted by or at the instigation of or with the consent of acquiescence of a public official or other person acting in an official capacity.* It does not include pain or suffering arising only from, inherent in or incidental to lawful sanctions."[47]

This definition was drawn from the 1975 UN Declaration against Torture[48] and it is clear that, under the UN instrument, the offence of torture is certainly an offence for which the State is responsible under international law. Indeed, if one accepts this definition it is impossible to commit an act of torture for which the State is not also responsible. It is true that others see the international

---

[45] UN Security Council Resolution 748, 31 Mar. 1992.

[46] Draft Code of Crimes Against the Peace and Security of Mankind, Commentary to Art. 8, para. 3.

[47] UN Convention Again Torture and other Cruel, Inhuman or Degrading Treatment or Punishment (1984), Art. 1 (emphasis added).

[48] Declaration on the Protection of All Persons from being Subjected to Torture and Other Cruel, Inhuman or Degrading Treatment or Punishment, GA Res. 3452(XXX), 9 Dec. 1975. The definition in the Convention goes beyond that found in Art. 1 of the Declaration, which does not extend to acts committed with the consent or acquiesence of public officials, or those acting in an official capacity.

prohibition of torture as extending to the private acts of individuals. Indeed, the UN Human Rights Committee has interpreted the more generalised wording of Article 7 of the 1966 UN Covenant on Civil and Political Rights[49] as meaning that "[i]t is the duty of the State party to afford everyone protection through legislative and other measures as may be necessary against the acts prohibited by Article 7, whether inflicted by people acting in their official capacity, outside their official capacity or in a private capacity".[50] This appears to be a deliberate attempt to expand the ambit of Article 7 into the "private sphere",[51] and it is too soon to say whether this reflects a new understanding of what is embraced within the term "torture". Certainly, it is moving beyond existing state practice, which considers the 1984 Convention definition to reflect customary international law.[52] Whatever the position may be in the future, it is certainly true that the core of the obligation is that States should not permit those acting under their authority or with their approval to engage in acts of torture. In any case, the argument that torture may occur in the "private" sphere does not absolve the State from responsibility on the international plane.[53] Rather, state responsibility expands to embrace it.[54]

If the State is truly committed to fulfilling its international obligation to eradicate torture within its jurisdiction, it should take action against those against whom allegations are made, and this is expressly provided for in the 1984 Torture Convention[55] (as it is in equivalent situations in other *aut dedere aut judicare* instruments). The 1948 Genocide Convention also contains an undertaking that States will enact the necessary legislation to give effect to their obligation to punish those committing offences punishable under the Convention,[56]

---

[49] This simply provides that "[n]o one shall be subjected to torture or to cruel, inhuman or degrading treatment or punishment. In particular no one shall be subjected without his free consent to medical or scientific experimentation".

[50] General Comment No. 22 (44) (Art. 7) adopted by the Human Rights Committee on 3 Apr. 1992 (CCPR/C/21/Rev.1/Add.3, para. 2).

[51] General Comment No. 7(16) (Art. 7) adopted by the Human Rights Committee in 1982, and which was replaced by General Comment No. 22 (44), did not make this claim.

[52] See, e.g., in the UK the 1988 Criminal Justice Act (1988, c.33), s. 134 and *Al Adsani* v. *Government of Kuwait*, 103 ILR 420 at 424 (QBD) and in the USA the Torture Victim Protection Act (1992, 28 USC §1350) and, *inter alia*, *Kadic* v. *Karadzic*, 70 F 3d 232 (1995), 104 ILR 136, all of which emphasise that official torture is prohibited under international law, citing the 1984 UN convention definition.

[53] See A. Clapham, *Human Rights in the Private Sphere* (Clarendon Press, Oxford, 1993), 104–7, 188 and 189–203 where the consequences of the application of the ECHR in the "private sphere" are worked out in the context of Art. 3 of that convention. See also D. Shelton, "Private Violence, Public Wrongs and the Responsibility of States", 13 *Fordham Journal of International Law* 1 at 14–26.

[54] It may be that in such cases the responsibility of the State is not engaged by the act of torture itself but for its failure to protect the victim from an act of torture, or inhuman or degrading treatment or punishment. Viewed from this perspective, the "official" nature of the act recedes into the background and the nature of the treatment sustained attains prominence. *Cf.* the approach of the European Commission on Human Rights when finding the UK in breach of its obligations under the ECHR for an act of corporal punishment meted out in a domestic context in *A.* v. *UK*, Comm. Rep., 18 Sept. 1997, paras. 42–5.

[55] UN Convention Against Torture, Art. 4.

[56] Convention on the Prevention and Punishment of Genocide, Arts. III and IV.

but, unlike the later instruments, it was not considered necessary to look for enforcement by domestic courts of States other than those of the State in whose territory the acts had taken place.[57] Why has this development come about? The case for universal jurisdiction can only be based upon the belief that States either do not fulfil their existing international obligations or, if the existence of the obligation was previously in doubt, will not fulfil those which they undertake on becoming a party to the relevant Convention. Taking this one stage further, translating these grants of universal jurisdiction into the heads of jurisdiction of an International Criminal Court exercising jurisdiction over individuals points up the question already evident from the creation of the ICTFY: what is the appropriate judicial response to those States which, under existing principals of international law, are responsible for acts which also attract individual responsibility?[58] Some answers to these questions may emerge when the ICJ gives its judgment at the merits phase of the *Genocide case*.[59] However, the ILC has made it clear that it does not believe that the punishment of the individual by the international community, by either international or domestic courts, absolves the State from liability for its failure to prevent (or its act in encouraging) the activity in the first place.[60]

But is this what happens in reality? Currently, States resort to universal jurisdiction in order to exact "justice" upon those whose activities run counter to the international conscience. But when those involved are little more than pawns in the hands of those who exercise authority over them, is this enough (setting

[57] *Ibid.*, Art. VI. This also provides for the exercise of jurisdiction "by such international penal tribunal as may have jurisdiction . . ." and this is now realised in the ILC draft Statute of the ICC. The ICJ itself has attempted to subvert the clear meaning of these words by arguing that, since obligations under the Convention are owed *erga omnes*, "the obligation that each State thus has to prevent and to punish the crime of genocide is not territorially limited by the Convention": *Application of the Convention on the Prevention and Punishment of the Crime of Genocide (Bosnia and Herzegovina* v. *Yugoslavia)*, Preliminary objections, Judgment ICJ Reports 1996, 595, para. 31. While this may be the case as a matter of customary international law, it is difficult to see how this can be the case under the Convention. Judge *ad hoc* Kreca pointed out that the principle of universal jurisdiction had been considered and rejected (Dissenting Opinion, paras. 101–2).

[58] It is now known what might happen to those tried by the Tribunal—and what may potentially happen to those tried under the domestic laws of States exercising jurisdiction in accordance with generally accepted principles of international law: see nn. 31 and 32 above.

[59] In its Memorial, Bosnia has requested:
"6. That the Federal Republic of Yugoslavia (Serbia and Montenegro) must wipe out the consequences of its international wrongful acts and must restore the situation existing before the violations of the Convention on the Prevention and Punishment of the Crime of Genocide were committed;
7. That, as a result of the international responsibility incurred for the above violations . . . the Federal Republic of Yugoslavia (Serbia and Montenegro) is required to pay, and the Republic of Bosnia and Herzegovina is entitled to receive, in its own right and as *parens patriae* for its citizens, full compensation for the damages and losses caused, in the amount to be determined by the Court in a subsequent phase of the proceedings in this case."

[60] See, e.g., Art. 4 of the Draft Code of Crimes Against the Peace and Security of Mankind ("the responsibility of individuals for crimes against the peace and security of mankind is without prejudice to any question of the responsibility of States under international law") and the Commentary to Art. 19 of the ILC Draft Arts. on State Responsibility which makes the same point (see [1976] YBILC, Vol. II, Pt. 2, 103–4).

aside the question of whether it is right)? It is important not to lose sight of the fact that the State may itself be in breach of a primary obligation and the individual cannot be treated as its *alter ego* within the international system.[61] Indeed, it could be argued that the concept of individual responsibility in international law is only needed because of the inability of the international system to ensure that the obligations it places upon States are complied with. If the rise of individual responsibility and universal jurisdiction has been used at least in part as a surrogate for the effective enforcement of international norms on the international plane, the development of more effective mechanisms might call for a reappraisal of these trends.[62] The other side of this coin is that the failure to construct a more effective and rational system through which appropriate judicial action may be taken against the delinquent State may further encourage this surrogate tendency.

5.   DOMESTIC COURTS: ANOTHER HIDING PLACE FOR THE STATE?

There is an alternative strategy. Rather than (or at least in addition to) letting municipal fora exercise jurisdiction over the individuals, let them do so over the State. This may not seem a particularly radical innovation, given that States are regularly impleaded before domestic courts on a whole host of issues as a consequence of the application of the doctrine of restrictive State immunity. Of course, the essence of such cases is that the State is not acting (or is not deemed to be acting) as a State, whereas the circumstances which have been considered so far in this chapter relate to instances in which the responsibility of the State is engaged *iure imperii*: and the idea that one State can be subject to even the civil—let alone criminal—jurisdiction of another in such circumstances verges upon doctrinal heresy. The application of principles of State immunity have acted as a barrier preventing the assertion of universal jurisdiction over individuals acting in violation of international norms which give rise to individual responsibility from spilling over into assertions of jurisdiction over States. This is well illustrated by a number of cases decided in recent years in the USA and the UK.

In 1980 the US Court of Appeals, Second Circuit, decided in the now famous case of *Filartiga* v. *Pena-Irala*[63] that the United States Judiciary Act 1789, and the Alien Tort Claims Act,[64] enabled aliens who were victims or relatives of victims to claim damages in the USA for acts of torture committed outside the USA in violation of international law, irrespective of the nationality of the

---

[61]   See n. 2 above.

[62]   *Cf.* the view, expressed in the ILC, that "the attribution of criminal responsibility to a State was furthermore viewed as inconceivable in the absence of a legal organ to try and punish States" [1994] ILCYB Vol. II, Pt. 2, 139.

[63]   630 F 2d 876 (1980), 77 ILR 169.

[64]   28 USC §1350. This provides federal district courts with original jurisdiction over "all cases where an alien sues for a tort . . . [committed] in violation of the Law of Nations".

torturers.[65] The 1992 Torture Victim Protection Act[66] extended the cause of action under this head of jurisdiction to US citizens.[67] However, the US courts have not been prepared to accept that acts of torture committed by private individuals amount to a violation of international law, stressing that the prohibition extends only to acts of *official* torture. This makes it quite clear that the responsibility of the State is engaged by these actions—but the US courts have been equally emphatic in insisting that the State itself cannot be brought before them on this basis alone. In *Argentine Republic* v. *Amerada Hess Shipping Corp.*[68] the US Supreme Court determined that the sole basis for obtaining jurisdiction over a foreign State was under the Foreign Sovereign Immunity Act, which preserves the immunity of the State for acts undertaken *iure imperii*. This stumbling block was challenged in *Siderman de Blake* v. *Argentine Republic*, in which it was argued that the international prohibition of official torture was a norm of *ius cogens* and that the FSIA did not grant immunity to States acting in violation of such norms.[69] The Court accepted that official torture was indeed a norm of *ius cogens*, but concluded that:

> "if violations of *ius cogens* committed outside the United States are to be exceptions to immunity, Congress must make them so. The fact that there has been a violation of *ius cogens* does not confer jurisdiction under the FSIA".[70]

This decision was mirrored in the English case of *Al Adsani* v. *Government of Kuwait*.[71] The applicant, a British and Kuwaiti national, alleged that he had been tortured in Kuwait by government officials. Leave to serve proceedings out of the jurisdiction was granted, but when the substance of the case was heard it was decided—drawing on *Siderman*—that Kuwait was immune from process. Article 1 of the 1978 State Immunity Act provides that foreign States are "immune from the jurisdiction of the Courts . . . except as provided" and the only relevant exception is found in Article 5, which lifts their immunity for tortious acts resulting in death or personal injury which occurred in the United Kingdom, but not elsewhere. Once again, it was argued that the drafters could not have intended to exclude the courts from

---

[65] In *Filartiga* itself, the acts of torture had taken place in Paraguay and all concerned—plaintiffs, defendants and victim (the son and brother of the victim who had been tortured in death) were citizens of Paraguay.

[66] Pub. L. No. 102–256, 106 Stat. 73 (1992).

[67] See *Kadic* v. *Karadzic*, 70 F 3d 232 (1995) at 246, 104 ILC 136 at 159.

[68] 109 S. Ct. 683 (1989), 81 ILR 658.

[69] 699 F 2d 699 (1992) at 714, 103 ILR 454 at 470.

[70] 699 F 2d 699 (1992) at 179, 103 ILR 454 at 475. The Court did, however, decide that on the facts of the case the actions of the Argentine Republic in seeking to use the US courts to execute a judgment against the plaintiffs meant that the plaintiffs' action fell within the implied waiver exception and so could proceed.

[71] Judgment of Mantell J (QBD), 15 Mar. 1995, 103 ILR 420, affirmed on appeal, 12 Mar. 1996 (*The Times*, 29 Mar. 1996). For comment see S. Marks, "Torture and the Jurisdictional Immunity of Foreign States", 56 *CLJ* 8; M. Byers, "Decisions of British Courts During 1996", 67 *BYIL* 536. This case has now been submitted to the European Commission of Human Rights. See App. No. 35763/97 v. *UK*.

exercising jurisdiction over acts in violation of norms of *ius cogens*, but, once again, this was not accepted.[72]

In the light of these decisions, it seems clear that there is little prospect of the State being held liable before the domestic fora of another State for acts which violate the most fundamental principals of international law and which give rise to individual liability. At the same time, the liability of the individual remains. It has, however, been argued in the USA that the immunity of the State under the FSIA also extends to state officials acting within the lawful scope of their activities.[73] This was left open in the case of *Xuncax* v. *Gramajo*, which took refuge in the argument that "such immunity would in any event be unavailable in suits against an official arising from acts that were beyond the scope of the official's authority" and that the acts of torture in question could not be considered "officially authorised".[74] But does this lack of official authorisation mean that such acts cease to be "official torture" for the purposes of the Alien Torts and Torture Victims Protection Acts, thus effectively shutting the door on *Filartiga*-style claims (unless and until the courts finally determine the position of the individual under the FSIA)? The answer is no, because such acts, although outside the scope of the lawful authority of the official are still conducted "under the colour of law" for the purposes of these statutes.[75] Of course, this means that the responsibility of the State is still engaged for those actions on the international plane, but that does not mean that a remedy can be sought before the domestic courts. The "lockout" seems complete.

At first sight, the amendments made to the FSIA by the Antiterrorism and Effective Death Penalty Act (1996) might seem to indicate a significant development, since it lifts the immunity of the State in cases:

> ". . . in which money damages are sought against a foreign state for personal injury or death that was caused by an act of torture, extrajudicial killing, aircraft sabotage, hostage taking, or the provision of material support or resources . . . for such an act if such act or provision of material support is engaged in by an official, employee, or agent of such foreign state while acting within the scope of his or her office, employment, or agency . . ."[76]

This indeed means that the State can no longer hide behind the cloak of immunity when impleaded before the US courts. However, this amendment is not of general application. It has effect only with respect to foreign States which have

---

[72] For criticism of this see Byers, n. 71 above, 540–1.

[73] See T.R. Posner, 90 *AJIL* 658 at 662.

[74] 886 F Suppl. 162 (1995) at 175, 104 ILR 165 at 176.

[75] *Ibid*. See also *Kadic* v. *Karadzic*, it was said that the mere "semblance of official authority" was sufficient. Indeed, the view was expressed that even the semblance of authority given by an unrecognised state would be sufficient since "[t]he inquiry, after all, is whether a person purporting to wield official power has exceeded internationally recognized standards of civilized conduct, not whether statehood in all its formal aspects exists". At this level, it is difficult to see quite how these differ from the acts of private individuals, although the Court denies that this is the case: see 70 F 3d 232 (1995) at 244, 104 ILR 136 at 157–8.

[76] Pub. L. No. 104–32, s. 211, 24 April 1996, becoming 28 USC 1605(a)(7). See 36 ILM 759.

been "designed as a state sponsor of terrorism".[77] In short, immunity will be lifted only with respect to those States which have incurred the political opprobrium of the international community (or of the United States). Rather than indicate a greater willingness to see the State as well as the individual before domestic courts, this amendment to the FSIA tends to underline the limited degree to which this is likely to occur.

If the international community is prepared to countenance the use of domestic legal fora when individuals breach norms of international law giving rise to individual responsibility, why does it find it difficult to countenance the use of those fora when States themselves stand accused of the same offence for which state responsibility also exists? Certainly, as regards torture, it is difficult to understand the equities of a situation in which an individual's responsibility is conditional upon their acting under the auspices or with the acquiescence of public authority; that domestic courts can legitimately exercise jurisdiction (civil or criminal) over the alleged torturer irrespective of the *locus* or nationality of the perpetrator or victim; but that the State remains "immune" from process. The finding that the individual is indeed liable will usually presuppose a finding of state responsibility. The State in question is *de facto*, "on trial" and may certainly consider itself to be so. To that extent, the domestic courts can— and do—provide a forum in which even these forms of violations of international law can be examined, but, once again, in a surrogate fashion.

6. A SALUTARY CONCLUSION

Rather than press this case further, it is worth recalling the Code of Crimes once again—for it provides a salutary lesson. Under that Code, jurisdiction with regard to the crime of aggression would not be universal and shared with national courts. Rather, apart from instances involving the nationals of each State, it would pass into the hands of the International Criminal Court. Is this because it is so great a crime that consistent and co-ordinated international action is essential? It seems not. The Commentary to the draft article says:

> The aggression attributed to State is a *sine qua non* for the responsibility of an individual for his participation in the crime of aggression. An individual cannot incur the responsibility for this crime in the absence of aggression committed by a State. Thus a court cannot determine the question of individual criminal responsibility for this crime without considering as a preliminary matter the question of aggression by the State. The determination by a national court of one State of the question whether another State has committed aggression would be contrary to the fundamental

[77] 28 USC 1605(a)(7)(A). Subs. (B) adds further limitations: (i) that if the claim is brought against the State in which the act occurred then that State must be given "a reasonable opportunity to arbitrate the claim in accordance with accepted international rules of arbitration" and (ii) that the claimant or victim was a US national at the time of the act. This rather suggests that the principle thrust of the Act is aimed at States with which the USA is unable to exercise a normal protective function with regard to its nationals abroad (e.g. in the absence of diplomatic relations).

principle of international law, *par in parem imperium non habet*. Moreover, the exercise of jurisdiction by the national court of a State which entails consideration of the commission of aggression by another State would have serious implications relations and international peace and security.

At least it is honest. In consequence, the exercise of jurisdiction would depend upon the relevant consents being given under the Statute of the ICC, which, one suspects, might rarely be the case. The consequence seems to be that the more serious the offence, and the closer the responsibility for its commission rests on the State rather than upon the individual, the less likely it is that effective mechanisms of judicial redress—let alone remedies—will be in place. It seems that at the root of these objections to the use of municipal courts to enforce international obligations lies the "outmoded" model of the international system outlined at the start of this chapter. It may have evolved as far as rights are concerned; it may have evolved as far as responsibility is concerned. But if it has evolved at all as regards remedies, then it is into a chameleon.

Certainly, individuals can assert their rights through a wide variety of international treaty mechanisms which can themselves be extremely innovative and effective. But this simply raises the question at the heart of this argument, but from another angle. Why does it have to be done by the individual when the obligations in question are also owed to States? Could it be—on both sides of the equation—that States are not as interested in the true position of the individual under international law as they say they are? Perhaps it is not what "they", States, see international law as being about, after all. And perhaps the interests of the individual as a subject or as an object, or as part of the dynamic, of international law would be well served by developing and refining the implementation of inter-State obligations at the inter-State level, not as a replacement for individual—or, indeed, State—responsibility before domestic fora, but as a complement; and not only as regards international crimes for which there might be both individual and State responsibility, but for all forms of international obligations.

12

The Treaty of Amsterdam: Towards a More Effective Enforcement of International Obligations?

NANETTE A. NEUWAHL

1. INTRODUCTION

A book on remedies against breaches of international law by States would not be complete without a reflection on the European Union. This is so for various reasons.

First of all, the European legal system may teach something about effectiveness and efficiency as a reason for the creation of remedies. Within the European Union, the law on remedies against breaches of Community law has had life breathed into it by the European Court of Justice for the purpose of enhancing the effectiveness of the legal order established by the Treaties, and this in particular for the benefit of the private individual. The *Van Gend en Loos* case[1] permitted the Member States to let diplomacy prevail in mutual relations within the European Community, and allowed the European institutions to concentrate on different tasks; rather than the enforcement of the law for the benefit of individuals in general, the Commission would henceforth be able to concentrate more on initiating legislation, as well as on increased administrative enforcement in some areas. Effectiveness and efficiency of administration clearly played a role in creating remedies in the European Community. It also determined their continued expansion. In several ways, national legal systems have come under pressure from the Community legal system. These developments are well known. On the one hand, the harmonisation of national remedies was required,[2] and, on the other hand, in the pro-active case law of the Court of Justice the distinction between obligations on States and obligations on individuals became increasingly (though not totally) blurred. Although in theory the same mechanisms could be applied to international treaties, it does not usually occur because, as a rule, States would not agree to let this happen.

---

[1] Case 26/62, *Van Gend en Loos* v. *Nederlandse Administratie der Belastingen* [1963] ECR 1.

[2] See also J. Temple Lang, "The Duties of National Courts under Community Constitutional Law", 22 *ELRev*. 3–18; and C.M.G. Himsworth, "Things Fall Apart: The Harmonisation of Community Judicial Procedural Protection Revisited", 22 *ELRev*. 291–311.

Secondly, a book on remedies would not be complete without investigating EU law because, within the international legal system, this area stands somewhat apart. European Union law is a distinct area of the law. Although derived from international treaty, it cannot simply be equated, lock, stock and barrel, with international law because of the supra-national characteristics of the parts which constitute European Community law. By "supra-national" I mean the capacity of the law to be both enacted and enforced over a Member State without the consent of its government. This quality is absent as of principle from the international legal order. As EU law cannot be assimilated to national law either—again, for the same reasons—the EU is sometimes characterised as something "in between": in between an international organisation and a State, in between a confederation and a federal State. Alternatively, it is sometimes called a process, thereby implying it is travelling in a certain direction, although the desitnation, the route and the timetable remain undetermined. Because of this special in-between situation of EU law, solutions may be found within European Union law which can be extrapolated and used for purposes of comparison with, contrast to or use in either type of legal system.

In relation to remedies in particular, it will be noted that the special "compact" which exists between the EC judiciary and the "Van Gend individual" is an extraordinary one. To be sure, European Union law itself is not a homogeneous area of the law. There used to be a distinction between the First Pillar of the Union (EC law) on the one hand and the Second and Third Pillars (respectively the Common Foreign and Security Policy and Justice and Home Affairs) on the other. The Second and Third Pillars, it was thought, were intergovernmental in character and therefore had a legal status akin to international law. Under the Treaty of Amsterdam this distinction still exists, although important subject matters have been transferred from the intergovernmental to the supranational arena. However, supra-national "Community" remedies, upheld by the ECJ because they are inherent in the Community treaties, do not cover all areas of the law. The jurisdiction of the ECJ is concentrated on subjects falling within the area of application of, notably, the EC Treaty, although it is in the process of expanding. In this connection it might be interesting to see, for example, why the jurisdiction of the ECJ does not extend to some subjects, and why under the Treaty of Amsterdam the principle of uniformity of procedures within the EC Treaty has been abandoned. Will the new provisions significantly enhance the availability of remedies for individuals under municipal law? What does this tell us about the preparedness of the Member States to create international remedies in general?

Thirdly, the law relating to remedies in the European Union is in a state of flux, bringing to the fore new, topical issues which may be relevant beyond the scope of EC law itself. Recently, the European integration process has started to bring about quests for remedies that are not based on the effectiveness of some fundamental principles of EC law and are unrelated to the efficiency of the EC legal system. That system itself is under pressures of a social and normative political nature. As balances of interest are changing, past solutions as regards the system of remedies may no longer appear valid. For example, the effectiveness of administration may recede in importance now that the core of the Single Market is a reality, or it may increase with enlarged competence or territorial application of the Treaties. The progress or stagnation of integration may call for greater equality or greater diversity in the law; it may allow other groups to be protected, not only through a larger field of application of the law, but also through the furtherance of legal action by new interest groups for which hitherto there was no place. These are some of the possible consequences of the dynamic character of European integration, which make it such a fertile area of study.

Of course, the division of powers between the Member States and the European institutions also raises questions concerning the relationship between Member State responsibility and EC or EU responsibility, both on the international plane and within the Union itself.

It will be clear that within the context of a single chapter all the above matters cannot be covered, though a start can certainly be made. For that reason, attention will be focused on some matters which have arisen in the previous chapter to see how they might apply in the context of the European Union.

2. CONFINES AND STRUCTURE OF THE PRESENT INVESTIGATION

It was suggested by Malcolm Evans[3] that there is a tendency in international law to develop mechanisms through which the responsibility of the individual can be enforced, while leaving the State whose responsibility might also be engaged by the very act in question "beyond the reach" of the judicial machinery. Thus, it seems incongruent that jurisdiction for international crimes committed by individuals tends to be made universal, i.e. does not depend on the *locus* or nationality of the perpetrator, whereas scant provision is made for inter-State settlement of such disputes, thus leaving the acts of States largely beyond the reach of judicial determination. If one should take a negative standpoint on these developments, one might want to call this lip-service by States to their international obligations. If one should want to portray events in a more positive light, one would suggest that the international system is moving towards a low-key, though admittedly perhaps less than effective system, of dispute settlement, in which State responsibility is marginalised or avoided. The examples used by Malcolm Evans are in the field of international criminal law, but it was suggested that the principle applies on a much broader scale. The present chapter therefore tentatively explores the same area and investigates what, if anything, European law has to contribute to this hypothesis.

---

[3] See Ch. 11 above.

194   *Nanette A. Neuwahl*

The Distinction Between the Active and the Passive Side

In the European Community, where a very elaborate system of remedies exists, perhaps a distinction needs to be made between active and passive responsibility. As regards the passive side, it is probably true to say that in the Community obligations on individuals are used to complement obligations on Member States. Several obligations under the EC Treaty which are literally incumbent only on Member States have been found to apply also to individuals. For instance, this is so with regard to Article 119 EC on equal treatment between men and women,[4] and it can apply to a variety of legal instruments, including Regulations and Directives. The legal instrument of the Directive is not suitable for creating direct obligations on individuals,[5] but there are ways, indirectly, of bringing about the same result, in particular through the workings of indirect effect.[6]

There are limits to the extent to which individuals can be held liable for breaches of Community law, especially when it comes to aggravating his or her liability under criminal law which has in the past been ruled out.[7] Yet there is no doubt that obligations on individuals are used by the ECJ to reinforce the efficacy of Community law. This seems wholly salutary, without it being possible to speak of Member States being able to "hide" behind this phenomenon. Direct effect of Community law (enforceability before courts) does not free the Member States from their own obligations, nor from liability, under certain circumstances, for breaches of Community law.[8] It may be considered a pity from the viewpoint of legal certainty and effectiveness that Article 48 EC on the free movement of workers has not been held to impose obligations for individuals, but there is no evidence that the enforcement over Member States of their own obligations under the same Article would suffer as a consequence.

On the *active* side of the legal relationship, the question whether individual action replaces that of States is slightly more complicated. The picture is rendered somewhat complex because of the interposition of a Community body that is explicitly charged with the duty of supervising the application of the law, namely, the European Commission.[9] Since we are concerned with the hypothesis that States prefer to avoid contentious litigation at the international level, the assumption is that they will do so within the framework of the Community as well, avoiding action for breach by the Commission in favour of the more low-

[4] Case 43/75, *Defrenne* v. *Sabena* [1976] ECR 455.
[5] Case C–271/91, *Marshall* v. *Southampton and South West Hampshire Area Health Authority (Teaching)* (*No. 2*) [1993] ECR I–4367.
[6] Case C–106/89, *Marleasing SA* v. *La Commercial Internacional de Alimentación SA* [1990] ECR I–4135.
[7] Case 80/86, *Officier van Justitie* v. *Kolpinghuis Nijmegen* [1987] ECR 3969. Recently see Case C–168/95, *Arcaro* [1997] 1 CMLR 179.
[8] Joined Cases C–46/93 & 48/93, *Firma Brasserie du Pêcheur* v. *Germany* and R. v. *Secretary of State for Transport, ex parte Factortame* [1996] ECR I–1029.
[9] Art. 155 EC Treaty.

profile solution of litigation before municipal courts. Indeed, within the Community, judicial claims by individuals before national courts are preferred in many respects. Yet again, it seems to be a case of the individual complementing, notably, the Commission, rather than anything else. On paper, contentious international litigation is there, and it is certainly used by the Commission. One must therefore conclude that within the EC context the movements which Evans suggests are detectable on the international level do not really apply.

The Distinction Between EC Law and Broader European Law

A further distinction needs to be made, however, between the European Community and the larger context of the European Union. It is illuminating to dwell on the developments regarding co-operation in areas just outside the Community, in what is called the "intergovernmental" part of the Treaty on European Union. More particularly, in the "Justice and Home Affairs" pillar, as will be seen, there is an ongoing search for adequate judicial remedies. Most recently this has culminated in the proposal, in the context of the draft Treaty of Amsterdam, to transfer certain subject matters to the Community pillar. It may be interesting to reflect on what could motivate the drafters to opt for particular forms of remedies against breaches of international obligations by States. To what extent are remedies for individuals included, and how could this affect the responsibility of States?

3. REMEDIES IN THE FIELD OF JUSTICE AND HOME AFFAIRS CO-OPERATION BEFORE AMSTERDAM

If one is considering remedies under the Third Pillar it is useful to recall what is currently included in this field, i.e. before the entry into force of the Treaty of Amsterdam. Although there is currently no definition of Justice and Home Affairs (JHA), Article K.1 of the Treaty on European Union (TEU) lists a number of items declared to be "of common interest" within the so-called Third Pillar:

> "For the purposes of achieving the objectives of the Union, in particular the free movement of person, and without prejudice to the powers of the European Community, Member States shall regard the following areas as matters of common interest:
> 1. asylum policy;
> 2. rules governing the crossing by persons of the external borders of the Member States and the exercise of controls thereon;
> 3. immigration policy and policy regarding nationals of third countries:
>   a. conditions of entry and movement by nationals of third countries on the territory of Member States;

    b. conditions of residence by nationals of third countries on the territory of the Member States, including family reunion and access to employment;

    c. combating unauthorised immigration, residence and work by nationals of third countries on the territory of Member States;

4. combating drug addiction in so far as this is not covered by 7 to 9;

5. combating fraud on an international scale in so far as this is not covered by 7 to 9;

6. judicial cooperation in civil matters;

7. judicial cooperation in criminal matters;

8. customs cooperation;

9. police cooperation for the purposes of preventing and combating terrorism, unlawful drug trafficking and other serious forms of international crime, including if necessary certain aspects of customs cooperation, in connection with the organisation of a Union-wide system for exchanging information within a European Police Office (Europol)."

The area of Justice and Home Affairs is characterised not only by a variety of policy aims, but also by a number of policy instruments (in particular, joint actions, joint positions and conventions) which are specific to the Third Pillar. However, the field is also covered by other sets of regulations, including, in part, the EC Treaty, as well as ancillary agreements between Member States concluded in accordance with Article 220 EC. This Article, in the section headed "General and Final Provisions" of the EC Treaty, provides that:

"Member States shall, so far as necessary, enter into negotiations with each other with a view to securing for the benefit of their nationals:
    —the protection of persons and the enjoyment and protection of rights under the same conditions as those accorded to their own nationals;
    —the abolition of double taxation;
    —the mutual recognition of companies [. . .];
    —the simplification of formalities governing the reciprocal recognition and enforcement of judgements of courts or tribunals and of arbitration awards."

It will be clear that some of the matters concerned here are matters of Justice and Home Affairs, so that there may be an overlap between what is achieved here and the work done currently under the Third Pillar. Furthermore, in some areas such as in matters of asylum, there may be three or more different sets of regulations—for example, the Schengen agreements, the Dublin Convention, the Third Pillar of the TEU and European Community law.

Dispute settlement is hardly addressed under the Third Pillar, except that Article K.3 TEU provides that conventions drawn up under the Justice and Home Affairs title may stipulate that the Court of Justice shall have jurisdiction to interpret and to rule on any disputes regarding their application in accordance with such arrangements as they may lay down. As we shall see, this option is seldom used. There is, however, a host of dispute settlement mechanisms operating in the field covered by the Third Pillar, which is not explicitly provided in the Treaty on European Union. Dispute settlement can take the form of political or judicial dispute settlement; in the latter case it can sometimes take place at the initiative of private individuals.

Litigation may first of all take place before national courts. Title VI TEU consists of international treaty provisions which can be applied in those national courts which are empowered to do so.

International dispute-settlement mechanisms come in a variety of forms, as is illustrated in particular by several international agreements in the field under consideration. Many treaties do not rely on diplomacy alone but entrust an international body with special functions in the context of dispute settlement. These may range from advisory functions to the power to take binding decisions. For example, the K.4 Committee of the TEU may give opinions; the Executive Committee provided for in Article 131 of the Convention applying the Schengen Agreement on the Gradual Abolition of Checks at their Common Borders is entrusted with the task of ensuring that the Convention is implemented correctly.[10] Also the Committee provided for by Article 18 of the "Dublin Convention", has important powers, including in extreme cases that of authorising a Member State temporarily to suspend the application of the Convention.[11]

What is striking, however, is the absence in the field of specialised international courts. Examples of judicial dispute-settlement organs in the field covered by the Third Pillar include the Benelux Court and the European Court of Human Rights. The Benelux Court has jurisdiction *inter alia* in matters of immigration into the territory concerned, i.e. Belgium, the Netherlands and Luxembourg. Since all the Member States are parties to the European Convention on Human Rights (ECHR), the European Court of Human Rights in Strasbourg provides a valuable course of action for individuals against breaches of that convention by Member States' authorities. The jurisdiction of the International Court of Justice is not as restricted as that of the Strasbourg institutions in terms of subject matter, but neither individuals nor the Community have standing before it, and using it as a regular avenue of dispute settlement has its disadvantages. The jurisdiction of the ECJ is in principle restricted to the EC Treaty and to cases where it has expressly been given a role in conventions concluded among the Member States.

On the basis of Article 220 of the EC Treaty (EC) several conventions have been negotiated under the terms of which the ECJ has been entrusted with jurisdiction, in particular the Brussels Convention on the Jurisdiction of Courts and the Recognition and Enforcement of Judgements in Civil and Commercial

[10] *Cf.* Art. 131 of the Convention Applying the Schengen Agreement of 14 June 1985 between the Governments of the States of the Benelux Economic Union, the Federal Republic of Germany and the French Republic on the Gradual Abolition of Checks at their Common Borders; text in H. Meijers (ed.), *Internationalisation of Central Chapters of the Law of Aliens, Refugees, Security and Police* (2nd edn., NJCM-Boekerij, No. 21, Leiden, 1992), at 155–92.

[11] *Cf.* Art. 17 of the Convention Determining the State Responsible for Examining Applications for Asylum Lodged in One of the Member States of the European Communities: text in Meijers, n. 10 above, at 147–54.

Matters,[12] the Convention of 29 February 1968 concerning the Mutual Recognition of Companies and Legal Persons,[13] and the Rome Convention on the Law Applicable to Contractual Obligations.[14] This practice inspired the inclusion of Article K.3(2)(c) in the Maastricht Treaty. According to Article K.3(2)(c), conventions which the Member States may adopt in the field of Justice and Home Affairs "in accordance with their respective constitutional requirements" may stipulate that the Court shall have jurisdiction to interpret their provisions and to rule on any disputes regarding the application of such conventions. This is without prejudice to Article 220 EC. Thus, Article 29 of the Draft Convention on the Crossing of External Frontiers provides that[15]:

> "The Court of Justice of the European Communities shall have jurisdiction:
> —to give preliminary rulings concerning the interpretation of this Convention; references shall be made as provided in the second and third paragraphs of Article 177 of the Treaty establishing the European Community.
> —in disputes concerning the implementation of this Convention, on application by a Member State or the Commission."

Of all Third Pillar measures, this Convention is the most far-reaching as regards the conferment of jurisdiction on the Court of Justice. However, as is well known, the signing of the Dublin Convention has been temporarily delayed following a dispute between the United Kingdom and Spain over Gibraltar. Furthermore, as the example of the Europol Convention shows, the negotiation of appropriate clauses in conventions under Article K.3 has proved tortuous and has had little effect.

The Court of Justice may acquire full jurisdiction under Community law over any of the areas listed in Article K.1(1) to (6) to which the Member States may decide, by virtue of Article K.9 TEU, to apply Article 100C EC. Such decisions are to be adopted by the Member States "in accordance with their respective constitutional requirements". Yet, since Justice and Home Affairs are core elements of national sovereignty, it is hardly astonishing that the Member States have so far not been eager to make use of Article K.9, which entails a transfer of legislative potential to the Community.[16]

The procedure of Article K.3(2)(c)—*ad hoc* provisions in international conventions—is clearly preferred by the majority of Member States. Needless to say this procedure also requires the approval of all Member States and ratification in accordance with the respective national requirements. In addition it is worth

---

[12] *Cf.* the Protocol of 3 June 1971 on giving the Court of Justice power to interpret the Convention, entered into force Sept. 1975, OJ 1975, L204/28, subsequently amended by reason of accession of new Member States to the Community.

[13] Cf. Protocol of 3 June 1971 on giving the Court of Justice jurisdiction to interpret the Convention.

[14] *Cf.* OJ 1990, C219/1.

[15] Text in J. Monar and R. Morgan (eds.), *The Third Pillar of the European Union—Cooperation in the Fields of Justice and Home Affairs* (The Bruges Conferences No. 5. European Interuniversity Press, Brussels, 1994), 151–72 at 171.

[16] *Europe*, 15 July 1994, 10.

noting that it is not limited to the matters listed in Article K.1(1) to (6). It can cover all matters of common interest listed in Article K.1 TEU. It does not entail a transfer of legislative potential to the Community, only an extension of the jurisdiction of the ECJ.

On the other hand there have been several arguments against the involvement of the ECJ, which may explain the resistance of some of the Member States to going down that route. Only the most important ones need to be mentioned here. In particular it is sometimes said that the Court of Justice should not be overburdened, as it is already overloaded with work. This argument is controversial, as it is somehow putting the cart before the horse. Delays at the Court have always been a matter for concern, averaging about one and a half years. However, it is far from certain that another jurisdictional layer will be able to deal with its case-load more speedily.

Yet the greatest obstacle appears to be the lack of will to go forward and the apparent loss of sovereignty in the field. It has been pointed out that the extension of the jurisdiction of the Court requires the consent of all the Member States. However, the requirement that all the Member States have to agree on an enlargement of the jurisdiction of the Court of Justice need not be prohibitive. One may resort to the instrument of the Optional Protocol, allowing a limited number of States to have access to a body established by a larger number of States. The fact that this option has not been used with success has to be attributed to a great extent to a lack of political will. As will be seen below, this appears to have been overcome to some extent in the Treaty of Amsterdam.

4. REASONS FOR CHANGE

The reasons for seeking progress in the field of the Third Pillar is in part the wish to proceed in terms of substantive policy-making and, secondly, the desire to provide for a more effective system of settling disputes and securing observance of the law. I have had the occasion to deal elsewhere[17] with the advantages of involving the ECJ, and there is no need to go over the same ground except in order to recall the main considerations.

First, without the involvement of an international court capable of taking binding decisions there is a risk of divergent or conflicting interpretations and applications of intergovernmental rules.

Secondly, national judges may not grant the most effective protection of the individual as they are reluctant to interfere with intergovernmental decisions which are the result of diplomatic compromise.[18] Because an international court

---

[17] "Judicial Control in Matters of Justice and Home Affairs: What Role for the Court of Justice?", in R. Bieber and J. Monar, *Justice and Home Affairs in the European Union. The Development of the Third Pillar* (European Interuniversity Press, Brussels, 1995), 301–20.

[18] C.A. Groenendijk in H.G. Schermers *et al.* (eds.), *Free Movement of Persons in Europe. Legal Problems and Experiences*, Asser Institute Colloquium on European Law 1992 (Dordrecht, Nijhoff, 1993), 391–402 at 393.

does not need to be reticent in this respect, the protection of the individual would be enhanced, whether or not private persons themselves have direct or indirect access to that court.

Thirdly, the creation of a variety of international jurisdictions should be avoided so as to minimise the risk of conflicting case law and uncertainty as to which law is to be observed.

Fourthly, from the Community point of view, the involvement of the Court of Justice in areas related to the Community's aims is generally to be preferred in order to guarantee the uniform interpretation of Community law. The borderline between Community competence and Member States' competence may be hard to draw for an external jurisdiction, so that it may be induced to pronounce also on aspects of Community law. This might detract from the authority of Community law and undermine Community solidarity.

Fifthly, the Court of Justice is a well-established institution whose decisions are generally respected. Specialised courts will have to face the difficulty of establishing a similar reputation especially where such delicate matters as Justice and Home Affairs are concerned.

Sixthly, the ECJ can deal with disputes between Member States as well as with disputes between them and the EC institutions. The existing co-operation procedures between the national courts and the Court of Justice can be extended to guarantee the most effective protection to individuals and, conversely, to make use of the vigilance of the individual as plaintiff so as to obtain a most effective system of supervision.

Finally, endowing the Court of Justice with jurisdiction may in practice be the only way to ensure that European institutions can be held responsible for their acts under Title VI. To the extent that such acts do not infringe primary Community law, the activity of organs of the Union will in practice not be subject to judicial review, the only exception being the possibility that individuals complain in Strasbourg of an infringement of their human rights in an action against (the collectivity of) the Member States.

These are all reasons to move ahead as regards judicial enforcement of the provisions in this field. Yet they would have applied already before the negotiation of the Treaty of Amsterdam. So why was it not sufficient for the ECJ to be endowed with jurisdiction through *ad hoc* provisions in international agreements?

Perhaps the single most negative aspect of *ad hoc* provision in Third Pillar agreements is that they remain Third Pillar agreements, not Community instruments. The reliance on national courts will only work if the individual has an effective remedy under the national legal system. For instance, preliminary rulings will be of little use if individuals cannot avail themselves of legal redress before a national court or tribunal in the first place. Thus, it has been observed that in some countries formal procedures for legally challenging immigration decisions are virtually non-existent.[19] Whereas in the case of Community law

[19] P. Bartram, "European Aspects of the Admission and Expulsion of Asylum-Seekers", 6 (1) *Immigration and Nationality Law & Practice* 40–3 at 42.

the creation of effective remedies is a justiciable obligation of the Member States, it is doubtful whether the same applies more generally in the field of Justice and Home Affairs. Implementation of an intergovernmental convention would be required in relation to disputes involving individuals if their national legal system requires international agreements to be incorporated into national law before they can be justiciable.

5. THE TREATY OF AMSTERDAM

In the following section I shall discuss the new provisions of the Treaty of Amsterdam regarding the involvement of the Court of Justice in matters which are currently regulated by the Third Pillar of the Treaty on European Union. Since the provisions lay down important principles it is worthwhile quoting the two main Articles at length:

Article K.7 [New Article 35]:

"1. The Court of Justice of the European Communities shall have jurisdiction, subject to the conditions laid down in this Article, to give preliminary rulings on the validity and interpretation of framework decisions and decisions, on the interpretation of conventions established under this Title and on the validity and interpretation of the measures implementing them.

2. By a declaration made at the time of signature of the Treaty of Amsterdam or any time thereafter, any Member State shall be able to accept the jurisdiction of the Court of Justice to give preliminary rulings as specified in paragraph 1.

3. A Member State making a declaration pursuant to paragraph 2 shall specify that either:

(a) any court or tribunal of that State against whose decisions there is no judicial remedy under national law may request the Court of Justice to give a preliminary ruling on a question raised in a case pending before it and concerning the validity or interpretation of an act referred to in paragraph 1 if that court or tribunal considers that a decision on the question is necessary to enable it to give judgment, or

(b) any court or tribunal of that State may request the Court of Justice to give a preliminary ruling on a question raised in a case pending before it and concerning the validity or interpretation of an act referred to in paragraph 1 if that court or tribunal considers that a decision on the case is necessary to enable it to give judgment.

4. Any Member State, whether or not it has made a declaration pursuant to paragraph 2, shall be entitled to submit statements of case or written observations to the Court in cases which arise under paragraph 1.

5. The Court of Justice shall have no jurisdiction to review the validity or proportionality of operations carried out by the police or other law enforcement services of a Member State or the exercise of the responsibilities incumbent upon Member States with regard to the maintenance of law and order and the safeguarding of internal security.

6. The Court of Justice shall have jurisdiction to review the legality of framework decisions and decisions in actions brought by a Member State or the Commission on

grounds of lack of competence, infringement of an essential procedural requirement, infringement of this Treaty or of any rule of law relating to its application, or misuse of powers. The proceedings provided for in this paragraph shall be instituted within two months of the publication of the measure.

7. The Court of Justice shall have jurisdiction to rule on any dispute between Member States regarding the interpretation or application of acts adopted under article K.6(2) whenever such dispute cannot be settled by the Council within six months of its being referred to the Council by one of its members. The Court shall also have jurisdiction to rule on any dispute between Member States and the Commission regarding the interpretation or the application of conventions established under Article K.6(2)(d)."

Article 73p [68 new numbering]:
"1. Article 177 shall apply to this Title (on visas, asylum, immigration and other policies related to free movement of persons) under the following circumstances and conditions: where a question on the interpretation of this Title or on the validity or interpretation of acts of the institutions of the Community based on this Title is raised in a case pending before a court or tribunal of a Member State against whose decisions there is no judicial remedy under national law, that court or tribunal shall, if it considers that a decision on the question is necessary to enable it to give judgment, request the Court of Justice to give a ruling thereon.

2. In any event, the Court of Justice shall not have jurisdiction to rule on any measure or decision taken pursuant to Article 73j(1) relating to the maintenance of law and order and the safeguarding of internal security.

3. The Council, the Commission or a Member State may request the Court of Justice to give a ruling on a question of interpretation of this Title or of acts of the institutions of the Community based on this title. The ruling given by the Court of Justice in response to such a request shall not apply to judgments of courts or tribunals of the Member States which have become *res judicata*."

Judicial Control in Matters Transferred to the First Pillar

If we read Article 73p EC closely and do so in the larger context of the EC, we must observe that in Third Pillar matters transferred to the First Pillar the jurisdiction of the ECJ is broader than before, although on the whole it not as broad as would be the case in respect to the bulk of Community law. With Article 73p, the newly designed Title IIIa (Title IV under the new numbering) "on visas, asylum, immigration and other policies related to free movement of persons" contains a few provisions on the Court of Justice which are more restrictive than those applying in respect to the EC Treaty in general.

It is to be noted that the subjects coming within this new EC title are specified in Article 73i (61 under the new numbering) and further worked out in Articles 73j to 73n (62–68 under the new numbering). They include, generally, matters which hitherto came under items 1–6 of Article K.1 of the present TEU. Customs co-operation, mentioned under item 8 in the current Article K.1, is transferred to Article 116 EC (135 in the new numbering), and comes in a new Title of its own. Customs co-operation is therefore not subject to the particular provisions of Title IIIa but rather comes under the general provisions of the EC Treaty regarding jurisdiction of the Court. It thereby has achieved "full Community treatment".

Article 73p (68 in the new numbering) provides in its first paragraph for a duty of national courts of last resort to refer questions of Community law to the ECJ. This probably implies a principle of direct effect as well, as this would enhance the useful effect of the provision, much as in any *Van Gend en Loos* type of situation. Under Article 73p, lower courts are not given the power to refer questions to the Court of Justice. A contextual interpretation of the provision—comparing it with the general provisions of the current Article 177—would suggest that their power cannot be implied, because otherwise, the first paragraph would lose most of its useful effect.

The second paragraph of Article 73p provides that the Court of Justice shall not have jurisdiction to rule on any measure or decision taken pursuant to Article 73j(1) relating to the maintenance of law and order and the safeguarding of internal security. This paragraph is difficult to interpret as it is not clear whether it applies to Community acts only, or also to Member State measures. However this may be, for present purposes it is sufficient that it shows that the drafters were against endowing the Court with jurisdiction in this field, even if this could be to the benefit of individuals. The words "in any event" seem to say that the internal security exception would hold, within the framework of this title, with regard to all jurisdictions of the ECJ, not merely that under Article 177. Since the new Title on visas can be seen as *lex specialis* in relation to the general provisions on the jurisdiction of the ECJ, the Court is likely to be asked further to clarify the extent of the exception within the framework of the new Title.

The third paragraph of Article 73p lays down a totally new non-contentious procedure. Hitherto, within the framework of the EC Treaty the institutions had only a very limited power to refer to the Court for advisory opinions. This power mainly concerned the question of the compatibility with the Treaty of international agreements to which the Community intends to become a party.[20] Now, a new facility is introduced: the Council, the Commission or a Member State may request the Court of Justice to give a ruling on a question of interpretation of the new Title or of acts of the institutions of the Community based on it. The purpose of such rulings is not further clarified, so that the reasons for asking for a ruling seem limitless. The fact that the ruling given by the Court of Justice in response to such a request shall not apply to judgments of courts or tribunals of the Member States which have become *res judicata* is unprecedented and will be considered further below.

In addition to the provisions in the new title, there are the more general provisions of the Treaty on the jurisdiction of the Court of Justice. The provisions

---

[20] Currently, Art. 228(6) EC.

regarding the jurisdiction of the ECJ in the new Title on visas, asylum and other policies relating to the free movement of persons are *lex specialis* in relation to the general rules on the jurisdictions of the ECJ which will remain unchanged except for their numbering (currently Articles 164–188 EC, 220–245 in the new numbering). As neither the latter provisions nor those laid down in the new title of the EC Treaty regulate the matters exhaustively, both sets of provisions will apply in relation to matters transferred to the new title. Within this framework, due to Article 73p, the preliminary rulings procedure is refurbished, but the other jurisdictions, notably those under Articles 169, 170 and 173 EC, remain unaffected. If this is true, it must be concluded that contentious litigation at the international level is expanded by the new provisions. Similarly, the availability of remedies for individuals is increased by giving highest national courts access to the European Court. The expansion of the jurisdiction of the Court will prove an effective additional incentive, on all levels, to the enforcement of the law.

The leap forward in this field can be seen as a recognition by the Member States that something needed to be done in this field which is so closely connected to the realisation of an area without internal frontiers. In some respects, however, the arrangements agreed upon are a compromise.

First of all, the lower courts are not given the power to refer questions to the Court of Justice. This is to be regretted. Whereas references by lower courts are not absolutely necessary for ensuring the uniform application and interpretation of the Treaty—although they can greatly help to speed up the process—it is to be regretted that an asymmetrical procedure will now apply across the Treaty. This may lead to the Court increasingly having to question the appropriateness of a reference, especially when it relates in any respect to the new title. This may undermine confidence in the Article 177 procedure itself, and therefore work negatively on the system of dispute settlement as a whole.

Secondly, because of the introduction of the second paragraph of Article 73p, the Court will tread carefully in relation to matters pertaining to the maintenance of law and order and the safeguarding of internal security. This in turn may affect also the willingness of municipal courts to interfere in the same area.

Thirdly, there are opt-outs from the substantive provisions of the Treaty, namely, in relation to Title IIIa and Schengen. In particular, the United Kingdom and Ireland can opt in later.[21] This means that with respect to the subjects concerned the international remedies provided for under the Treaties are not really available with respect to these countries, and municipal remedies are also more difficult to obtain.

Fourthly, the fact that the rulings requested by the Member States, Council or Commission shall not affect judgments of courts or tribunals of the Member States which have become *res judicata* does not sit easily with the current relationship between Community law and national law. The qualification in relation to earlier judgments of national courts can be seen as an obligation on the

---

[21] Denmark's situation is rather special. See the Protocol on Denmark to the Treaty of Amsterdam.

part of the Court of Justice to limit the retro-active effect of this type of ruling, though the Article is silent on the effect of a judgment on facts occurring prior to the ruling but not yet subject to national jurisprudence. The qualification is clearly intended to take away any misgivings which Member States might have as to the effects of the rulings, and to lower the threshold of the use of the procedure. At the same time, it illustrates that the rulings are not to be seen as simple advisory opinions but are binding upon the Community. This makes it a promising avenue for the settlement of disputes, which allows for an authoritative clarification of responsibility by way of a non-contentious procedure. The most attractive aspect of Article 73p, making its use preferable, more specifically, over that of the current Article 169 or 170 EC, seems to be the lower threshold connected with the *res judicata* exception. However, the relationship of judgments under the first and third paragraph of Article 73p remains unclear. In particular, it seems difficult to reconcile the new exception with the supremacy of Community law as a whole and with the binding character of preliminary rulings at the request of the highest national courts. At first sight it therefore seems as if a similar phenomenon occurs, as was suggested by Malcolm Evans[22]: there is a subtle curtailment (in the third paragraph) of international responsibility, which contrasts with the expansion of remedies for individuals brought about by the first paragraph of Article 73p. Nevertheless, with the variety of avenues available, it is probably more correct to state that the new provisions are an improvement in terms of effective enforcement procedures.

On the whole, it is felt that the provisions are definitely a step ahead. There are now ways to obtain a uniform interpretation and enforcement of the law. It is true that not all Member States are involved in the substantive obligations, but at least these Member States will no longer be in a position to put obstacles in the way of the jurisdiction of the ECJ in relation to the other Member States. Overall, this is a positive contribution to the effectiveness of the rules applicable in the field.

Title on Police and Judicial Co-operation in Criminal Matters

The Treaty of Amsterdam also brings a greater involvement of the ECJ in the field of intergovernmental co-operation, which is now reduced in scope to the extent that matters have been transferred to the First Pillar. This comprises judicial co-operation in criminal matters and "police co-operation for the purpose of combating terrorism, unlawful drug-trafficking and other forms of international crime, including if necessary some aspects of customs cooperation, in connection with the organization of a Union-wide system for exchanging information within a European Police Office (Europol)".

It should be noted that the distinction between the First and Third Pillars may be subtle. Moreover, through the "passerelle" of Article K.14 (42 in the new

---

[22] See Ch. 11 above.

numbering) TEU, further chunks of the Third Pillar can be transferred to Title IIIa (IV) of the EC Treaty.

The provisions relating to the involvement of the ECJ in the "rump" of the Third Pillar are laid down in Article K.7 (new Article 35). The Article is longer than the corresponding provisions of the new title in the EC Treaty, but, as might be expected, they are more restrictive. In order to assess their impact it is necessary to look closely at these provisions, the more so because they are not supplemented by the *lex generalis* of the EC Treaty.

The first three paragraphs of Article K.7 lay down and regulate anew the jurisdiction of the Court of Justice to give preliminary rulings in this field. It will be subject only to a declaration made by Member States. A Member State making a declaration accepting the preliminary rulings option shall specify either that a court or tribunal of last resort or any court or tribunal may request a preliminary ruling. The provisions are definitely an improvement because the jurisdiction of the ECJ no longer depends on the negotiation of a provision in an international convention in the field. The negative experiences made in the context of the Europol Convention are therefore vindicated.

Obviously, the creation of a preliminary rulings facility would not directly increase the enforceability of the provisions concerned, also because, unlike the First Pillar, Third Pillar law is not of itself supreme. Third Pillar law does not trump national law and is not necessarily directly applicable. The possibility of obtaining a preliminary ruling from the ECJ may have an indirect effect on national courts by increasing their willingness to adjudicate if they can obtain the opinion of an independent judicial organ, i.e. the ECJ. But it does not directly increase enforcement possibilities. This seems to be underlined also by the absence of an obligation on national courts of last resort to refer questions to the Court of Justice. Of course, if Member States wanted they could provide for this obligation themselves, for instance when making the declaration granting the power to request preliminary rulings. It does however seem to make much less sense to provide for an obligation to refer in the context of the Community where there is a striving towards a uniform application of Community law. If there is no fixed hierarchy between the intergovernmental measures and national law, there is indeed no real guarantee of a uniform application.

The progress obtained in respect of matters remaining in the Third Pillar is therefore much less marked than it might appear at first sight, although it is of course a slight improvement. The jurisdiction of the Court of Justice is in principle agreed and there is no need to establish it on a case-by-case basis in individual conventions.

Not insignificantly, the fifth paragraph of Article K.7, like Article 73p EC, excludes from the jurisdiction of the Court of Justice responsibilities incumbent upon Member States with regard to the maintenance of law and order and the safeguarding of internal security, while also excepting questions regarding the validity or proportionality of operations carried out by the police and other law enforcement services.

Paragraph 6 is a provision on judicial review. It establishes a direct action for annulment against the "inter-governmental" acts at issue which is open to the Member States and the Commission. There is no direct action on the part of private individuals; according to the first paragraph of Article K.7 a somewhat similar effect can be obtained through the preliminary rulings procedure, but this is not at the discretion of individuals.

Finally, paragraph 7 provides for contentious dispute settlement, showing yet again a clear preference for negotiated settlements. Where there is a dispute between the Commission and (one or more of) the Member States regarding the interpretation or application of conventions established under Article K.6(2)(d), the ECJ can immediately be called upon to resolve it. In other instances, Member States cannot simply access the Court but have to refer a dispute with other Member States to the Council first. This means that disputes between Member States should be solved if possible by negotiation. Only if that is not possible within six months of it being referred to the Council can the Court take over. One assumes that there will still be a need for an explicit reference by a Member State or the Council.

6. CONCLUSIONS

Improvements in the field of remedies are noticeable both with regard to matters which under the Treaty of Amsterdam are transferred to the EC Pillar and with regard to matters which will stay in the Third Pillar.

With regard to the free movement of persons, first of all, the possibility of preliminary rulings is introduced into the Treaty. We have seen that this encourages dispute settlement before national courts. The law with respect to the free movement of persons will also have direct effect in principle, and it will be subject to the fundamental principles of equal treatment and effective enjoyment of rights in the same way as applies to Community law in general. This greatly enhances the effectiveness of remedies and of the substantive law in the field under consideration, albeit that it excludes matters of internal security and is subject, in the main, to variable geometry. Matters coming under Articles 116 (customs union) and 220 (conventions) are not included in this option. The effect of "variable geometry" in relation to the substantive law (opt-ins especially for the UK and Ireland) is that the consequences of communitarisation are not quite the same for every Member State of the Union. Yet temporarily "severing" the Member States concerned has allowed the other Member States to go ahead as well as to agree on the involvement of the ECJ. In the long run, moreover, the provisions should have a positive effect on the application of the law by all Member States.

Contentious proceedings also exist in the First Pillar, as a matter of last resort. In the majority of the Member States, the preliminary rulings procedure will be a useful complement to the other proceedings, even though only courts of last resort have a duty/power to make references. The involvement of individuals in enforcing the law may still be regarded with suspicion in some Member States, but it looks as if it is regarded as salutary by most of the others. The only Member States that could be said to "hide" are those that are not prepared to subscribe to the substantive part of the Treaty concerned by those provisions.

As regards matters that have remained under the Third Pillar—the provisions of the TEU on Police and Judicial Co-operation in Criminal Matters—things are more complex. There is some progress here as well, although less markedly so. Unlike under the new title of the EC Treaty on visas, asylum, immigration and other policies relating to the free movement of persons, here the availability of preliminary rulings depends on individual Member States making a declaration empowering national courts to refer questions to the ECJ. So too, because Community principles do not apply to the intergovernmental context, the route of litigation by private individuals is not secured under the Third Pillar in a way comparable to the Community, even in Member States that would allow (or even oblige some of) their courts to refer to the ECJ. Remedies under the Third Pillar therefore continue to be uncertain.

Contentious dispute settlement before the ECJ is provided for, as well as dispute settlement before national courts. Yet in places the effectiveness of the remedies for individuals is lagging behind. Within the Third Pillar, this is noticeable from the fact that the provisions need not have the same effect in every Member State.

In respect of the Third Pillar as regards the matters transferred to the EC sphere, one notes the inability of the drafters to agree to entrust the ECJ with jurisdiction over matters of internal security. Particularly in the field of human rights protection in the Community, this is a severe shortcoming.

Within the Community there is a complementarity of remedies for individuals and States. Within the Third Pillar we are still some way off that ideal. Yet the overall impression is that in terms of judicial enforcement the Treaty of Amsterdam is a step ahead. It is evident that the Union is seeking to improve the availability of remedies in the whole area under consideration.

Studying the relevant provisions it emerges that the Treaty of Amsterdam has become very compartmentalised. Arguably, this compartmentalisation should be taken into account when judging the efficacy of the system as a whole. But that is a different chapter altogether.[23]

---

[23] On this matter see further N. Neuwahl, "Judicial Cooperation within the European Union: An Appraisal", Grotius Programme Seminar Paper, Liverpool, 10 Jan. 1998 (to be published).

13

The Communities, the Union and Beyond: Community Law in the International Sphere?

WILLIAM ROBINSON*

1. INTRODUCTION

"[T]he EEC Treaty, albeit concluded in the form of an international agreement, none the less constitutes the constitutional charter of a Community based upon the rule of law. As the Court of Justice has consistently held, the Community treaties established a new legal order for the benefit of which the States have limited their sovereign rights, in ever wider fields, and the subjects of which comprise not only Member States but also their nationals. The essential characteristics of the Community legal order which has thus been established are in particular its primary over the law of the Member States and the direct effect of a whole series of provisions which are applicable to their nations and to the Member States themselves."[1]

This seminal passage from the Court of Justice's first opinion on the draft European Economic Area agreement draws together the key elements of the Community legal order as it stood at that time. Those principles had been enunciated primarily by the Court of Justice since the early 1960s.[2] The passage also illustrates why Community law has not generally found favour with either international or national lawyers and scholars. Community law has been bound by the scriptures of neither national nor international law. Ironically, it nevertheless remains dependent on both: national courts are the "Community courts of general jurisdiction"[3] and "constitutional" amendments require international agreements.[4]

As a hybrid operating in both spheres, the Community legal order has drawn upon Member States' national laws, whether civil, criminal, constitutional or administrative, and principles of international law for its development. Indeed,

---

* All views expressed are personal to the author.

[1] Opinion 1/91, *Re the Draft Treaty in a European Economic Area* [1991] ECR I–6079, para. 21.

[2] Since, notably, Case 26/62, *Van Gend en Loos* v. *Nederlandse Administratie der Belastingen* [1963] ECR 21, to which para. 21 of *Opinion 1/91*, n. 1 above, made reference.

[3] Case T–51/89, *Tetra Pak* [1990] ECR II–309.

[4] Art. N TEU.

the Court relied upon the hybrid nature of Community law when announcing the principles of primacy and direct effect. The Court held in the landmark case of *Costa* v. *ENEL* that:

> "the law stemming from the Treaty, an independent source of law, could not, because of its *special and original nature*, be overridden by domestic legal provisions, however framed, without being deprived of its character as Community law and without the legal basis of the Community itself being called into question."[5]

Similarly, the Court stated in *ICC* v. *Amministrazione delle Finanze* that:

> "Uniform application of Community law is *imperative* not only when a national court is faced with a rule of Community law the meaning and scope of which need to be defined; it is just as imperative when the Court is confronted by a dispute as to the validity of an act of the institutions."[6]

However, the Communities and Community law are now merely one element of the European Union whose competencies, in Community and international terms, have increased markedly since the Court's pronouncements regarding the EEA Agreement. The Union has wedded together supranational political and judicial institutions and intergovernmental co-operation procedures. Tensions necessarily exist between the various actors in the Community legal order and the European Union: individuals, Member States, the Institutions, third countries and international organisations.

Three areas of tension are apparent: first, the relationship within the Community legal order between individuals and Member States, on the one hand, and national and Community courts, on the other; secondly, the line of demarcation within the Union between the Community legal order and intergovernmental competence; lastly, the interface between the Community legal order and third countries and international organisations.

It is against this background that this Chapter seeks to evaluate, from the perspective of the case law of the Court of Justice, the evolving relationship of Community law with international law and national law. While Community law fine-tunes its relationship with national law within the Member States, its approach to various international law obligations is in a period of flux. The Community legal order appears increasingly to be wrestling with its conception of Community law in the international arena.

2. STRUCTURAL TENSION

The structure of the European Union has been likened to that of a Greek temple. It comprises, essentially, three pillars and an overarching facade. Despite

---

[5] Case 6/64, *Costa* v. *ENEL* [1964] ECR 585, at 594, emphasis added.
[6] Case 66/80, *ICC* v. *Amministrazione delle Finanze* [1981] ECR 1191, para. 11, emphasis added.

severe criticism,[7] this structure persists and is the primary source of the three areas of tension mentioned above.

The temple is founded on the *Community pillar*, which comprises the Treaties establishing the European Community, the European Coal and Steel Community and the European Atomic Energy Community. The composition, jurisdiction and powers of the Court of Justice, together with those of the other institutions thereby established—the Council, the Commission, the European Parliament and the Court of Auditors—are prescribed and limited by these treaties.[8] Within this system, the Court of Justice acts, first, as a constitutional court evaluating disputes between the institutions and Member States; secondly, as an administrative court, when reviewing the actions of the institutions; and, lastly, as an organ of judicial co-operation to ensure the uniform interpretation of Community law for application by national courts. Its jurisdiction does not, however, extend appreciably beyond the Community pillar of the Union. Article L of the Treaty on European Union provides:

"the powers of the Court of Justice of the European Communities and the exercise of those powers shall apply only to the following provisions of this Treaty:

(a) provisions amending the [EC], [ECSC] and the [EAEC Treaties];
(b) the third subparagraph of Article K.3(2)(c);
(c) Articles L to S [the final provisions]."

The Treaty on European Union brought within the Union two intergovernmental pillars, namely *Common Foreign and Security Policy* (CFSP)[9] and *Co-operation in the Fields of Justice and Home Affairs* (CJHA).[10] Finally, the provisions on the nature of the Union are set out in the overarching facade, the "Common Provisions",[11] and in the plinth, the "Final Provisions".[12]

It is clear that both substantive and institutional overlaps exists. In particular, four differences and interactions should be noted. First, the Court has, *prima facie*, no jurisdiction over either the intergovernmental provisions or the common provisions of the Union. Secondly, while the Union as a whole is served by a "single institutional framework",[13] the roles of the Commission and Parliament are reduced under the CFSP and CJHA pillars to little more than implementation and consultation, respectively.[14] Thirdly, the Member States of

---

[7] See, notably, D. Curtin, "The Constitutional Structure of the union: a Europe of Bits and Pieces", 30 *CMLRev.* 17.

[8] The first para. of Art. 3b EC states: "The Community shall act within the limits of the powers conferred upon it by this Treaty and of the objectives assigned to it therein". Art. 4(1) EC provides that "[e]ach institution shall act within the limits of the powers conferred upon it by this Treaty". See also Art. E TEU.

[9] Title V, Art. J TEU.

[10] Title VI, Art. K TEU.

[11] Title I, Arts. A to F TEU.

[12] Title VII, Arts. L to S TEU.

[13] Arts. C, J.11 and K.8 TEU.

[14] On the Commission, see Arts. J.5(3), J.8(3)(4)(5), K.3(2), K.4(2) and K.9 TEU. On the European Parliament, see Arts. J.7 and K.6 TEU.

the Communities have undertaken not to submit a dispute concerning the interpretation or application of those treaties to any method of settlement other than
those provided for therein.[15] Accordingly, disputes between institutions and
Member States and, indeed, between the Member States themselves must to be
adjudicated by the Court of Justice.[16] On the other hand, no method of dispute
resolution is included within the CFSP and CJHA pillars. Indeed, in the absence
of a self-limiting provision equivalent to that in the EC Treaty, it cannot be ruled
out, however unlikely in practice, that disputes between Member States within
the CFSP and CJHA pillars could fall for adjudication before the International
Court of Justice. Lastly, the three Communities have legal personality.[17]
The Union, however, has no legal personality and, as such, cannot undertake
international legal obligations. Furthermore, the institutions which serve the
Union have no international legal personality. It follows that the Union can only
enter into international legal obligations through its component parts, the
Communities and the Member States.

3. FINE-TUNING THE COMMUNITY LEGAL ORDER

The relationships between the Communities, Member States, national courts
and individuals are governed exclusively, within the territorial and substantive
scope of the Communities, by the Community legal order. The basic tenets of
primacy and direct effect have been accepted, somewhat reluctantly in certain
cases, by Member States and national judiciaries. Indeed, Member States have
now accepted, without objection, the equally far-reaching principles, first, that
the State is liable for loss and damage caused to individuals as a result of
breaches of Community law for which the State can be held responsible[18] and,
secondly, that national courts are obliged to interpret national law, as far as
possible, in conformity with Community law.[19]

Existing tensions within the Community legal order are more nuanced.
Battlegrounds include the principle of subsidiarity,[20] the appropriate forum for

---

[15] Art. 219 EC.

[16] The principal causes of action in this connection are: actions for failure to fulfil a Treaty obligation brought by either the Commission (Arts. 169 and 171 EC) or Member States (Art. 170 EC)
against a Member State; the action for annulment of Community acts (Art. 173 EC); and the action
for failure of a Community institution to act (Art. 175 EC).

[17] Art. 210 EC, Art. 184 Euratom, Art. 6 ECSC.

[18] See, in particular, Cases C–6/90 and C–9/90, *Francovich and Others* v. *Italian Republic* [1991]
ECR I–5357 and Joined Cases C–46/93 and C–48/93, *Firma Brasserie du Pêcheur* v. *Germany and R.*
v. *Secretary of State for Transport, ex parte Factortame* [1996] ECR I–1029.

[19] See, in particular, Case 14/83, *Von Colson and Kamann* v. *Land Nordrhein-Westfalen* [1984]
ECR 1891 and Case C–106/89, *Marleasing SA* v. *La Commercial Internacional de Alimentación SA*
[1990] ECR I–4135.

[20] The second para. of Art. 3b EC provides, "In areas which do not fall within its exclusive competence, the Community shall take action, in accordance with the principle of subsidiarity, only if
and in so far as the objectives of the proposed action cannot be sufficiently achieved by the Member
States and can therefore, by reason of the scale or effects of the proposed action, be better achieved

the judicial protection of individuals[21] and the extent of the rights which individuals may derive from Community directives. These conflicts concern essentially the competencies of Member States to act and the consequences of such actions or failures to act.

The Direct Effect of Directives

Article 189 of the EC Treaty states that directives "shall leave to the national authorities the choice of form and methods". Member States are obliged to take all the measures necessary to achieve the result prescribed by a Community directive within the period for transposition provided for therein.[22]

The doctrine of direct effect means that private parties are entitled to rely on rights derived from a Community measure in national courts, even if that measure has not been implemented by national legislation. The doctrine was conceived in relation to the express prohibitions provided for in the EC Treaty.[23] However, in 1974, the Court extended the application of that doctrine to directives.[24] The Court held that on the basis of the binding obligation on the Member States:

> "the *useful effect* of such an act [directive] would be weakened if individuals were prevented from relying on it before their national courts and if the latter were prevented from taking it into consideration as an element of Community law."[25]

Individuals could therefore claim substantive rights derived from Community directives against Member States. Under pressure from Member States, the underlying reasoning of the direct effect of directives evolved, in 1979, to a quasi-estoppel argument. That argument is based upon the relationship between the individual, Member State and Community, rather than on the "effectiveness" of the measure:

by the Community". The definition and application of "subsidiarity" have been considered in the Conclusions of the Edinburgh European Council of 11 and 12 Dec. 1992, the Inter-institutional Agreement of 25 Oct. 1993 between the Parliament, the Council and the Commission (OJ 1993 C329/135) and, further to the Amsterdam Treaty, the Protocol to the EC Treaty on the application of the principles of subsidiarity and proportionality (OJ 1997 C 340/105). See also Case C–233/94, *Germany* v. *European Parliament and Council* [1997] ECR I–2405, in which the Court essentially treated Germany's subsidiarity argument as an element of proportionality.

[21] See, e.g., Case 314/85, *Foto-Frost* [1987] ECR 4199 (Court of Justice alone may annul a Community act); Cases C–188/92, *TWD* [1994] ECR I–833 (in certain circumstances, an applicant must proceed by direct action before the Community courts and cannot avail themselves later of an Art. 177 reference) and C–68/95, *T. Port* [1996] ECR I–6065 (individuals may only seek interim measures before the Community courts for an alleged failure of a Community institution to act).

[22] See, on the obligations within the transposition period, Case C–129/96, *Inter-Environnement Wallonie ASBL*, [1997] ECR I-7411.

[23] Case 26/62, *Van Gend en Loos* v. *Nederkandse Administratie der Belastingen* [1963] ECR 1.

[24] Case 41/74, *Van Duyn* v. *Home Office* [1974] ECR 1337.

[25] *Ibid.*, para. 12, emphasis added.

"a Member State which has not adopted the implementing measures required by the directive in the prescribed periods may not rely, as against individuals, on its own failure to perform the obligations which the directive entails."[26]

According to authoritative analysis,[27] provisions of directives will therefore produce direct effects if they are (i) clear, precise and unconditional as to the result to be achieved, (ii) capable of producing rights for individuals, and (iii) the implementation period has expired.

That juridical basis and analysis of the direct effect of directives has since been frequently repeated, and has had the consequence that a directive may not impose obligations on an individual (the so-called "horizontal direct effect of directives").[28]

However, two recent cases, *Großkrotzenburg*[29] and *Aannemersbedriff P.K. Kraaijeveld BV*,[30] suggest that the Court has placed greater emphasis on the relationship between individual, Member State and Community than on the mechanical application of a formula. Both cases concerned the interpretation of Directive 85/337 on the assessment of the effects of certain public and private projects on the environment (the "Environmental Impact Assessment Directive").[31]

According to Article 2(1) of the Directive, Member States shall adopt measures to ensure that projects "likely to have a significant effect on the environment" are made subject to an assessment. However, Article 4(2) provides that for certain projects, such as that in issue, Member States may "establish the criteria and/or thresholds" necessary to determine which projects are to be subject to an assessment.

Kraaijeveld's business required access to navigable waterways. However, the Sliedrecht Municipal Council in the Netherlands adopted a dyke reinforcement and zoning plan which would have had the effect of cutting off that access. No environmental-impact assessment was carried out on the dyke modification, as the Dutch law implementing Article 4(2) provided that an assessment would only be necessary if the dyke was 5 km or more in length, with a cross-section of at least 250 m². Kraaijeveld challenged the decision approving the plan before the Dutch courts.

The Court held that Article 4(2) of the Directive conferred a discretion on the Member States. Such discretion would preclude direct effect, in the formulaic sense, as being conditional on national implementing measures.

However, the Court continued and stated that the Member States' discretion was limited by Article 2(1). A Member State which established criteria or thresholds at a level such that, in practice, all projects relating to dykes would be

---

[26] Case 148/78, *Ratti* [1979] ECR 1629, para. 22.
[27] See, e.g., M. Brealey and M. Hoskins, *Remedies in EC Law* (Longman, London, 1994).
[28] Case C–91/92, *Faccini Dori* [1994] ECR I–3325.
[29] Case C–431/92, *Commission v. Germany (Großkrotzenburg)* [1995] ECR I–2189.
[30] Case C–72/95, *Aannemersbedrijf P.K. Kraaijeveld BV* [1996] ECR I–5403.
[31] OJ 1985 L175/40.

exempted in advance from the requirement of an impact assessment would exceed the limits of its discretion under Articles 2(1) and 4(2) of the directive unless all projects excluded could, when viewed as a whole, be regarded as not being likely to have significant effects on the environment.

The national court was under a duty to review whether the national authorities had exceeded their discretion in the setting of the national thresholds or criteria. If so, the national provisions must be set aside. The national authorities must then take all the general or particular measures necessary to ensure that projects are examined in order to determine whether they are likely to have significant effects on the environment and, if so, to ensure that they are subject to an impact assessment.

The judgment is interesting, in the context of this chapter, in three respects. First, Kraaijeveld was not being granted substantive rights, such as a right to insist that an environmental-impact assessment is performed. Such substantive rights are usually associated with the direct effect of a provision of Community law. The Advocate General had suggested such an approach, based upon the Directive's information provisions, but was not followed by the Court. Instead, the Court conferred on Kraaijeveld a procedure right, through the obligation on the national court, to have the national implementing provisions reviewed. It remains to be seen how plaintiffs will use such a procedural right within the context of national judicial review procedures and *locus standi* rules.

Secondly, national courts are now required not only to set aside national laws which are incompatible with clear precise and unconditional Community directives, but also to review the exercise of a Member State's discretion. This clearly elevates their role within the Community legal order regarding the enforcement of Community law obligations against the Member States.

Lastly, the Court's reasoning is instructive. By reference to *Verbond van Nederlandse Ondernemingen*,[32] a case decided in 1977, the Court reintroduced the "effectiveness" reasoning into the doctrine of direct effect, if indeed that label can be applied to this case. The implication is that the doctrine of direct effect remains a flexible tool in the definition of the rights and obligations of the Community, Member States, national courts and individuals.

4. THE COMMUNITY AND THE UNION

The structural and substantive interrelationships which exist within the Union give rise to jurisdictional tensions. As noted above, the possibilities for democratic accountability, at a supranational level, and judicial protection of Community institutions, Member States and individuals are markedly different depending upon whether a matter falls within either the Community or intergovernmental pillars of the Union. Individuals are particularly prejudiced

---

[32] Case 51/76, *Verbond van Nederlandse Ondernemingen* [1977] ECR 113.

within the intergovernmental pillars, being dependent on the constitutional provisions, within each Member State, regarding rights derived from international law.

The Court has, to date, excluded its own jurisdiction in areas clearly outside the limits established in Article L of the Treaty on European Union: first, as to a purported breach of Article B of the Treaty on European Union regarding the objectives of the Union[33] and, secondly, as to acts of the European Council.[34]

However, substantive overlaps exist between, in particular, the CJHA pillar and the European Community's provisions on the free movement of persons.[35] The demarcation line between Community and intergovernmental competence is of crucial concern for the determination of the rights and obligations of the Community, the Member States and individuals. The Court has recently been seised of a series of judicial review cases concerning the CJHA pillar.[36]

The Member States have consistently argued that acts of the Member States adopted outwith the Community structure may not, in any circumstances, be reviewed by the Court of Justice. Can the fact that an act purports to be adopted outwith the Community legislative structures prevent judicial review by the Court of Justice of the author of that act? This issue arose prior to the creation of the Union in *Parliament* v. *Council and Commission (Bangladesh I)*.[37]

In that case the contested act granted emergency humanitarian aid to Bangladesh—a field in which the Community does not have exclusive competence. The act was adopted at a meeting of the Council, but was described as an "act of the representatives of the Governments of the Member States meeting in the Council". The Parliament argued that this act was in reality an act of the Council which had infringed its prerogatives, in particular regarding budgetary procedures.

The Parliament was unsuccessful in its application. However, the Court recalled that an action for annulment must be available in the case of all measures adopted by the institutions, whatever their nature or form, which are intended to have legal effects.[38] The Court then held, at paragraph 14, that:

> "it is not enough that an act should be described as a 'decision of the Member States' for it to be excluded from review under Article 173 of the Treaty. In order for such an act to be excluded from review, it must still be determined whether, having regard to

---

[33] Case C–167/94, *Grau Gomis* [1995] ECR I–1023, point 6.

[34] Case T–584/93, *Roujansky* v. *Council* [1994] ECR II–585, point 13.

[35] See, e.g., Arts. K.3 TEU and 100C EC.

[36] The exclusion of jurisdiction under the CFSP has been raised once, in Case C–120/94R, *Commission* v. *Greece* [1994] ECR I–3037 (former Yugoslav Republic of Macedonia). Greece argued that a mere link between Art. 224 EC and the CFSP would exclude the case from the jurisdiction of the Court (paras. 61 and 62 of the Order). The Court did not rule on this point. The substantive action was later removed from the Register (C–120/94, Order of the President [1996] ECR I–1513).

[37] Joined Cases C–181/91 and C–248/91, *European Parliament* v. *Council and Commission* [1993] ECR I–3685.

[38] Case 22/70, *Commission* v. *Council* [1971] ECR 263, para. 42.

its content and all the circumstances in which it was adopted, the act in question is not in reality a decision of the Council."

The determination of the Court's jurisdiction therefore necessitated an assessment of the merits of the act in question. In this case, the Court held that the act was not an act of the Council, but an act taken by the Member States collectively. The application was therefore inadmissible. Nevertheless, the Court clearly established its ability to determine the author of the contested act based upon the substance of the contested act rather its form, thereby endorsing Advocate General Jacobs' "functional approach" to judicial review.[39]

A related issue arose in *Parliament* v. *Council (supported by Spain)*.[40] That case concerned the adoption of an act by a Community institution on the basis of powers conferred outwith the Treaties. The Parliament sought the annulment of the financial regulation[41] applicable to development finance co-operation under the Fourth ACP–EEC Convention.[42] It argued that Lomé expenditure is Community expenditure, and must accordingly be governed by Treaty's financial regulations.

The Council and Spain did not dispute that the act is an act of the Council. However, they argued that no judicial review of the act was available under Article 173 as the act was not adopted pursuant to the Treaty, but rather pursuant to a power conferred on the Council by a provision of an internal agreement to which all the Member States are parties.

The Court disagreed. In broad terms the Court stated:

> "an action by the Parliament against an act of an institution intended to have legal effects is admissible irrespective of whether the act was adopted by the institution pursuant to Treaty provisions."

The Court relied upon the wording of Article 173, which provides that the Court of Justice shall review the legality of "acts of the Council". This power seemingly extends to those acts adopted by the Council outwith the scope of the Treaties.

These cases were lodged with the Court prior to the entry into force of the Treaty on European Union. However, the power of review thereby attributed to the Court of Justice is considerable. The question remains how the Court will apply this case law within the field of substantive overlap between the Community and, notably, the CJHA provisions. That relationship is governed by Article M of the Treaty on European Union, over which the Court has jurisdiction. It provides:

> "nothing in this treaty [on European Union] shall affect the Treaties establishing the European Communities or the subsequent Treaties and Acts modifying them."

[39] Joined Cases C–181/91 and C–248/91, *Parliament* v. *Council and Commission* [1993] ECR I–3685, Opinion at para. 21.
[40] Case C–316/91, *Parliament* v. *Council (supported by Spain)* [1994] ECR I–625.
[41] Financial Regulation 91/491/EEC (OJ 1991 L266/1).
[42] The Fourth ACP–EEC Convention was signed at Lomé on 15 Dec. 1989 (OJ 1991 L229/3).

The limits of the Court's powers were raised, for the first time, in the observations in *Parliament* v. *Council (supported by France)* concerning visa requirements for third country nationals when crossing external borders.[43] The Council Regulation in issue[44] was adopted under Article 100C of the EC Treaty, but was linked with a Convention on the crossing of external frontiers, whose legal basis was the CJHA intergovernmental pillar.

Advocate General Fennelly opined that the Court has jurisdiction regarding Article M, but argued that this case concerned only the procedural requirements applicable to the Parliament within the EC Treaty:

> "In reaching a conclusion about the scope of Community competence under Article 100C of the Treaty, the Court will look at that provision in its Treaty context and cannot, in my view, qualify or restrict that interpretation by reference to a provision which it is expressly prohibited from interpreting [CJHA].[45]

The Court followed the Advocate General's Opinion. It did not address the relationship with the provisions of the CJHA and confined itself to the legislative procedural requirements. The Court implicitly suggests that the prohibition on its power in Article L, in combination with Article M, allows it to ignore provisions of the CJHA when considering Community measures.

The foregoing precedents have been considered in a further case, *Commission (supported by the European Parliament)* v. *Council (supported by France, Denmark and the United Kingdom)* regarding airport transit visas.[46] The Council adopted, on its face, a joint action regarding airport transit visas under the CJHA intergovernmental provisions.

The Commission contends that the subject matter of this act correctly falls under Article 100C of the EC Treaty. Indeed, certain provisions of a Community regulation have been reproduced in the joint action. The Commission therefore seeks the annulment of the joint action.

Advocate General Fennelly argued that, in this case, the Court has jurisdiction, and that the admissibility of the action could only be examined in the light of the merits of the case. The Court has jurisdiction to ensure that, in exercising their powers under the CJHA and CFSP provisions, the Council and the Member States do not encroach on the powers attributed to the Communities under the founding treaties. The Court could not identify the purpose of the CJHA provisions, but could establish the proper construction of the Community provisions. In this case, the Advocate General found that Article

---

[43] Case C–392/95, *Parliament* v. *Council (supported by France)* [1997] ECR I–3213.

[44] Council Regulation 2317/95 of 25 Sept. 1995 determining the third countries whose nationals must be in possession of visas when crossing the external frontiers of the Member States (OJ 1995 L234/1).

[45] Case C–392/95, *Parliament* v. *Council* [1997] ECR I–3213, Opinion of Fennelly AG, at para. 36.

[46] Case C–170/96, *Commission (supported by the European Parliament)* v. *Council (supported by France, Denmark and the United Kingdom)*, pending (OJ 1996 C210/7), Opinion of Fennelly AG of 5 Feb. 1998. Judgment of 12 May 1998—see postscript.

100C did not extend to the provisions of the joint action in question. He therefore found the action to be inadmissible.

It remains to be seen whether the Court will follow the approach of the Advocate General, first, as to jurisdiction, and, secondly, as to the interpretation of Article 100C. If so, the Court will considerably alleviate the democratic accountability and judicial review restrictions placed upon the Community institutions by the structure of the Union. Furthermore, it would potentially open a further avenue of review for individuals before national courts, operable through the Article 177 reference procedure, of Community and national legislation. No such reference has yet been received by the Court of Justice.

Lastly, it should be noted that the Advocate General's approach relies upon classical Community law methods of interpretation. By turning a blind eye to the Union's intergovernmental provisions, the Court's analysis remains within its core area of operation. This conforms to the intentions of the Union's draughtsman, but does not assist in establishing the principles underlying the Court's approach to international law.

5. COMMUNITY LAW AND INTERNATIONAL LAW

In contrast to the Community legal order, the Communities' external relations do not need to be based on uniform principles. The Court of Justice has thus held that:

> "there is no general principle of Community law obliging the Community, in its external relations, to accord third countries equal treatment in all respects."[47]

This principle will necessarily entail certain limited differences of treatment within the Community:

> "if different treatment of third countries is compatible with Community law, then different treatment accorded to traders within the Community must also be regarded as compatible with Community law where that different treatment is merely an automatic consequence of the different treatment accorded to third countries with which such traders have entered into commercial relations."[48]

In addition to the binding nature of the Community's obligations in international law, Article 228(7) of the EC Treaty states that "[a]greements concluded under the conditions set out in this article shall be binding on the institutions of the Community and on Member States". In ensuring respect for commitments arising from an international agreement concluded by the Community, Member States fulfil an obligation not only in relation to the non-member country concerned, but also and above all in relation to the Community

---

[47] Case C–122/95, *Germany (supported by Belgium)* v. *Council (supported by Spain, France and the Commission)*, Judgment of 10 Mar. 1998, not yet reported, para. 56.

[48] Case 52/81, *Faust* v. *Commission* [1982] ECR 3745, para. 25.

which has assumed responsibility for the due performance of the agreement. Thus, the Court held that agreements concluded by the Community form an integral part of Community law,[49] and fall within its jurisdiction to ensure uniform interpretation throughout the Community.

In the hierarchy of norms, the Community's international legal obligations fall between the treaties and secondary legislation.[50] As such:

> "the Court is obliged to examine whether their [Community Regulations] validity may be affected by reason of the fact that they are contrary to a rule of international law."[51]

However, the Court held that before the incompatibility of a Community measure with a provision of international law can affect the former's validity, the Community must, first, be bound by that provision, and, secondly, the provision of international law must be directly effective.[52] These criteria are necessary irrespective of whether the validity of a Community measure is challenged in a direct action or in a reference for a preliminary ruling. Furthermore, reciprocity is no obstacle to direct application within the Communities.[53]

The Court's definition of the doctrine of direct effect for international provisions is almost identical to that for Community measures:

> "A provision in an agreement concluded by the Community with non-member countries must be regarded as being directly applicable when, *regard being had to its wording and the purpose and nature of the agreement itself*, the provision contains a clear and precise obligation which is not subject, in its implementation or effects, to the adoption of any subsequent measure."[54]

The distinguishing feature of the test of direct effect of international obligations is the greater reliance on the spirit, object, purpose and context of the international agreement in ascertaining whether its provisions can be directly effective. Thus, in *Polydor*, the Court held that provisions in an agreement between the Community and Portugal, despite being in identical textual terms to directly effective Community provisions, were not directly effective on account of the different objects, purposes and contexts of the two agreements.[55]

The case law of the Court of Justice has ebbed and flowed regarding the vigour with which it has applied the criteria for the direct effect of international legal obligations. This stems from the *prima facie* parallelism between the tests of direct effect of, on the one hand, Community measures and, on the other, international agreements. The Court has, in certain circumstances, been drawn into applying the Community notion of direct effect in the international sphere.

---

[49] Case 181/73, *Haegeman* v. *Belgium* [1974] ECR 449, paras. 4 and 5, as clarified in Case 104/81, *HZA Mainz* v. *Kupferberg* [1982] ECR 3641, para. 13.

[50] Joined Cases 31/85 & 35/86, *LAISA* [1988] ECR 2285.

[51] Joined Cases 21–24/72, *International Fruit Company* [1972] ECR 1219, para. 6.

[52] *Ibid.*, paras. 7 and 8.

[53] Case 104/81, *HZA Mainz* v. *Kupferberg* [1982] ECR 3641, para. 18.

[54] Case 12/86, *Demirel* [1987] ECR 3719, para. 14, emphasis added.

[55] Case 270/80, *Polydor* v. *Harlequin Record Shops* [1982] ECR 329.

Two examples demonstrate the Court's uneasy application of Community law principles, such as direct effect, to international obligations. First, the Community legal order's relationship with the GATT, in its various incarnations, has been highlighted by the ongoing banana saga. Secondly, in the progression towards the future enlargement of the Union, the Court appears to be in the midst of a re-appraisal of its relations with its nearest neighbours, namely those States with which it has signed co-operation, association and "Europe" agreements. These examples will be considered below.

GATT and Bananas

The Community has become embroiled in a continuing saga regarding the Community market and international trade in bananas. This has led to an almost impenetrable web of national and Community litigation.

The sage commenced in 1993 when the Community substituted a common market for bananas and a common regime governing trade with third countries for the various national regimes previously in force.[56] Community demand for bananas was previously met from Community production (the most expensive bananas),[57] ACP States[58] and third countries (extremely cheap "dollar" bananas from Central and South America), and organised within national regimes.

The Community banana regime established an import quota, common tariffs and a licensing requirement. The quota varied between traditional ACP imports, on the one hand, and third country and non-traditional ACP imports, on the other. Similarly the licensing regime divided the quota according to fixed percentages between three categories of importers: "A" third country banana/ non-traditional ACP importers; "B" Community/traditional ACP banana importers; and "C" new importers.

At the same time, trade negotiations were continuing in the Uruguay Round of the GATT. Within that context, Colombia, Costa Rica, Nicaragua and Venezuela asked the Community to open consultations and, subsequently, the dispute-settlement procedure of the GATT in relation to the new Community banana regime.[59] In January 1994 the panel set up under the latter procedure submitted a report concluding that the Community import regime was incompatible with the GATT rules. In order to resolve this dispute, the Community came to an agreement with those countries, in March 1994, in the form of the "Framework Agreement on Bananas". The Agreement notably fixed the percentage of the Community quota those countries are to receive and exempted category "B" importers from the export-licence system. The Framework

---

[56] Council Regulation 404/93 of 13 Feb. 1993 on the common organisation of the market in bananas (OJ 1993 L47/1).

[57] French overseas departments, Crete, the Algarve, etc.

[58] In particular, Cameroon and Jamaica.

[59] Art. XXII:1 and Art. XXIII:2 of the GATT, respectively.

Agreement was included within the Community customs concessions in the GATT.[60] The GATT was approved, within the WTO, by Council Decision.[61]

The Community, WTO and Lomé rules have been the subject of disputes before two jurisdictions. First, certain Member States, particularly Germany and Belgium, and individuals have sought to challenge the legality of the Community regime within the Community legal order. Secondly, a further dispute-settlement procedure has run its full course under the WTO rules.

Review within the Community Legal Order

With regard to the legality of the Community regime under Community law, the Court of Justice has rejected applications for the annulment of the Community regime for alleged breaches of procedural requirements, the Common Agricultural Policy, competition rights, fundamental human rights, general principles of law, the Lomé Convention, the GATT rules and the banana protocol annexed to the EC Treaty.[62] The Court has, however, more recently annulled the Council Decision approving the WTO to the extent that the Council thereby approved the Framework Agreement, in so far as that agreement exempts category B operators from the export-licence system.[63] The discrimination thereby created between operators was not the automatic consequence of any difference of treatment of certain third countries, and so was not justified. The remainder of the application regarding the Framework Agreement was rejected.

With regard to the GATT rules, the Court reiterated that, although the provisions of the GATT have the effect of binding the Community, in assessing the scope of GATT in the Community legal system, the spirit, the general scheme and the terms of the GATT must be considered. The Court noted, in particular, the flexibility of its provisions, the dispute-resolution procedures and the possibility for unilateral action. The Court found that the GATT rules do not display the unconditional nature which is an essential precondition for them to be recognised as rules of international law that are immediately applicable in the domestic law of the contracting parties. Neither individuals nor Member States could therefore rely on the GATT rules before the Court in order to challenge the lawfulness of a Community act.

Those observations were made in respect of the GATT 1947 rules. In one of the many cases brought by *T. Port*,[64] a German banana importer, the Court was

[60] The Framework Agreement on Bananas formed an annex to Sched. LXXX to GATT 1994, which itself constitutes Annex 1A to the Agreement Establishing the World Trade Organisation.

[61] Council Decision 94/800/EC of 22 Dec. 1994 concerning the conclusion on behalf of the European Community, as regards matters within its competence, of the agreements reached in the Uruguay Round multilateral negotiations (1986–94) (OJ 1994 L336/1).

[62] See, in particular, Case C–280/93, *Germany* v. *Council* [1994] ECR I–4973.

[63] Case C–122/95, *Germany (supported by Belgium)* v. *Council (supported by Spain, France and the Commission)*, Judgment of 10 Mar. 1998, not yet reported.

[64] Joined Cases C–364/95 and C–365/95, *T. Port GmbH & Co.*, Judgment of 10 Mar. 1998, not yet reported.

required to consider the GATT 1997 rules. Port argued that those rules contained significant amendments to the GATT 1947 to confer on them sufficient unconditionality so as to be immediately applicable in the Community legal order. This argument did not hold must sway with Advocate General Elmer.[65] He referred, *obiter*, to the consistent case law regarding the absence of direct effect of GATT 1947–92 and to the Council Decision approving the GATT 1997, which stated that the WTO is not susceptible to being invoked before national courts.[66] On this basis, he concluded that the jurisprudence relative to GATT 1947–92 should apply to GATT 1997. The Court did not need to address the issue, having found that the bananas in question originated from a non-GATT State.[67]

According to the jurisprudence, if the GATT rules are sufficiently unconditional then direct effect will be accorded to them. This approach is clearly derived from the Community internal legal order, and has not been specifically modelled on international legal obligations. It remains to be seen whether GATT 1997 can be invoked within the Community legal order, on account of its revised form, even though the Member States and the Council have clearly stated that, as part of a world trade organisation, GATT 1997's provisions should not have such effect.

Review under the World Trade Organisation Rules

At the request of the United States, Ecuador, Guatemala, Honduras and Mexico, a Panel was established by the WTO to consider the Community regime on bananas. The Panel issued its report on 29 April 1997. It found that a number of elements of the Community's banana regime are not in conformity with the WTO rules, namely the General Agreement of 1994 and the General Agreement on Trade in Services (GATS). The following elements were condemned: the import-licensing arrangements, the allocation of certain percentages of the tariff quota to the signatories of the Framework Agreement on bananas and the authorisation by the signatory countries to grant export licences as well as the share out of the quantities set for traditional imports from ACP States. The report also argued that respect for the Lomé Convention did not constitute a justification for the breaches of the GATT and the GATS.

The European Union appealed against the WTO ruling on 12 June 1997. The Appellate Body of the WTO adopted its report on 5 September 1997. It confirmed the Panel report and ruled that the Community regime was not in conformity with WTO rules. In response to this ruling, the Commission adopted, on 14 January 1998, a proposal to modify the regulation establishing the

---

[65] *Ibid.*, Opinion of Elmer AG of 24 June 1997, paras. 27–9.
[66] Council Decision 94/800, n. 61 above, preamble, recital 11.
[67] Joined Cases C–364/95 and C–365/95, *T. Port GmbH & Co.*, Judgment of 10 Mar. 1998, not yet reported, at para. 63.

common organisation of the market for bananas.[68] The proposal attempts to bring the Community regime into line with the Union's commitments under the World Trade Organisation agreements and the Fourth Lomé Convention, while also protecting the interests of the Community's producers and consumers.

The developments within the WTO settlement procedures indicate the difficulties facing the Court of Justice. On the one hand, the Court has not distanced itself from the GATT, by finding, for example, that direct effect could never be afforded to such an agreement due to its nature. On the other hand, it has not embraced fully the binding effect of the GATT rules. The middle ground is likely to be squeezed as the WTO agreements tend towards greater precision.

Association Agreements

Association and co-operation agreements have been concluded, pursuant to Articles 238 and 228(3) of the EC Treaty with several States, among which figure applicants for membership of the Union. The agreements signed with Eastern European States, the so-called "Europe Agreements", are specifically designed to prepare those States for accession to the Union. The agreements vary in the extent of desired integration with the Communities. Notably, all provide for association councils with decision-making power, composed of representatives from the signatory parties.

The Court has recognised the direct effect of the provisions of both the Association Agreements and the Decisions of the Association Councils.[69] As to Decisions, the Court held in *Sevince*:

> "since they are directly concerned with the Agreement to which they give effect, the decision of the Council of Association, in the same way as the Agreement itself, form an integral part, as from their entry into force, of the Community legal system."

The majority of the Court's jurisprudence in this field has concerned the Association Agreement with Turkey[70] which provides for the progressive establishment of a customs union and for the alignment of economic policies with the Union. The Europe Agreements similarly recognise the final objective of membership of the Community and the role of the agreement in achieving this objective.[71] The objective of these agreements may be contrasted to those of certain

---

[68] Proposal for a Council Regulation (EC) amending Regulation 404/93 on the common organisation of the market in bananas (COM(1998)4 final). A Council decision is expected in June 1998.

[69] See Case 12/86, *Demirel* [1987] ECR 3719 and Case C–192/89, *Sevince* [1990] ECR I–3461, respectively.

[70] Agreement establishing an association between EEC and Turkey, signed at Ankara on 12 Sept. 1963 and concluded on behalf of the Community by Decision of the Council of 23 Dec. 1963 (OJ 1973 C113/2).

[71] See, e.g., the Preamble to the Europe Agreement establishing an association between the European Communities and their Member States, of the one part, and the Republic of Poland, of the other part (OJ 1993 L348/2), approved by Decision 93/743/EC, ECSC, Euratom of the Council and the Commission of 13 Dec. 1993 (OJ 1993 L348/1).

co-operation agreements, whose objectives are to promote economic and trade co-operation between the Community and the third country.[72] Indeed, the majority of those third States would be ineligible for membership of the Union as not being "European States" within the meaning of Article O of the Treaty on European Union.

Two lines of jurisprudence have emerged regarding the direct effect of provisions of association agreements and the decisions adopted thereunder. On the one hand, the Court has recognised, in a series of cases,[73] the direct effect of the principle of equal treatment in social security matters, as enshrined in the Article 39(1) of the Co-operation Agreement with Algeria and, in the same terms, Article 41(1) of the Co-operation Agreement with Morocco.[74] Those provisions state:

> "workers of [Algerian] [Moroccan] nationality and any members of their families living with them shall enjoy, in the field of social security, treatment free from any discrimination based on nationality in relation to nationals of the Member States in which they are employed."

This line of jurisprudence was confirmed most recently by a judgment of 15 January 1998, *Babahenini*.[75]

On the other hand, the Court was requested, in *Taflan-Met*,[76] to rule on the direct effect of Articles 12 and 13 of Decision No. 3/80 of the EEC–Turkey Association Council on the application of the social security schemes to Turkish workers and members of their families.[77] Those Articles contained detailed rules, and made reference to the Community social security regime and its implementing provisions. On 10 September 1996, the Court held that those Articles were not capable of producing direct effect, on account of the need for specific implementing legislation. The Court then stated in general terms, although strictly *obiter*, that:

> "even though some of its provisions are clear and precise, Decision No. 3/80 cannot be applied so long as supplementary implementing measures have not been adopted by the Council."[78]

---

[72] See, e.g., the Co-operation Agreement between the European Economic Community and the People's Democratic Republic of Algeria, signed in Algiers on 26 Apr. 1976 and concluded on behalf of the Community by Council Regulation 2210/78 of 26 Sept. 1978 (OJ 1978 L263/1).

[73] Case C–103/94, *Krid* v. *CNAVTS* [1995] ECR I–719, and, by analogy, Case C–18/90, *ONEM* v. *Kziber* [1991] ECR I–199; Case C–58/93, *Yousfi* v. *Belgian State* [1994] ECR I–1353; and Case C–126/95, *Hallouzi-Choho* v. *Bestuur van de Sociale Verzekeringsbank* [1996] ECR I–4807.

[74] Co-operation Agreement between the European Economic Community and the Kingdom of Morocco, signed in Rabat on 27 Apr. 1976 and concluded on behalf of the Community by Council Regulation 2211/78 of 26 Sept. 1978 (OJ 1978 L264/1).

[75] Case C–113/97, *Babahenini* v. *The Belgian State*, [1998] ECR I-183, paras. 17 and 18.

[76] Case C–277/94, *Taflan-Met* [1996] ECR I–4085.

[77] Decision No. 3/80 of the EEC–Turkey Association Council of 19 Sept. 1980 on the application of the social security schemes of the Member States of the European Communities to Turkish workers and members of their families (OJ 1983 C110/60).

[78] Case C–277/94, *Taflan-Met* [1996] ECR I–4085, para. 37.

These two lines of jurisprudence must be considered by the Court in *Sürül*.[79] The Sürül family, of Turkish nationality but resident in Germany, was denied child benefit and its supplement for their child on the ground that Mrs Sürül did not hold a specific form of residence authorisation, which was not required of a German national. Mrs Sürül claims that she has been discriminated against contrary to Article 3(1) of the same Decision 3/80, which provides:

> "persons resident in the territory of one of the Member States to whom this Decision applies shall be subject to the same obligations and enjoy the same benefits under the legislation of any Member State as the nationals of that State."

The national court has asked the Court whether this provision has direct effect. Accordingly, a sharp contrast can be drawn between the case law on the Morocco and Algerian *co-operation* agreements, which found that a similarly worded obligation conferred direct effects, while that Court held that Decision 3/80 of the Turkish *association* agreement could not, as a whole, have such an effect.

Advocate General La Pergola opined that, as Community law does not distinguish between *ratio decidendi* and *obiter dictum*, the Court should over-rule *Taflan-Met* and find that Article 3(1) of Decision 3/80 confers direct effect.

This Opinion draws upon the fact that the object and purpose of the EEC–Turkey agreement foresaw greater integration than the Moroccan and Algerian co-operation agreements. This approach would clarify the intention that the conditions of direct effect should be more easily fulfilled the closer international agreements come to the objectives of the Community. Alternatively, the Court may wish to indicate a retreat from the extensive use of direct effect, in the Community law sense, in relations with associated States. The judgment may therefore indicate the Court's current attitude to the use of direct effect as a tool in the Community interpretation of international law obligations.

6. CONCLUSION

The three examples presented in this chapter indicate that the Court of Justice is most at ease in its role of interpreting Community law within the functional and territorial limits of the European Communities. However, the Court has attempted, not entirely convincingly, to apply the techniques developed within its "new legal order" to the interpretation of the Community's international law obligations. In the same way that the Court has merged national and international law techniques to create the Community legal order, so lawyers have seized upon the possibility of applying certain private law notions to international obligations through Community law. As the pending cases noted in this chapter show, there remains significant scope for clarification of the Community's international law obligations within the Community legal order.

[79] Case C–262/96, *Sürül*, pending (OJ 1996 C269/19), Opinion of La Pergola AG of 12 Feb. 1998.

Postscript: The Court of Justice handed down its judgment in Case C-170/96, *Commision v. Council (airport transit visas)* on 12 May 1998 (not yet reported). The Court held that it had jurisdiction to review the content of the Council Act on airport transit arrangements (adopted on the basis of Article K.3 CJHA) in the light of Article 100c of the EC Treaty in order to ascertain whether that Act affects the powers of Community under that provision and to annul the Act if it appears that it should have been based on Article 100c of the Treaty. As to the substance, the Court, first, analysed the provisions of the EC Treaty and, second, interpreted the Act as applying airport transit visas solely to passengers in international transit. Accordingly, the Act did not concern the crossing of external borders within the meaning of Article 100c of the EC Treaty, and the action was dismissed.

Index